MASTERING
REAL ESTATE
APPRAISAL

Dennis H. Carr, MAI
Jeff A. Lawson, MAI, SRA
J. Carl Schultz, Jr., MAI, SRA, CRE

Dearborn™
Real Estate Education

This publication is designed to provide accurate and authoritative information in regard to the subject matter covered. It is sold with the understanding that the publisher is not engaged in rendering legal, accounting, or other professional service. If legal advice or other expert assistance is required, the services of a competent professional person should be sought.

President: Roy Lipner
Publisher and Director of Distance Learning: Evan M. Butterfield
Development Editor: Amanda Rahn
Acting Editorial Production Manager: Daniel Frey
Creative Director: Lucy Jenkins

TABLE OF CONTENTS

The real estate appraiser's role is generally to render an unbiased, professionally derived opinion of a defined value of specified rights in the ownership of real property. Often called an art rather than a science, the appraisal process involves a structured procedure, coupled with experience and the application of sound judgment. Appraisers report rather than create value; as such, the "reporter" should have a thorough understanding of the economic principles and dynamics that drive buyers and sellers in the marketplace and a working knowledge of appraisal principles and techniques to properly report value conclusions on which financial decisions are made.

Mastering Real Estate Appraisal is designed to cover all of the topics established by the Appraiser Qualification Board of the Appraisal Foundation for the prelicensing appraisal course. The successful completion of this course satisfies the minimum requirements for state registration and is an integral portion of the education necessary to be a licensed or certified appraiser.

The course is interactive in its content, with numerous examples and illustrations presented to assist in mastering various learning objectives. Appraisal theory and application are emphasized to give the student not only the means to pass the state examination but a solid foundation on which to continually build professional competency.

Through the many classroom and homework questions, exercises, and practice examinations, student participation is emphasized. The course is practical, concise, and timely.

The authors would like to thank John Maggi, SRA, for his valuable feedback during his teaching of this course and his contributions of time and vast knowledge during the development of this text. His input is greatly appreciated. Thanks also go to the following members of the *Mastering Real Estate Appraisal* Review Board for their gracious participation in the development of this textbook, and their valuable contributions of time, criticisms, and suggestions:

Richard P. Bobbitt, Bobbitt and Company

Lynne L. Heiden, GRPA, Trans-American Appraisal & Real Estate, Kearney, Nebraska

Levin P. Messick, Professor, Mount San Antonio College

Wade R. Ragas, University of New Orleans

Dennis H. Carr, MAI

President of Carr, Lawson, Cantrell & Associates, Inc., an Atlanta-based real estate appraisal and consultation firm.

- 1971 Graduate of the University of Georgia—Bachelor of Business Administration, Real Estate.

- Involved exclusively in real estate valuation and consultation since 1972.

- Has appraised all types of real estate including office buildings, shopping centers, motels, warehouses, manufacturing facilities, subdivisions, and planned unit developments.

- Holds the MAI designation of the Appraisal Institute and Certified General classification of the State of Georgia.

- Has held numerous offices and chaired numerous committees of the Appraisal Institute. Was State President in 1990.

- Has authored numerous articles on appraisal and appraisal related topics.

- Taught various appraisal courses—served as staff instructor of the Georgia Institute of Real Estate of the Atlanta Board of REALTORS.®

- Has testified on real estate valuation matters in state and federal courts.

- Currently serves various clients including local, national, and international banks; federal, state, and local governments; insurance companies; law firms; and corporations.

Jeff A. Lawson, MAI, SRA

Vice President of Carr, Lawson, Cantrell & Associates, Inc. Formerly served as Senior Review Appraiser for Regions Bank.

- 1983 Honor Graduate of the University of Kentucky—Bachelor of Business Administration, Marketing.

- Has appraised all types of real estate including apartments, office buildings, retail properties, golf courses/land developments, warehouse/industrial properties, churches, farms, single-family residences, subdivisions, and various types of land.

- Holds the MAI and SRA designations of the Appraisal Institute and the Certified General classification of the State of Georgia.

- Has held numerous offices and chaired numerous committees of the Appraisal Institute. Was Atlanta Area President in 2002.

- Authored a continuing education course titled *Developing An Accurate Value Via The Cost Approach.*

- Approved instructor for the Appraisal Institute. Has taught various appraisal courses—Staff instructor of the Georgia Institute of Real Estate of the Atlanta Board of REALTORS.®

- Attended the First National Bancorp (now Regions Bank) Lender's Academy.

J. Carl Schultz, Jr., MAI, SRA, CRE, SGA

Managing Director of Integra Schultz-Northington, the Atlanta real estate appraisal and consulting office of Integra Realty Resources, which has 50 offices nationwide.

- 1963 Graduate of the University of Georgia—Bachelor of Business Administration, Real Estate

- Involved exclusively in real estate valuation and consultation since 1963.

- Has appraised all types of real estate including office buildings, shopping centers, hotels, manufacturing facilities, planned unit developments, and recreation and resort properties such as golf courses, marinas, tennis facilities, etc.

- Holds the MAI and SRA designations of the Appraisal Institute and the Certified General classification of the State of Georgia and six other southeastern states.

- Has held numerous offices and chaired numerous national committees of the Appraisal Institute. Was National President in 1989.

- Is a CRE-designated member of the Counselors of Real Estate and an SGA-designated member of the Society of Golf Course Appraisers.

- Has authored numerous articles on appraisal and appraisal-related topics including the national Uniform Standards of Professional Appraisal Practice (USPAP) Course for the Appraisal Foundation.

- Taught various appraisal courses—served as staff instructor of the Georgia Institute of Real Estate of the Atlanta Board of REALTORS.® Also teaches the Uniform Standards of Professional Appraisal Practices courses for the Appraisal Institute.

- Has testified on real estate valuation matters in state and federal courts.

- Has made numerous trips to Asia and eastern and central Europe to assist in the development of Standards and the regulation of appraisers of numerous former Soviet bloc countries.

CHAPTER ONE

Influences on Real Estate Value

■ LEARNING OBJECTIVES

Students will be able to

1. identify and understand the five attributes of land including the concept that land is unique in location and composition, is durable, is finite in supply, and is useful.

2. identify, understand, and give examples of the social, economic, physical/environmental, and governmental forces that impact real estate value.

3. recognize that categorizing the four forces (social, economic, physical/environmental and governmental) can sometimes be subjective. Being able to identify and measure the market reaction to the respective force is far more important than specifically categorizing the force.

■ KEY TERMS

durable	physical/environmental	unique in location
economic forces	forces	useful
finite in supply	social forces	
governmental forces	unique in composition	

■ INTRODUCTION

In order to perform competently, the appraiser must constantly observe and analyze influences that affect the value of land and/or improvements. This Chapter addresses some of the basic influences with which the appraiser must become familiar.

PART ONE   The Attributes of Land

Land (real estate) has characteristics that are different from all other assets. Land is

1. **unique in location**—no two parcels are identical in terms of location.

2. **unique in composition**—no two parcels are identical in their geological composition.

3. **durable**—land is long-lasting.

4. **finite in supply**—land is something that is not continually created.

5. **useful**—land has use or utility to people.

Because land has these five characteristics, it has value. Land's usefulness is especially critical to its value. Obviously, land that has a most logical use as a corn field has less value than land that has a realistic use as a downtown office building site. It is our job as appraisers to identify what factors and conditions create value, to analyze them, to formulate a conclusion, and to communicate these findings in an appraisal to our client.

PART TWO   The Four Forces

Academicians isolate the following four forces that impact real estate value:

a. Social

b. Economic

c. Physical/Environmental

d. Governmental

Identification may be confusing and overlapping sometimes, but all influences on property value can be classified into one or more of these four forces.

■ SOCIAL FORCES

Social forces relate to trends in society or culture. Sometimes these forces are imagined while at other times they are based on actual facts and figures. Some of the social forces that affect real estate value include the following:

Population Trends (Growth, Decline, Stability)

Many people tend to think that populations are always increasing, fueling the demand for real estate. In many rural areas, however, population is actually declining as modernization of the agricultural industry has lessened the demand for farm labor. Also, an individual neighborhood may be losing population even though the housing stock remains the same because children are growing up and leaving the households.

Family Composition

No one can argue that the traditional view of the American household and its composition is changing. This is not to say that the idea of the traditional household with working father, homemaking mother, and two well-adjusted children is obsolete. Many suburban neighborhoods are composed of 80 percent to 90 percent traditional-type households. Single-parent households, households with two working parents, empty nesters, and *DINKs* (double-income, no kids) are all on the increase. These redefined households demand a different housing type than that customarily viewed as proper for the traditional American household. Rather than the detached, single-family dwelling on a subdivision street somewhere in suburbia USA, these changing households have created demand for apartments, townhomes, cluster-type residences, and other housing alternatives.

Aging of America's Population

The aging of America's population has created the need for more retirement homes, assisted care living facilities, senior apartment communities, nursing homes, hospitals, medical offices, and so on. Empty nesters (mature couples whose children have left home) usually desire less spacious homes, but homes that are high quality on small, easy-to-maintain lots with retirement amenities such as golf courses, lakes, tennis facilities, nature trails, etc.

Evolution of Home Offices

The high-tech age in which we are living has allowed many individuals to work partially or totally at home. Fax machines, computer networks, and advanced communications have led to reduced demand for office space in many metropolitan areas as well as a trend toward less office space per worker than ever before.

Environmental Consciousness

Homes today are more environmentally friendly than ever with increased awareness of builders and homebuyers alike in the construction of homes. Examples include more efficient mechanical systems, extra insulation, and low-consumption water devices.

Security Consciousness

The perception of an ever-increasing crime rate has drastically affected consciousness of security. Homes today are often prewired for security systems and fire protection.

Many communities emphasize the security aspect through guard gates, surveillance equipment, and so on.

Leisure Time

With the focus on leisure time since the 1960s, unprecedented demand is expected for second homes such as vacation retreats, weekend rentals, and homes and/or lots on lakes, beaches, and mountains.

The Family and Functional Utility

New homes are now built with more functional living areas such as the *great room* versus the former separate living room and den. More expensive homes also offer *keeping rooms*, rooms just off the kitchen where families can read, watch TV, study, or work while other members prepare meals. Another evolution has been the media room with its home entertainment system with TV, VCR, DVD, and stereo equipment. Home designs of the 1980s and 1990s have focused on the master bedroom and bath along with more bathrooms serving other living areas. Another trend of the 1980s was the movement toward larger and more functional kitchens.

Conversely, the theme of the 1970s was on living rooms, dens, and car storage (evolution of the garage and the garage door with automatic opener).

■ ECONOMIC FORCES

Economic forces relate to the fact that land has value because of its productivity. Land may be used to grow crops, support single-family residential subdivisions, or support highrise office buildings. Virtually all land has some use and therefore some desirability. Because of this desirability, land has value. Because different sites have different desirability, values differ from site to site and from period to period. For this reason, an appraisal must be site specific as of a specific date.

Economic influences also relate to consumers' ability to purchase and use real estate. Economic forces are always present on national, regional, and local market levels. Presented in the following paragraphs are some examples of economic forces.

Income Levels

Regardless of how much someone wants to purchase or rent an item, service, or parcel of real estate, the desire does not translate into market activity until there is adequate purchasing power. Personal income levels are vital in the valuation of real estate. A proposed single-family subdivision with homes priced from $300,000 to $350,000 will not be viable if the prevalent purchaser in the area has a gross income level in the $30,000 to $50,000 per year range.

Employment

The nature of employment is a critical economic factor which should always be considered in an appraisal. Unemployment rates should of course be noted, but the stability of employment should also be addressed. Most communities strive for employment diversity with no major dependence on a single industry. The economic base of an area can be a stabilizing one such as a governmental center. Conversely, the economic base of a community can be an unstable one such as tourism.

For years, communities with a dependence upon military installations were deemed as very stable; however, the early 1990s witnessed the downsizing of the military and the closing of numerous military installations. Major economic recessions occurred in most of those communities that experienced such closings. Southern California is an example of such an area. On the other hand, military conflicts, potential military conflicts, and new military technology could have beneficial effects on a community.

Another example of dependence upon a single industry is the southwestern United States where, to a large degree, the economy was dependent upon oil. Many communities suffered catastrophic downturns in their economies when oil prices plummeted in the 1980s, thus affecting employment. Stabilized oil prices or rapidly escalating oil prices can have the opposite affect.

Housing Construction Costs

The construction cost of housing directly and indirectly influences real estate prices. The costs for items such as wood, concrete, and steel are obvious influences. Less obvious ones are financing costs, land costs, and indirect costs (building permit fees, sewer tap fees, or re-zoning costs). Sometimes, stringent governmental regulations and impact fees increase the cost associated with residential as well as commercial and industrial construction, perhaps restricting the growth and development of a particular location.

Credit Availability

The availability of debt money also influences real estate. When credit is plentiful, as in the 1980s, loans are easy to obtain, and the availability of money results in an active market. When credit is scarce, as in the early 1990s, illiquidity occurs, and prices often decline because only a few people can pay cash or qualify to borrow or find a bank to loan them money. In the early 2000s, interest rates declined drastically, and this trend expanded the borrowing power of many people. The unstable economy also prevalent during this time period served to dampen purchasing, a mitigating factor.

Interest Rates

Trends in interest rates affect housing affordability and thus demand for new and resale homes. A person making $25,000 per year may qualify to buy a $70,000 home if the interest rate on the borrowed funds is available at 7 percent. If the interest rate increases to 10 percent, however, the same home may not be affordable. This lack of affordability drastically impacts new housing construction and resale activity. A less obvious influence is the interest rate a builder must pay on borrowed funds during the construction period (indirect costs).

Utility Costs

The cost for utilities can also influence the supply and demand and pricing of real estate, particularly for industrial and commercial customers whose utility bills may be in the hundreds of thousands of dollars per year.

■ PHYSICAL/ENVIRONMENTAL FORCES

Physical/environmental forces on real estate values are the easiest to identify. Variances in location, topographical features, climate, and other similar factors are easily observable by even the casual buyer or seller.

Certain physical factors may be desirable or undesirable, depending upon the property use type.

> For example, a site with excellent visibility and substantial frontage along a major commercial highway may be advantageous for a retail outlet but very disadvantageous for a residential use. Level, street grade topography may be very desirable for a fast-food restaurant, whereas rolling topography may bring a premium in a residential community.

Some examples of environmental forces on real estate include:

Location

Every particular parcel of real estate is uniquely different in that it occupies a geographically defined location on the earth's surface. In practicality, however, many properties share the same major locational influences.

An old-time cliché in the real estate industry is that there are three important value determinants. These are "location, location, and location." Obviously, this is a redundant statement, but it does illustrate the importance of location in the real estate industry. Essentially duplicate houses can have vastly different prices if located in different neighborhoods.

Transportation

In our mobile society, the primary linkages are highways. In selecting a house, most purchasers look initially for a good neighborhood but also for one with easy access to shopping, employment, recreation, and other points that are visited on a regular basis. The development of the interstate highway system has had a major impact on national, regional, and local economies in that long distances can be traveled in a relatively short period of time.

Public transportation is also important to some cities. In recent years, many cities have developed rapid rail systems which are frequently augmented by bus networks.

Other transportation alternatives relate directly to other land uses. Industrial facilities often locate along rail lines or interstate highways. The relocation of a corporate headquarters to a certain city may well be dependent upon that city's air transportation facilities.

Topography

The topography is important not only to the development of the land, but also to the desirability of the land. Rolling, wooded topography may be highly desirable for residential usage, but the grading costs required to produce a level site may preclude utilization of the land for commercial or industrial development. A property's drainage is important, as well as its soil and subsoil conditions. Extreme topographical problems may in fact preclude any development, rendering the property useful only for aesthetic purposes.

Topography also relates directly to farmland. Gently rolling to level land may be well suited for cropland, whereas more severely rolling contours may limit the agricultural use to pasture.

Climate/Weather

The climate/weather of an area can have a direct influence on the nature of the development pattern. Florida has become a vacation and retirement center because of its tropic-like weather, coupled with its abundance of coastline. Central Florida has become a major tourist attraction as theme parks have located there because there are few days during the year when the climate is intolerable.

■ GOVERNMENTAL FORCES

Whether on a national, state, or local level, **governmental forces** on real estate values can be significant. The very essence of our private real property ownership system relates to historical governmental evolution. Even subtle changes in monetary policy can have far-reaching implications on values. Governmental forces on real estate may include:

Taxes

Higher city and/or state income taxes result in less disposable income for real estate purchases. Although high income taxes are not good for homebuilders, apartment landlords may fare quite well because their tenants cannot afford to buy homes.

Freeport (no taxes on inventory) status, allowable depreciation schedules for capital write-offs, and capital gains tax treatment are other tax-related government factors.

Federal Monetary Policy

Although interest on borrowed funds and savings is usually considered to be an economic influence, the federal government can definitely affect the level of interest rates. The federal government generally seeks to maintain a proper balance between economic growth and inflation and tends to manipulate monetary policy to this end. By changing the discount rate for funds furnished to member banks, the Federal Reserve can have a direct influence on the level of interest charged for these funds to be loaned to individual consumers for construction loans or mortgages. More discussion about the Fed is found in Chapter 5.

In recent years, the federal monetary policy has been impacted by worldwide monetary phenomenon in that funds are now competing in a world market.

Real Estate Taxes and Assessments

Local real estate taxes affect the supply and demand of homes and land in a certain area as well as commercial properties and industrial projects.

Labor Issues

Labor issues can have a major influence on a business's choice when building or relocating a facility. A company may decide for (or against) a certain location because of certain labor laws and regulations, including whether or not labor unions are prevalent.

Quality of Schools

The quality of schools in a certain area may place a neighborhood, area, or even an entire county or state in a competitive advantage or disadvantage relative to another neighborhood, area, county, or state. Test scores at different grade levels, percent of students who finish high school and go to college, expenditures per student, and ratio of students to teachers are important factors in determining the quality of schools within a system or comparing system to system.

Quality of Services

Similar to schools, a government's quality of services can be an influence. These include such items as police and fire protection, the availability of health care, and municipal recreational facilities.

■ IDENTIFICATION OF FORCES

In most cases, a particular force is easily identifiable and categorized as social, economic, physical/environmental, or governmental. In other cases, however, identification of the force is not as easily recognized. Consider the following:

1. Is the lack of utilities in an area a governmental or environmental force?

2. Zoning requires a minimum 20,000 square foot site to develop whereas the subject property contains only 15,000 square feet. Is this an environmental or governmental force coming into play?

3. The Federal Reserve has reduced the discount rate charged to member banks, and interest rates begin to fall. Is this a governmental or economic implication?

4. An increase in the income tax rate has reduced demand for starter housing in a certain community. Is is an economic or governmental factor?

In these examples, there is no clear classification, and identification of the force may vary according to the person doing the interpretation. The most important thing is to recognize that the four forces often interact and overlap. It is more important for the appraiser to measure the market reaction to these forces than to spend time identifying the classification of the force.

1. Which of the following would be an example of an economic force?
   a. A trend toward smaller household sizes
   b. A city ordinance banning outdoor advertising
   c. A city's favorable climate
   d. A manufacturing plant reopening after closing

2. Which of the following would be an example of a social force?
   a. Higher utility rates for a certain area
   b. Lower interest rates
   c. An increasing divorce rate
   d. Recurring flooding of a certain few homes in a subdivision

3. Which of the following would be an example of a governmental force?
   a. An area's abundant natural resources that results in lower lumber costs
   b. Strict building codes requiring poured concrete foundations for homes within the city
   c. The development of a new private country club golf course
   d. The opening of a new grocery store

4. Which of the following is NOT a governmental influence?
   a. Development of a new subdivision by a local builder
   b. Sales tax increase for a certain area
   c. A hotel occupancy tax
   d. Development of a new sports arena financed by city bonds

5. An area has a reputation for being a neighborhood with a low crime rate and an excellent quality of life. What force is this an example of?
   a. Social   c. Governmental
   b. Economic   d. Environmental

6. A neighborhood has excellent views of the ocean. What force does this exhibit?
   a. Social   c. Governmental
   b. Economic   d. Environmental

7. A city has a zoning code that does not allow satellite dishes in the front yard. This is an example of which kind of force?
   a. Social   c. Governmental
   b. Economic   d. Environmental

8. San Francisco is a city influenced by its strategic location along the Pacific Coast and its favorable climate. Which of the four forces are these part of?
   a. Social   c. Governmental
   b. Economic   d. Environmental

9. Los Angeles had some major obstacles in its economic expansion in the 1980s including civil rights issues, crime, and illegal immigration. Which of the four forces were these part of?
   a. Social   c. Governmental
   b. Economic   d. Environmental

10. A severe hurricane damaged the Miami region in August 1991. Which of the four forces does this represent?
    a. Social   c. Governmental
    b. Economic   d. Environmental

11. The Disney theme park outside Orlando has had a significant impact on uses of land in southwest Orlando for many years and an influence on the value of that land. Which of the four forces does this represent?
    a. Social   c. Governmental
    b. Economic   d. Environmental

12. The King's Bay Submarine Base in southeastern Georgia is one of the largest developments in America. It was created by the Department of Defense to build nuclear submarines for the Navy. What force does this represent?
    a. Social   c.   Governmental
    b. Economic   d   Environmental

13. The Tax Reform Act of 1986 had a dramatic impact on real estate by eliminating many of the tax advantages for passive real estate investors. This is an example of which kind of force?
    a. Social   c.   Governmental
    b   Economic   d.   Environmental

14. A real estate mall developer purchases a site with the intent of building a regional mall because the immediate area has a significant number of households and the income level of those households is affluent. What type of force is the neighborhood going through?
    a. Social   c.   Governmental
    b. Economic   d.   Environmental

15. Families are more aware of recycling their consumer wastes than ever before. This is an example of which kind of force:
    a. Social   c.   Governmental
    b. Economic   d.   Environmental

2 Legal Considerations in Appraisal

■ LEARNING OBJECTIVES

Students will be able to

1. recognize the important legal considerations that affect real estate appraisal.

2. define and understand the differences among real estate, real property, personal property, and fixtures.

3. identify and understand the limitations on ownership of real estate including police power, eminent domain, escheat, and taxation.

4. identify and understand private restrictions on real estate including deed restrictions, easements, leases, mortgages, and liens.

5. define and understand encroachments and adverse possession.

6. understand the concept of fee simple ownership, as well as ownership interests that are less than fee simple such as life estate, leased fee estate, leasehold estate, air rights, and surface/subsurface rights.

7. understand the various forms of property ownership including joint tenancy, tenancy in common, tenancy by the entirety, as well as special forms of ownership such as condominiums, cooperatives, and timeshares.

8. understand the various forms of legal descriptions and how to identify property according to the specific form of legal description.

9. understand the types of title transfers including general warranty, special warranty, and quitclaim deeds.

■ KEY TERMS

adverse possession	general warranty deed	personal property
air rights	government (rectangular)	police power
bundle of rights	survey	purchase money mort-
condemnation	joint tenancy	gage
condominium	lease	quitclaim deed
cooperative	leased fee estate	real estate
deed restriction	leasehold estate	real property
easement	lien	special warranty deed
easement appurtenant	life estate	surface/subsurface rights
easement in gross	limited warranty deed	taxation
eminent domain	lot-and-block system	tenancy
encroachment	metes-and-bounds	tenancy by the entirety
escheat	description	tenancy in common
fee simple estate	monument system	time-share
fixture	mortgage	

■ INTRODUCTION

Ownership of real estate in the United States of America is a direct function of constitutional guarantees. Our governmental heritage, especially related to the ownership of real estate, is English in its origin, and legal implications that affect ownership evolved from this heritage.

This Chapter focuses on the various legal considerations involved in the ownership of real property that a professional appraiser must understand. Covered in this Chapter are the following six legal considerations:

1. Fundamental definitions of legal interests

2. Limitations on ownership of real estate

3. Forms of legal interests

4. Property ownership forms

5. Four types of legal descriptions

6. Types of real estate transfers

PART ONE   Fundamental Definitions of Legal Interests

In understanding the ownership of real estate, a clear distinction must be made between real estate and real property:

■ REAL ESTATE

Real estate relates to the land and all improvements permanently attached to the land, either by nature or by people.

As discussed in Chapter 1, real estate has the following five unique characteristics that distinguish it from other asset types:

1. Unique in location

2. Unique in composition

3. Durable

4. Finite in supply

5. Useful

These five unique characteristics all relate to the physical attributes of land and/or improvements.

■ REAL PROPERTY

Real property relates to the interests, benefits, and rights inherent in the ownership of real estate.

Based on this distinction between real estate and real property, those involved in the valuation of real estate are technically real property appraisers as opposed to real estate appraisers.

Consistent with the concept of real property is **the bundle of rights** concept, a view of real property ownership suggesting that the rights inherent in the ownership of a parcel of real estate can be compared to a bundle of sticks whereby each stick represents a separate and distinct right in the ownership of that real estate.

Rights generally inherent in the ownership of real estate include but are not limited to the following six:

1. The right to sell

2. The right to lease

3. The right to mortgage

4. The right to sell or lease a partial interest

5. The right to build improvements thereon

6. The right not to do any of the above

The bundle of rights can be divided through various instruments including leases, easements, and mortgages. Through these instruments, one party owns or controls certain rights whereby another party owns or controls other rights.

For example, in a lease arrangement, the person leasing the property (lessee) generally acquires the right to use and occupy the premises for a certain reason, for a certain period of time, usually at a specified rental rate. The owner of the property (lessor) retains the right to receive rent for giving up the use of the property but also retains the right to the reversion, or the right to get the property back after the lease has ended.

■ PERSONAL PROPERTY

Personal property is an item that is not real property.

It usually falls outside the subject of an appraisal. Three examples of personal property that may appear to be related to the real estate are the following:

1. A portable microwave oven

2. A window air-conditioning unit

3. Furniture

■ FIXTURE

A **fixture** is an item that was once personal property that has become part of the real estate.

When a dishwasher has been delivered to a construction site and is awaiting installation, it is personal property. When installed, however, it becomes a fixture and is considered part of the real estate. Following are four examples of fixtures:

1. Light fixtures

2. Stoves

3. Basketball goals (permanently installed)

4. An irrigation system

In deciding whether or not personal property has become a fixture, there are generally the following three tests:

1. The manner in which the item is attached

2. The intent of the parties

3. Tradition/character of the item

A builder removes a ceiling fan from the box, installs it on the ceiling, and sells it along with the house. This item has satisfied all three tests for becoming a fixture. But what about curtains and other window treatments? In many cases, a purchaser of a home has been disappointed to find out the curtains he or she assumed would go with the house have been removed once the premises become vacated. The purchase contract should specify what the buyer and seller are considering as a fixture or personal property.

Although furniture is generally considered as personal property, motels and hotels are usually sold with room furnishings included. In this instance, furniture is considered a fixture and part of the real property.

When confronted with uncertainties as to the treatment of property, the appraiser should address the problem, consult the client, and agree upon proper treatment.

PART TWO   Limitations on Ownership of Real Estate

The purest and most complete form of real estate ownership is **fee simple**. Yet, even though an individual may own a parcel of real estate in fee simple with no mortgage encumbrance, he or she does not have exclusive use of that property. There can be private restrictions placed on the property by the previous owner. Such restrictions may require a minimum floor area, architectural controls, and placement of improvements.

There can also be governmental controls. When purchasing real estate, one should recognize that the purchase is being made subject to these restrictions which are inherent in the ownership of the property.

■ PUBLIC RESTRICTIONS ON REAL ESTATE OWNERSHIP

There are four public or governmental restrictions known as the four powers of government. These limit the ownership of all real property in the United States. The four powers are as follows:

1. Police power

2. Eminent domain

3. Escheat

4. Taxation

Police Power

Police power is the right of government to regulate land use for the public good. There are numerous examples of police power, but the most obvious ones are zoning and building codes.

Zoning is intended to promote orderly development of land. Zoning may allow commercial development along a major highway but may restrict adjoining land to single-family residential usage. By promoting orderly development, zoning generally tends to maximize and maintain an individual parcel's value.

Building codes are intended to protect the consumer from inappropriate or faulty construction. The requirement of sprinkler systems in office buildings over four stories high may have a significant impact on construction costs and rental rates. The requirement to reinforce foundation footings may insure the viability of a residential structure for years to come whereas the average consumer may be unaware of its importance.

Eminent Domain

Eminent domain is the right of governments to acquire private property for public use, such as a road widening. The process of acquiring private property for public use is called **condemnation**, whereas the right of government to acquire the property is eminent domain. Whether we agree or disagree with this right as individuals, it is inherent in the United States Constitution.

Laws in many states recognize the power of eminent domain but go on to state that *just compensation* must be paid to the owner. Examples in which the power of eminent domain is employed may include the following:

1. Highway construction

2. Parks

3. Governmental building sites

4. Airport expansion

5. Reservoirs

6. Utility construction

Escheat

Escheat actually means *going to the state*. If a person dies without a will, that person is said to have died *intestate*, and that person's property transfers to the state.

Taxation

Governments are granted the right of **taxation**, that is, they are allowed to levy taxes on properties. In many communities, property taxes are the primary funding basis for local operations including schools. If property taxes are not paid, governments have the right to acquire the properties, although proper legal procedures must be followed.

■ PRIVATE RESTRICTIONS ON REAL ESTATE OWNERSHIP

In addition to governmental restrictions, individuals may place private limitations on property, and these restrictions may or may not transfer with the property when it sells.

Following are five examples of private restrictions:

1. Deed restrictions

2. Easements

3. Leases

4. Mortgages

5. Liens

Deed Restrictions

A **deed restriction** is a limitation on the use of real estate through a written legal document that is usually recorded. The recording document is usually referred to or stated in the transfer agreement such as a deed. While a zoning restriction usually applies to many parcels, a deed restriction usually relates to a specific parcel or even a defined subdivision or planned use development. When deed restrictions are in conflict with zoning, usually the more restrictive prevails.

One of the most common deed restrictions is a subdivision *restrictive covenant*. A subdivision deed restriction may state that the minimum size of a home must be 2,000 square feet, even though zoning may only require a minimum of 1,500 square feet. Usually deed restrictions have time limitations, but under certain circumstances, they can be extended.

Easements

An **easement** conveys the right to use part of the land for a specific purpose. Easements thus divide the bundle of rights.

Utility companies have to acquire easements to extend utility lines through property. In order to widen an existing highway, a governmental authority may have to acquire a *temporary* easement alongside the highway for construction purposes.

In Figure 2.1, a parcel that would otherwise have no access or be *landlocked* has attained access through an access easement across the adjoining property. In Figure 2.1, the owner of Tract B has given an easement to the owner of Tract D.

An easement typically does not convey ownership of the majority of the rights in the bundle of rights; easements relate to specifically identified rights usually identifying a temporary or perpetual use. An easement that runs with the land and can be conveyed from a seller to a buyer is called an *easement appurtenant*. An easement that serves only one person that cannot be conveyed from a seller to a buyer is called an *easement in gross*.

Leases

A **lease** is a contractual agreement between a property owner (lessor) and a tenant (lessee). It specifies the use of a property for an identified period of time. The tenant acquires the right to occupy and use a property. The owner usually receives the right to

FIGURE 2.1 ■ Access Easement Example

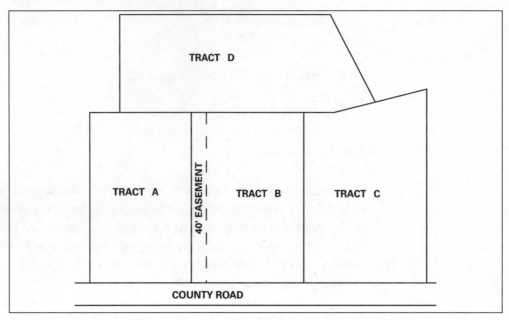

collect rent from the tenant and also has the right of reversion, that is, the right to get the property back at the end of the lease. Usually, sales of property do not nullify leases. This concept is particularly important when valuing properties that are subject to leases as will be discussed later in Chapter 15.

Mortgages

When real estate is purchased, there are usually some borrowed funds involved as part of the purchase price. When part or all of this money is borrowed from a lending institution, a mortgage instrument is usually created.

A **mortgage** is a loan or promissory note that is secured by the real estate. If the loan is not paid back according to the agreed upon terms and conditions, the lending institution providing the funds can acquire title to the property through foreclosure.

Frequently, the seller of real estate takes back a mortgage as part of the purchase price. This form of *seller financing* is often referred to as a *purchase money mortgage*. The terms and conditions are often more advantageous to the buyer than the terms and conditions available for borrowed funds from traditional lending institutions.

Liens

A charge against a property in which the property is security for payment of a debt is called a **lien**. There are many forms of liens such as a mechanic's lien, materialman's lien, or liens which may be placed on a property through a condominium association for nonpayment of mandatory association fees. All mortgages are liens, but all liens are not mortgages (mechanic's lien).

■ RELATED TERMS

Encroachments

An **encroachment** is a trespass on another's land. If a fence has been installed over the property line onto the adjacent property, an encroachment has been created. A house that extends over a property line is also an example of an encroachment. In most cases, the person doing the encroaching can be forced to correct the encroachment.

Adverse Possession

Adverse possession is a method of acquiring ownership through possession: If a person utilizes another person's property openly for an extended period of time, that property may be transferred as to ownership. Several requirements are necessary for one to acquire title through adverse possession. Possession must involve all of the following:

a. Be apparent (open and visible)

b. Be continuous and uninterrupted for a certain period of time

c. Be exclusive

d. Be claimed, i.e., the person who has the apparent possession must make a claim to that possession

e. Be hostile with denial or opposition to the original owner's title

A frequent situation where property is claimed through adverse possession involves abandoned railway lines. If a rail company abandons a rail line and removes the rail, and an adjacent property owner fences in the area and utilizes it for agricultural purposes for an extended period of time, that property owner may have claim to the abandoned railway line through adverse possession.

PART THREE   Forms of Legal Interest

Several forms of ownership of real property exist, varying from state to state. As noted previously, because we are technically appraising real property rather than real estate, we must have a clear understanding of the ownership interest being appraised.

■ FEE SIMPLE ESTATE

The most complete form of ownership is a **fee simple estate**. Although the purest form of ownership without any claims by heirs or private restrictions, a fee simple estate is limited by the aforementioned four powers of government. Usually, an appraisal of any interest less than fee simple begins with an analysis of the fee simple value.

■ PARTIAL INTERESTS

Any interest less than a fee simple interest is known as a partial interest. Several forms of partial interests are discussed in the following paragraphs.

Life Estate

A **life estate** is created when an owner of real property grants the right to another to use the property for his or her life. To illustrate, say a grandmother wants to live in her house until her death. She could sell the property to another but retain the right to occupy the house until her death. In this case, all of the bundle of rights have not transferred because the grandmother will continue to use and occupy the property for some duration.

Leased Fee Estate

A landlord's (lessor's) interest in a property when there is a lease encumbering the property is called a **leased fee estate**. The lease document itself has divided the bundle of rights.

The landlord usually retains the right to receive rent in exchange for giving up use of the property for a specified period of time; the landlord also retains the right to get the property back at the end of the lease (reversion). In such an arrangement, the obligations accruing to the landlord and the obligations accruing to the tenant are usually specified by the lease.

> For example, either the landlord or the tenant can be contractually obligated to pay the taxes, insurance, heating and cooling equipment maintenance, structural maintenance, grounds maintenance, etc.

Leasehold Estate

In contrast to the leased fee estate, the tenant's (lessee's) interest in a leased property is called a **leasehold estate**. The tenant usually obtains the right to use and occupy the property but assumes the obligation to pay rent. A leasehold estate can have a positive value (tenant has an advantage) if the contract rent (rent specified in the lease) is less than economic or market rent (rent which could be achieved in an open market). A leasehold interest can have a negative value (tenant is at a disadvantage) if the contract rent is more than the economic or market rent.

Air Rights

Air rights are particularly important in urban areas. In many cases, buildings are constructed within an identified air space.

For example, a highrise office building could be constructed over parking decks. Usually, air rights also include *touch down* rights where suitable building supports can be constructed.

Air rights do not extend indefinitely. There are height limitations imposed by the Federal Aviation Administration related to air traffic control.

Surface/Subsurface Rights

Surface/subsurface rights also come into play more in urban areas. A government agency may acquire (through eminent domain) subsurface rights for the construction of an underground rapid rail system. An owner of a parcel of land may retain the surface rights for use as parking and sell the air rights for an overhead walkway connecting to adjacent buildings. Often, a seller may transfer his land but retain the subsurface mineral rights.

PART FOUR   Property Ownership Forms

As appraisers, we are concerned with the valuation of an ownership interest (real property) in specified real estate. The bundle of rights relates to real property and, as discussed, can be divided. In addition to understanding rights, an appraiser should also understand the various types of ownership.

■ INDIVIDUAL (SEVERALTY)

This is the most common form of ownership where one person or corporation owns the entire bundle of rights, still subject to governmental and private restrictions.

■ TENANCIES AND UNDIVIDED INTERESTS

Tenancy is created when the bundle of rights is divided, and in real estate generally has the following two meanings:

1. The possession of title or other ownership form

2. The right to use and occupy property

As discussed, the second meaning relates to leased property in which the lessee has the right to use and occupy the property, and the landlord has the right to receive rent and get the property back at lease termination.

Related to the ownership of real property, there are several important ownership forms that warrant explanation. They relate to an "undivided interest" in the real property. The undivided interest concept is difficult for many people to comprehend. What this means is that the property itself cannot be divided, only the ownership interest.

For example, if an individual purchases a 50% undivided interest in 20 acres of land, his or her ownership relates to a partial interest (50%) in the entire 20 acres, not exclusive (100%) ownership of 10 acres.

Following are the three most common forms of tenancies related to ownership:

1. Joint tenancy

2. Tenancy in common

3. Tenancy by the entirety

Joint Tenancy

Ownership by **joint tenancy** occurs when two or more persons have inseparable or undivided interests in property. Upon the death of one of the owners, title to the deceased owner's portion of the property automatically passes to the surviving owner(s). This is referred to as the *right of survivorship*.

Tenancy in Common

The **tenancy in common** form of ownership also relates to two or more persons who have undivided interests. The undivided interest may or may not be equally distributed to the estate holders. This form of ownership is different from joint tenancy in that there is no right of survivorship. In other words, if one owner dies, title would pass to that owner's heirs rather than to the surviving owner(s) automatically.

Tenancy by the Entirety

Tenancy by the entirety relates to a husband and wife who own a particular property. In this case, neither party can sell his or her interest individually; the property can sell only as a unit. This ownership interest is usually reserved for married couples.

■ SPECIAL FORMS OF OWNERSHIP

The following three special types of ownership evolved in recent years as the bundle of rights separated in more creative ways:

1. Condominium

2. Cooperative

3. Time-share

Condominium

The term **condominium** describes a type of ownership, not a type of building. This is a form of ownership in which an owner has an interest (usually fee simple) in a certain unit defined such as the space between the interior walls, the ceiling, and the floor of that unit; the owner also owns a pro-rata share of the common areas (drives, grounds, recreational amenities, etc.) within the development.

> For example, assume Martha owns a condominium within an 80-unit development. Martha would own the interior of her unit and 1/80 of the common areas.

Cooperative

A **cooperative** is a form of ownership in which a corporation owns the land and improvements, and the residents own stock in the corporation. Then, the corporation signs an exclusive lease with the tenant-stockholder. Cooperatives are common in certain regions of the country. This type of ownership allows tenant-stockholders to *select* their neighbors, voting on whether to allow or deny a prospective buyer to be allowed into the corporation, and thus occupancy of a unit in the building.

Time-Share

A **time-share** is a partial form of ownership in which other time-share owners (tenants in common) purchase the right of use/occupancy for a specified period of time, say one week per year. Typically, 50 weeks per year are sold, with the other two weeks reserved for maintenance. Thus, an owner who buys one week will have a 2 percent ownership (1/50) in the unit, but his ownership/occupancy may be restricted to a certain period or week of the year. A Miami time-share week is likely more expensive in January than is a week in July; hence, a buyer cannot purchase an inexpensive week in July and expect to use it during a more expensive January week.

PART FIVE   Forms of Legal Descriptions

Legal descriptions are methods of describing real estate so that each property can be recognized from all other properties, recognizing its unique characteristics with regard to location. Because land is a unique commodity in that it is immobile, it must be described specifically. Following are the four types of legal land descriptions:

1. Metes-and-bounds description

2. Government (rectangular) survey system

3. Lot-and-block system

4. Monuments system

■ METES-AND-BOUNDS DESCRIPTION

A **metes-and-bounds description** begins at a point of beginning (POB), and the terms metes and bounds relate to distance and direction. From the POB, the reader of the legal description is walked around the perimeter of the parcel using angles and distances, eventually returning to the POB. A basic understanding of plane geometry is needed in this system because of the emphasis on angles and distances.

In addition to defining the geometric shape, a metes-and-bounds description also makes reference to a specific land lot, within a district, within a county.

Generally, all counties are divided into several districts for identification purposes, with the districts being subdivided into land lots of 20-acre to 40-acre plots identified by a predetermined grid system.

Figure 2.2 is an example of a metes and bounds legal description.

■ GOVERNMENT (RECTANGULAR) SURVEY SYSTEM

The **government (rectangular) survey** description utilizes a predetermined governmental survey of a county. In this system, horizontal and vertical boundary lines have been surveyed by the federal government and are assumed to be permanently in place. Townships are six miles square (36 square miles). Each township is divided into 36 sections (one square mile each). Each section has 640 acres. These predetermined lines form the basis for describing a parcel of land.

■ LOT-AND-BLOCK SYSTEM

Under the **lot-and-block system**, a certain plot of land is subdivided. The key is the recording of the subdivision plat into public records. Within each subdivision, the lots

FIGURE 2.2 ■ Example of Metes-and-Bounds Description

All that parcel of land lying within Land Lot 23 of the 6th District, in Fulton County, Georgia, and more particularly described as beginning at a point located at the northeast corner of the intersection of Jones Street and Smith Street (POB); running thence north 90 degrees, 0 minutes along the east right-of-way of Jones Street, 100 feet to a point; thence east 90 degrees, 0 minutes, 200 feet to a point; thence south 90 degrees, 0 minutes, 100 feet to a point along the north side of Smith Street; thence west along the north right-of-way of Smith Street 200 feet to the point of beginning.

and blocks are identified, making reference to the recorded plat. Figure 2.3 shows an example of a legal description utilizing the lot-and-block system.

■ MONUMENT SYSTEM

The **monument system** utilizes natural and human-made landmarks to describe land. It is similar to a metes-and-bounds description; however, the points of reference are human-made or natural landmarks such as rivers, lakes, or human-placed monuments. The monument system is generally no longer used.

P A R T   S I X   Types of Title Transfers

Title is conveyed by deeds. A deed is an instrument that conveys ownership of property. Title refers to the right to possess or control property. In real estate title is a concept rather than a written document. The following are three types of deeds:

1. General warranty deeds

2. Special warranty deeds

3. Quitclaim deeds

FIGURE 2.3 ■ Example of Lot-and-Block System

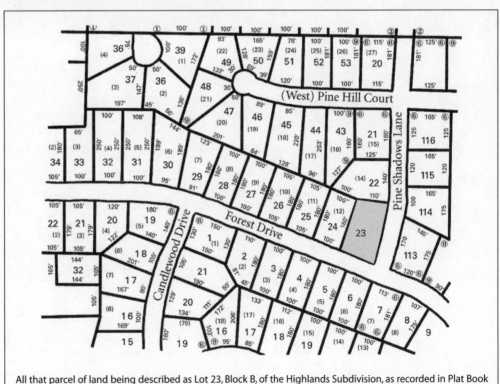

All that parcel of land being described as Lot 23, Block B, of the Highlands Subdivision, as recorded in Plat Book 23, Page 11, of the Monroe County records.

Deeds are recorded in most states for the conveyance to be legal and valid. In some states, however, the transfer is valid when delivered by the grantor and accepted by the grantee.

■ GENERAL WARRANTY DEED

The **general warranty deed** conveys a covenant of warranty in which the seller guarantees to the buyer that the title is *unclouded*, or clean of any prior claims or heirs.

■ SPECIAL WARRANTY DEED

A **special warranty deed** warrants to the grantee by the grantor that the seller will defend the buyer against all claims by the actions or omissions of the grantor, but not any claims that precede the grantor's ownership; thus, the warranty is limited to the seller's ownership period and not prior to the time before the seller obtained title. This type of deed is also frequently referred to as a **limited warranty deed**.

■ QUITCLAIM DEED

A **quitclaim deed** is a conveyance in which the grantor ceases any claim against the property to the grantee. The grantor relinquishes his or her claim against the property, if any. In effect, the grantor conveys whatever interest he or she may have in the property.

1. Which of the following is *NOT* one of the three tests of when personal property becomes a fixture and thus part of the real estate?
   a. Cost of the item
   b. Manner of attachment
   c. Intent of the parties
   d. Character of the item

2. A fee simple interest in a property is an example of
   a. real property.
   b. real estate.
   c. personal property.
   d. emblement.

3. A window air conditioner that is permanently attached to a home and built-in with caulked, side/top/bottom molding and screwed to the window frame is an example of a(n)
   a. trade fixture.
   b. fixture.
   c. personal property.
   d. encroachment.

4. Which of the following is *NOT* a form of a private limitation?
   a. Lease
   b. Mortgage
   c. Severalty
   d. Easement

5. A tenant or lessee may most likely possess which type of interest?
   a. Life estate
   b. Leased fee estate
   c. Lien
   d. Leasehold estate

6. Which of the following is *NOT* a form of an ownership limitation?
   a. Lease
   b. Tenancy
   c. Mortgage
   d. Easement

7. Which of the following is *NOT* a type of special ownership?
   a. Escheat
   b. Condominium
   c. Co-operative
   d. Time-share

8. Which type of title transfer offers a guarantee of the title from the seller to the buyer?
   a. Quitclaim
   b. Title insurance
   c. General warranty
   d. Adverse possession

9. Real property is
   a. the same as real estate.
   b. different than unreal property.
   c. an intangible interest in real estate.
   d. the bricks and mortar.

10. Real estate is
    a. the tangible bricks and mortar and land.
    b. different than unreal estate.
    c. an intangible interest.
    d. a microwave sitting on top of a kitchen counter.

11. Which of the following is used in determining when personal property becomes a fixture?
    a. Weight of the item
    b. Size of the item
    c. Cost of the item
    d. Manner of attachment

12. A ceiling fan installed in a home is
    a. personal property.
    b. a trade fixture.
    c. a fixture that is now part of the real estate.
    d. real property.

13. Building codes and zoning represent which of the four powers of government?
   a. Police power
   b. Eminent domain
   c. Escheat
   d. Taxation

14. A lease and a mortgage are considered to be
   a. deed restrictions.
   b. powers of government.
   c. personal property.
   d. private restrictions.

15. A toolshed that is partly on a neighbor's lot is known as a(n)
   a. lien.
   b. encroachment.
   c. deed restriction.
   d. easement.

16. A leased-fee estate is an interest controlled by the
   a. mortgagee.
   b. management company.
   c. landlord.
   d. tenant.

17. A leasehold estate is created by a(n)
   a. mortgage.
   b. lease.
   c. easement.
   d. life estate.

18. Which is the most common form of ownership?
   a. Severalty
   b. Joint tenants
   c. Tenants by the entireties
   d. Tenancy in common

19. A condominium is known as
   a. tenancy in common.
   b. partial ownership.
   c. joint tenancy.
   d. a type of special ownership.

20. Which is *NOT* a form of a legal description?
   a. Metes-and-bounds method
   b. Special warranty deed
   c. Monument system
   d. Government survey system

CHAPTER THREE

Types of Value

■ LEARNING OBJECTIVES

Students will be able to

1. understand that there are objective and subjective views of value and know which applies to real estate valuation.

2. understand and differentiate between price and value.

3. understand and differentiate between the types of value with special consideration accorded the definition of market value.

4. cover in detail and understand the various fundamental conditions in the standard market value definition.

■ KEY TERMS

assessed value	liquidation value	subjective value
going concern value	market value	value in use
insurable value	objective value	
investment value	price	

■ INTRODUCTION

In order to perform competently, the appraiser must constantly observe and analyze influences that affect the value of land and/or improvements. Following are the two major philosophical views of value:

a. Objective

b. Subjective

Objective Value

The **objective value** view holds that value is inherent in the object itself. Because something is, it has value. This school of philosophical thought emphasizes the cost to produce a commodity as the primary value determinant.

Subjective Value

The **subjective value** philosophical position holds that value is in the eyes of the beholder, not in the object itself. It is often said that *the worth of a thing is what it will bring*. The subjective value concept represents the more modern school of thought that is emphasized in modern day appraisal. Because of this concept, forces outside the property itself have a direct bearing on its value.

The difference between objective and subjective value can be illustrated by a gallon of bottled water. This product required certain cost factors in its creation. It is put on a shelf with competing products in a supermarket to compete for consumer dollars. Hopefully, the sales price will be greater than the cost to produce and deliver this product to the supermarket. This product may have appeal to a particular purchaser who shops comparatively, then makes the decision to purchase this product from among competing products. At the time of the purchase, the product had a certain level of desirability.

Let's suppose that during the night a water main bursts, and all the homes along the street are left without water. The next morning, the purchaser of the bottled water gets out of bed to brush his or her teeth. Has the desirability and utility of the bottled water increased?

In an extreme example, let's suppose a person has been stranded in Death Valley for three days and is at the point of total dehydration. This same bottled water, if available, may have an entirely different value to the person dying of thirst.

In these three instances, the product is the same. Under the objective school of thought, the value would be the same in all three cases. Under the subjective school of thought, however, the value would change considerably in the three instances. The value may increase to the shopper if no other means of water were available; the price would escalate dramatically to the dehydrated person dying of thirst. In all cases, however, the product is the same.

Real estate is evaluated on a subjective, not objective, basis. A home or warehouse does not have value just because it is there (objective); it has value due to numerous characteristics, such as the location, the quality, and the size, among other items.

Consistent with the concept that value is more subjective in nature, this Chapter focuses on real estate influences from a subjective point of view.

P A R T   O N E   Value Versus Price

The appraiser must have a clear understanding of the difference between *price* and *value*. Often, these terms are used interchangeably; however, economic theory makes a clear distinction. The terms are identified as follows:

■ PRICE

Price relates to the actual number of dollars a commodity or service brings when it is sold. Price is therefore a fact and not a theoretical concept.

> For example, a price would be: 1050 Main Street sold for $100,000. It may have been sold from parents to son, and its value could have been $125,000.

■ VALUE

Value relates to the worth of a commodity. This is more of a theoretical concept rather than an actual fact. The value would be an estimate, such as in the example below:

> The market value estimate of the fee simple interest in the property located at 1000 Second Avenue is $125,000, as of January 1, 1995.

When studying markets, appraisers often become aware of price levels that may or may not be reflective of the values of the individual properties. In practical application, appraisers study price levels under the concept that most are occurring at or near their actual values; the value of a parcel of real estate can be estimated utilizing sales prices of other similar properties.

P A R T   T W O   Types of Value

There are many types of value that an appraiser can estimate. The most common is market value; however, there are other types of value that can be estimated for various reasons. It is a good idea for the appraiser to never use the term *value* without a modifier (such as market, investment, insurable, etc.) so that the reader has a clear understanding of the value which the appraiser is reporting.

■ MARKET VALUE

Market value is the most common value estimated by appraisers. At least 90 percent of all appraisals address this value concept. Although the exact definition of market value has changed through the years, it has become more standardized in the recent past.

The most widely accepted definition of market value is that used in the *Uniform Standards of Professional Appraisal Practice* (USPAP). According to this source, the market value definition follows:

> "Market Value" means: The most probable price which a property should bring in a competitive and open market under all conditions requisite to a fair sale, the buyer and seller, each acting prudently, knowledgeably, and assuming the price is not affected by undue stimulus. Implicit in this definition is the consummation of a sale as of a specified date and the passing of title from seller to buyer under conditions whereby:
>
> a. Buyer and seller are typically motivated;
>
> b. Both parties are well informed or well advised and are acting in what they consider their own best interests;
>
> c. A reasonable time is allowed for exposure in the open market;
>
> d. Payment is made in terms of cash in U.S. dollars or in terms of financial arrangements comparable thereto; and
>
> e. The price represents the normal consideration for the property sold unaffected by special or creative financing or sale concessions granted by anyone associated with the sale.

In some states, the market value definition may vary slightly from that specified in the *Uniform Standards of Professional Appraisal Practice* (USPAP), the most commonly cited source. In these instances, the appraiser should cite the actual definition and be sure that his value conclusion is consistent with the definition employed.

This value concept is generally held to be synonymous with the term *value in exchange*. This latter concept, however, is not as widely utilized.

■ INVESTMENT VALUE

Investment value is the worth to a particular investor, using a specific investor's parameters or assumptions as seen in the following examples.

> An example of investment value would be an insurance company that purchases income-producing type property and is willing to pay more for it, resulting in a lower net return, because the insurance company does not pay income taxes. This particular investor would be expected to pay more for a property and have a different internal investment value than the typical market participant.

Another example of investment value could involve a situation in which a developer is renovating an older apartment building that is on the historic register. In this instance, certain federal income tax credits may be available to promote such an endeavor. Without consideration of the investment tax credits, the net benefits derived from the rental of this apartment complex may not justify the cost to renovate the building. By factoring in the investment tax credits, however, the endeavor could well be financially feasible to this developer. In this case, the market value without consideration of the tax credits would be substantially less than the investment value which takes into account the tax credits.

■ VALUE IN USE

Value in use relates to value to a specific user rather than the market in general. It does not relate to the price level most individuals would be willing to pay (see the examples below).

For example, a homeowner with a physical disability may choose to install a $15,000 heated swimming pool for physical therapy reasons. His value in use would be commensurate with the cost of $15,000. The house may be located in a neighborhood where most homes are generally in the $125,000 to $150,000 range. In this neighborhood, the market may react to the existence of a swimming pool by paying only a $3,000 premium. The contributory value of this pool is $3,000, which reflects the incremental difference in market value. The value in use, however, is $15,000.

Another example of value in use is an industrial building that has 40-foot ceilings to accommodate overhead cranes that service a particular manufacturing function. The excessively high ceilings and overhead cranes could very well contribute to value in use commensurate with the cost of these items if there is market demand for these peculiarities; however, the market may be dominated by typical warehouse users who require 24-foot ceilings and no overhead cranes. In this case, typical purchasers would not be willing to pay a significant premium, if any, for the higher ceilings and overhead cranes.

■ INSURABLE VALUE

Insurable value relates to the cost to reproduce improvements. Insurance proceeds for building reconstruction for damages caused by fire, flood, or other hazard, are usually based on the cost to reproduce the structure. When estimating insurable value, the appraiser is therefore interested in estimating costs to reproduce a building or component. Insurable value usually does not relate to land which is generally considered to be unaffected by hazards.

■ ASSESSED VALUE

Assessed value relates to the value of property established by municipalities for purposes of establishing a basis for taxation. Real estate taxes generally comprise a major source of revenues for local municipalities. Assessed value usually relates to market value.

> For example, a municipality's assessed value may be 40% of the market value as estimated by the county tax assessor.

The following is an example of a tax valuation, assessment, and ultimate tax determination:

Market Value (Tax Assessor's Office)	$100,000
Assessment Factor	× 0.40
Assessed Value	$40,000
Millage Rate ($35.00 Per $1,000 of Assessment)	× 0.0350
Tax Charge	$1,400

Because of the magnitude of most tax valuation programs, there are often numerous inconsistencies and errors in the assessor's reported market value of individual parcels. For this reason, tax valuations may or may not be consistent with the actual market value of properties.

A related term is *ad valorem* tax. The term *ad valorem* means *based on value*. The intent to relate the tax charge to the market value of property is thus illustrated.

■ GOING CONCERN VALUE

Going concern value relates to an ongoing, established business operation. Implicit in this value concept is the premise that the business will continue to operate. A McDonald's restaurant may have a certain going concern value which includes all the business aspects of the enterprise whereas the market value of the real estate may be restricted to the land and buildings.

When estimating going concern value, appraisers are often called upon to allocate the total going concern value among the basic components of the enterprise, which could be:

a.   Land

b.   Building improvements

c.   Franchise

d.   Furniture, fixtures, and equipment (FF&E)

e.   Goodwill

Because going concern value encompasses all aspects of the enterprise, it usually exceeds the capacity of most real estate appraisers and requires a separate discipline known as *business valuation*.

■ LIQUIDATION VALUE

Liquidation value relates to the concept that the property requires immediate transfer. Liquidation value would result with an abbreviated marketing period such as an auction or bank foreclosure sale. This would not meet the criteria of the market value definition that *a reasonable time is allowed for exposure in the open market*. To estimate liquidation value, a discount is usually applied to the property's market value; the discount is based on other liquidation sales.

PART THREE   Fundamental Conditions of Market Value

Because the most common purpose of an appraisal is to estimate market value, this definition requires additional attention. Conditions implicit in the market value definition are addressed in the following paragraphs.

■ BUYER AND SELLER ARE TYPICALLY MOTIVATED

The two parties should be acting for typical reasons such as a buyer of a home purchasing for shelter or investment and a seller disposing to move to a different location or to another home. One example of an atypical motivation would be a bank receiving the property via foreclosure and deciding to sell the property via auction. Another example is the case in which a seller sells a property for a price that appears to be less than market days before the seller declares bankruptcy or experiences foreclosure. It will not always be readily apparent what the motivations are; the appraiser will likely find out in the data verification process, in which an appraiser confirms the details of a transaction for accuracy and motivations (discussed in Chapter 12).

■ BOTH PARTIES ARE WELL-INFORMED

The buyer and seller should have sufficient knowledge and information to make an informed decision that is self-serving. An example of an uninformed buyer is a job transferee who flies into the new job market on Friday and has the weekend to find a home, negotiate the price, and offer a contract on the home by Sunday afternoon. Although the buyers are acting in their best interest, they are not informed purchasers and may pay too much (full list price or close to it) when an appraisal may have saved them thousands of dollars. If higher quality data does not exist, an appraiser may still use this sale, but a comment or even an adjustment may be necessary, especially if the buyer/seller/agent discloses the buyer's duress and could offer a dollar figure for the premium that was paid versus the price that normal market negotiations would have likely produced.

■ REASONABLE TIME

The property must be exposed on the open market (via typical market channels which differ from local market to local market) for a time that is typical for sales in that market. The typical rule-of-thumb is 60 days to 120 days for a home that is priced appropriately in an active market and with available financing and, quite importantly, marketed professionally. Professional marketing includes real estate listing publications and online computer services and a well-distributed flyer, as well as an accessible, professional, and cooperative real estate agent.

> For example, it would be improper and inconsistent for a banker to direct an appraiser to estimate the market value of a home in a neighborhood of $1,000,000 homes with a marketing period of 30 days if it normally takes such a home 120 days to 240 days in that market to effect a sale that would meet the test of market value. The 30-day assumption is unreasonable and would be asking the appraiser to estimate the liquidation value, not the market value.

■ PAYMENT IN CASH

Payment is based on United States dollars or in terms of financial arrangements comparable thereto—the exchange used in the sale is cash or terms equivalent to cash.

> For example, assume the sale of a $100,000 house in which the seller received $100,000 cash; obviously that meets this criteria. But suppose the seller received $94,000 in cash and a truck worth $6,000; this is still $100,000 cash equivalent, assuming of course that the truck really is worth $6,000, which may take some additional research.

■ NORMAL CONSIDERATION

If the sale involved some part of the consideration being noncash equivalent, an adjustment is necessary for "cash equivalency" for terms conceded or granted in the sale.

Say a home sells for "$100,000." In your verification process, you find out the buyer obtained a $90,000 loan from a bank and gave $2,000 in cash to the seller with the remaining $8,000 in the form of a second mortgage (for five years) that the seller financed at a below market interest rate of 5 percent. The market rate at the time of sale was 8.5 percent. If the cash equivalency of that $8,000 second mortgage is $6,500, then an adjustment should be made to the sale in the amount of $1,500, that is, the cash equivalent sales price is $98,500, not $100,000.

In its original form, the sale did not meet the definition of market value; however, it could still be used as a comparable after an adjustment for the below market financing.

Another example of cash equivalency would be the instance in which a home sells for $300,000. In the verification process, the appraiser finds out that the buyer obtained a $250,000 loan from a bank and gave the seller $40,000 in cash. The remaining $10,000 was paid in cash to the seller for the seller's country club membership. This sale, in its original form, did not meet the definition of market value. It could still be used as a comparable. However, after an adjustment of $10,000 was made for the country club membership, an effective cash equivalent price of $290,000 was indicated.

1. Which is the most common value estimate provided in an appraisal of a single-family residence?
   a. Market value
   b. Value in use
   c. Going concern value
   d. Insurable value

2. Which type of value would likely be sought in the appraisal of an established business operation?
   a. Investment value
   b. Liquidation value
   c. Value in exchange
   d. Going concern value

3. Which valuation would be based on a limited marketing period?
   a. Assessed value
   b. Liquidation value
   c. Value in use
   d. Going concern value

4. Which value provides the basis of the real estate tax liability for a property?
   a. Going concern value
   b. Value in exchange
   c. Assessed value
   d. Insured value

5. Which is a condition in the definition of market value?
   a. Availability of credit
   b. Buyer and seller are absolutely fully informed about every detail of every transaction within the last five years
   c. Buyer and seller are typically motivated
   d. Buyer and seller are not related in any way

6. What is a reasonable marketing period for a single-family residence?
   a. 90 days
   b. 180 days
   c. Until the seller gets his or her asking price
   d. Unknown; each individual market is different and a reasonable marketing period depends upon an analysis of each market

7. By definition, market value is
   a. always the absolute highest price.
   b. always the absolute lowest price.
   c. the most probable price.
   d. cost plus profit.

8. A $50,000 mortgage has a $5,000 cash equivalency adjustment of $5,000 because of below market financing. The down payment was $3,000. What is the cash equivalent sales price?
   a. $50,000
   b. $55,000
   c. $48,000
   d. $58,000

9. What is the value to a specific occupant?
   a. Market value
   b. Value in use
   c. Value in exchange
   d. Assessed value

10. The value to a particular investor is
    a. market value
    b. assessed value
    c. insurable value
    d. investment value

4 Economic Principles

■ LEARNING OBJECTIVES

Students will be able to

1. understand, be able to differentiate, and give examples of the fifteen economic principles that drive real estate valuation.

2. understand the four agents of production including land, labor, capital, and entrepreneurship, and how they relate to the principle of surplus productivity.

3. understand and give examples of the five economic characteristics of value including utility, scarcity, desirability, effective purchasing power, and demand unit.

■ KEY TERMS

anticipation	desirability	land
balance	economics of scale	opportunity costs
capital	effective purchasing	scarcity
change	power	substitution
competition	entrepreneurship	supply and demand
conformity	externalities	surplus productivity
consistent use theory	increasing and decreasing	utility
contribution	returns	
demand unit	labor	

■ INTRODUCTION

Literally volumes have been written on economics. It is obviously impossible to convey in this book the total expanse of knowledge related to economics.

It is important to remember, however, that the appraiser is reporting the market and in a sense emulating buyers and sellers in a particular marketplace. An understanding of some basic economic principles that most buyers and sellers intuitively possess is the goal of this Chapter.

This Chapter focuses on the following three basic areas:

1. Economic principles

2. Four agents of production

3. Five economic characteristics of value

PART ONE   Economic Principles

■ SUPPLY AND DEMAND

In a free market, buyers and sellers tend to set the price or value of an item based on the relative supply of the product and the demand for it. The following three interrelated terms explain the principle of supply and demand:

1. Supply

2. Demand

3. Price

Given Level of Supply

At a given level of supply, if demand increases, then the price increases. Conversely, given that same level of supply, if demand decreases, then price decreases.

Given Level of Demand

At a certain level of demand, if the supply increases, then the price decreases. Given the same level of demand, if the supply decreases, then the price increases.

Specifically related to real estate, assume that the population in a certain community is growing by 100 households per year. If there are no additions to the existing housing stock (supply), the demand will certainly increase, and prices will accordingly escalate. If the supply is increased by 200 homes per year, then supply will exceed demand, and prices will tend to decline.

In open and competitive markets, supply and demand tend to fluctuate and get out of balance for short periods of time, but they do tend to be in balance over long periods of time. This concept is particularly true in real estate markets where supply generally takes a long time to create; also, factors that affect demand are also often broad-based and extend over long periods of time.

■ ANTICIPATION

The principle of **anticipation** holds that value is simply a function of the present worth of future benefits, that is, people are paying current dollars for future benefits. These future benefits may take the form of intangibles, as seen in the example below.

> For example, when purchasing a home, buyers tend to look for aesthetics, livability, convenience to shopping and employment, neighborhood, and other intangible factors.

When purchasing investment type property (shopping centers, office buildings, hotels), the anticipated benefits are future dollars. In other words, the buyer is exchanging present dollars for property that will hopefully produce more dollars in the future. The principle of anticipation is the basis for the income approach, discussed in Chapter 10.

Under this principle, the past is only important because it tends to give an indication of what is to be expected in the future (see example below).

> For example, a purchaser of a 40-unit apartment complex may look at its income and expenses over the last three years to give an indication of what the property can be expected to generate in terms of income and expenses over the next several years.

A buyer for a home may look at standardized school test scores, trends in home prices, and community growth patterns, all of which have occurred in the past, in order to determine which way the neighborhood is likely to continue in the future. This past information gives the buyer insight as to what to pay for the property today.

■ BALANCE

The principle of **balance** relates both to the property as well as the environment in which the property is located. Related to the property itself, this principle holds that value is achieved and maintained when all elements are in proper proportion.

Consider a builder constructing a single-family residence in a neighborhood of 2,000 square-foot to 2,500 square-foot homes priced from $125,000 to $150,000. Assuming lot prices are consistent, the builder would expect to receive more money for a larger home.

The builder actually experiences the following activity:

Plan	Size in SF	Total Cost	Cost per SF	Sales Price	Price per SF	Difference	Profit
A	2,000	$114,000	$57.00	$126,000	$63.00	$12,000	10.5%
B	2,200	$123,200	$56.00	$143,000	$65.00	$19,800	16.1%
C	2,400	$132,000	$55.00	$148,800	$62.00	$16,800	12.7%
D	3,100	$160,000	$51.61	$182,000	$58.71	$22,000	13.8%

Although the builder receives the highest price for Plan D, the greatest return is reflected by Plan B. In this case, the principle of balance would hold that the proper home would be more related to Plan B. Note that Plan D can achieve a $22,000 profit, but it is only a 13.8 percent return on cost; it also is much riskier given the large size and absolute ($) cost and price (hence, conformity to the neighborhood would be an issue worth investigating before building Plan D).

The principle of balance also relates to land use. Under the optimum land use concept, there would be a proper blend of single-family residences, apartments, complementary shopping centers, nearby employment centers, and reasonably accessible recreational facilities. Conversely, a neighborhood that features no convenient access to shopping, places of worship, or employment would be considered inferior and result in lower demand and in lower prices.

■ CONFORMITY

The principle of **conformity** is similar to the principle of balance, but it relates more to real estate characteristics. It holds that maximum value is achieved and maintained when there is reasonable conformity and not monotonous uniformity among properties.

A Williamsburg or colonial style home in a neighborhood that features all Williamsburg style homes with some individual variance is desirable. A California contemporary ranch style within this neighborhood would be a nonconforming use; the market would likely pay less for this contemporary house in this Williamsburg neighborhood. This California contemporary residence would likely sell for more in a neighborhood that is dominated by California contemporary residences. Conversely, a traditional neighborhood with 300 essentially duplicate houses would be somewhat monotonous and again result in value loss.

■ SURPLUS PRODUCTIVITY

The **surplus productivity** principle recognizes the four agents of production, which are subsequently discussed in this Chapter. The four agents of production are as follows:

1. Land

2. Labor

3. Capital

4. Entrepreneurship

In any enterprise, labor must be paid first, with capital paid after that under the surplus productivity concept. Entrepreneurship is then paid. After returns have been made for these three items, the residual income is attributed to the land (including buildings where appropriate). This residual income is attributed to the real estate and tends to set the value of the land and/or buildings.

An example of surplus productivity would be a motel. Income is derived from room rents, telephone charges, restaurant sales, and other departmental sources. All of the motel labor is paid first. After that, payments due on borrowed funds are made (capital). The entrepreneur is usually paid last.

If there is residual income, this residual income is considered to be attributed to the motel itself (building and land). This residual income can then be converted into a current value indication based on the principle of surplus productivity.

■ CONTRIBUTION

The principle of **contribution** holds that the value of a component is a function of its contribution to the whole rather than as a separate component. The cost of an item does not necessarily equal its contributory value.

Take a swimming pool. In the vast majority of neighborhoods, swimming pools do not add to property value commensurate with their costs. A swimming pool may cost $5,000 to $10,000 to construct, but it may add only $1,000 to $2,000 in value, and in some neighborhoods a pool can actually detract from value.

In other instances, contributory value may exceed the cost. An example can be energy conservation features. Insulating windows, extra ceiling and floor insulation, and extra thick walls may result in added construction costs of $10,000; however, the market may pay a $15,000 premium for a home with all of these features.

Often, as in the example below, home additions do not reflect contributory value commensurate with their costs.

> For example, enclosing a garage may cost $10,000, but the market may pay little, if any, premium for an enclosed garage if market preference in this neighborhood is to have a garage available for its intended use.

In some instances, a whole building may not contribute to value. In transitional areas, an old deteriorated house may detract from value if the most probable purchaser is a fast food restaurant developer who is seeking only the land.

Related to the principle of contribution is the concept of **interim use**. At a certain point in time, improvements no longer contribute to overall property value because of age, loss in functional utility, change in land economics, or other factors. Identification of the exact point in time when the improvements do not contribute to value is virtually impossible. Properties usually go through a transition period in which the improvements are utilized on an interim basis prior to ultimate site redevelopment. A rental house may generate income for a three-year period if demand for the underlying land for an alternate use is going to be deferred four years to five years because of changing land economics.

■ INCREASING AND DECREASING RETURNS

The principle of **increasing and decreasing returns** relates to the principle of balance as well as to the principle of contribution. This principle holds that as capital units are added, a certain point is reached where the added units do not contribute value commensurate with their costs.

An instance of increasing and decreasing returns is adding fertilizer to a row crop field. In this instance, spending $100 per acre in fertilizer on a field may increase the crop yield by $120 per acre. Spending $105 per acre in fertilizer may increase the crop yield by $130 per acre. If fertilizer is added at a cost of $160 per acre, however, the crop yield may not increase by the same $160 per acre spent. In fact, crop yield could decline because of overfertilization. There is no economic reason to spend more than $105 per acre in this example because this expenditure results in the maximum crop yield.

This represents the point of increasing and decreasing returns; hence, balance and maximum contribution have been achieved. Spending more per acre in fertilizer does not necessarily result in a proportionate increase in the crop yield.

The law of increasing and decreasing returns also applies to the maximum-size building that should be placed on a parcel of land. Adding stories to an office building may result in property value exceeding costs until the point is reached that an elevator must be added. From this point, the added cost may not result in added value commensurate with the cost.

■ CHANGE

The principle of **change** holds that as time and market conditions change, so does supply and demand for real estate, and thus, the value of real estate. All elements around us are constantly in a state of change, and a valuation represents a photograph at a certain point in time within its constantly changing environment.

It is important to remember that the appraiser's role is to report market reaction in this constantly changing environment, recognizing buyers' and sellers' anticipation of changing conditions rather than emphasizing the appraiser's own perception.

■ SUBSTITUTION

The principle of **substitution** is the basis for all decisions made by real estate buyers and should thus be the basis of every appraisal and every appraiser's thought process. Substitution is the process of identifying alternatives that would satisfy the same need, want, or desire. A prudent purchaser would pay no more for a home than it would cost him or her to build or buy another one. Substitution keeps the market in balance. For instance, if a buyer could purchase a house for $100,000, why would the purchaser build one for $110,000, assuming both offered the same utility and satisfaction?

Substitution is the key to the following three approaches to real estate valuation, all of which will be discussed in detail in Chapter 12 through Chapter 15:

1. The Cost Approach—A buyer would pay no more for a property if he or she could build one for less.

2. The Sales Comparison Approach—A property with the lowest price generally will yield the greatest demand if the properties are competitive and similar in terms of utility.

3. The Income Capitalization Approach—A renter would rent another equal property if it provided the same utility and satisfaction for less money. Likewise, if two properties reflected similar risk, return, and management capabilities, an investor would select the property which is priced less.

■ CONSISTENT USE THEORY

Consistent use theory involves the concept that land cannot be valued under one highest and best use while the improvements are valued based on another highest and best use.

> For example, if a residence is located in a commercial area, it cannot be appraised based on a residential use (improvements) plus another value for the underlying land (commercial). The value must be based on its highest and best use—either as a residence with commercial potential based on sales of similar properties with similar potential, or as a commercial site giving no value to the improvements. There may in fact be some deduction in value because of the required demolition costs of the house.

Recognizing that properties normally undergo an extended period in transition from one use to another, the interim use concept is not a violation of the consistent use principle.

■ OPPORTUNITY COSTS

The principle of opportunity costs holds that money allocated to a certain use cannot be used for an alternative.

> For example, a bond purchased for $10,000 may be producing a satisfactory return of 7%. If the purchaser of the bond later finds out that he or she could have invested the $10,000 in commodity futures and could have received a 25% return, the opportunity cost is the incremental 18% return (25% − 7%). The 18% "lost" is the opportunity cost, although the risk of the other opportunity should also be considered and analyzed.

■ EXTERNALITIES

The principle of **externalities** holds that there are the following four major forces outside the property limits that influence value:

1. Social

2. Economic

3. Physical/environmental

4. Governmental

These outside forces are explored more fully in Chapter 1. The important concept is that value is subjective in its nature, and the actions of buyers and sellers that create and maintain value are influenced by forces outside the limits of the subject property's boundaries.

■ HIGHEST AND BEST USE

Highest and best use is defined as that logical, legal, and most probable use which will yield the greatest net income to the land over a sustained period of time. Simply put, it is the most profitable, logical, and legal use. The four standard tests for highest and best use relate to that use which is physically possible, legally permissible, financially feasible, and maximally productive. Properties are normally appraised at their highest and best use. This is a complex concept that is more fully explored in Chapter 8.

■ COMPETITION

The principle of **competition** holds that profits tend to spur competition. The more profitable a venture may appear, the more competition will be created. In other words, success breeds competition, and extremely high success breeds excess competition.

> For example, if builders are experiencing 10% to 12% profit margins in a particular suburban expansion area outside a major metropolitan area, and demand increases to the point that builders are able to increase their profit margins to 15% to 20%, there is a high probability that the principle of competition will come into play, and more builders will begin to construct houses in this market.

■ ECONOMICS OF SCALE

This theory, **economies of scale**, is based on the idea that the greater the volume of an item, the less each incremental volume should cost. For instance, which would cost less: a single can of cola or each can in a case of colas? Probably the latter, due to the quantity discount. The same holds true for real estate. Which is more expensive per square foot, all things being equal: a 2,000 square foot home, or a 2,800 square foot home?

P A R T   T W O   Four Agents Of Production

To produce anything privately in a capitalistic society, the following four agents of production must be present:

1. Land

2. Labor

3. Capital

4. Entrepreneurship

Regardless of what is produced, whether it be an automobile, single-family residence, office building, or an appraisal report, all four agents of production come into play.

■ LAND

Land is the real estate component. Land can function by itself, or it can be used to support a building. Land is necessary for any building improvements. The cost or payment for the land and improvements usually is covered by a lease or mortgage payment.

■ LABOR

Labor relates to the direct and indirect costs and wages associated with workers. In addition, this agent of production includes materials utilized by labor in the production of a commodity.

■ CAPITAL

Capital is the cost of borrowing money and relates to the availability of credit. Venture capital for startup companies, securitized credit from Wall Street, and a bank loan from the local institution can all be sources of capital. Cash in one's savings account can also be capital, although the management of this capital is done by the bank lending officer.

■ ENTREPRENEURSHIP

This term means *coordination* or *management*. **Entrepreneurship** is the process of orchestrating land, labor, and capital to produce an item. It is usually the last position for which a return is paid (see Chapter 10).

A simple example of the four agents of production interacting is the construction of a single-family residence. A land developer acquires a large tract of unimproved land, constructs the streets and utility lines, and subdivides the parcel into smaller lots. A builder purchases a lot (land) and begins construction of a single-family home. During the process, materials are purchased, and all labor is paid (labor). Most of the construction monies come from local bank loans (capital). The builder is expected to pay fees and interest for use of these borrowed funds. When the house is completed, the builder hopes to sell the home for a profit. This profit becomes the reward for the builder's efforts (entrepreneurship).

P A R T   T H R E E   Economic Characteristics of Value

For an item to have value, it must possess the following five characteristics:

1. Utility

2. Scarcity

3. Desirability

4. Effective Purchasing Power

5. Demand Unit

■ UTILITY

Utility relates to a product or service's ability to satisfy a want, need, or desire. It is essential that an item have utility to have value; hence, it must have a use to the consumer. Many items have utility (home) while some items do not (hazardous waste).

■ SCARCITY

For an item to have value, it must not be readily available. Air can be seen as a good example of **scarcity**: It is essential that people have air to breathe, yet air is abundant, around us all the time, so no one is willing to pay for air. But when scuba diving in 100 feet of water, air has a tremendous value because in a breathable state, it is scarce. Sand is abundant, but there is little demand for it. Other items are in demand but are very scarce or unavailable (a magic carpet). Real estate, particularly land, is very scarce: It may appear to be abundant, but no additional land is being created.

■ DESIRABILITY

For something to have value, it must be desired. Real estate has value because it is a rare commodity that satisfies human desires. It is in demand because of **desirability**.

Certain types of homes may be quite desirable, while others may not be. For instance, an adobe home in Atlanta, Georgia, would more than likely be undesirable, but the standard in Albuquerque, New Mexico. Conversely, one probably should not build a two-story brick traditional or Cape Cod style home in Miami, Florida, but it may be perfectly desirable (and conforming) in Charlotte, North Carolina.

■ EFFECTIVE PURCHASING POWER

Although many items may have utility, be scarce, and be in demand, they may not have a realistic, achievable value because there are not enough consumers with adequate purchasing power. Many people would like a ski chalet in Aspen, Colorado, but few can afford it. **Effective purchasing power** is basically the ability to participate, economically speaking, in an activity. The methods of calculating what products people can afford vary from product to product and industry to industry. A general rule-of-thumb is that one-third (33 percent) of a household's income is available for housing, be it for rent or mortgage payments. Other ratios may be based on disposable income. Disposable income is income remaining after deductions made by the government, such as taxes or Social Security payments. It is basically money that can be spent.

■ DEMAND UNIT

A **demand unit** is simply the combination of desirability and effective purchasing power, that is, a member of a population of data (person, family, household, business, etc.) that desires a product and can afford it.

1. The four agents of production are
   a. scarcity, utility, desire, and effective purchasing power.
   b. land, improvements, labor, and capital.
   c. land, labor, capital, and entrepreneurship.
   d. land, labor, materials, and entrepreneurship.

2. To have value, an item must possess what characteristics?
   a. Land, labor, materials, and entrepreneurship
   b. Scarcity, utility, demand, and effective purchasing power
   c. Scarcity, utility, effective demand, and transferability
   d. Scarcity, utility, effective purchasing power, and desirability

3. Comparing an item's value to the item's cost is an evaluation of the item's
   a. conformance.
   b. highest and best use.
   c. change.
   d. contribution.

4. What two components comprise effective demand?
   a. Cost and value
   b. Desire and effective purchasing power
   c. Desire and need
   d. Desire and satisfaction

5. Appraising an improved property, an appraiser values the improvements as one use and the site as another use. This violates the theory of
   a. contribution.
   b. conforming use.
   c. consistent use.
   d. highest and best use.

6. Issues concerning a site's physical possibilities, legal permissibility, financial feasibility, and maximally productive uses relate to
   a. agents of production.
   b. factors that create value.
   c. supply and demand.
   d. highest and best use.

7. Scarcity, utility, effective purchasing power, and desire all relate to
   a. agents of production.
   b. economic characteristics of value.
   c. supply and demand.
   d. highest and best use.

8. When the yield of a product falls as the cost is increased, this is called
   a. decreasing returns.
   b. supply and demand.
   c. balance.
   d. change.

9. Assume a swimming pool cost $15,000 to install; however, the increase in market value of the property is only $3,000. Which principle is illustrated?
   a. Conformity
   b. Consistent use theory
   c. Contribution
   d. Balance

10. Which is one of the four criteria of highest and best use?
    a. Financially feasible
    b. Supply and demand
    c. Contribution
    d. Competition

11. Substitution is the primary basis of which approach to value?
    a. Cost approach
    b. Income capitalization approach
    c. Sales comparison approach
    d. All of the above

12. Entrepreneurial incentive is the same as
    a. contribution.
    b. profit.
    c. anticipation.
    d. competition.

13. Which of the following is NOT one of the four economic characteristics of value?
    a. Utility
    b. Effective purchasing power
    c. Anticipation
    d. Scarcity

14. The combination of desirability and effective purchasing power is called
    a. demand unit.
    b. supply unit.
    c. balance.
    d. unit of comparison.

15. The theory that each incremental item becomes less expensive as the volume is increased is called
    a. efficiency.
    b. economies of scale.
    c. profit.
    d. marginal utility.

CHAPTER FIVE

Real Estate Markets and Analysis

■ LEARNING OBJECTIVES

Students will be able to

1. understand and differentiate the difference between districts and neighborhoods.

2. understand the relationship of the four value forces as they relate to districts and neighborhoods.

3. understand and be able to identify the four stages in a neighborhood's life cycle.

4. understand the concept of market segmentation.

5. understand and explain the difference between efficient and inefficient markets, giving examples of each.

6. identify the three different types of market analysis.

7. identify the types and sources of data.

8. understand the basic steps in performing a market analysis.

9. understand the basic impact of federal monetary and fiscal policy with special emphasis on the three credit regulation devices used by the Federal Reserve to impact the price and supply of money.

10. understand and differentiate between money and capital markets, giving examples of each.

11. understand the basics of real estate finance including the basic terms, types of loans, and various forms of mortgages.

■ KEY TERMS

amortization	Federal Open Market	market study
buydowns	Committee (FOMC)	money markets
capital markets	fiscal policy	original loan amount
conclusion	growth	neighborhood
decline	inefficient market	payment
district	interest	points
efficient market	life cycle	reserve requirements
equity	loan-to-value (LTV) ratio	revitalization
feasibility study	market analysis	stability
federal discount rate	market segmentation	

■ INTRODUCTION

As we have already learned in this course, value influences can generally be broken down into the following four basic forces or categories:

1. Social

2. Economic

3. Physical/Environmental

4. Governmental

In recognizing these four forces, it is noted that the physical attributes of the real estate component of a particular property being appraised comprise only part of one of these four forces, that being physical/environmental. We have also learned that value is subjective in its nature rather than objective. With these two concepts in mind, it is obvious that value is significantly influenced by occurrences outside the property limits. The interaction of the four forces creates a "real estate market." This Chapter focuses on the identification and analysis of real estate markets, with consideration also accorded the influence of federal monetary and fiscal policy, as well as real estate finance, allowing the appraiser to proceed efficiently through the appraisal process.

PART ONE   Districts and Neighborhoods

Recognizing that most factors that influence value occur outside of the actual real estate, the appraiser must undertake a study of the market factors that affect a certain parcel of real estate. Before doing this, however, the appraiser must identify the particular market in which the four forces interact to create value of a particular property. An understanding of districts and neighborhoods is essential for this task to be completed efficiently and thoroughly.

■ DISTRICT

A **district** is a group of *homogenous* land uses. The most obvious district with which most people are familiar is the immediate subdivision in which a family or individual lives. Most subdivisions are planned with the idea of grouping similar and compatible structures. Developers often seek to maintain congruity as to house styles, sizes, price ranges, and configuration.

There are, however, other types of districts. Many of us work in well-defined industrial districts. Consistent with residential subdivisions, an industrial district is composed of similar buildings on similar sites, with similar manufacturing or warehousing orientation.

Another example of a district would be a heavily developed corridor featuring strip commercial development. Here, the homogenous land uses are all retail in their character.

■ NEIGHBORHOOD

A **neighborhood** is a group of complementary land uses. Uses that would be complementary to a residential subdivision may include those destinations or places frequented by families or individuals living in the subdivision. Schools, shopping facilities, places of worship, and employment centers are all complementary to single-family usage.

The term used to describe the connecting of complementary uses to the homogenous land uses (district) is **linkage**. Linkage is the element that joins districts to complementary uses, creating neighborhoods. Linkages that would apply to a residential district (subdivision) would include nearby schools, shopping facilities, employment centers, and places of worship.

Linkages that would transform an industrial district into a neighborhood would include access routes to interstate highways, airports, other transportation facilities, residential areas that provide an employment base, and possibly financial services.

Linkages that transform a commercial district into a neighborhood would include transportation routes to wholesalers, nearby residential areas (customers), etc.

■ THE FOUR VALUE FORCES

Both neighborhoods and districts are influenced by the four value forces. The identification of a district or a neighborhood is usually based on the physical/environmental forces that affect value; however, it is quite common for one or more of the other three forces to be the most dominant determinant when identifying a district or neighborhood. The following are examples:

Social

Family composition
Community and neighborhood organizations
Cultural or ethnic groups

Economic

Income levels of residents
Development trends
Employment

Physical/Environmental

Topography
Subsurface (Rock, marsh, etc.)

Governmental

Zoning
School districts
Police and fire protection
Land use plan

Even though a district or neighborhood may be most clearly identifiable by a social, economic, or governmental force, the appraiser usually relates these forces to a specific area defined geographically.

> For example, a neighborhood may be most easily identifiable by the predominance of a particular age or occupational group such as young professionals; however, the appraiser would usually "frame" the defined district or neighborhood through street boundaries or other geographic means.

■ LIFE CYCLE

Neighborhoods and districts alike generally exist in one of four life cycle stages; these are growth, stability, decline, and revitalization.

Growth

Growth is typically the initial stage in a neighborhood or district's life cycle. This refers to the period in which the neighborhood or district is expanding and developing. An example would be a suburban bedroom community where numerous houses are being constructed, along with complementary schools, shopping facilities, and other uses. Compared to the other stages in the life cycle, the growth stage is usually fairly rapid.

Stability

After the growth stage, an area typically matures and grows at a slower rate. The **stability** stage in the life cycle may occur when it is no longer profitable to build, and/or the supply of vacant land is depleted.

Decline

When a neighborhood can no longer compete with other comparable neighborhoods, it usually enters the **decline** stage of its life cycle. Improvements may become functionally inadequate and lose market appeal, and maintenance levels frequently decrease.

Revitalization

After decline, a neighborhood or district sometimes shows **revitalization**, that is, it regains momentum or sees rebirth. Often, this occurs because of an area's proximity to employment or other conveniences. Many fringe areas around older downtown business districts are being revitalized. In a sense, a district or neighborhood such as this re-enters the "growth" stage of the life cycle.

When older structures are revitalized, with rehabilitation and renovation occurring, the area is said to be undergoing *gentrification*.

Sometimes, a neighborhood or district may go through a long, extended growth stage, then mature and stabilize, never going through the decline or revitalization stages. Stability may dominate the life cycle for many years, with the area never declining to the point that revitalization occurs.

■ MARKET SEGMENTATION

The act of distinguishing or delineating markets that the appraiser should consider in his data program is called **market segmentation**.

When appraising a typical, single-family residence, the market segmentation process may relate only to identifying the specific neighborhood in which the subject property is located, along with the comparable sales, rentals, and land sales.

Market segmentation can also become very complex. If an appraiser is involved in an appraisal of a limited market property, such as a food processing facility, cold storage warehouse, concrete plant, etc., the breadth of the market research may well be expanded to include several states, a region, and in some cases the entire United States. When market segmentation requires expansion of the research program into such a broad area, the appraiser should concentrate on cities, counties, or regions with economic characteristics similar to the area in which the subject is located.

For example, an appraiser who is appraising a poultry processing plant in Georgia, may have to expand his data search into Arkansas as both states have significant poultry industries.

PART TWO   Efficient/Inefficient Market

An **efficient market** is one that is characterized by goods or services that are easily produced and readily transferable, with a large number of buyers and sellers. An **inefficient market**, on the other hand, is just the opposite. Goods and services are not readily produced or easily transferable, with no readily identified group of buyers and sellers active in a particular marketplace. The differences between an efficient market and an inefficient market are illustrated in Table 5.1.

Based on these characteristics, described in Table 5.1, real estate tends to operate in an inefficient market. Often, real estate transactions are confidential, and limited information is available via public records, making the data collection and verification process crucial in real estate appraisal.

When a market is undersupplied, an extended time period is usually required to bring a particular type of real estate to the market for sale. Conversely, oversupplied conditions can occur because the time period required from initial conception to final delivery of real estate may encompass a number of years, and demand could possibly decline during the period that it takes to create the real estate product.

TABLE 5.1 ■ Contrasts of an Efficient Market and Inefficient Market

Characteristic	Efficient Market (stock market)	Inefficient Market (real estate)
Products	Homogeneous	Unique
Inventory of Buyers and Sellers	Large number	Few
Prices	Uniform/Stable/Low (most can afford)/ Quality Tends to Uniformity at a Set Price	Variable/Inconsistent/High (limited affordability)
Restrictions	Self Regulating/ Few Government Restrictions	Many Restrictions
Supply and Demand	Balanced (daily) due to competition	Often Unbalanced (for months/years)
Information/Intelligence	Fully Informed Participants	Limited Accurate Information
Organized Conduit	An Exchange	None
Goods	Readily Available/Consumed Quickly/ Supplied Easily/Transportable	Years to Consume/Months or Years to Supply/Immobile

Although technology has enhanced the marketability of real estate tremendously in recent years, most buyers still want to personally view the product they are buying, as well as a number of alternative properties. This activity is very time consuming, especially since the "shopping" time may well be restricted to weekends and other off work times.

All of these tendencies make real estate an inefficient market.

PART THREE   Market Analysis

Market analysis is the study of a specific market. It is the collection and dissection of data and the conversion of that data to information that can be used for analysis and decision-making by an appraiser or analyst.

■ TYPES OF MARKET ANALYSIS

The following three types of market analysis are available:

1. Market study

2. Marketability study

3. Feasibility study

All are performed by appraisers either separately or as part of a complete appraisal.

Market Study

A **market study** is the analysis of an environment of buyers/sellers and/or landlords/tenants (lessors/lessees). A market study is not site specific. It usually relates to a certain property type or geographic area.

> For example, a bank may want a market study of a certain city or region indicating what the region's trends are related to housing. The bank may be interested as to whether the area is dominated by condominiums, detached starter homes, detached move-up homes, or estate homes. Based on this information, the bank could tailor its loan portfolio to the product type likely to be most successful in a particular area.

As a second example, a developer interested in developing a shopping center in a certain suburban area of a metropolitan community would likely want to know the origin of the potential customers. To perform this, a market study of the housing in the area may be performed. Based on this study, a developer could ascertain whether or not the area was growing, what the prevailing income levels were, whether or not there were families with children, or a wide variety of other informative data.

Marketability Study

A **marketability study** relates to a more specific product type within a defined market. A marketability study often addresses the time required to absorb a particular product, and the price or rent level at which that product would be accepted into the marketplace.

A marketability study is usually both site specific and property type specific. However, the appraiser usually begins with a broad market, then reduces this down to an individual submarket.

For example, if an appraiser is performing a marketability study to determine whether or not 30,000 square feet of minor tenant space in an anchored shopping center in a metropolitan suburban bedroom community would be absorbed in a reasonable period of time, the analysis may begin with a retail overview (supply and demand) of the overall metropolitan area. From here, the appraiser may study the county retail market, then focus on the immediate neighborhood or submarket.

A single-family residential subdivision developer may have recently acquired a 50-acre parcel. By studying demographic trends, income levels, and other factors, the developer may conclude that the most logical and probable use for the site is to subdivide the parcel into one-half acre lots with curvilinear subdivision streets and cul-de-sacs. The marketability study would give the developer an indication as to how long it would take to sell the lots, and at what general price level the lots would sell. A marketability study may also reveal that a subdivision amenity package (pool and tennis courts) is a necessity if a developer is expected to market more than 100 lots comprising a subdivision.

Another example would be an office developer considering constructing a speculative office building in the downtown area. A marketability analysis may indicate that the current market is oversupplied, with a five-year inventory remaining at current absorption levels. Based on the implied demand that is expected to be unmet five years hence, the office building developer may choose to postpone construction for three years so that a two-year construction period would coincide with the absorption of the excess space currently existing in inventory. Then, there should be demand when the office building is completed.

Feasibility Study

A **feasibility study** is simply a comparison of cost versus the value if the project is undertaken. If cost exceeds the value, the proposal is not feasible. If the value exceeds cost, the proposal is feasible.

Cost feasibility is incorporated into the highest and best use analysis, as subsequently discussed. There may be numerous feasible uses, but there is usually one that is most profitable, that ultimately being the highest and best use.

An example would be a builder who acquires a building lot for $30,000. His construction costs, including all hard and soft expenditures, may total $100,000. If the prevailing price range for similar houses in the neighborhood is $100,000 to $110,000, the builder's total investment of $130,000 indicates that this project is not feasible. On the other hand, if the prevailing price range is $140,000 to $160,000 for similar houses, the value obviously exceeds costs, leaving the developer with a profit for having undertaken the venture.

A feasibility study is of course property type as well as site specific.

■ TYPES AND SOURCES OF DATA

When proceeding through the data collection process, the appraiser should be aware of how to categorize all the information obtained. One general means is to classify the data by type and by source.

Types of Data

1. *General Data*—General data relates to collected information that would be appropriate for many properties. General data usually encompasses all of the four forces (social, economic, environmental/physical, and governmental).

   A demographic printout from a demographic service is an example of general data.

Other examples of general data include labor statistics, weather studies, transportation studies, etc.

2. *Specific Data*—This relates to information that is used directly in the analysis of the subject property. Specific data thus relates to the subject property itself as well as the comparables that will be used in the actual valuation process.

> For example, information on the subject itself would include site data such as legal description, survey, environmental report, etc. Information on the comparables may include data related to land sales similar to the subject site, sales of improved properties with improvements similar to the subject, and comparable rentals.

Sources of Data

1. *Secondary Data*—Secondary data encompasses publications and other sources of information that were prepared by someone other than the appraiser. Sources of secondary data may include chamber of commerce publications, census reports, rent studies, published sales data services, etc.

2. *Primary Data*—Primary data relates to information that was collected directly by the appraiser. Examples of primary data may include a sketch prepared by the appraiser based on actual building measurements, subject photographs, sales information procured directly by the appraiser, area rentals obtained directly by the appraiser, etc.

In the course of performing an appraisal, an appraiser usually starts with a variety of secondary data sources, then chooses the items that must be verified and/or inspected directly by the appraiser. When this step occurs, primary data may be produced from the secondary data source.

> For example, a multiple-listing service (MLS) sold book may be an example of secondary data, but when the sale is confirmed firsthand by the appraiser, then inspected and photographed by the appraiser, it then becomes primary data.

■ STEPS IN MARKET ANALYSIS

Market analysis includes an evaluation of the market boundaries and then of its supply and demand for one or more products.

Market Boundaries

Identifying the market area is the first step in market analysis. Although the boundaries may be more clearly defined by social, economic, or governmental factors, the **market boundaries** are usually identified by some geographical (physical/environmental) means. Geographical boundaries may include streets, rivers, lakes, rail lines, etc.

Establishing boundaries does not necessarily mean that the appraiser cannot go outside the boundaries for appropriate data.

> For example, there may be insufficient data within a specific residential subdivision for a meaningful application of the sales comparison approach. The appraiser may have to go to a nearby similar but geographically distinct subdivision for sales data.

Forces outside the subject site boundaries are called external forces or external economies, and thus, could include the market area, but would be outside the subject site itself.

In other instances, neighborhood boundaries may be more readily identifiable by linkages.

> For example, a resort destination may be more appropriately defined by the areas from which the buyers come. This may be statewide, regionwide, or even nation-wide. Because of this phenomenon, a resort community in Colorado may have as its direct competition a resort in Utah.

Supply

The existing inventory represents the most easily identifiable component of **supply**. There are other more subtle indications of supply, however, that must also be analyzed. Properties under construction, properties planned, or properties that are capable of being converted all represent supply alternatives. A study of housing permits in a certain geographic area could be a very valuable indicator of what the inventory may be several months hence. Most major developments such as office buildings, shopping centers, or industrial parks become known through public announcements.

Demand

Demand relates to occupancy and absorption of a particular product in the defined area. Occupancy is the count of the units that are physically occupied as of a certain period while absorption is best described as the change (positive or negative) of occupied units over a specified period of time.

In performing a demand analysis, the appraiser usually starts with a broad market, then continually condenses the analysis into a smaller, well-defined area.

> For example, a proposed single-family subdivision in a certain census tract may require the appraiser to first consider population trends based on census data and county projections, household composition, and income levels. A census tract may be expected to add 500 households over the next five years, with the family composition indicating two children per household. This may well indicate demand for single-family detached dwellings.

If household income levels are $50,000, one could reasonably anticipate demand for detached single-family homes priced in the $100,000 to $125,000 range based on historic price levels/income earnings relationships. A more concentrated study of five subdivisions in the subject's immediate area may indicate that all the subdivisions are selling two to four houses per month within this identified price level. Assuming continuation of this demand and a proper supply, it may be concluded that the time is right to proceed with a single-family subdivision development on the subject site.

Conclusion

The **conclusion** of a market analysis reconciles or correlates the results of the supply and demand analysis in the identified market. This step is necessary for market studies as well as marketability studies.

PART FOUR   Monetary and Fiscal Policy

When real property is sold, a defined interest in real estate is exchanged for a defined amount of money. Usually, the money exchanged is free to float in an open market, competing for other goods and services. Most of the time, a portion of the money used to acquire a real property comes from borrowed funds, most often from banks or other traditional lending institutions. Money should not be viewed as a fixed, static commodity, but rather one that is constantly changing in its availability and cost.

The United States operates on a fractional reserve banking system in which deposits are made to banks, and the banks lend from the deposits. Although most of the deposits are loaned to various customers, the banks are required to keep some of the deposits in reserve. Loans and reserves are directly influenced by federal monetary policy. The supply and cost of money in the United States is significantly affected by the Federal Reserve, commonly known as the Fed. This is not a direct part of the federal government; however, the President of the United States does appoint the Federal Reserve board members.

■ CREDIT REGULATION DEVICES

The Fed impacts the price (interest rate) and the supply of money in the three ways described on the following page. By affecting the price and supply, demand is also affected.

Federal Discount Rate

The **federal discount rate** is the rate at which member banks can borrow funds from the Fed to loan to other customers. Banks compete in the open market for deposits and must pay a certain level of interest. Banks also must charge customers higher rates than the rates being paid for deposits so that profit can be made. If the Fed lowers its discount rate, member banks are allowed to pass the savings onto customers through lower interest rates. This spurs economic demand since the cost of acquiring borrowed funds has been lessened. Conversely, if the discount rate is increased, credit tends to become tight, and economic activity declines. An economy that is expanding too rapidly may lead to inflationary conditions. The Fed is constantly trying to maintain a balance between economic growth through lowering rates and controlling inflation through raising rates.

Reserve Requirement

The **reserve requirement** is the percentage of deposits that must be retained by banks. If the reserve requirement is increased, credit tends to tighten. Because of the limited amount of available funds, interest rates tend to rise, and economic activity decreases. If the reserve requirement is lowered, more funds are made available for borrowers. Interest rates tend to come down, and economic expansion occurs. Again, a balance between economic expansion and inflation control is the ultimate goal of the Fed.

Federal Open Market Committee (FOMC)

The **Federal Open Market Committee (FOMC)** is the part of the Fed that buys and sells government securities. If the FOMC buys government securities, money flows into the economy, spurring economic expansion. If the FOMC sells securities, funds are funneled into the Fed from the general economy, and credit becomes scarce, increasing interest rates and decreasing economic activity.

All three of these mechanisms influence the money supply and the price of credit (interest). The most direct influence is the federal discount rate because many banks tie their prime lending rate to the discount rate. Discount rates are changed frequently during the year. Reserve requirements, on the other hand, have a lagging effect on the economy, but a change can have a powerful and long-term impact on the supply and demand for money. The FOMC buys and sells securities every business day. Although not immediately evident to the public, the effects are similar to the discount rate in that they are current and sometimes dramatic.

■ FISCAL POLICY

The government's management of revenues (taxes) and expenses (appropriations) is called **fiscal policy**. The United States fiscal policy is managed by the Office of Management and Budget (OMB). The budget management and fiscal spending also affect interest rates. Generally, the higher the amount of debt, the higher the inflation rate, which means the higher the interest rate. Conversely, the lower the debt amount for the nation, the lower the inflation rate and the lower the interest rate.

P A R T   F I V E   **Money and Capital Markets**

Money markets and capital markets are both sources of funds and differ only in the types of instruments and the maturities of these instruments. Money markets are financial instruments that have a maturity of less than one year; capital market instruments have maturities of more than one year. Money markets and capital markets are important because they both compete with real estate for investment dollars. Prevailing interest rates are a direct consequence of the activity in both of these markets. Interest rates also have a direct impact on the demand for real estate because real estate purchases usually involve the use of borrowed funds that are repaid with interest. When interest rates are down, demand for real estate tends to be up; when interest rates are up, demand tends to be down. Assuming a stable supply of a product, prices increase when demand increases, and prices decrease when demand decreases.

■ MONEY MARKETS

Money markets are financial vehicles with traditional maturities or investment periods of less than one year. Some examples of money market instruments are short-term certificates of deposit (a bank's CDs), federal funds (member banks' short-term borrowing from the Fed), Treasury bills (short term government securities), and commercial paper (corporate promissory notes). Money market instruments tend to influence short-term financing rates, such as loans for construction and/or development of real estate.

■ CAPITAL MARKETS

Capital markets include financial vehicles with usual maturities of more than one year. Examples of capital market instruments include bonds, stocks, mortgages, and deeds of trust. Capital market instruments tend to influence long-term financing rates, as well as required rates of return on real estate investments.

P A R T   S I X   **Real Estate Finance**

Real estate transfers usually involve the use of dollars as opposed to other assets. Also, most real estate acquisitions involve both the buyer's investment in the property as well as the use of borrowed funds for the balance. The buyer's contribution is called equity, whereas the borrowed money is called a mortgage. Mortgages are generally considered to be capital instruments because payback periods are usually 15 years or more.

■ MORTGAGE FINANCING TERMS

To understand the ramifications of mortgage financing, some basic terms must be understood.

Original Loan Amount

The **original loan amount** is the face amount of the original loan.

Equity

Equity is the down payment or the cash paid by the buyer.

Amortization

Amortization is the process of retiring a mortgage or debt over a specified time period. An amortization usually calls for the systematic repayment of principal plus interest at some specified rate.

Interest

Interest represents the money earned for the right to use capital. Mortgages in the United States are generally paid on a compound interest method in which interest is paid each month on the outstanding balance at the contractual interest rate.

Payment

Payment is also known as *debt service*. A payment on an amortizing mortgage is comprised of both interest and principal. Dividing the annual debt service by the original loan amount equates to the mortgage constant. For instance, if a mortgage payment is $1,300 per month, or $15,600 per year, and if the original loan amount was $200,000, the annual constant is .078 ($15,600 ÷ $200,000).

Loan-to-Value

The **loan-to-value (LTV)** ratio is a percentage of the original or proposed loan to the value of a property (loan amount ÷ property value). Mortgages are usually based on a loan-to-value concept that protects the lender from loaning too much on a property. If a lender has a program that loans 90 percent LTV, and the property value is $100,000, the maximum loan will be $90,000. The remaining $10,000 is derived from a down payment (equity) or some form of other financing.

Points

Points are prepaid interest to the lender and are calculated based on the loan amount. Each point is 1 percent of the loan amount. To qualify at a lower interest rate, a buyer might pay cash to the lender at closing (points). Assuming a buyer wants to prepay interest to buy down the rate on the mortgage in the first three years, it may cost two points on the $100,000 mortgage. The buyer's cost will be $2,000 ($100,000 × 0.02 = $2,000).

■ TYPES OF LOANS

Loans vary by region and the dynamics of the market. Traditionally, there were only 30-year self-amortizing loans available; in the 1980s, adjustable rate mortgages (ARMs) became popular; today, an array of mortgage programs are available, and new ones are announced frequently. The following loan programs are the most popular.

Fixed Rate Mortgages

In a *fixed rate mortgage*, the interest rate is fixed, usually for the term of the loan. Other programs are available in which the rate is fixed for five or seven years, then readjusted for the remainder of the term; the initial interest rate is less on these loans as the lender is committed only to the contractual rate for five or seven years versus being committed to the entire term.

Adjustable Rate Mortgages (ARMs)

An *adjustable rate mortgage (ARM)* is a loan in which the interest paid is based on a certain index (one year Treasury bill, for instance) plus a "spread" or amount over the index. An ARM might be 200 basis points (or 2.00%) over the 1-year T-bill. Assuming the one-year T-bill is 4.0%, the interest rate would be 6.0%. It adjusts on the anniversary of the loan to the then-current T-bill rate. ARMs typically have annual and lifetime "caps" that keep the mortgage within an acceptable range. A common program is a 2% annual cap and a 6% lifetime cap. In the example noted here, the highest it could go in Year 2 is 8.0%, then 10.0% in Year 3, and so on to a maximum of 12.0% over the life of the loan. Keep in mind, however, that the ARM "floats" with the indexed rate; the rate and payment could also decrease if the T-bill rate falls.

Buydowns

Buydowns are a variation of ARMS or fixed-rate mortgages, but interest is prepaid to lower the payments in the early years of the term. The interest is sometimes prepaid by the builder or developer in order for prospective homeowners to qualify.

■ FORMS OF MORTGAGES

There are various forms of mortgages available, such as conventional, insured, purchase money mortgages, and blanket, chattel, and package mortgages.

Conventional Mortgages

Conventional mortgages are the most common mortgage instruments and are available through mortgage bankers, banks, and savings and loan institutions. These types of mortgages are originated by these groups but are usually bought and sold by the following three entities:

1. FNMA (Federal National Mortgage Association)

2. FHLMC (Federal Home Loan Mortgage Corporation)

3. GNMA (Government National Mortgage Association)

This is known as the *secondary market* for mortgages. Because these are promissory notes secured by real estate, they have value which is based on the yield and the maturity date of the note. Due to the stringent requirements of these agencies/corporations, these loans and the mortgages, properties, appraisals, and documents that go along with them must fit certain criteria. Loans fitting their criteria are traded on the secondary market since they are backed by these groups. Loans not meeting their criteria are termed non-conventional loans. Nonconventional loans are also traded on the secondary market, but without the backing of FNMA, FHLMC, and GNMA, and are thus considered more risky.

Insured Loans

Insured loans are mortgages which include a guarantee or insurance to protect the lender in case of default by the borrower. The Federal Housing Authority (FHA) and the Department of Veterans Affairs (VA) both offer loan programs to qualifying individuals.

Blanket Mortgages

A *blanket mortgage* is a mortgage secured by a group of properties or a number of lots. Suppose a person owns ten rental houses; she may want a blanket mortgage on all ten homes, with one loan, one payment, and one lender.

Chattel Mortgages

A *chattel mortgage* is a loan for personal property and secured by personal property.

For example, a restaurant owner may put a chattel mortgage on the restaurant equipment.

Package Mortgages

A *package mortgage* is a loan on both real and personal property. The same restaurant owner may put a package mortgage on the restaurant equipment and the real estate.

Purchase Money Mortgages

A *purchase money mortgage (PMM)* is a loan or note taken back by the seller and part of the purchase price. For instance, say Joe wants to buy a home and can qualify for a $90,000 mortgage at today's interest rates; he has $12,000 for a down payment and closing costs; closing costs are estimated to total $3,000; hence, he can afford a $99,000 home; he finds a home he likes and contracts to buy it at $110,000; to effect the sale, the seller could take back a PMM for $11,000 to make up the difference.

1. A group of complementary land uses is called a(n)
   a. area.
   b. neighborhood.
   c. district.
   d. region.

2. Which component does NOT comprise demand?
   a. Buyer/tenant profiles
   b. Occupancy
   c. Properties under construction
   d. Absorption

3. Which of the following is NOT a credit regulation device controlled by the Fed?
   a. Federal funds rate
   b. Prime rate
   c. Reserve requirements
   d. Federal Open Market Committee

4. Which of the following is a capital market instrument?
   a. Treasury bills
   b. Short-term bank CD
   c. Federal funds
   d. Mortgage

5. Which is the systematic reduction of debt over time?
   a. Points
   b. Payment
   c. Amortization
   d. Principal

6. A point equals which of the following?
   a. 1 percent of the interest
   b. 1 percent of the payments
   c. 1 percent of the value
   d. 1 percent of the loan amount

7. Which characteristic is indicative of an efficient market?
   a. Having a unique product
   b. Numerous governmental restrictions
   c. Often unbalanced supply and demand
   d. An organized exchange conduit

8. Which study examines the profitability of a proposed property?
   a. Feasibility study
   b. Market study
   c. Marketability study
   d. Trade area analysis

9. Which component does NOT comprise supply?
   a. Absorption
   b. Existing inventory
   c. Properties under construction
   d. Planned properties

10. Which body of government controls fiscal policy?
    a. Office of Management and Budget
    b. The President
    c. The Committee of Back-Slapping, Back-Stabbing Idiots (CBSBSI)
    d. Congress

11. Payments on an amortizing mortgage are comprised of
    a. Principal
    b. Utility costs
    c. Interest
    d. Both A and C

12. A mortgage in which the interest rate floats with an indexed rate is a(n)
    a. adjustable rate mortgage.
    b. package mortgage.
    c. fixed rate mortgage.
    d. buydown mortgage.

13. General data relates to what?
    a. All data gathered in the research process.
    b. The four forces on real estate—social, economic, physical/environmental, governmental
    c. Data relating to the subject property only.
    d. All primary and secondary data.

14. What is data that is gathered in the analysis of a certain property?
    a. Primary data
    b. General data
    c. Specific data
    d. Secondary data

15. Data that the appraiser personally collects is called
    a. specific data.
    b. general data.
    c. secondary data.
    d. primary data.

CHAPTER SIX

The Valuation Process

■ LEARNING OBJECTIVES

Students will be able to

1. understand the entire valuation process, recognizing the significance of each step.

2. understand the importance of properly defining the valuation problem including the identification of the real estate, identification of the real property, value definition, function, etc.

3. recognize the data program that will be required for the valuation at hand including the data collection and verification, as well as data analysis.

4. comprehend the basic concept of highest and best use, together with its various tests, recognizing that the highest and best use analysis must address the land if vacant and property as improved.

5. understand the appropriateness of valuing the land if vacant.

6. recognize the importance and applicability of the three approaches to value.

7. recognize the importance of the reconciliation as this function relates to the three value approaches.

8. recognize that various report alternatives are available, with these covered subsequently in the course.

■ KEY TERMS

collection	general data	scope
current data	income approach	specific data
data analysis	previous date	submission of report
function	purpose	verification
future date	reconciliation	

■ INTRODUCTION

The valuation process is a systematic, orderly procedure to address a valuation problem and convey the findings. To this point, this book has dwelt on real estate value influences, legal considerations, various types of value, economic principles, and real estate market analysis. This Chapter represents the bridge between this "background" and the actual valuation and conveyance (reporting) of the value conclusion to the user of the appraisal.

The basic valuation process can generally be outlined as in Figure 6.1.

Ideally, the appraiser proceeds through the valuation process in an orderly fashion; however, on a practical basis, many of the steps have to be performed out of sequence because of missing subject property information, time lag in procuring data, personnel availability, or other factors. Often, the actual appraisal assignment may be modified during the course of the appraisal process because of information obtained by the appraiser in his normal course of investigating the subject property or market area.

P A R T   O N E   Definition of the Problem

■ IDENTIFICATION OF REAL ESTATE

The term *real estate* relates to the physical attributes of the property, generally land and improvements.

The identification of the real estate usually begins with some form of legal documentation describing the land. Because improvements are subject to change (expansion, modification, or demolition), the improvements are seldom mentioned in a legal description. The appraiser is not a title attorney and should never assume this role. The responsibility of identifying the real estate resides in the user of the report or person ordering the appraisal. It is the responsibility of the appraiser, however, to advise the client as to where the responsibility lies. Also, when the legal description and physical characteristics of the property appear to be inconsistent, the appraiser should notify the client for direction.

As noted in Chapter 2, following are the three basic methods to legally identify the real estate:

1. Metes-and-bounds description

2. Governmental (rectangular) survey system

3. Lot-and-block system

A fourth form, the monument system, is archaic and is generally not currently used.

FIGURE 6.1 ■ Outline of the Basic Valuation Process

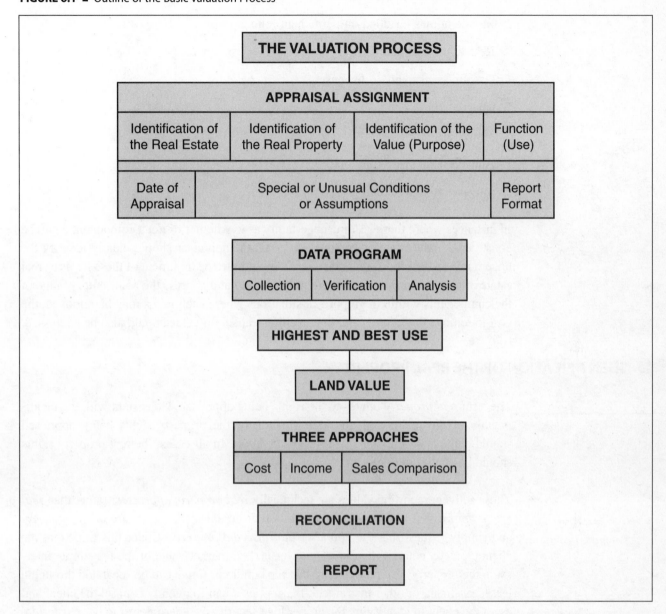

A surveyor's plat is usually a graphic representation of one of the methods and is often considered legally acceptable in most municipalities, assuming the plat is properly recorded in public records.

Tax plats are generally not documented to the extent that they can be assumed to be graphically correct; in fact, most tax plats have a qualifying assumption addressing the limitation of their accuracy.

Even though tax plats are generally not held to be legally correct, they can be utilized for visual interpretation. In instances where the appraiser does have a surveyor's plat, it is usually beneficial to present a tax plat in the report with deviations as well as consistencies with the legal description noted.

In the process of identifying the real estate, questions often arise as to items that may be considered real estate or personal property. Examples of these include the following:

1. Signs and supporting structures

2. Mobile homes installed on permanent foundations

3. Restaurant equipment

4. Gasoline tanks and/or dispensers

5. Chandeliers

6. Motel furniture

7. Aboveground swimming pool

8. Movable storage building

In instances where there is some uncertainty as to whether or not a component could be construed as real estate or personal property, the appraiser should clearly identify the uncertainty in the report, seek the client's input as to the treatment of these items as real estate or personal property, then properly identify and address the contributory value of the components within the report. In situations where such items may be removed, the cost to remove these items and the resulting impact on value should also be addressed.

■ IDENTIFICATION OF THE REAL PROPERTY

The term *real property* relates to the rights being appraised. Consistent with the identification of the real estate, the identification of the property rights being appraised should come from the client or user of the report. In all cases, the real property rights should be clearly defined.

Those actively reporting values are technically *real property appraisers* rather than *real estate appraisers*. Frequently, those who order appraisals are unaware of this concept and simply request that the appraiser *appraise the property*. Under this direction, the client typically equates *the property* to mean "the market value of the fee simple interest in the property." By recognizing that the bundle of rights can be separated through a lease, easement, or other instrument, the appraiser can frequently counsel the client and assist the client in identifying the proper loan security or other interest to be transferred.

The vast majority of appraisal assignments involve the fee simple interest in a parcel of real estate. In appraising fractional interest, it is usually helpful for the appraiser to begin with a fee simple value estimate. This fee simple value represents the entire bundle of rights, subject to the four powers of government. By having the fee simple value as the beginning point, the value of a fractional interest can be analyzed as it relates to the value of the entire bundle of rights. In some instances, the value of a partial interest can exceed the value of the entire bundle of rights.

> For example, a property could be leased at a rental rate above market to a creditworthy tenant. The owner of the leased fee interest could in such case be entitled to a premium over and above what the property would sell for if it were not encumbered with a lease favorable to the owner.

■ IDENTIFICATION OF THE VALUE ADDRESSED (PURPOSE)

As noted in Chapter 3, there are numerous types of value for which appraisals are requested. Although the vast majority of appraisal assignments are concerned with market value, assignments involving insurable value, liquidation value, going concern value, value in use, or other values are common.

One important factor to consider is this:

The term *value* should never be used in an appraisal report without a modifier.

The identification of the real property and identification of the value addressed combine to form a section of the appraisal frequently called **Purpose**. Examples of "Purpose of the Appraisal" are as follows:

1. The purpose of this appraisal is to estimate the market value of the fee simple interest in the real estate identified as. . .

2. The purpose of this appraisal is to estimate the market value of the leased fee interest in the real estate identified as. . .

3. The purpose of this appraisal is to estimate the going concern value of the leasehold interest in the real estate identified as. . .

■ FUNCTION OF THE REPORT

The term **function** relates to the use of the appraisal. For years, many practitioners in the appraisal industry argued that the function should not be made a part of the appraisal process because the use of the report should have no bearing on the value being sought; that is, market value for a sales transaction should be the same as market value for estate tax purposes, condemnation, or any other reason.

More modern appraisers, however, do recognize the need for this section in that it tends to customize the appraisal to the needs of the client.

> For example, a client may request a market value appraisal when in fact the client is an insurance company that is more interested in replacement costs; a clear understanding of the function of the report would have led the appraiser to verify with the user of the report that insurable value may be needed as opposed to market value.

■ DATE OF APPRAISAL

There are obviously three broad date alternatives for conveying a value conclusion. These are as follows:

1. Current date

2. Previous date

3. Future date

Current Date

The vast majority of appraisal assignments involve the **current date**. Under most circumstances, the appraiser utilizes the actual date of inspection and conveys his or her value conclusion as of that date.

Frequently, the appraiser may be asked to assume hypothetical conditions on the current date. This is generally an acceptable appraisal request and is presented in the *Uniform Standards of Professional Appraisal Practice (USPAP)*.

Previous Date

Occasionally, an appraiser may be asked to appraise a property as of a **previous date**. Three instances requiring a *back-dated* appraisal are the following:

1. Appraisal for estate purposes (normally the date of death)

2. Condemnation proceedings (established date of taking)

3. Property donation purposes (date donation was made)

One of the most difficult concepts for appraisers to grasp is that under the traditional market value definition, the appraiser, in effect, mirrors actions of buyers and sellers in the marketplace as of a specific point in time. Typical buyers and sellers in the marketplace would, of course, not have knowledge of future events that would have occurred after the date of valuation.

When appraising as of a previous date, appraisers must therefore place themselves back in time to the appraisal date and interpret the market based on general market knowledge and activity prevalent at that time. Major economic events that occurred subsequent to the valuation date cannot be taken into consideration; however, the appraisers can certainly report market reaction to facts that were perceptions on the date of valuation.

Because the appraiser normally does not have the opportunity for a full, formal inspection on the date of valuation when appraising as of a previous date, efforts must be made to ascertain the condition of the real estate on the actual valuation date. In this effort, the appraiser can consider the existing improvements on the date of inspection, but also must rely on other documentation such as interviews with knowledgeable people, examination of records including photographs and building plans, etc. When this is necessary, the appraiser should always include a special limiting condition addressing the assumption as to quality and condition of the real estate on the date of valuation.

Future Date

It is also necessary to occasionally estimate market value as of a prospective **future date**. Examples in which a future valuation date may be needed are as follows:

1. Appraising a proposed building; the lender will likely fund the loan according to degree of completion.

2. Estimating the reversionary value when valuing leased property; the reversion represents the property that will revert back to the lessor upon lease termination.

In addressing future values, the appraiser must rely on historic evidence and be able to interpret trends. Real estate market behavior has historically been cyclical in nature, but the duration and extremities of the cycles have varied greatly.

As in the case of valuations as of a past date, valuations of a future date should carry appropriate qualifiers such as:

> This valuation assumes that the improvements will be constructed in accordance with plans and specifications furnished to the appraisers, and that the work will be completed in a market acceptable, workmanlike manner.

◼ LIMITING CONDITIONS AND ASSUMPTIONS

Every appraisal is contingent upon a series of conditions that are generally beyond the professional capacity or control of the appraiser. Limiting conditions are covered in the *Uniform Standards of Professional Appraisal Practice (USPAP)*.

In addition to typical limiting conditions, the appraiser is often asked to assume hypothetical conditions.

◼ IDENTIFICATION OF THE APPRAISAL REPORT FORMAT

In the past, report formats have been varied, ranging from the fully documented self-contained narrative appraisal report, the most complete report format, to a verbal conveyance of value. Various other formats between these two extremes have been used on occasion.

On July 1, 1994, the standard appraisal format alternatives as proposed by The Standards Board of The Appraisal Foundation became the policy for all federally related transactions. These formats have become the industry standards and have been adopted by all state licensing bodies.

The time-tested and accepted position in the appraisal industry, however, is that the appraisal document itself represents a summary of the appraisal process and should not be considered representative of the full extent of the work that has been performed. The degree of documentation can of course vary, but the appraisal process should not, if in fact a "complete appraisal" is being conveyed. In other words, an abbreviated format does not mean an abbreviated run through the appraisal process.

A clear understanding of the appraisal report format to be submitted to the client eliminates much confusion.

P A R T   T W O   Data Program (Scope)

Under the Uniform Standards of Professional Appraisal Practice, the appraiser must include a **scope** section. The term "Scope of the Appraisal" means the extent of the process of collecting, confirming, and reporting appraisal data. The appraiser must disclose the extent of the research program. Scope is explored more fully in the USPAP section of this course.

■ COLLECTION

As noted in Chapter 5, there is no one standard procedure in the data collection process; rather, the appraiser makes full use of the data sources available. The data **collection** process is not just a random gathering of information. During this process, the appraiser becomes aware of trends and formulates opinions on numerous items that will ultimately impact the final value conclusion.

General Data

General data relates to those broad concepts where the appraiser begins to understand ramifications of the following four forces:

1. Social

2. Economic

3. Physical/environmental

4. Governmental

Most of the data the appraiser comes in contact with will not be formatted into these four classic categories. Rather, various studies are generally available in which all influences are intermingled. For example, the appraiser may attain historical listing data on housing starts in a particular census tract. While primarily categorized as economic data, the number of housing starts also relates directly to social factors such as population trends, family sizes, income levels, and a variety of other factors.

The availability of sewer service can have a direct impact on the number of housing starts, and this "governmental" influence may currently be impacted by sewer moratoriums, school expansion programs, or road improvements.

Seldom does an appraiser initiate the general data research from the absolute beginning of an appraisal assignment. Typically, this is an ongoing process as the appraiser continually updates the appraisal "plant" by subscribing to pertinent demographic services, news releases, etc.

When working in a town or community with which the appraiser has little familiarity, the process of gathering general data is even more pronounced as the appraiser does not have the opportunity for ongoing knowledge of a particular market.

Specific Data

Specific data relates to the subject property itself as well as the comparable land sales, improved sales, and rent comparables utilized in the three approaches to value.

As a general rule, the appraiser should gather the same data on the comparable properties that are relevant characteristics of the subject property. Additionally, the data collection analysis involves obtaining relative price information for sales, rent levels for rent comparables, etc. Differences between the subject property and comparable properties should be reflected in varying price or rent levels.

■ VERIFICATION

In most instances, general data can be accepted at its face value, assuming the data source is reliable and reputable. Specific data, on the other hand, is usually obtained first in an unconfirmed status and needs **verification**.

> For example, a real estate sales service may report transfer prices based on transfer amounts specified in deeds, transfer tax, prices specified in multiple listing services, or other sources.

In the comparative adjustment process, the following seven items of potential dissimilarity must be addressed:

1. Property rights conveyed

2. Financing

3. Conditions of sale

4. Market conditions (time)

5. Location

6. Physical characteristics

7. Income variances

The comparable adjustment process is detailed more fully in Chapter 11 and Chapter 12. A review of the adjustment process, however, reveals very few variables that are obvious from published data sources.

Property Rights Conveyed

Few data sources denote the actual interest that was conveyed. Appraiser verification must be done to ascertain whether or not fee simple or some other interest was actually sold.

Financing

Most deeds and reporting services seldom indicate whether or not the transfer was cash or cash equivalent. Appraiser verification is needed to ascertain whether or not the transaction was cash and consistent with the market value definition, or if some owner financing was involved.

Conditions of Sale

It is virtually impossible to ascertain from published records whether or not the buyer or seller was acting under duress, if the parties were related, or if there were other factors that would render the transaction something less than arm's length, consistent with the market value definition.

Market Conditions (Time)

Although published information may specify a transfer date, there can be factors pertinent to the date of sale that only appraiser verification can detect.

For example, a current sale may have resulted from the exercising of a purchase option at a predetermined price in a lease that was signed ten years ago, or from a contract negotiated months or even years prior to the closing of the sale.

Another example: Suppose a home next door to the property being appraised is under contract, but the sale has not "closed" or been concluded. The agent shared the approximate contract price, but instructed the appraiser that the price remains confidential. What should the appraiser do? Should the "sale" be used? Yes, the sale can be used, with the sale price labeled "confidential" and not disclosed verbally or narratively, but the list price can be disclosed, similar to the data that would be available to another sales agent or purchaser. The appraiser should make an additional note in the "Limiting Conditions and Assumptions" of the appraisal that the sale has not yet closed, and the agent disclosed the price only to remain confidential.

Location

Location is one of the few factors that generally does not require appraiser verification to ascertain any hidden factors. However, there can be circumstances in which appraiser verification uncovers undisclosed factors.

> For example, a parcel in a remote area may reflect a premium purchase price because of a nearby, unannounced road relocation.

Physical Characteristics

The appraiser very seldom has the opportunity to view the comparable property on the actual date of transfer. Substantial improvements may have been made since the transfer date, or the improvement may have been demolished. Appraiser verification leads to a reasonable understanding of the physical characteristics of the property on the date of transfer.

For example, a level commercial lot may have had topographical problems at the time of the transfer, but subsequent grading produced a level lot viewed by the appraiser on the inspection date.

Income Characteristics

Few published data sources, if any, reveal any rental or expense information on sale properties. In most instances, appraiser verification is the only means to ascertain income and expense projections on which income producing properties were purchased, allowing the appraiser to abstract rates of return.

■ DATA ANALYSIS

It is during the **data analysis** program that the appraiser begins to identify and understand trends and to focus in on those specific items of data that are most appropriate leading to the final value conclusion.

As a part of the data analysis program, the appraiser develops units of comparison. Often, the data can be analyzed utilizing several units of comparison, and market trends and tendencies can be ascertained by studying the various units. Through the "Verification" process, the appraiser usually attains some insight as to what are the most appropriate units of comparison, and analyzing the sales through the units of comparison identifies and isolates market tendencies.

For example, buyers and sellers for commercial land may respond in the verification process by quoting prices per front foot, and this unit of comparison will likely bear out this tendency. In other markets, land prices per square foot may be more appropriate.

PART THREE   Highest and Best Use

The **highest and best use** analysis is essential to the final value conclusion. As documented subsequently, the highest and best use generally is the optimum use to which land or improved property can be put. It is also the available use or most probable use alternative that results in the highest present land value. The highest and best use must be the following:

1. Physically possible

2. Legally permissible

3. Financially feasible

4. Maximally productive

The highest and best use also relates to the data collection and analysis program in that it tends to identify the markets for comparable land sales, improved sales, and rent comparables.

The highest and best use addresses both of the following:

1. Land if vacant

2. Property as improved

Frequently, the appraiser cannot make a reasonable conclusion as to the highest and best use until the property is valued under several use alternatives, with market supply and demand factors for each use being considered.

PART FOUR   Land Value

Even though the appraisal assignment may involve improved property, a separate underlying land valuation is usually conveyed. By estimating the land value separately, the appraiser can gain insight into the highest and best use of the property as well as gaining a more thorough understanding of the improvement contribution to total property value. Separate land values are particularly important when properties appear to be in transition from one use to another.

Generally, the following six methods are used to estimate land value. A brief overview of each follows, with a more thorough presentation in Chapter 11.

1. Sales comparison approach

2. Allocation

3. Extraction

4. Subdivision analysis

5. Land residual

6. Ground rent capitalization

■ SALES COMPARISON APPROACH

In this procedure, sales of similar competitive land parcels are compared to the subject. Appropriate units of comparison are developed, with appropriate adjustments required for dissimilarities as compared to the subject property.

■ ALLOCATION

This procedure encompasses an allocation of total sales price of improved properties that have sold between land and improvements. This is usually employed when land and improvement contribution relationships are known.

> For example, it may be observable that subdivision lot prices contribute 20% of finished home prices in a certain subdivision submarket. This 20% can then be applied to the home price to isolate the land value. If a new house in the subdivision sold for $100,000, the lot value could be established at $20,000 ($100,000 × 0.20).

■ EXTRACTION

This procedure also involves sales of improved properties. The land contribution is isolated by estimating the improvement contribution by a cost analysis and deducting the improvement contribution from the known sales price. Say a house sold for $80,000, and the improvements reflected a depreciated cost of $50,000, then the lot value would be $30,000 ($80,000 − $50,000).

■ SUBDIVISION ANALYSIS

In this procedure, the land is viewed as if subdivided. The gross sales proceeds are estimated based on the anticipated sales of lots or other components. Appropriate deductions are made from the projected income stream (cost to develop, selling costs, and carrying costs), and the net proceeds are converted into a current land value indication through a discounted cash flow model, a technique of the income approach.

■ LAND RESIDUAL

This is a technique of the income approach in which total net operating income attributed to the property is separated into the land and improvement components. After deducting the appropriate return to the improvements, generally based on depreciated cost, the resulting residual income is assumed to be attributed to the land and is capitalized into a current land value indication by use of a land capitalization rate.

■ GROUND RENT CAPITALIZATION

In this technique, a vacant land parcel's market rent potential is estimated based on leases of similar land parcels, appropriate deductions are made, and the resulting net income is capitalized into a value indication by an appropriate technique of the income approach.

P A R T   F I V E   Application of the Three Approaches

Historically, the appraisal process has focused on the following three generally accepted approaches to value:

1. Cost Approach

2. Income Approach

3. Sales Comparison Approach

Although presented as three separate approaches, it is important to note that all are market driven, utilizing market extracted data.

■ COST APPROACH

The *Cost Approach* is based on the premise that the total property value can be derived by adding the depreciated reproduction cost or replacement cost of the improvements to the value of the underlying land. For the Cost Approach to be applicable and reliable, the following two factors must be present:

1. The improvements must be new or nearly new.

2. The improvements must represent the highest and best use of the site, if vacant.

The Cost Approach basically involves the following five steps:

1. Estimate reproduction or replacement cost of the improvements.

2. Estimate accrued depreciation form all sources (physical deterioration, functional obsolescence, external or economic obsolescence).

3. Deduct accrued depreciation from the reproduction or replacement cost to arrive at the depreciated improvement cost.

4. Estimate land value.

5. Add the depreciated improvement cost to the land value to arrive at a total property value indication.

■ INCOME APPROACH

The *Income Approach* emphasizes the principle of anticipation. Related to investment type properties, the anticipated benefits are commensurate with anticipated rental income. This approach views real estate as an investment vehicle, with current dollars (purchase price or value) exchanged for the right to receive future dollars (net rental income). The five basic steps of the income approach are as follows:

1. Estimate potential gross revenue via contract or market rents.

2. Estimate and deduct a vacancy and credit loss allowance to yield effective gross revenue.

3. Estimate and deduct appropriate fixed and operating expenses that would be paid by the owner or lessor of the property to arrive at an indication of the property's net operating income or revenue.

4. Identify the appropriate capitalization technique and abstract the appropriate rates of return from market data.

5. Apply the appropriate capitalization technique to the subject's net operating income potential.

■ SALES COMPARISON APPROACH

The *Sales Comparison Approach* is the most direct and easily understood approach. Sales and listings of similar properties are gathered and analyzed, with appropriate units of comparison made. Items of dissimilarity are accounted for, with appropriate adjustments made.

The seven elements of comparison are summarized as follows:

1. Property rights conveyed

2. Financing

3. Conditions of sale

4. Market conditions (time)

5. Location

6. Physical variances

7. Income variances

After adjusting each sale, a range of values for the subject will result. The appraiser then correlates the range into a value indication by the sales comparison approach based on qualitative analysis of the data.

PART SIX   Reconciliation

In the **reconciliation** section, the appraiser summarizes the results of each approach, and weighs the validity of the value indication from each approach leading to the final value conclusion. In different property types and different instances, one approach may have more validity than another. The "reconciliation" section is absolutely *not* a simple *averaging* process.

PART SEVEN   Submission of Report

Generally, the report format will be specified by the client. Although the **submission of the report** is presented as the last item in the valuation process, most appraisers work continually on the appraisal report during the entire valuation process. The allowed report formats are outlined in Standard 2 of the *Uniform Standards of Professional Appraisal Practice (USPAP)*.

1. In identifying the real estate, the appraiser should consider which of the following?
   a. Interest to be appraised
   b. Location of the land
   c. Market trends
   d. Zoning

2. All of the following are forms of identifying real estate *EXCEPT*
   a. governmental survey.
   b. lot and block system.
   c. metes and bounds.
   d. street address.

3. Tax plats may be used to identify the real estate
   a. at the authorization of the client.
   b. always.
   c. at the request of the borrower.
   d. never.

4. If an appraiser is uncertain as to whether a fixture is to be treated as real or personal property, he should
   a. check state law and make a determination.
   b. ask the seller about his or her intentions.
   c. use force to see if the item is in fact movable.
   d. consult with the client as to treatment of the item.

5. Real estate and real property are
   a. separate and distinct.
   b. synonymous.
   c. immovable fixtures.
   d. both used to describe land and improvements.

6. Most real estate appraisal assignments involve the valuation of which interests?
   a. Leased fee
   b. Leasehold
   c. Fee simple
   d. Life estate

7. When appraising fractional interests, the appraiser usually begins with
   a. the entire bundle-of-rights (fee simple).
   b. the opposite position (leased fee versus leasehold).
   c. an analysis of all easements.
   d. the intent of the owner.

8. When is the use of "value" without a modifier allowed in an appraisal report?
   a. Always
   b. Occasionally
   c. Never
   d. At the appraiser's discretion

9. The value to be addressed and the interest to be addressed combine to form what section of the appraisal?
   a. Physical description
   b. Purpose
   c. Function
   d. Highest and best use

10. When would market value for estate tax purposes be different from market value for refinancing?
    a. Never
    b. Sometimes
    c. At the discretion of the client
    d. At the discretion of the appraiser

11. Which of the following can be requested appraisal dates?
    a. Current date
    b. Previous date
    c. Future date
    d. All of the above

12. When appraising a property as of a previous date, the appraiser should
    a. assume physical condition consistent with the current physical condition.
    b. attempt to ascertain physical condition on the appraisal date through interviews or other means.
    c. assume no improvements were in place.
    d. assume the improvements were new.

13. When might a future valuation date be appropriate?
    a. In appraising proposed buildings
    b. When there is no current market data and sales are expected to occur several months hence
    c. When a natural disaster is anticipated
    d. Never

14. The appraisal format is determined by
    a. the appraiser.
    b. the client.
    c. the property owner.
    d. governmental agencies.

15. Which word below describes the extent of the process of collecting, confirming, and reporting appraisal data?
    a. Function
    b. Purpose
    c. Scope
    d. Highest and best use

16. When does the appraiser normally find general data classified into the four broad categories (social, economic, physical/environmental, and governmental)?
    a. Seldom
    b. Always
    c. Depends upon other appraisers' files
    d. Only on Fridays

17. In working in an appraiser's home community, general data is
    a. completely reanalyzed upon every appraisal assignment.
    b. an ongoing process which is updated continuously.
    c. only considered quarterly.
    d. never considered.

18. In the comparative adjustment process, the elements of comparison in correct order are
    a. Conditions of sale, market conditions (time), rights conveyed, financing, income variances, physical variances, location
    b. Rights conveyed, conditions of sale, financing, income variances, market conditions (time), physical variances, location
    c. Rights conveyed, financing, conditions of sale, market conditions (time), location, physical variances, income variances
    d. Conditions of sale, location, physical variances, income variances, financing, market conditions (time), rights conveyed

19. When appraising improved properties, a highest and best use analysis should address
    a. the property as improved.
    b. the site if vacant.
    c. both A and B.
    d. none of the above.

20. All of the following are methods utilized to appraise land EXCEPT
    a. allocation
    b. subdivision analysis
    c. sales comparison approach
    d. syndication

21. Which of the following is NOT one of the three traditionally accepted approaches to value?
    a. Income approach
    b. Functional analysis
    c. Cost approach
    d. Sales comparison approach

22. Scope in the appraisal process is defined as
    a. the extent of the process of collecting, confirming, and reporting appraisal data.
    b. the purpose for which a client requests the appraisal.
    c. the function and intended use of the appraisal.
    d. the fine print in an appraisal that explains the valuation process.

23. To apply the cost approach, the improvements should
    a. be new or nearly new.
    b. represent the highest and best use of the site if vacant.
    c. be both A and B.
    d. be none of the above.

24. Which approach emphasizes the principle of anticipation with the anticipated benefits identified as rental revenue?
    a. Cost approach
    b. Sales comparison approach
    c. Income approach
    d. None of the above

25. The reconciliation is always which of the following?
    a. A weighing process
    b. An averaging process
    c. A multiple choice process
    d. None of the above

26. When would the appraisal report represent the exhausting details of each and every one of the appraiser's efforts?
    a. At the client's discretion
    b. At the appraiser's discretion
    c. Never (appraisal report is a summary to the client, not the entire appraisal process)
    d. Always

27. What is the first step in the valuation process?
    a. Sending the invoice
    b. Property inspection
    c. Writing the report
    d. Defining the problem

28. The type of appraisal report produced is determined by the
    a. use or function of the appraisal.
    b. owner.
    c. appraiser.
    d. fee.

29. The most common type of report format is
    a. narrative.
    b. form.
    c. letter.
    d. oral.

30. The appraiser learns of a current contract for a home similar to the subject property. Can the contract be used as a "sale"?
    a. No, it has not closed.
    b. No, it is not a comparable.
    c. Yes, with a statement that it is a contract and a note in the "Limiting Conditions and Assumptions," and a guarantee not to disclose the price or information learned in confidence if the source so desires.
    d. Yes, it is a sale and can be used unconditionally.

7

Real Estate Description

■ LEARNING OBJECTIVES

Students will be able to

1. recognize the difference between a tract and site.

2. recognize, analyze, and report the characteristics that define a tract or site such as frontage, size, shape, etc.

3. recognize the difference between building improvements and site improvements.

4. recognize the importance of a building inspection, recognizing the various building styles and components.

5. identify and examine the functional utility of a building.

6. recognize the difference between actual age and effective age for subsequent utilization in the cost approach.

■ KEY TERMS

access	floodplain	site improvements
actual age	frontage	tract
building improvements	functional utility	topography
building inspection	quality/condition survey	utilities
drainage	shape	wetlands
effective age	site	
environmental hazards	size	

■ INTRODUCTION

Regardless of the appraisal format, an appraisal usually contains a fairly detailed description of the subject land and improvements. Not only is the conveyance of a detailed description of the land and improvements pertinent to the subject property, but it also establishes the relationship of the subject land and improvements to competing properties that are rented or have sold. For sales and rentals of competing properties to be adjusted to the subject as value indicators, the relationship of the subject to the comparables as to the physical attributes must be established.

Most appraisers are neither surveyors nor builders; however, a basic understanding of physical attributes of land and improvements is necessary when performing appraisals at a competent level. The appraiser must be able to distinguish between favorable and unfavorable characteristics and measure the market reaction to these variables.

This Chapter is intended to provide the student with a basic knowledge of land and improvement attributes. Most of the appraiser's competency comes primarily from experience in the field. Geographic areas differ as to prevailing construction techniques and materials, and the appraiser must become aware of local peculiarities.

The appraiser must also recognize that construction techniques and materials change over the years as does market preference related to style, design, and functional utility.

Influences that are outside of the subject site boundaries are called external forces or external economies. Only forces within the subject site boundaries will be discussed in this Chapter.

PART ONE   Land or Site Description

■ TRACT VERSUS SITE

Although frequently used synonymously, the terms tract and site are separate and distinct. The two definitions follow:

1. **Tract**: Land in an unimproved state.

2. **Site**: A parcel of land that has been improved to the point suitable to support building improvements.

Improvements necessary to change a tract to a site include road improvements and utilities such as electricity, natural gas, telephone service, water, and sewer.

■ FRONTAGE

Frontage relates to the portion of the land adjoining a public or private roadway. Also, borders along other focal points such as streams, lakes, or golf courses can be important, depending upon market preference.

For example, road frontage may not be an important factor for a house that also fronts the ocean; the amount of ocean frontage is likely to be a more important factor.

■ SIZE

If not conveyed in a legal description or plat, the appraiser must estimate the **size** of the land parcel. Of importance is the size of the parcel related to zoning requirements. Size is usually expressed in terms of square feet or acres (43,560 square feet equals one acre).

■ SHAPE

The parcel's **shape** can follow any geometric configuration. Of importance is market preference and utility attributed to the shape as it relates to the highest and best use of the land.

■ TOPOGRAPHY

A parcel's **topography** can be level, rolling, hilly, moderately sloping, or severely sloping, or a blend of these. Of importance is the parcel's topography as it relates to the ultimate development potential.

For example, level topography at street grade may be desirable for a commercial use, whereas gently rolling, elevated topography may be more desirable for residential use.

■ DRAINAGE

Drainage is, according to *Language of Real Estate*, "a system of gradually drawing off water and moisture from land, naturally or artificially, by means of pipes and conduits." The appraiser should be aware of existing and potential drainage hazards, particularly as drainage relates to the improvements located on a particular parcel and neighboring parcels.

■ FUNCTIONAL UTILITY

All of the variables noted above relate to the **functional utility** of the parcel. Again, functional utility can vary according to use.

For example, substantial frontage may be desirable for commercial property, whereas limited cul-de-sac frontage may be desirable for residential usage.

■ FLOODPLAIN

The Federal Emergency Management Agency (FEMA) has prepared nationwide flood-plain studies indicating areas prone to flooding. The areas designated as **floodplain** are documented on FEMA topographical maps; however, the scale on the FEMA maps is often small and difficult to relate to a specific property. Ultimate determination as to whether or not a parcel lies within a floodplain often requires the services of a surveyor or engineer. While a parcel may be located in the flood hazard zone area, it may never flood, and this designation alerts the public only to a potential hazard. Owners of properties with improvements that lie within floodplain designated areas are generally permitted to purchase flood insurance from the federal government.

In recognizing that the appraiser's role is that of a reporter of market actions, careful analysis should be made isolating the market's reaction to flood hazard zones.

■ WETLANDS

Wetlands have become an increasingly important factor affecting real property values in recent years. The term *wetland* implies hydraulic (water) influence; however, other factors such as soil type and vegetation can lead to wetland designations. These areas are generally protected from development. This is not to say that they have no value in that there is often a market for the preservation of wildlife and the aesthetics offered by such wetland areas. Wetland areas can in some cases be relocated if proper procedures are followed.

■ ENVIRONMENTAL HAZARDS

The appraiser is generally not trained in detecting **environmental hazards** including materials and conditions; however, the appraiser is often asked to complete a checklist noting obvious potential hazards such as chemical spills, unusual debris, or other factors. While the appraiser generally acknowledges his or her lack of expertise in hazardous materials detection, the obvious should be reported and the client consulted for direction.

■ UTILITIES

The appraiser should be aware of all public and private **utilities** available at the site and the access for the developer of a site to tap into the utility lines if needed. Also, the capacity should be verified. Public officials can be contacted for the presence and accessibility of public utilities. Often, the property owner has to be interviewed about septic tanks or wells, as opposed to public sewer and water on the property.

■ ACCESS

Access or ingress and egress to the property being appraised is important. Again, accessibility relates to the use potential.

For example, circuitous accessibility may be perfectly acceptable for single-family residential usage, whereas commercial property generally emphasizes high-volume direct accessibility. Public transportation may be important in urban areas. Also, accessible rapid rail or bus lines may become an important factor in suburban communities.

After all of the intricate variables of the site can be ascertained, an overall judgment should be made as to the adaptability of the site for the most logical use potential.

P A R T   T W O   Improvement Description

Not only is an improvement description important for documentation of the appraiser's files, information about the improvements becomes important later on in the appraisal process when the appraiser is making judgmental decisions about the quality, condition, and functional utility of structures and site improvements.

Generally, all improvements are either of the following two:

1. Building improvements

2. Site improvements

Building improvements relate to the structure itself while site improvements encompass things around the perimeter of the building such as drives, walks, landscaping, etc.

■ BUILDING IMPROVEMENTS

Although there are various ways to classify **building improvements,** a suggested format is to subdivide the structure into the following three major components:

1.   Exterior

2.   Interior

3.   Equipment and mechanical

Exterior

Generally, all exterior construction components can be subdivided into the following two:

1.   Substructure—construction components below ground

2.   Superstructure—construction components above ground

FIGURE 7.1 ■ Some Parts of a Building's Substructure

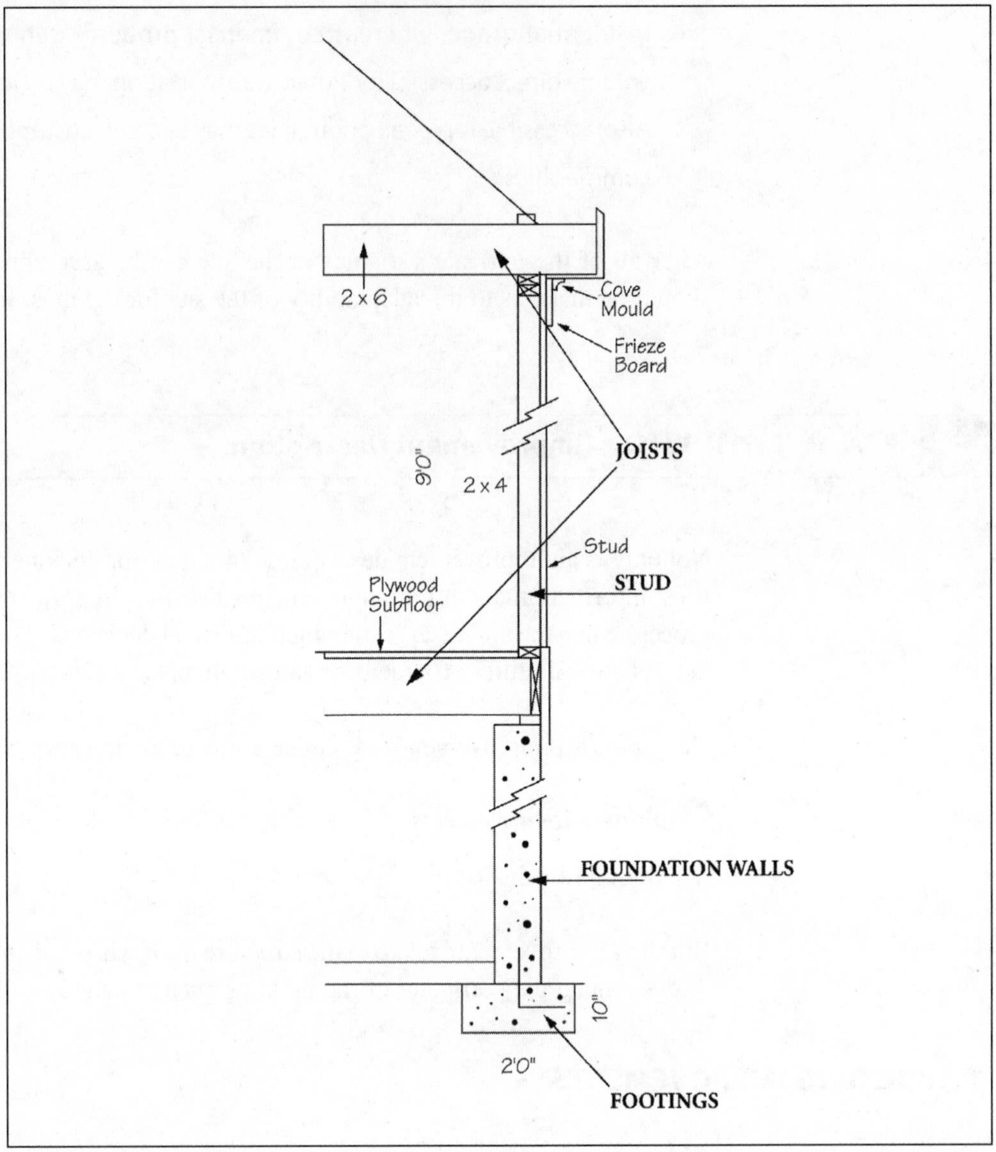

Substructure **Substructure** components support the superstructure or part of the structure that is visible.

Footings Footings are supporting components, usually of poured concrete, frequently reinforced. Footings are generally wider than the foundation walls that they support for proper load bearing. Often, footings are bordered by foundation drains that divert water away from the footings.

Foundation walls Foundation walls are usually continuous perimeter walls that are either poured in place concrete or concrete block. Foundation walls are usually reinforced. Usually, the portion of the foundation walls below grade is left unfinished, although normally they are waterproofed. The foundation walls are the basement walls.

In many municipalities, building codes will require that all foundation walls above grade be covered with some sort of decorative material such as brick, stone, or stucco.

Superstructure The **superstructure** is the part of the building that is visible and supported by the substructure.

Frames Most residences utilize wood frame construction. Historically, the predominant framing members have been 2″ x 4″, although 2″ x 6″ wall framing with the added width for greater potential for insulation has become widely used. There are generally two types of framing members:

1. Studs—These are vertical framing members.

2. Joists—These are horizontal framing members. Floor joists usually rest on the foundation walls and support the floor as well as wall studs. Joists have traditionally been solid wood, usually 2″ x 10″ or 2″ x 12″ but laminated plywood-type joists and truss (pre-engineered) joists are also common.

Roof trusses These are usually factory-built systems that are placed on the roof joists on-site.

Sheathing Usually plywood or insulation board, this is the exterior facing of a structure. Neither wall sheathing nor roof sheathing are visible after construction completion.

Roof design Of the many building roof designs in use today, five of the most popular are shown in Figure 7.2: flat, gable, mansard, gambrel, and hip.

Exterior walls There are a variety of exterior materials and design variations. Most are either masonry, vinyl, or wood or wood product.

FIGURE 7.2 ■ Five Popular Roof Designs

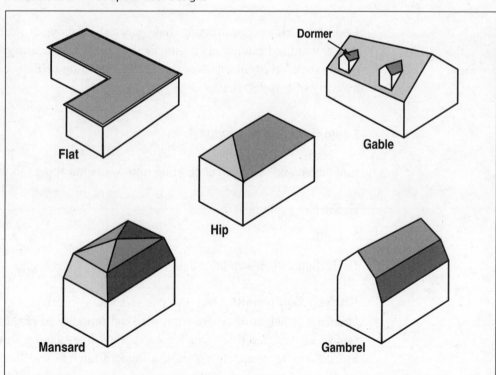

Interior

Interior components of a structure consist basically of the following three:

1. Floors

2. Interior walls

3. Ceilings

Floors Generally, floor structures consist of subflooring material over wood joists with some type of floor finish. Throughout most of the 1900s, subfloors were diagonal planks constructed directly over the wood joists. Since the 1960s, however, plywood has become more extensively used. Builders either used plywood alone or a combination of plywood and particle board, nailed and/or glued directly to the joists.

Floor finish varies widely but generally consists of carpet over foam pad, vinyl, hardwood, or tile. Most surfaces subject to water (kitchens and baths) typically have some form of vinyl or ceramic tile as opposed to carpet.

Interior Walls Until the 1950s, interior walls were mostly plaster over wood lath. This finish required highly skilled workmen, and construction was extremely tedious. Cracks occurred during settlement, and repairs were often needed. During the 1950s, drywall began to be substituted for plaster. In drywall construction, sheets of material similar in substance to plaster are shipped directly to the building site and installed by workmen. Consisting of nailing, taping, and painting, the degree of workmanship required for drywall is generally less than plaster.

Other forms of interior walls include wood paneling, tongue-in-groove planks, or ceramic tile.

Ceilings Ceiling construction has generally followed interior wall construction. Plaster was used extensively during the first part of the century, but drywall has become more extensively utilized since the 1950s. Finish on ceilings can vary from smooth to a variety of textured finishes.

Equipment and Mechanical

Equipment and mechanical building improvements appear in three main areas:

1. Kitchen equipment

2. Baths

3. Heating and air-conditioning

Kitchen Equipment Over the past 30 years to 50 years, the trend has been for kitchen equipment to evolve from personal property to real property. In the 1930s, a typical kitchen had a few built-in cabinets, a freestanding stove and refrigerator, and limited counter space. In contrast, a modern kitchen will likely have a sink complex with one or more bowls, garbage disposal, rinsing facilities, built-in dishwasher, one or more built-in ovens, microwave, built-in surface burners, ice-maker, and garbage compactor, as well as extensive built-in cabinets and counter space. Occasionally, a refrigerator may also be built in. Because of the manner in which these items are affixed, they often become real estate rather than personal property, and their contributory value should be reflected in the final value conclusion.

Baths Similar to kitchen evolution, baths have progressed from functional rooms with a toilet, tub, and sink to elaborate living centers with one or more vanities, separate shower stalls and tubs, Jacuzzis, and other features. As with kitchens, all bath equipment should be considered according to its contribution to the market value of the whole.

Heating and Air-Conditioning Heating systems have also evolved consistently with other components of the residence. For hundreds of years, wood was the primary fuel for heating, and most residences constructed prior to the turn of the century depended solely upon fireplaces for heating. Freestanding stoves were a great improvement because of their more effective use of wood as a fuel. It was during the early part of the century that fossil fuels became widely utilized for heat. Coal-burning fireplaces gradually replaced wood-burning fireplaces, and coal furnaces became popular. The earliest furnaces were based on hot water systems where hot water was circulated throughout the residence and heat distributed to the individual rooms through radiators. Later, forced heated air utilizing furnaces became more popular. Modern systems are generally central in configuration with the heat source being electricity, natural gas, propane gas, and occasionally heating oil, coal, or other fuel.

Air-conditioning in residences originally took on the form of window units, and these were occasionally placed permanently in walls. When placed in a window, the units were generally considered moveable and were not considered part of the real estate. During the last 20 years to 30 years, however, central air-conditioning systems utilizing remote condenser/compressors have been almost universally utilized in new construction because of the energy efficiency advantage as well as more uniform cooled air disbursement.

In evaluating kitchen and bath equipment and finish as well as heating and air-conditioning systems, the appraiser must recognize that the acceptability of the system relates to the market in which the property is located. A gas-fired hot water radiator system with window air-conditioning units may be very well accepted in an older, in-town neighborhood, whereas such a system would be functionally obsolete in a new suburban neighborhood in the same town. The ultimate test of the acceptance lies in the market reaction to these physical attributes.

■ SITE IMPROVEMENTS

As noted earlier, **site improvements** encompass things around the perimeter of the building such as drives, walks, landscaping, etc. They can have a significant impact on both the cost and contributory value of the total improvements. In some cases, the site improvements can in fact exceed the building improvements as to cost and contributory value. A builder constructing a convenience store with gasoline operation may well find that the cost of the paving, curbing, underground utility lines, and other site improvements are a substantial part of total improvement costs. In most property types, however, site improvements are not the most significant part of the total construction cost or contributory value.

When analyzing site improvements, the appraiser must always be aware that the contributory value of a particular component must be emphasized rather than cost. A swimming pool, for example, almost always contributes less to property value than its cost in most residential properties. Extensive oriental gardens in a neighborhood of homes ranging from $125,000 to $150,000 may have significant appeal to the current owner, but a typical buyer may choose to give little relevance to such site improvements.

■ BUILDING INSPECTION

During the appraiser's inspection, the improvements are normally measured, and detailed notes are taken as to construction features. An appraiser's **building inspection** is generally divided into the following two components:

1. Exterior inspection

2. Interior inspection

Exterior Inspection

Usually, the first step in the inspection process is measurement of the exterior dimensions of the building. The appraiser generally utilizes a flexible measuring tape with a hook on one end so that the measurement can be performed by a single person. Often, a sketch is made of the residence as the measurements are being taken. The appraiser usually utilizes "grid" type paper that is lined to a certain scale so that a reasonably accurate graphic depiction of the exterior is created as measurements are taken.

The appraiser then notes all critical exterior construction components, usually starting top to bottom or bottom to top. Most appraisers find that a checklist is helpful so that individual construction components will not be omitted. The appraisal may start with the foundation, record exterior walls, windows, and doors, then go on to note the roof type and cover.

Interior Inspection

Utilizing the exterior perimeter sketch drawn to scale, the appraiser can then proceed to the interior. It is recommended that the floor plan sketch be completed first, then individual construction details should be recorded. Most appraisers do not measure each interior wall, because approximations are usually adequate.

After the interior sketch is made, the appraiser then goes on to record construction materials and condition. Some appraisers use portable recording devices while other appraisers prefer to take handwritten notes. In either case, however, it is recommended that a checklist also be utilized.

Usually, the owner is the most knowledgeable about physical quality and condition of the improvements, and the appraiser should never hesitate to ask questions. During the inspection, the appraiser may notice things that prompt questions. For example, the appraiser may ask: When was the house painted? Have there been any major heating and air-conditioning improvements in recent years? Are any major replacements anticipated in the near future? The appraiser should be aware that proper reporting of the physical characteristics of the improvements, with particular focus on condition and those items that will require corrections or replacement in the future, could prove to be very valuable information for the client in the decision-making process.

■ RESIDENTIAL STYLES

Residential house styles vary from era to era. However, as illustrated in Figure 7.3, the following five basic "classic" styles emerged in the United States to provide shelter here since colonial times:

1. The 1 Story, or Ranch Style

2. The 2 Story, or Colonial

FIGURE 7.3 ■ Five Basic Residential Styles

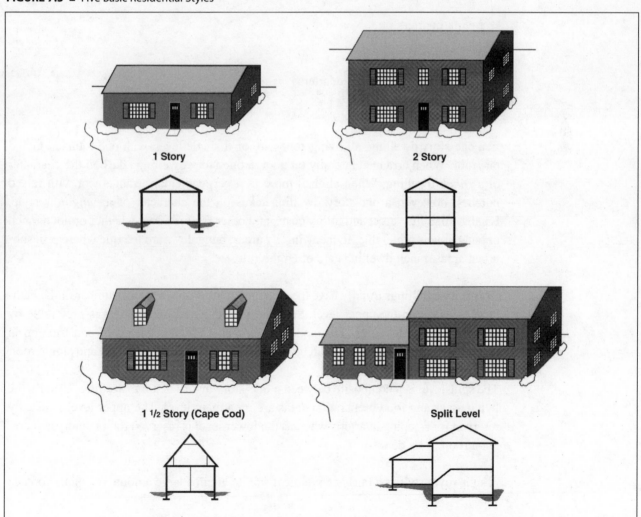

1 Story

2 Story

1 ½ Story (Cape Cod)

Split Level

FIGURE 7.3 ■ Five Basic Residential Styles (cont'd)

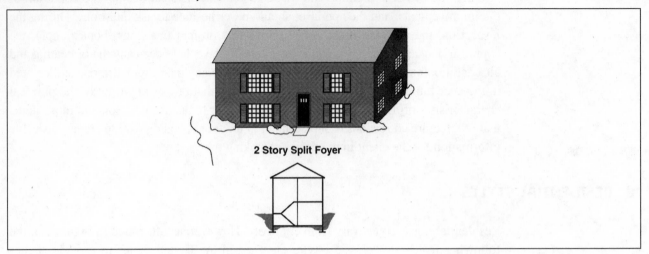

2 Story Split Foyer

3. The 1½ Story, or Cape Cod

4. The Split Level, or Tri-Level

5. The 2 Story Split Foyer, or Raised Ranch

In all residential styles, the interiors are divided into the following four basic sections:

1. Living quarters

2. Sleeping quarters

3. Food preparation/dining quarters

4. Bathroom quarters

In a one-story dwelling, all living zones are on a single level, with one foundation and one roof. When arranged laterally on a lot, a one-story dwelling takes on the character of a *ranch* dwelling. When aligned more in a perpendicular arrangement with raised porches, however, a one-story dwelling takes on the character of a *bungalow* style. Land availability, street and utility costs, and other factors affect whether or not a ranch or bungalow is preferable. In many in-city areas, bungalows are the rule whereas in suburban areas, ranch dwellings are often the rule.

Two-story dwellings usually have the sleeping quarters and a major number of the bathroom quarters on the upper level. Separation of the sleeping quarters is preferable by many market participants. This style also is a cost-efficient means of construction in that additional square footage can be erected with a smaller foundation and single roof.

The split-level is a composite between a one-story and two-story dwelling. Usually the living areas and food preparation areas are on a main level. The upper level is usually reserved for sleeping quarters, whereas the lower level is reserved for a laundry, a recreation room, or a den.

A split-foyer style is a fairly economical way to attain a large amount of square footage with limited costs. The lower level is essentially low-cost basement-type construction whereas the upper level is similar to a one-story dwelling as to its construction characteristics. Often a major portion of the lower level is reserved for a garage.

■ FUNCTIONAL UTILITY

The term **functional utility** means: *The ability of a component or item to perform its intended task.*

Conversely, when an item is judged to have *functional inutility*, it does not function well in performing the task for which it was intended. Moreover, a home may suffer functional inutility if it is not designed to meet current market standards. Generally, the kitchen and bathrooms will suffer the greatest inutility first. Think how market standards have changed over the past 20 years to 30 years for these two rooms versus, say, a dining room or bedroom. Dining rooms and bedrooms have changed little, but kitchens have changed dramatically, contrasting a home built in the 1960s to a recently constructed home.

Functional utility and functional inutility do have an effect on a property's value. It is therefore necessary for the appraiser to analyze items that may become functional problems and to interpret the market reaction to these items. As subsequently presented in the cost approach, there are ways to measure items of functional obsolescence. Also, the appraiser can be made aware of market reaction to items of functional inutility through paired sales analysis.

Functional inutility can lie in the substructure or superstructure as well as the equipment and mechanical systems.

It is also important to note the following items of functional inutility:

1. Excessiveness

2. Inadequacy

Some specific items of functional inutility can be found in Table 7.1.

TABLE 7.1 ■ Functional Inutility Items

	Excessiveness	Inadequacy
Substructure	1) Thicker than required foundation walls	1) Lack of foundation drains
	2) Over-reinforced footings	2) Poor compaction
	3) Costly foundation wall finish	3) Improper materials
Superstructure	1) Excessive energy conservation	1) Limited energy conservation materials
	2) Excessive trim	2) Insufficient number of baths
	3) Excessively high ceilings	3) Insufficient storage area

For example, the appraiser must always be aware that an item by itself may or may not be a functional problem. For example, a swimming pool in a neighborhood of $400,000 to $500,000 houses may not be an over-improvement, whereas a swimming pool in a neighborhood of $70,000 to $90,000 houses may contribute nothing to value and, in some cases, detract from value because of the added maintenance cost. Upgraded interior finish such as countertops and floor surface may reflect contributory value equal to or greater than cost in upscale subdivisions but contribute substantially less than cost in moderate quality subdivisions.

In the floor plan in Figure 7.4, the appraiser is attempting to isolate items of functional inutility. What may be a consideration?

FIGURE 7.4 ■ Functional Inutility Problem

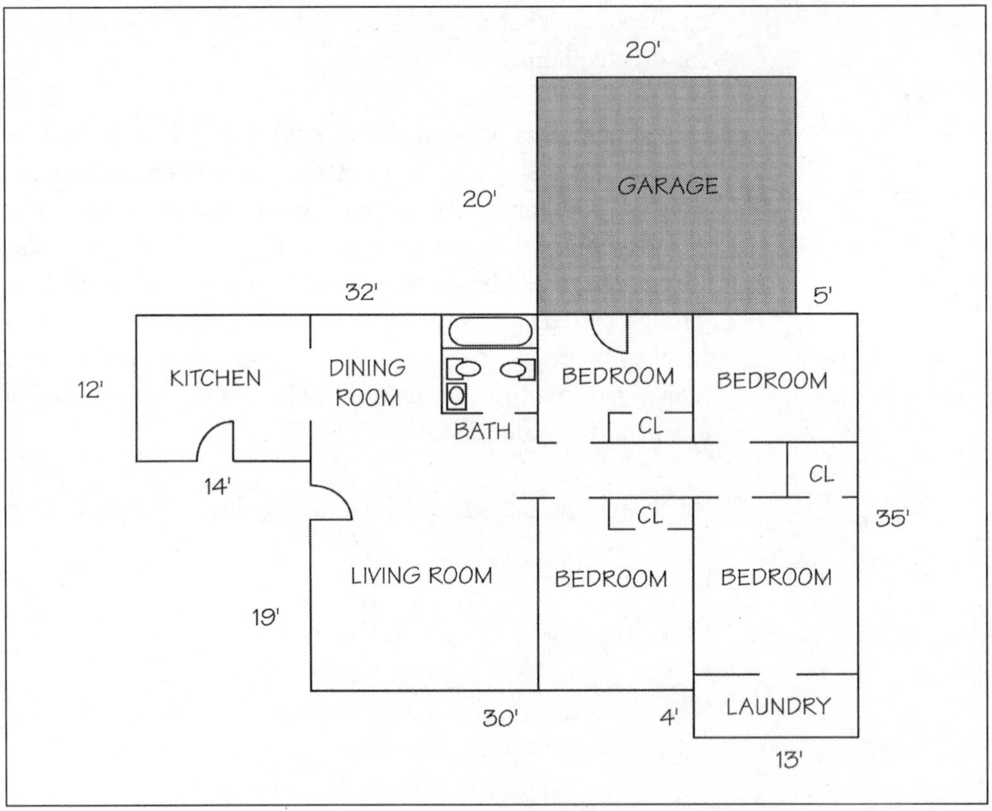

Items for consideration:

1. Entry from garage leads directly into a bedroom

2. Laundry room accessible only through bedroom

3. Entrance to sole bathroom off living room

4. Too many fixtures in bathroom for space allocated

5. Bedroom-to-bathroom ratio is high

■ ENERGY EFFICIENCY

Since the oil crisis in the 1970s, there has been extreme awareness of energy conservation in building construction. Wall insulation, ceiling insulation, and multi-paned insulating windows have all become important features in residential construction. Additionally, energy efficient heating and air-conditioning systems have become more important. As energy costs continue to rise, it is logical to conclude that energy conservation awareness will increase.

It is not the role of the appraiser to measure energy efficiency; rather, the appraiser must attempt to measure the market reaction to perceived energy efficient and energy inefficient construction materials and techniques.

■ QUALITY/CONDITION SURVEY

One item that is vital to the description of the improvements and the adjustments of comparables is the quality and condition of the subject property. In the **quality/condition** survey, the appraiser surveys the subject improvements noting quality standards met, or ones that are lacking or are above-standard for the market. The same is noted for condition of the property, particularly *short-lived* items, discussed later, such as paint, gutters, appliances, carpet, and other items that have lives less than the home itself. They will need replacing before *long-lived* items such as the foundation or roof trusses need replacing, if ever.

■ ACTUAL AGE

Actual age is the amount of time that has passed between the construction of an improvement and the date of appraisal. Also known as *historical age* or *chronological age*, it is a fact or objective figure.

■ EFFECTIVE AGE

Effective age is a subjective estimate of age made by the appraiser that considers both the physical condition and functional utility of an improvement; may be less than, greater than, or equal to the actual age depending upon design, quality, workmanship, materials used, maintenance, etc.

1. Related to construction knowledge, the appraiser's level of expertise should be
   a. that of a builder.
   b. that of a high school student.
   c. somewhere in between A and B.
   d. that of a real estate salesperson.

2. Over the years, construction materials and techniques
   a. remain constant.
   b. change.
   c. vary depending upon builder preference.
   d. experience none of the above.

3. A parcel of land that has been improved to the point suitable to support building improvements is a
   a. tract.
   b. site.
   c. real property.
   d. subdivision.

4. The relationship between road frontage and value is determined by
   a. the appraiser.
   b. the banker.
   c. the developer.
   d. buyers and sellers in the marketplace.

5. When is it the appraiser's job to accurately survey and properly report the exact acreage of a parcel of land?
   a. Never
   b. Always
   c. At the discretion of the appraiser
   d. At the discretion of the client

6. Level, at street grade topography, is most desirable for
   a. commercial uses.
   b. golf courses.
   c. residential uses.
   d. ski resorts.

7. Floodplain can only be accurately determined by
   a. the appraiser.
   b. a builder.
   c. an engineer or surveyor.
   d. an environmentalist.

8. For part of a land tract to be located in floodplain, it must
   a. always flood.
   b. sometimes flood.
   c. be designated as such by the Federal Emergency Management Agency (FEMA).
   d. look like it might have potential as a good fishing hole.

9. For a property to be designated wetlands, it must
   a. always be under water.
   b. be occasionally under water.
   c. possess the hydraulic, soil type, or vegetation influences that lead to a wetlands designation by the federal government.
   d. lie in a floodplain.

10. The best way for an appraiser to check for available utilities is to
    a. consult the local municipality or body responsible for installing the lines.
    b. use a back hoe.
    c. ask the owner.
    d. check FEMA maps.

11. Construction components below ground are part of the
    a. superstructure.
    b. substructure.
    c. functional utility.
    d. land.

12. Footings are part of the
    a. substructure.
    b. superstructure.
    c. building structure.
    d. land.

13. Vertical framing members are called
    a. studs.
    b. joists.
    c. substructure components.
    d. flooring.

14. Factory built systems that support the roof are called
    a. studs.
    b. joists.
    c. roof trusses.
    d. sheathing.

15. Most interior walls and ceilings in today's construction are
    a. plaster.
    b. drywall.
    c. concrete block.
    d. masonite.

16. The trend in kitchens and bathrooms is to have
    a. more built-in components.
    b. fewer built-in components.
    c. fireplaces.
    d. none of the above.

17. The four basic sections of a house are
    a. living quarters, food preparation/dining quarters, mechanical equipment, plumbing.
    b. living quarters, bathroom quarters, substructure, superstructure.
    c. living quarters, sleeping quarters, food preparation/dining quarters, bathroom quarters.
    d. bathroom quarters, sleeping quarters, meeting rooms, recreation rooms.

18. The ability of a component or item to perform its intended task is called
    a. functional utility.
    b. functional inutility.
    c. functional superadequacy.
    d. functional inadequacy.

19. Functional inutility can be attributed to
    a. excessiveness.
    b. inadequacy.
    c. both A and B.
    d. neither A nor B.

20. Which two rooms generally suffer the greatest amount of functional inutility, when contrasting a home built in the 1950s or 1960s to today?
    a. Dining room and bedroom
    b. Living room and dining room
    c. Den and laundry room
    d. Kitchen and bathroom

CHAPTER EIGHT

Highest and Best Use

■ LEARNING OBJECTIVES

Students will be able to

1. define highest and best use and understand the significant components of the definition.

2. appreciate the importance of the concept of highest present land value.

3. understand and apply the four tests in analyzing the highest and best use of the site as vacant.

4. understand and apply the four tests for the highest and best use of the property as improved.

5. understand concepts related to highest and best use including interim use, holding, plottage, excess land, and surplus land.

■ KEY TERMS

excess land	interim use	plottage
financially feasible	legally permissible	surplus land
highest and best use	maximally productive	surplus productivity
holding	physically possible	

■ INTRODUCTION

The highest and best use of a property is probably the most critical factor leading to ultimate valuation. In many instances, the highest and best use is obvious. For example, a single-family home on a one-half acre lot situated within a large neighborhood composed of 300 similar homes on similar lots requires little in the analysis of highest and best use, assuming the subdivision is stable with the housing price levels being maintained. Other properties, such as a residence along a strip emerging as a commercial corridor, may require an in-depth highest and best use analysis.

This Chapter focuses on those elements essential to the highest and best use conclusion and attempts to quantify and clarify concepts that appear somewhat vague on the surface.

As in the ultimate appraised value conveyance, the highest and best use conclusion is an estimate by the appraiser, not an absolute fact. Also consistent with the appraisal process, the highest and best use conclusions should be based on sound analysis and reasoning rather than simply an unsupported opinion.

PART ONE   Definition of Highest and Best Use

The **highest and best use** generally is the optimum use to which land or improved property can legally be put. It is also that available use or most probable use alternative that results in the highest present land value. The highest and best use must meet the following four tests:

1. Physically possible

2. Legally permissible

3. Financially feasible

4. Maximally productive

The highest and best use conclusion must also be logical, and there must be economic demand for this use.

The highest and best use analysis applies in the following two instances:

1. Land as though vacant (even if improved)

2. Property as improved

PART TWO   Highest Present Land Value

One of the most difficult concepts for the appraiser to grasp is the concept that the highest and best use must produce the highest present land value. The foundation of this concept lies in the premise that land is permanent, whereas buildings are not permanent. The underlying land has some economic use, and its use potential may vary as time goes on. Land formerly utilized as forestland can become cleared for cropland production. The cropland can, in turn, be engulfed by suburban sprawl and used to support a single-family residential subdivision; the single-family residential subdivision can be affected by urban growth and be purchased for an office park development. Throughout this cycle, the land has retained its permanence, although the highest and best use potential has changed.

The underlying economic principle related to the maximum land value concept is the principle of **surplus productivity**. This principle holds that after all factors of production have been paid (capital, labor, entrepreneurship), the residual income is assumed to be attributed to the underlying land. After deducting an allowance for a return on the improvements, the residual return to the land (income) tends to establish the value for the land.

Take for example a small entrepreneur who decides to go into the used car business. The family owns a vacant lot on a commercial corridor. The small businessman borrows money to buy a modular office building, pave the lot, and stock the lot with vehicles to be sold. After the small businessman reconciles the income and expenses at the end of the month, he finds that he has indeed made enough money to pay his hired help (labor), the monthly bank note (capital), pay himself a salary (entrepreneurship), and have money left over. The entrepreneur has satisfied the entrepreneurial risk, paid for all labor, and satisfied the monthly obligation for the bank loan which was utilized for inventory and property improvements.

The residual income thus accrues to the land. Anyone purchasing the land would review this entrepreneur's monthly income and expense statements to anticipate what the long-term earnings potential would be for this land, then pay a lump-sum price for the land.

If the earnings history of this land produces a value of around $5 per square foot, and other land parcels along the corridor have been selling for $8 to $10 per square foot, it is likely that the used car operation is not the highest and best use of the site, as if vacant, assuming there is demand for alternative uses such as fast-food restaurants, branch banks, or convenience stores.

If land parcels along this corridor are selling for around $5 per square foot, it could be said that the used car lot operation is a reasonable representation of the highest and best use of the site. This is why a compatible property such as fast-food restaurants, branch banks, and convenience stores often pay similar prices for competing sites, even though each competing site may have its own absolute highest and best use.

Although every parcel theoretically has one absolute highest and best use, from a practical standpoint, the appraiser usually decides on a range of uses that would be compatible with the highest and best use of the site. This is why compatible properties such as fast-food restaurants, branch banks, and convenience stores often pay similar prices for competing sites.

PART THREE   Land as Though Vacant

■ PHYSICALLY POSSIBLE

To determine the **physically possible** the appraiser must thoroughly analyze the physical attributes of the land. In the identification of the real estate, the appraiser becomes aware of the size of the parcel, road frontages, and topographical features, as well as off-site characteristics such as adjoining roadways, access, and availability of utilities.

The presence of floodplain and wetlands are important issues that must be addressed. Sometimes floodplain and wetlands areas appear to be unusable, but may in fact be able to be incorporated into a large site development for walking trails, parking, yard storage, or other complementary uses.

■ LEGALLY PERMISSIBLE

While zoning is considered to be the most important factor related to allowable and **legally permissible** uses, it is not the only factor. Other factors include private limitations such as deed restrictions, building codes, and easements.

Zoning is human-made and is subject to change. Frequently, existing zoning lags behind underlying land economics, signaling a change in use. Existing zoning and a municipality's future land use plan may be in contradiction in that the land use plan represents future use whereas zoning indicates current use or current use potential.

Although zoning is usually a critical factor, it does not absolutely dictate highest and best use. The appraiser frequently concludes that the highest and best use of a parcel is inconsistent with current zoning; then, the probability of rezoning must be addressed. Discussions with zoning officials, analysis of land use plans, and other factors may lead the appraiser to conclude that a zoning change is highly likely or highly unlikely. In such instances, the final concluded value must address the degree of uncertainty.

> For example, physical limitations are frequently intertwined with legal limitations. A residential lot containing 10,000 square feet may be physically suitable to support a residence and related site improvements; however, existing zoning may require a minimum lot area of 15,000 square feet. While it is not critical for the appraiser to decide whether or not this is a physical or legal restriction, the limitation must be recognized and the influence on value addressed accordingly. An office site may be physically adaptable to support a highrise building at 100,000 square feet per acre, but zoning could limit development of the site to 40,000 square feet per acre.

■ FINANCIALLY FEASIBLE

When exploring use alternatives of a site, the highest and best use definition requires that the physically possible and legally permitted uses be **financially feasible**. Financial feasibility relates to two things—cost and value.

If the cost of a venture exceeds its value, the venture is not feasible. If the value exceeds cost, the venture is feasible.

For example, a builder purchases a lot in a subdivision for $20,000 and constructs a residence on the lot at a cost of $80,000. At this point, the builder has a total investment of $100,000. If the house can be sold in a reasonable time for $120,000, the venture is, of course, feasible. If market conditions change, and the ultimate sales price plummets to $90,000, the venture is not feasible.

In normal markets, entrepreneurs prejustify construction before acquiring sites and building improvements. If a reasonable profit margin is experienced by entrepreneurs, construction goes on and supply and demand maintain reasonable equilibrium. When excess profits are realized, the principle of competition comes into play. As more improvements are constructed, the price levels tend to decline because of supply and demand factors, and profit margins are squeezed. When profit margins are squeezed to a certain level, construction ceases, projects are put on hold, and proper equilibrium is allowed to return. Pent-up demand can then increase prices, spurring additional construction, with the whole cycle repeating.

One of the basic principles appraisers often fail to grasp is the principle of supply and demand. An appraiser may conclude that a one-acre site is an ideal fast-food location because of the numerous fast-food sites that have been sold in the area and prevailing price levels that are higher compared to sites purchased for other uses. Further investigation, however, may disclose that all the restaurants are operating at a minimal sales volume level, and population and market demand are on the decline. This may signal demand for a lower or less intense use, and a corresponding lower land value.

Another example could be the saturation of grocery stores in a neighborhood. If four grocers are the main competitors in a metropolitan area, and all four operate modern stores within a neighborhood, a vacant site in that area is not likely to have a highest and best use as a grocery store anchored shopping center.

A thorough supply and demand analysis is therefore critical to the highest and best use study.

■ MAXIMALLY PRODUCTIVE

In reality, the appraiser may conclude a number of use alternatives are financially feasible; that is, their value exceeds cost. Of these uses, however, the appraiser can usually narrow these feasible alternatives down to a few selected uses that are **maximally productive**, i.e., that yield the greatest return on dollars invested. Consider the example in Table 8.1 for varying floor plans/designs of a home on the same lot.

Although all three homes are financially feasible (value or sales price is greater than cost), Floor Plan 1 produces the highest land value. It also produces the highest return or profit (total sales price divided by total cost, less 1).

In practical application, builders discover quickly that building the maximally productive house may not always be possible in that there may not be enough qualifying buyers with demand for the product type in a specific price range.

In other words, building a $400,000 home may suggest a maximally productive improvement, but in reality, the market for such a home may be so limited that a $250,000 home is more accepted in the marketplace and thus, less risky.

In the normal course of appraisal activity, appraisers do not consider all use alternatives for every site. Broad ranges of potential uses can generally be narrowed down by utilizing logic and observing land use patterns. It is impractical to analyze supply and demand factors for a resort motel in the middle of the Florida Everglades or in the Canadian wilderness. Likewise, it would be impractical for an appraiser to analyze the crop production capabilities of a one-acre parcel in the heart of a thriving downtown community or adjacent to a regional mall.

Logic is also a key ingredient to a meaningful highest and best use analysis. If a use is not physically possible, such as a shopping center on a certain site, then there is no need to test the legal permissibility or the financial feasibility of that shopping center use on the site. The same can be said for a use that may be physically possible but is not legally permissible. If it is not a potentially legal use, there is no need to explore the finan-

TABLE 8.1 ■ Floor Plan Cost Analysis

	Floor Plan 1	Floor Plan 2	Floor Plan 3
Sales Price	$155,000	$160,000	$145,000
Construction Cost	97,650	103,800	96,500
Selling Expenses (7%)	10,850	11,200	10,500
Builder Profit (10%)	15,500	16,000	15,000
Total Cost	$124,000	$131,000	$122,000
Indicated Land Contribution	$31,000	$29,000	$23,000
Return (Land Contribution ÷ Total Cost)	25%	22%	19%

cial feasibility of a certain use on the site. The appraiser should go to the next physically possible and legally permissible use to test feasibility.

Generally, the highest and best use alternatives tend to present themselves during the data collection and analysis process. While it is often stated that the highest and best use conclusion sets the stage for the selection of data, the opposite is often true. During the course of verifying market information, the appraiser becomes aware of market trends, tendencies, and facts that may not be evident upon casual observation.

The extent of the highest and best use analysis relates to the appraisal problem at hand. A 2,000 square foot single-family residence, three years in age, in a two-year-old to five-year-old subdivision of 300 houses, all of which have been well accepted in the market, requires little highest and best use analysis. A forty-year-old residence along a commercial strip where numerous residences have been converted to office or demolished for site redevelopment would likely require extensive highest and best use analysis.

At the conclusion of the highest and best use analysis, as if vacant, the appraiser should have an approximate conclusion as to what the ideal improvement would be on the site. That is, what hypothetical improvement would maximally utilize the site? The difference between the ideal improvement and the existing improvement would equate to the functional obsolescence in the existing improvements.

PART FOUR   Property as Improved

The same four tests apply to the property as improved that apply to the site as though vacant. Critical to the analysis of the property as improved is the principle of consistent use. Although a building may be existing and functioning, analysis considering the four tests should still be applied as in the highest and best use of the land as though vacant.

■ PHYSICALLY POSSIBLE

Although a building may be existing, certain physical modifications may be appropriate. Physically possible changes may include modernization, additions, restorations, or renovations. It may be that supply and demand factors in an area warrant the conversion of an old apartment building to a hotel. The lack of room to install utility lines and heating and air-conditioning ducts, however, may preclude this venture because of the physical deficiencies. Another example would be in an urban area where land economics would justify adding three or four stories to an existing three-story building; however, the existing foundation may not be sufficient to support the extra weight.

■ LEGALLY PERMISSIBLE

In most cases, buildings conform with zoning restrictions. In cases where buildings were constructed prior to current zoning restrictions, uses that are not in compliance are generally *grandfathered in* and are considered legal, nonconforming uses. In this case, while it may be physically possible to convert a building through expansion or other means, it may not be legally permissible.

> For example, a building producing $500 per month rent as a dress shop may be capable of producing $900 per month rent if converted to a liquor store. Zoning, however, may prohibit the liquor store at this location, even though there may be economic demand for such a retail outlet. Therefore, a liquor store would not be legally permissible, and thus, the property could not have a highest and best use as a liquor store with the higher rental rate and likely corresponding higher value.

■ FINANCIALLY FEASIBLE

As in the case of the land as though vacant concept, there may be a wide variety of financially feasible uses when considering changing or altering existing buildings. One important factor to remember is that the existing use without modifications or additions may in fact be the maximally productive use.

Items could be curable (financially feasible) or incurable (not financially feasible) in terms of the feasibility to replace or modernize. For instance, say you have a home that is 20 years old. Many homes in the neighborhood have modernized their kitchens (new appliances, countertops, cabinets, flooring, and lighting) at a cost of $8,000. If the increase in value were less than $8,000, the project would be infeasible or incurable; if more than $8,000, it would be feasible, or curable.

■ MAXIMALLY PRODUCTIVE

Again, the maximally productive use is the use that creates the most profitable current return that is both physically possible and legally permissible.

P A R T   F I V E   Related Concepts

■ INTERIM USE

In recognizing neighborhood life cycles (growth, stability and maturation, decline, and revitalization), properties frequently undergo a change in highest and best use. Rarely can the point in time when the highest and best use changes be specifically identified. Properties tend to go through **interim use** periods in which highest and best use is uncertain.

A one-acre site with an old residence currently rented for $400 along a commercial strip may not yet be ready for redevelopment. Population may be growing in the area, but existing commercial facilities may be adequate to serve the population needs. It may take two years to three years before another fast-food restaurant, branch bank, or convenience store is needed along the corridor. It is illogical to assume that the property would sell as a residence because possible buyers and sellers would be aware of the commercial potential of the land. Likewise, it is illogical to conclude that the house would be demolished if the property has potential to generate $400 per month as improved during the holding period compared to no rental return if the improvements were demolished.

Properties similar to this are said to be interim in nature, having interim improvements. The income potential not reflective of the ultimate use potential of the site is interim income potential. Following are examples of uses that may be considered interim in nature:

1. Christmas tree stand

2. Used car lot

3. House converted to an office

4. Abandoned gas station utilized as a repair shop

5. House on a commercial lot

6. Golf driving range

7. Produce stand

Just because the former use is not reflective of the highest and best use, the second-generation use, or what appears to be an interim use, could in fact be the highest and best use. A gasoline station converted to an auto repair garage may be the property's highest and best use if the population has declined to the point that no other use is demanded for the foreseeable future.

■ HOLDING

Not every parcel has a highest and best use that is current. Frequently, a parcel of real estate may be in an area in which the ultimate highest and best use may not be logically concluded. It could be an outlying parcel is being affected by trends toward developing multifamily, industrial, and commercial land uses, with changes in supply and demand factors within each sector.

In such cases when the markets are not well defined in a particular area, the appraiser can conclude that the highest and best use is speculative **holding** until such point in time when the underlying land economics mature to the point to justify a more clear determination of the use that is physically possible, legally permissible, financially feasible, and maximally productive. Ideally, the appraiser will have sales of other properties that reflect similar questionable highest and best uses, with the measurement of value reflected directly by market perceptions of the most probable land use.

■ PLOTTAGE

Frequently, a parcel may satisfy the legally permissible, financially feasible, and maximally productive tests; however, the parcel may not be large enough by itself to support the highest and best use. In such cases, the appraiser may conclude that the highest and best use is to assemble the parcel with adjoining properties (*assemblage*) that may or may not have the same physical limitations. In such cases, the appraiser usually concludes a value if assembled, then makes an adjustment for the uncertainty associated with potential assemblage difficulties. In these cases, the sum of the values of the parts may be less than the value of the assembled whole. Although many parcels may be suitable for assemblage, **plottage** is said to occur only when there is some incremental increase in value, over and above the value of each parcel individually if not assembled.

> For example, the values, individually, for the adjacent parcels are as follows:
>
> | | |
> |---|---|
> | A. | $200,000 |
> | B. | $250,000 |
> | C. | $200,000 |
> | D. | $300,000 |
> | Total | $950,000 |
>
> The value for the entire tract, assembled Parcels A, B, C, and D, may be $1,200,000. The incremental $250,000 ($1,200,000 – $950,000) is the plottage value.

■ EXCESS LAND

Excess land is land that is available for a separate use, separate and distinct from supporting the primary improvement.

> For example, if a neighborhood is dominated by 0.5-acre lots, and the subject property contains 1.0 acres, there may be excess land present. If the site configuration and location of the improvements, if any, allow sell-off of the 0.5-acre additional land, then it is considered excess land in that it is not needed for support of the primary improvements and use.

■ SURPLUS LAND

Similar to the concept of excess land is the concept of **surplus land**. The difference, however, relates to the fact that surplus land cannot be sold off as a separate use; simply, it is additional land over and above what is typical for a specific property type in an area. In the preceding illustration, that being a 1.0-acre parcel in a 0.5-acre lot subdivision, let us assume that a residence was placed on the center of the 1.0-acre parcel, effectively eliminating the sell-off of the remaining 0.5 acre of land that is over and above typical land area. In this case, there would be surplus land as opposed to excess land in that it could not be spun off for a separate use.

1. Which of the following is *NOT* a requirement of highest and best use?
    a. Physically possible
    b. Legally permissible
    c. Financially feasible
    d. Functional by design

2. The highest and best use must also result in
    a. reasonable current land value.
    b. highest current land value.
    c. lowest current land value.
    d. none of the above.

3. The four tests of highest and best use; that is, physically possible, legally permissible, economically feasible, and maximally productive, apply to
    a. site as if vacant.
    b. property as improved.
    c. both A and B.
    d. A only.

4. When analyzing potential use alternatives, the appraiser may conclude there are (is) _____ financially feasible use(s)?
    a. One and only one
    b. Several
    c. The use determined by the banker
    d. The use determined by the client

5. Of the uses that may be economically feasible, there can be only one that is
    a. physically possible.
    b. legally permissible.
    c. maximally productive.
    d. worthy of consideration.

6. The anticipated sales price of a house is $150,000. The construction cost is $125,000, with $15,000 in anticipated selling expenses and $20,000 for the land. This project is
    a. marginally feasible.
    b. unfeasible.
    c. profitable.
    d. uncertain.

7. The point in time in which a property's highest and best use changes is
    a. easily identifiable.
    b. usually somewhat subjective to determine.
    c. recorded in the courthouse.
    d. runs with the mortgage.

8. A use that is generating some income but not reflective of the ultimate use potential of the site is
    a. an interim use.
    b. a highest and best use.
    c. noneconomic use.
    d. consistent use.

9. When two parcels have a higher economic value combined, what comes into play?
    a. Plottage
    b. Highest and best use
    c. Interim use
    d. Speculative holding

10. What is the difference between the "ideal improvement" and the "existing improvement"?
    a. Functional obsolescence
    b. Highest and best use
    c. Financially feasible
    d. Maximally productive

CHAPTER NINE

Appraisal Mathematics

9

■ LEARNING OBJECTIVES

Students will be able to

1. recognize the importance of accurate area and volume calculations.

2. perform basic area and volume calculations.

3. recognize the importance and applicability of units of comparison.

4. understand the difference between decimals, percentages, and fractions.

5. understand and calculate basic statistical terms such as mean, median, mode, range, and weighted average.

■ KEY TERMS

absolute mean	gross building area	paired sales
adjustment process	(GBA)	percentage adjustments
application	gross living area (GLA)	percentages
area	heated areas	range
cash equivalency	mean	standard deviation
decimals	median	statistical analysis
extraction	mode	volume
fractions	paired rentals	weighted average

■ INTRODUCTION

Appraisers are generally not required to be PhD-equivalent mathematicians; however, appraisers do need a working knowledge of some basic mathematical functions both for data interpretation and application of the three approaches to value. Except for some more advanced applications in the income approach, statistical analysis, or use of a financial calculator, appraisers generally need to master only the following four basic mathematical functions:

1. Addition

2. Subtraction

3. Multiplication

4. Division

In the more advanced statistical analysis programs, as well as more advanced capitalization techniques, the math competency level required is somewhat higher.

Mathematical functions performed by the appraiser on a daily basis can generally be broken down into the following five categories:

1. Area and volume calculation

2. Units of comparison

3. Decimals, percentages, and fractions

4. Basic statistical analysis

5. Adjustments

P A R T   O N E   Area and Volume Calculation

More often than not, appraisers have to calculate areas and volumes because areas and volumes may not be evident from most data sources. While not intended to be a geometry lesson, this section does introduce some basic geometric formulas and leads the student through several area and volume calculations.

■ AREA CALCULATION

Area refers to an identified surface, either land or improvements, and the area of land is generally measured in two units:

1. Square feet

2. Acres

An acre encompasses 43,560 square feet, about the size of a football field. The areas of smaller parcels of land such as a commercial site, residential lot, etc., are generally expressed in square feet whereas the areas of larger tracts are generally expressed in acres. Improvement areas are usually expressed in terms of square footage.

The **gross building area (GBA)** is that measured area within the exterior walls, excluding unenclosed areas. **Heated areas** include enclosed, heated areas measured from the exterior walls. **Gross living area (GLA)** generally includes the above-grade, heated areas of finished space, measured from the exterior walls. Means of expressing area may vary from market to market. It is best to familiarize yourself with the standards for measuring homes and buildings in the area of your property.

Most land and improvements have dimensions generally following straight lines. Most areas can therefore be calculated by breaking the land or building down into a series of rectangles or triangles.

Rectangle

A rectangle is a four-sided figure with both pairs of opposite lines being parallel. Examples of rectangles can be found in Figure 9.1.

The area of a rectangle is calculated by the following formula:

$$\text{Length} \times \text{Width} = \text{Area}$$

In the examples found in Figure 9.1, the areas of the rectangles would be calculated as follows:

A. 20 Feet × 20 Feet = 400 Square Feet

B. 20 Feet × 40 Feet = 800 Square Feet

C. 100 Feet × 300 Feet = 30,000 Square Feet

To convert square footage to acres, the appraiser simply *divides the square footage calculation* by 43,560. Figure 9.2 is an example of how a land parcel 300 feet x 400 feet can be converted to square footage and acreage:

FIGURE 9.1 ■ Rectangle Examples

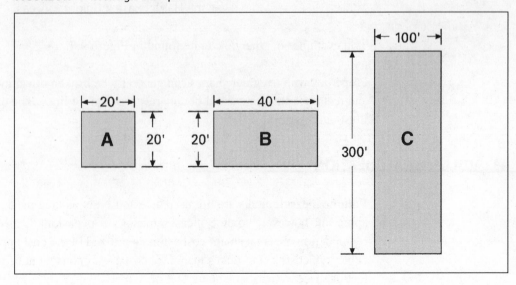

FIGURE 9.2 ■ Square Footage Conversion Example

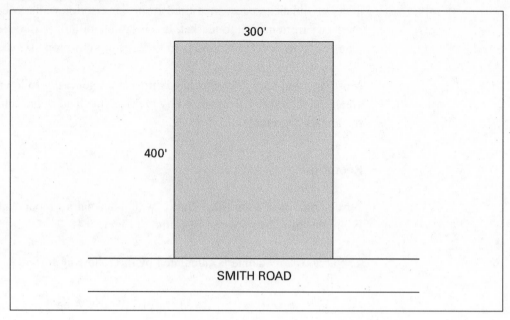

300 Feet × 400 Feet = 120,000 Square Feet

Converted to Acres: 120,000 Square Feet ÷ 43,560 = 2.7548 Acres

Frequently, the appraiser subdivides a land parcel or house into various rectangles, calculates the area of each rectangle, and then adds the results together to yield the total area. Figure 9.3 shows two examples.

Triangle

While dividing land or building into a series of rectangles is an easy method to calculate area, diagonal property lines or walls frequently create angles other than 90 degrees. When this occurs, the surface area can be broken down into triangles rather than rectangles for area calculation. The formula for calculating the area of a triangle is:

½ (One-Half) × Base × Height = Area

Two examples of triangle can be found in Figure 9.4.

Properties with irregular shapes can generally be broken down into a series of triangles and rectangles, as long as all boundaries are straight lines. The examples in Figure 9.5 illustrate this point.

■ VOLUME CALCULATION

Volume measurements are not used as extensively as area measurements in real estate appraisal; however, volume measurements are occasionally needed for buildings. A reproduction or replacement cost estimate utilized in the cost approach may emphasize cubic foot costs rather than square foot costs; warehouse rentals may be based on cubic feet of space rather than square feet of space.

FIGURE 9.3 ■ Calculating Total Area of Land and/or House

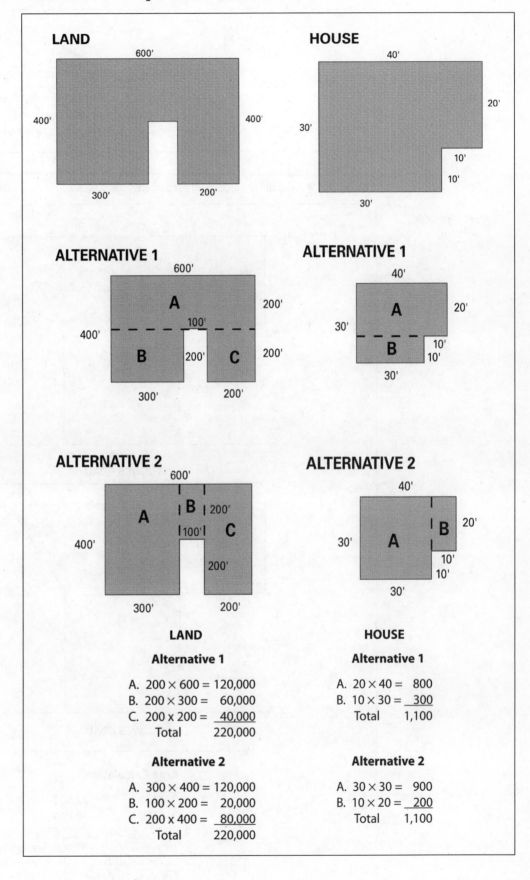

LAND

600'
400'   400'
300'   200'

HOUSE

40'
20'
30'
10'
10'
30'

ALTERNATIVE 1

600'
A   200'
100'
400'
B   200'   C   200'
200'
300'   200'

ALTERNATIVE 1

40'
A   20'
30'
B   10'
10'
30'

ALTERNATIVE 2

600'
A   B   200'
100'
400'   C
200'
300'   200'

ALTERNATIVE 2

40'
A   B   20'
30'
10'
10'
30'

LAND

Alternative 1

A. 200 × 600 = 120,000
B. 200 × 300 = 60,000
C. 200 × 200 = 40,000
Total   220,000

Alternative 2

A. 300 × 400 = 120,000
B. 100 × 200 = 20,000
C. 200 × 400 = 80,000
Total   220,000

HOUSE

Alternative 1

A. 20 × 40 = 800
B. 10 × 30 = 300
Total   1,100

Alternative 2

A. 30 × 30 = 900
B. 10 × 20 = 200
Total   1,100

FIGURE 9.4 ■ Triangle Examples

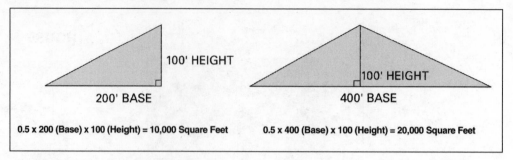

0.5 x 200 (Base) x 100 (Height) = 10,000 Square Feet　　　0.5 x 400 (Base) x 100 (Height) = 20,000 Square Feet

FIGURE 9.5 ■ Example of Calculating Area of Irregular Shape

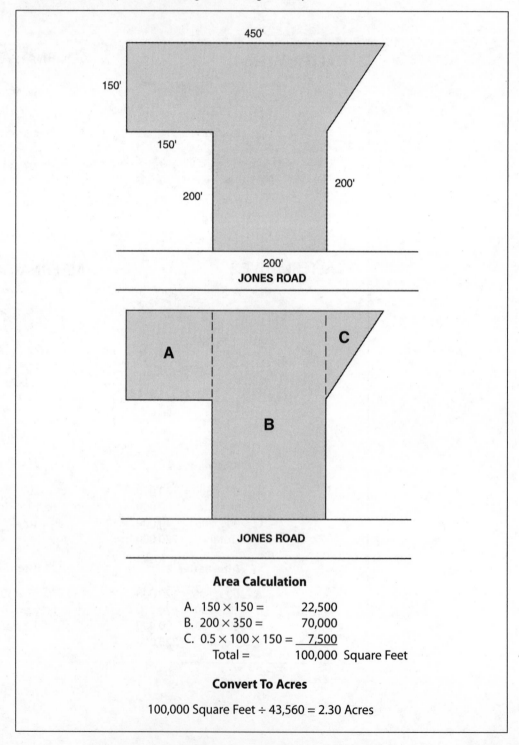

Area Calculation

A. $150 \times 150 =$　　22,500
B. $200 \times 350 =$　　70,000
C. $0.5 \times 100 \times 150 =$　　7,500
　　Total =　　100,000　Square Feet

Convert To Acres

100,000 Square Feet ÷ 43,560 = 2.30 Acres

FIGURE 9.6 ■ Example of Calculating Volume

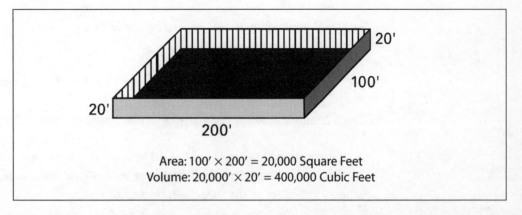

Area: 100' × 200' = 20,000 Square Feet
Volume: 20,000' × 20' = 400,000 Cubic Feet

In instances where volume calculations are needed, the appraiser simply multiplies the surface area by the height, as seen in Figure 9.6.

PART TWO   Units of Comparison

In the open market, virtually all commodities are comparatively priced on some type of per unit basis. Examples follow:

Beef—per pound

Eggs—per dozen

Orange Juice—per quart

Doughnuts—per dozen

Bread—per loaf

Likewise, appraisers work on a daily basis with **units of comparison** throughout the data collection and analysis program as well as through application of the three value approaches. An appraiser frequently analyzes data using a variety of per unit indicators. The indicators themselves frequently tend to identify market preference.

For example, the appraiser may not be aware of how commercial land along a commercial corridor is being bought and sold until all applicable units of comparison are analyzed and market participants are interviewed. The price per square foot indications may reflect an erratic pattern whereas the price per front foot indications may show a more consistent pattern. Buyer/seller verification should be considered to further understand market tendencies.

In order to convert data to units of comparison, the appraiser simply divides the price or rental by the unit being analyzed. For example, a commercial site that sold for $100,000 containing 20,000 square feet reflects a per unit sales price of $5 per square foot:

$$\$100,000 \div 20,000 \text{ Square Feet} = \$5 \text{ Per Square Foot}$$

Some common units of comparison can be found in Table 9.2.

As illustrated in Chapters 12, 13 and 15, *units of comparison* are also utilized in reproduction and replacement cost estimates in the *cost approach* as well as rental and expense estimates in the *Income Approach* to value.

PART THREE   Decimals, Percentages, and Fractions

Decimals, **percentages**, and **fractions** are all similar in that they represent parts of a whole. These mathematical expressions become important in measurements of land and improvements. Most electronic calculators operate on a decimal basis; therefore, it becomes necessary to convert a fraction to a decimal. This is done by dividing the numerator by the denominator. Take for example a five-inch measurement related to 12 inches in a foot. This would be converted to a decimal as follows:

$$\frac{5 \text{ (Numerator)}}{12 \text{ (Denominator)}} = 0.42 \text{ of a foot}$$

When the decimal is shifted two places to the right, it becomes a percentage. A percentage is simply a means to express a decimal in hundredths (two decimal places).

TABLE 9.2 ■ Common Units of Comparison

		LAND		
Agricultural	**Single-Family Residential**	**Multifamily Residential**	**Commercial**	**Industrial**
Acre	Acre	Acre	Front Foot	Acre
	Potential Lot	Potential Unit	Per Site	Square Foot

	IMPROVEMENTS		
Single-Family Residential	**Multifamily Residential**	**Commercial**	**Industrial**
Room	Unit	Square Foot	Square Foot
Square Foot	Room	Suite	Cubic Foot
Bedroom	Square Foot	Room	
	Bedroom		

Consider the following:

$$0.3500 = 35.00\%$$

$$0.2000 = 20.00\%$$

$$0.7194 = 71.94\%$$

$$1.3200 = 132\%, \text{ or } 132.00\%$$

For example, a room measurement is expressed in feet and inches converted to decimals, then multiplied to calculate area.

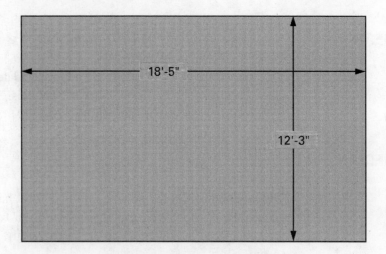

$\frac{5}{12} = 0.42 + 18 = 18.42$ Feet
$\frac{3}{12} = 0.25 + 12 = 12.25$ Feet
18.42 Feet × 12.25 Feet = 225.65 Square Feet, or
226 Square Feet (Rounded)

PART FOUR   Basic Statistical Analysis

The appraiser is often involved in analyzing large samples of data. As an aid in analyzing such data, there are mathematical relationships available to the appraiser that can be used to isolate market trends and tendencies. The process is called **statistical analysis**. Important terms in statistical analysis are as follows:

a.   Mean (also known as the average)

b.   Median

c.   Mode

   d. Range

   e. Standard Deviation

   f. Weighted Average

The *mean*, *median*, and *mode* are measurements of central tendency that form the basis for advanced linear regression and multiple regression analysis, which usually require the use of computer programs; however, these measurements can also be utilized for small samples of data using a calculator.

Although these mathematical expressions can be utilized to study market trends and tendencies, they should never be used as absolutes; rather, these mathematical relationships should be tempered with the appraiser's judgment in formulating conclusions.

■ MEAN

The **mean** is the same as the *average*. It is calculated by adding the value of all the variables, then dividing by the number of variables. Table 9.3 illustrates the mean apartment rent derived from a data sample.

■ MEDIAN

The **median** divides the sample into two equal halves, just as a median in a highway divides the lanes into two equal numbers. Prior to computing the median, the sample must be placed in numerical order. Table 9.4 gives an example of residence sales per square foot.

■ MODE

The **mode** represents a third way to interpret data. The mode represents the most frequently occurring variable in the sample. Table 9.5 gives an example of residential acreage sales expressed on a per acre basis.

TABLE 9.3 ■ Calculating the Mean

Comparable	Rent/Month
1	$450
2	$420
3	$435
4	$475
5	<u>$480</u>
	$2,260

$2,260 (Sum) ÷ 5 = $452 Per Month

■ RANGE

Range refers to the absolute low and absolute high within a sample. For instance, in the previous illustration in Table 9.5, the *range* is 8,100 to 9,300.

■ STANDARD DEVIATION

The **standard deviation** is a further refinement of describing the variance from central tendency. Mathematically, the standard deviation is the square of the difference between each point and the mean of the points.

TABLE 9.4 ■ Calculating the Median

Sample	Arrange Sample in Numerical Order	
38.10	#1 32.25	
37.90	#2 32.50	
32.25	#3 32.60	4 Samples
32.60	#4 33.75	
38.75		
37.72	#5 35.80	Median
35.80		
32.50	#6 37.72	
33.75	#7 37.90	4 Samples
	#8 38.10	
	#9 38.75	

TABLE 9.5 ■ Determining the Mode

8,100	
8,100	
8,150	
8,200	
8,300	
8,500	
8,500	Mode
8,500	
8,500	
8,600	
8,600	
8,900	
9,100	
9,150	
9,200	
9,300	

■ WEIGHTED AVERAGE

The **weighted average** takes into consideration the relative position of all the variables. For example, in the following subdivision analysis, three comparables were located. Pertinent lot absorption data is summarized:

Subdivision	Lot Sales	Months	Sales per Month
1	50	20	2.50
2	40	18	2.22
3	165	8	20.62
Totals	255	46	

The **absolute mean**, or average, would be calculated as follows:

$$
\begin{array}{r}
2.50 \\
2.22 \\
+\ 20.62 \\
\hline
25.34
\end{array}
$$

$$25.34 \div 3 = 8.45 \text{ Lot Sales Per Month}$$

The **weighted average**, on the other hand, would be the same as the total number of lot sales (255) divided by the total months (46), or:

$$255 \div 46 = 5.54 \text{ Lot Sales Per Month}$$

When analyzing large samples of data, most appraisers look at absolute averages as well as weighted averages; however, due to discrepancies in data samples analyzed, the weighted average usually proves to be the more reliable indicator of activity. In the preceding illustration, the *simple* or *absolute average* is 8.45, while the *weighted average* is 5.54.

The difference between the two is the success of Subdivision 3, or the lack of success of Subdivisions 1 and 2. Let's say Subdivision 3 is more comparable to the subject than Subdivisions 1 or 2. Emphasis should be placed in this case on Subdivision 3, as it is most relevant to the subject property.

P A R T   F I V E   Adjustments

Obviously, every property is unique to some degree. If two residences are constructed from the exact same building plans on two 100′ x 200′ adjacent level lots, there are still minor differences. If for no other reason, the two lots are different in that each occupies a separate portion of the earth's surface. Although the houses may appear to be duplicates, there can be minor variations in finish detail or workmanship. After a period of time, there can certainly develop differences in upkeep or modifications.

Whether dealing with comparable rentals, land sales, or improved sales, the appraiser must reconcile differences between the competitive property and the subject property.

The **adjustment process** is the means by which the appraisers measure market reaction to items of dissimilarity.

The *adjustment process* consists of the following two major components:

1. Adjustment extraction

2. Adjustment application

Within this process, there are the following two means by which adjustments can be mathematically extracted and applied:

1. Dollar (lump sum) adjustments

2. Percentage adjustments

■ DOLLAR ADJUSTMENTS

Extraction

The **extraction** process involves the use of **paired sales** or **paired rentals** analysis. This procedure simply involves the comparing of two properties that are highly similar to each other in all pertinent characteristics other than one factor.

The difference in price or rental rate can be attributed to this one item of dissimilarity. In the normal course of business, appraisers are constantly performing matched pair analysis so that market tendencies can be ascertained.

> For example, numerous comparisons may indicate that buyers are paying a premium for homes with basements in a certain neighborhood.

The most significant economic principle relating to the adjustment process is the concept of *contributory value*. This concept holds that the worth of a component is a function of its contribution to the whole entity.

When extracting adjustments, the mathematical process tends to isolate contributory value, or the value the component contributes to the overall entity. This contributory value may be less than, equal to, or greater than the cost of the component.

Extracting dollar adjustments requires a simple comparison procedure. Figure 9.7 illustrates this concept.

FIGURE 9.7 ■ Example of Contributory Value Concept

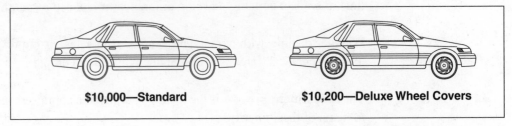

$10,000—Standard $10,200—Deluxe Wheel Covers

The first vehicle in Figure 9.7 is a standard model that sold for $10,000. The second vehicle has been upgraded by the addition of premium wheel covers. This vehicle sold for $10,200. The vehicles are highly similar to each other in all other respects. The only significant variance is the wheel covers. The difference in price is calculated as follows:

$10,200   (with wheel covers)
− $10,000   (without wheel covers)
  $200   Difference (contributory value of wheel covers)

The price variance of $200 is the contributory value of the wheel covers. The contributory value was borne out by market activity. This $200 contributory value may be equal to the added cost, less than the added cost, or more than the added cost.

The same concept holds true for analyzing real property. Consider the example in Figure 9.8.

In the example in Figure 9.8, the first residence sold for $90,000, while the second residence sold for $97,500. These are essentially duplicate residences on essentially duplicate lots. The only major variance is the added feature of the garage on the second residence. The contributory value of the garage is isolated as follows:

$97,500   (with garage)
− $90,000   (without garage)
  $7,500   Difference (contributory value of garage)

FIGURE 9.8 ■ Contributory Value Concept in Real Estate

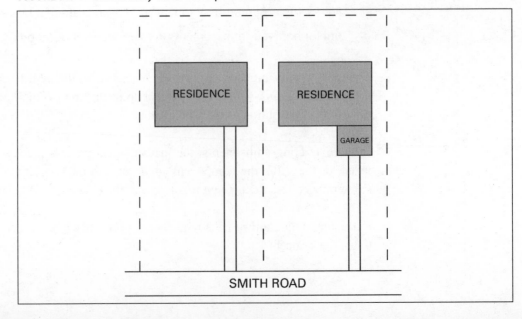

SMITH ROAD

Application

Once the contributory value of a property variable can be isolated, the appraiser then must apply the adjustment in the comparative process. Following are *three critical rules* to remember in the **application** of the adjustment process:

1. Always adjust the comparable to the subject (*never* adjust the subject).

2. If the comparable has a superiority, the adjustment is downward (CBS).

3. If the comparable has an inferiority, the adjustment is upward (CIA).

The easiest way to remember 2 and 3 above is an exercise called CBS and CIA. CBS is an acronym for Comparable Better, Subtract—if the comparable is better (superior) in some respect to the subject, you will subtract from the comparable's sale price, to adjust it "down" to the level of the subject. CIA is for Comparable Inferior, Add—if the comparable is inferior to the subject, you will add to the comparable's sale price, to adjust it "up" to the level of the subject.

In the following example, the appraiser is most concerned with whether or not a lot is lakefront or nonlakefront.

It is obvious from Figure 9.9 that the lakefront lots tend to sell for a premium over the nonlakefront lots. The premium is calculated as follows:

$$
\begin{array}{ll}
\$40,000 & \text{(Lakefront)} \\
-\ \underline{\$25,000} & \text{(Typical—nonlakefront)} \\
\$15,000 & \text{Lake premium (Contributory Value of lake frontage)}
\end{array}
$$

Confusion may arise as to whether or not the adjustment should be upward or downward. Refer back to the *three critical rules* to eliminate any confusion. If the appraiser

FIGURE 9.9 ■ Lakefront Versus Nonlakefront Value

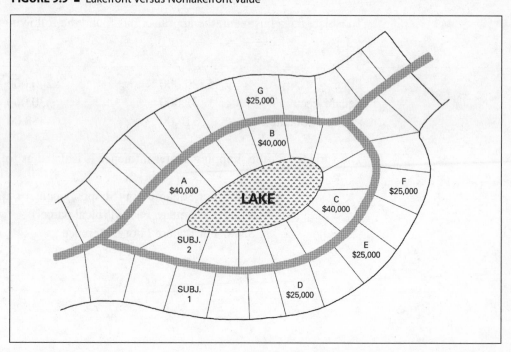

is involved in the valuation of Subject Property 1, and only Sales A, D, and E were available, the following would be concluded:

	Subject 1	A	D	E
Lakefront	No	Yes	No	No
Price		$40,000	$25,000	$25,000
Adjustment		– $15,000	$0	$0
Adjusted Price		$25,000	$25,000	$25,000

By contrast, suppose the appraiser is appraising Subject Property 2 and had available only Sales D, E, and B. The following would be concluded:

	Subject 2	D	E	B
Lakefront	Yes	No	No	Yes
Price		$25,000	$25,000	$40,000
Adjustment		+ $15,000	+ $15,000	$0
Adjusted Price		$40,000	$40,000	$40,000

■ PERCENTAGE ADJUSTMENTS

Percentage adjustments are essentially the same as dollar adjustments. The appraiser must be concerned with the percentage adjustment abstraction as well as the percentage adjustment application. One feature that does require careful consideration is the calculation of the percentage adjustment and application of the percentage adjustment.

In the following example illustrated in Figure 9.10, the appraiser has observed that shopping center "out parcels" tend to sell for more per square foot than typical commercial sites along the remainder of the commercial corridor. The appraiser has determined that the price per square foot is the most applicable unit of comparison. Because this is the case, dollar adjustments are not appropriate because all of the sales vary somewhat in size.

To isolate the adjustment, the appraiser has found the following paired sales analysis:

Sale	A	B
Price	$320,000	$240,000
Square Feet	32,000	30,000
Price Per Square Foot	$10.00	$8.00

The variance for the shopping center influence is isolated as follows:

$10.00 Per Square Foot (Shopping center out parcel)
– $8.00 Per Square Foot (Typical parcel)
$2.00 Per Square Foot Difference

FIGURE 9.10 ■ Percentage Adjustment Example

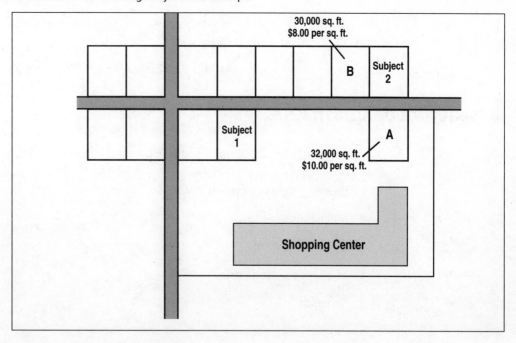

When trying to convert the difference to a percentage adjustment, the following calculations are made:

A. $2.00 ÷ $10.00 = 20%

B. $2.00 ÷ $ 8.00 = 25%

The question is: Is the adjustment 20 percent or 25 percent?

The answer is: *It depends on which way the adjustment is being made.*

If the appraiser is appraising Subject Property 1 and is employing Sale B, the appraiser is adjusting a sale upward for an inferior location or attribute. In the percentage calculation, Alternative B represents the means by which an inferiority is accounted for. To adjust the sale price of Sale B upward 25 percent, the mathematical calculation is:

$8.00 Per Square Foot × 1.25 = $10.00

or

$8.00 Per Square Foot ×125% = $10.00

If the appraiser is appraising Subject Property 2 and utilizing Sale A, the opposite would be true. The price of Sale A would thus have to be adjusted downward 20 percent to reflect the sale's superiority in comparison to the subject. To adjust downward 20 percent, the appraiser simply performs the following mathematical calculation:

$$\$10.00 \text{ Per Square Foot} \times 0.80 = \$8.00$$

or

$$\$10.00 \text{ Per Square Foot} \times 80\% = \$8.00$$

■ SEQUENCE OF ADJUSTMENTS

As noted in Chapter 6, there is a seven-step adjustment order, recapped as follows:

1. Property rights conveyed

2. Financing

3. Conditions of sale

4. Market conditions (time)

5. Location

6. Physical variances

7. Income variances

Although the sequence of adjustments may look somewhat arbitrary and confusing at first, an analysis of each component reveals that it is logical and appropriate.

An easy way to remember the steps is a statement that makes a lot of sense! **Private First Class Means Low Pay Initially.**

Property Rights Conveyed

The first step is to convert the sale property to a fee simple transfer. Even when the appraiser is concerned with appraising something less than fee simple, the appraiser usually begins with a fee simple value. Also, the vast majority of all appraisal assignments are concerned with fee simple. Accordingly, the sale must be converted to a fee simple transfer. On a practical basis, there are very few transfers of partial interests that occur based on a market value perception of the fee simple interest. Partial interests generally do not openly transfer in the market. The failure of a sale to meet the fee simple test would normally disqualify this as a meaningful market sale, and the appraiser would simply discard this sale and move to another. Once the sale has been verified as a fee simple transfer, or it has been adjusted to fee simple, the appraiser moves on to the next step.

Financing

Inherent in the definition of market value, the value most often sought, is the concept that the value concluded is based on a cash to seller arrangement. This does not mean that the buyer must pay all equity cash, but through the use of third party borrowed funds, the seller must receive cash or cash equivalency at the time of the sale. If the seller chooses to finance a portion of the sale by taking back a note, and the note is commensurate with the third party financing market as to terms and conditions, then no adjustment may be necessary. The vast majority of all real estate transfers, however, involve a significant portion of the purchase price being paid with third party financing with the seller receiving cash at closing.

Say a sale needs to be adjusted for cash equivalency, or financing that was favorable to the purchaser and atypical for the market. The sale price was $100,000. The mortgage amount was $85,000, but was financed entirely by the seller at a below market rate, and it is determined the adjustment for financing is $5,000. The $5,000 should be deducted from the sales price of $100,000, or a "cash equivalent" sales price of $95,000.

> Adjusting for financing is tricky. It is easiest to base the decision on financing adjustment only if a concession (below market financing, for example) is made by a person directly involved in the sale itself—seller, buyer, or agent. If someone outside that "triangle" provides the financing, no adjustment is necessary.

> For example, if a newlywed couple is given a 3 percent mortgage on a home by a wealthy uncle, no adjustment is necessary. The uncle has nothing to do with the triangle of parties involved in the sale. The seller still got cash at closing, no matter where the cash came from.

Conditions of Sale

After the sale has been confirmed as being a fee simple transfer at cash or cash equivalency, the appraiser must then determine whether or not the buyer and seller were typically motivated, with both satisfying the inherent underlying assumptions in the market value definition.

Although a pure market value sale under the strict interpretation of the market value definition seldom occurs, the appraiser must apply judgment to see if reasonable seller/buyer knowledge, reasonable buyer/seller motivation, etc., were satisfied.

Frequently, the adjustments for financing and conditions of sale are handled simultaneously. A highly motivated seller may have offered a special, lucrative financing package to the buyer as an inducement to transfer the property.

Market Conditions (Time)

The appraiser is most often charged with the task of conveying the value as of a current date. The data from which the value is concluded, however, is historical in nature, with a judgment applied for market tendencies and trends. It therefore becomes necessary to convert historic data to current price levels, recognizing that prices may be increasing, decreasing, or stable.

Location

An often-used expression in the real estate industry is: *"There are three major factors that influence value—location, location, and location."*

While this statement is somewhat redundant, it does stress the importance of locational variances in real estate markets. Judging locational similarities and dissimilarities does require some exercise of judgment. A thorough understanding of the influences on value, however, can reduce improper judgments in most cases.

Physical Variances

Although the most obvious to detect, physical variances are not accounted for until the sixth step in the adjustment process. This does not lessen the importance of physical variances, but points out the other differences that may be more subtle and difficult to detect. In the normal course of applying the appraisal process, the first five elements of comparison are often inherently allowed for as the appraiser usually begins by choosing nearby sale properties (location) that sold recently (market conditions).

The appraiser would have discarded all other sales that are not fee simple transfers (rights conveyed) that occurred at a cash or cash equivalent price level (financing); also, the appraiser would have likely discarded all non-arm's length transfers (conditions of sale).

In the allowance for physical factors, the appraiser usually reduces all of the variables into a few critical categories, rather than adjusting for every single minor item of dissimilarity.

Income Variances

Income variables relate more to income-type producing properties. This element of comparison is more fully explored in other books.

■ DOLLAR VERSUS PERCENTAGE ADJUSTMENTS

When does the appraiser abstract and apply dollar adjustments, and when does the appraiser abstract and apply percentage adjustments? The answer: It depends. The variance can be by the following two:

1. Property type
2. Elements of comparison

Property Type

Although there is no hard and fast rule, appraisers usually utilize dollar adjustments in making comparisons related to improvement variances. Dollar adjustments may be useful to reconcile differences in the following: square footage variances, rooms, bathrooms, garages/carports, basements, quality, and condition.

The dollar adjustments can further be broken down into units of comparison such as the following: price per square foot of basement area, price per square foot of garage area, living area adjustment, and yard area adjustment.

Elements of Comparison

Generally, the appraiser adjusts the first four elements of comparison (rights conveyed, financing, conditions of sale, market conditions) through percentage adjustments. Also, it is important to note that a new adjusted base is produced every time a percentage adjustment is applied in the analysis of each of the first four steps. The appraiser should never lump adjustments for the first four items of dissimilarity together.

Adjustments for location and physical variances can be made either utilizing dollar or percentage adjustments. Both are employed extensively in the valuation process.

■ IMPORTANT CONSIDERATIONS IN THE ADJUSTMENT PROCESS

Market Trends

One comparison does not constitute a market trend. Rather than relying on one comparison, the appraiser is constantly seeking paired sales from which adjustments can be abstracted. Based on multiple comparisons, the appraiser may conclude that a swimming pool contributes substantially in an upscale neighborhood, but a swimming pool may tend to have negative value in a lower-priced neighborhood.

Always Temper Adjustments with Logic

One set of paired sales may reveal that a lakefront lot is inferior to a nonlakefront lot. Market tendencies, however, tend to support the premise that water frontage is a desirable characteristic, one that will command a premium in the marketplace. If a set of data indicates an adjustment contrary to logic, the appraiser should analyze the market more fully, interviewing buyers and sellers in that particular marketplace for further explanation.

Do Not Confuse Cost with Contributory Value

For example, swimming pools generally do not reflect contributory value commensurate with their cost. The cost to maintain a pool, potential liability, or other factors may influence this tendency.

Do Not Let Personal Preference Interfere with Open-Minded Market Analysis

The appraiser may have a passion for Californian-contemporary residential construction in a community dominated by traditional styles. Do not assume that the market is ever out of touch or unreasonable related to the appraiser's view. Always remember the following: the market is the teacher; the appraiser is the student.

■ MULTIPLE ADJUSTMENTS

Frequently, the appraiser is unable to isolate two properties that are exactly the same except for the variable that the appraiser is attempting to isolate as an adjustment. The appraiser frequently has to perform one or two initial adjustments so that a second or third adjustment can be isolated. Figure 9.11 illustrates this point.

FIGURE 9.11 ■ Multiple Adjustment Example

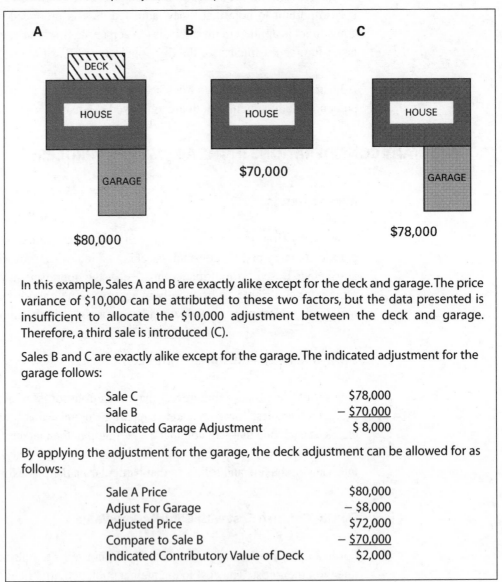

In this example, Sales A and B are exactly alike except for the deck and garage. The price variance of $10,000 can be attributed to these two factors, but the data presented is insufficient to allocate the $10,000 adjustment between the deck and garage. Therefore, a third sale is introduced (C).

Sales B and C are exactly alike except for the garage. The indicated adjustment for the garage follows:

Sale C	$78,000
Sale B	− $70,000
Indicated Garage Adjustment	$ 8,000

By applying the adjustment for the garage, the deck adjustment can be allowed for as follows:

Sale A Price	$80,000
Adjust For Garage	− $8,000
Adjusted Price	$72,000
Compare to Sale B	− $70,000
Indicated Contributory Value of Deck	$2,000

In the adjustment abstraction process, the appraiser should always seek to pair those sales that are different in only one respect prior to considering sale properties that are different in two or more respects. The best comparables, however, are comparables that require no adjustments.

P A R T   S I X   Cash Equivalency

Inherent in the definition of market value is the consummation of a sale whereby the seller receives all cash or its equivalent at closing. When the seller receives part of the price in consideration that is something less than a **cash equivalency**, an adjustment must be made to convert the transaction to an all cash basis.

There are many examples in which the seller might receive less than cash equivalency. The seller may take back a note for all or significantly part of the purchase price at an interest rate less than the prevailing market interest rate; the seller may pay for a mortgage buydown, allowing the buyer to obtain a mortgage at an interest rate less than the prevailing market rate for several years, enabling that buyer to qualify; a seller may pay all or a portion of the discount points charged to the buyer for the mortgage used in the sales transaction; the seller could offer nonreal property benefits associated with the transaction such as a free vacation as an enticement to purchase the property.

In all of these examples, there are mathematical means to convert the actual consideration to a cash equivalency sale. Although the mathematical computation can be made by the appraiser, there is one important rule to remember: the adjustment for cash equivalency should always be based on market extraction rather than a simple mathematical computation.

POINTS PAID BY SELLER

Assume that in a subdivision of starter homes in the $90,000 to $110,000 range a builder is marketing homes to first-time homebuyers who tend to have difficulty qualifying for loans because of up-front cash requirements. The builder/seller may choose to pay the mortgage discount points of 2 percent rather than having the buyer incur this expense. Assuming a $100,000 purchase price and a 90 percent ($90,000) mortgage, the discount points would equate to an up-front cost of $1,800 ($90,000 mortgage × 0.02). In this example, the actual cash equivalent price is $98,200 ($100,000 − $1,800).

By pairing sales, however, the appraiser may find that properties sold in this fashion sell for $99,000, whereas properties without builder/seller paid points sell for $100,000. Although the actual cash equivalent price by mathematical computation is $98,200, the adjustment applicable in the sales comparison approach would be $1,000 because the market reaction to this benefit is not dollar for dollar.

FAVORABLE SELLER FINANCING

In periods of high interest rates and/or scarcity of mortgage funds, sellers often provide financing for a portion of the sales price. This method of financing is also prevalent in rural land tracts.

For example, assume that the prevailing market interest rate is 10 percent. A seller may choose to finance 80 percent of the purchase price at an interest rate of 8 percent. The actual cash equivalent variance by mathematical computation between the two interest rates over the term of the mortgage might equate to a 7 percent difference in converting the stated sales price to a cash equivalent sales price. Again, the appraiser must measure the market reaction to such financing. By pairing sales that sold for cash with similar properties that sold with seller financing, one may find an extracted adjustment of 4 percent. Again, the appraiser's job is to measure the market reaction to the variance and adjust the sale accordingly, rather than applying a dollar for dollar cash equivalent adjustment. Accordingly, the adjustment would be 4 percent, not 7 percent.

■ MORTGAGE BUYDOWNS

Frequently, the seller funds the difference between a below market interest rate and the market interest rate for several years payable on the mortgage procured by the buyer to facilitate the sale of the property. The mathematical computation for the difference in the interest rates can be converted to a current cash equivalent difference between the stated sales price and cash equivalent price; however, the appraiser must attempt to isolate the market reaction to this financing that is favorable for the buyer.

■ FAVORABLE FINANCING FROM A PARTY UNRELATED TO THE TRANSACTION

Frequently, a purchaser is able to procure mortgage funds at a below market interest rate from a relative, employer, or other party. The critical factor, however, is that the seller still receives all cash at closing, regardless of where the money was obtained. Even though a buyer receives a $100,000 loan for 30 years at 3 percent from a relative, if all $100,000 is conveyed to the seller at closing, the transaction is cash equivalent, and no adjustment is needed.

■ REAL ESTATE COMMISSIONS AND CLOSING COSTS

In a normal real estate transaction, the seller never receives all the purchase price. Typical seller expenses such as real estate commissions and closing costs are generally held to be necessary to consummate the transaction, and no adjustment is needed. Just remember, the sales price is not what the seller actually gets in most cases.

1. Most appraisers need to achieve which level of mathematical competency?
   a. PhD
   b. Fifth grade education
   c. Working knowledge of basic mathematical functions
   d. Southeastern Conference Football fan

2. In typical appraisal assignments, appraisers are concerned with area and volume calculations for which of the following?
   a. Data analysis
   b. Application of approaches
   c. A and B
   d. None of the above

3. Given the following, what is the area?

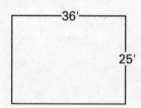

   a. 800 square feet
   b. 400 square feet
   c. 350 square feet
   d. 900 square feet

4. Given the following, what is the area expressed in acres?

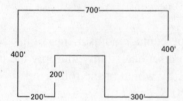

   a. 5.51 acres
   b. 4.38 acres
   c. 6.43 acres
   d. 5.08 acres

5. Given the following, what is the area of the triangle expressed in acres?

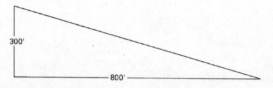

   a. 1.23 acres
   b. 4.82 acres
   c. 5.51 acres
   d. 2.75 acres

6. Given the following, what is the area?

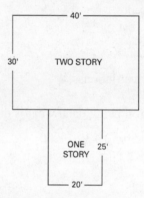

   a. 2,900 square feet
   b. 1,700 square feet
   c. 2,400 square feet
   d. 1,900 square feet

7. Your subject property contains 1.23 acres; what is the area expressed in square footage?
   a. 43,560 square feet
   b. 80,000 square feet
   c. 53,579 square feet
   d. 37,323 square feet

8. Given the following warehouse, what is the volume expressed in cubic feet?

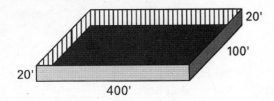

   a. 40,000 cubic feet
   b. 600,000 cubic feet
   c. 896,000 cubic feet
   d. 800,000 cubic feet

9. Developing units of comparison is important for
   a. data analysis.
   b. application of the three approaches.
   c. both A and B.
   d. none of the above.

10. The following are units of comparison applicable to land except
   a. square feet.
   b. front feet.
   c. acre.
   d. height restrictions.

11. Given the following data, what is the mean?

     9.00   10.50   10.33   8.00   7.20   9.00

   a. 8.50
   b. 9.01
   c. 7.20
   d. 7.75

12. Given the same data, what is the median?
   a. 9.00
   b. 7.75
   c. 8.50
   d. 10.50

13. Given the same data, what is the mode?
   a. 8.00
   b. 10.50
   c. 9.00
   d. 8.25

14. There are two types of adjustments; these are
   a. percentage and leased fee.
   b. dollar (lump sum) and percentage.
   c. dollar (lump sum) and off-site.
   d. percentage and rational.

15. Always adjust the
   a. comparable to the subject.
   b. subject to the comparable.
   c. comparable to the comparable.
   d. subject to the subject.

16. Given the following, what is the indicated adjustment for corner influence?

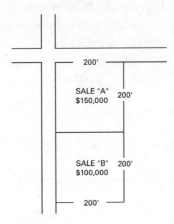

   a. $20,000
   b. $30,000
   c. $50,000
   d. $100,000

17. Given the same data for the previous question, what is the percentage adjustment to sale "B" if the subject is a corner lot?
   a. +50 percent
   b. −33 percent
   c. No adjustment needed
   d. −50 percent

18. If the percentage adjustment is plus 10 percent, the appraiser can simply multiply the unadjusted number by which of the following?
   a. 1.10
   b. 0.90
   c. 0.99
   d. 1.01

19. If the percentage adjustment is down 35 percent, the appraiser can simply multiply the unadjusted number by which of the following?
    a. 0.65
    b. 0.75
    c. 1.35
    d. 1.25

20. If the percentage adjustment is down 25 percent, the appraiser can simply multiply the unadjusted number by which of the following?
    a. 0.65
    b. 1.25
    c. 0.75
    d. 0.85

CHAPTER TEN

Relationships Between Time and Money

■ LEARNING OBJECTIVES

Students will be able to

1. understand the basic functions of a financial calculator

2. understand compounding and perform basic compounding calculations

3. recognize discounting and perform basic discounting calculations

4. calculate mortgage payments, terms, interest rates, and constants

■ KEY TERMS

annual debt service	mortgage constant (Rm)	present value of $1 per
compounding	mortgage interest rate	period
discounting	mortgage payment	reserves for replacement
future benefits	mortgage term	
future value of $1	periodic payment to grow	
future value of $1 per	to $1	
period		

■ INTRODUCTION

Value is often expressed as the present worth of future benefits. Related to investment properties, **future benefits** are monies that are to be received at a later date in exchange for the purchase of the present ownership. This Chapter deals with how investments compound or grow over time, and how dollars that are to be collected in the future can be converted to present value. Even though many mathematical functions are performed by computers or financial calculators, the appraiser should have a thorough understanding of the mathematics involved in order to detect errors.

P A R T   O N E   Relationships Between Time and Money

■ INTRODUCTION TO THE FINANCIAL CALCULATOR

There are five basic keys on a financial calculator with which an appraiser must become familiar. Generally, the keys are located at or near the top of the calculator and are in the following order from left to right:

(N)   Number of payments
(I)   Periodic interest rate as a percent
(PV)   Present value
(PMT)   Periodic payment
(FV)   Future value

When the information is known and entered for any of the three or four items, you can solve for the fourth or fifth unknown item. However, there are four general rules described below that must be followed to insure the accuracy of the calculation(s).

1. Always remember to clear the financial registers of the calculator before beginning calculations, even if you have just turned the calculator on. Many financial calculators retain inputs until the register is cleared using the appropriate steps. Once the register is cleared, you are ready to begin.

2. When solving mortgage calculations, the input for number of payments (N) is the sum of all periodic payments. For instance, if the loan were a 30-year loan with monthly payments, the number of payments (N) would be 360, or 30 years times 12 payments per year. If the loan were a 15-year loan with semiannual payments, the number of payments (N) would be 30, or 15 years times 2 payments per year.

3. Interest rates are expressed as an annual rate. When solving mortgage calculations, it is essential to keep the interest rate and the frequency of the payments consistent. To accomplish this, the annual interest rate must always be divided by the number of payments to be made during the year. This is called the *periodic interest rate*.

> For example, when payments are monthly, the interest rate must be converted from an annual rate to a monthly periodic rate (divide interest rate by 12) prior to being input into the calculator as (I). When payments are quarterly, the annual interest rate must be divided by four prior to being input into the calculator. When payments are semiannual, the annual interest rate must be divided by two prior to being input into the calculator, and so on.

4. When entering the (PV), (PMT), and (FV) cash flows, the quantities must be keyed into the calculator with the proper sign, + (plus) or − (minus).

> For example, money received is entered or displayed as a positive value (+). Money paid out is entered or displayed as a negative value (−). If you were solving for a mortgage payment, for instance, the loan received would be entered as a positive (+) value because that is an inflow of cash (assumes a borrower's perspective). Then when you solve for payment (PMT), the payment would be expressed as a negative (−) value because that is an outflow of cash from the borrower's perspective.

All calculators come with an owner's handbook and problem-solving guide. It is the responsibility of the user to become acquainted with the individual peculiarities of his or her own calculator.

■ COMPOUNDING (FUTURE VALUE OF $1)

Most people have heard the term *compound interest* associated with various accounts they may have at a financial institution. What is compounding? **Compounding** is best illustrated as the **Future Value of $1**, or what an investment or deposit will grow to in a given number of time periods at a specified rate of interest, including the accumulation of interest on interest.

Suppose you deposit $100 at the beginning of the year in an account that bears a nominal interest rate of 10 percent with annual compounding. At the end of three years, how much has your investment increased? The solution, done arithmetically, would look like this:

Original investment	$100.00
Interest earned at 10% during Year 1	+ $10.00
Worth of investment after Year 1	$110.00
Interest earned at 10% during Year 2	+ $11.00
Worth of investment after Year 2	$121.00
Interest earned at 10% during Year 3	+ $12.10
Worth of investment after Year 3	$133.10

You can solve this problem easily by using your financial calculator* as follows:

Step	Entry	Comments	Display
1		Clear Financial Registers	0.00
2	3 (N)	Number of Periods	3.00
3	10 (I)	Periodic Interest Rate	10.00
4	−100 (PV)	Present Value of Investment	−100.00
5	Solve for (FV)	Future Value of Investment	133.10

Of course, the reason the $100 is input into the calculator as a negative (−) value is because we are viewing this transaction from the depositor's perspective. The depositor invests the $100 with the bank (outflow), and at the end of three years receives $133.10 (inflow).

*Using a Hewlett-Packard 12-C financial calculator; other calculators may function differently.

■ DISCOUNTING (PRESENT VALUE OF $1)

While compounding views an investment that begins at time 0 and grows into the future, discounting is just the opposite. **Discounting** answers the question, "If I am to receive a specified amount of money at a specified time in the future, and I require a specified rate of return on my investment, what am I willing to pay for that right in today's dollars?" As previously discussed, the principle of *anticipation* is the underlying principle of the Income Approach to value. Investors often base the price they are willing to pay for an investment on the anticipated monetary benefits to be derived in the future, taking into account the perceived risk associated with receiving those monetary benefits. Simply stated, an investor pays present dollars for an investment based on their estimate of the future benefit(s) to be derived from the ownership of the investment. In order to estimate the market value of an investment, an appraiser is often required to *discount* forecasted monetary benefits into a present value estimate for the property being appraised.

For example, you forecast that at the end of three years, you will receive a one lump-sum payment of $133.10. Further, you require a 10 percent rate of return on your investment. What is the most you can pay for this investment and get your required rate of return? This problem can best be solved using your financial calculator as follows:

Step	Entry	Comments	Display
1		Clear Financial Registers	0.00
2	3 (N)	Number of Periods	3.00
3	10 (I)	Periodic Interest Rate	10.00
4	133.10 (FV)	Future Value of Benefits Received	+133.10
5	Solve for (PV)	Present Dollars to be Paid at 10%	-100.00

In this problem, you will receive $133.10 at the end of three years (inflow), therefore, the $133.10 would be input into the calculator as a positive (+) value. Solving for present value (PV) suggests you can only pay $100.00 today for the said investment (outflow) if you desire a 10 percent rate of return. Since the $100.00 is an outflow to the investor, the number is displayed in the calculator as a negative (-) value.

■ FUTURE VALUE OF $1 PER PERIOD

The **future value of $1 per period** represents the total accumulation of both principal and interest on a series of installments of $1 per period for a given number of periods with interest at the periodic interest rate.

For example, how much money would be accumulated if you were able to deposit $100 at the end of each month for a period of 5 years assuming an 8.0% interest rate? The accumulated amount of money can be calculated using your financial calculator as follows:

Step	Entry	Comments	Display
1		Clear Financial Registers	0.00
2	5×12 (N)	Number of Periods	60.00
3	$8 \div 12$ (I)	Periodic Interest Rate	0.667
4	−100 (PMT)	Periodic Payment Applied	−100.00
5	Solve for (FV)	Accumulated Amount at 8%	7,347.69

Although the periodic payments made into the investment total only $6,000 (60 payments at $100 each), the accumulated investment (principal and interest) at the end of five years totals $7,347.69, assuming a rate of return of 8.0%.

PRESENT VALUE OF $1 PER PERIOD

Suppose you were interested in purchasing a mortgage which has 8 years left before being fully amortized, with monthly payments of $1,135. Further, you require a return on investment of 10 percent. How would you determine the price to be paid, or **present value of $1**, for such an investment?

The price could be determined by using your financial calculator as follows:

Step	Entry	Comments	Display
1		Clear Financial Registers	0.00
2	8×12 (N)	Number of Periods	96.00
3	$10 \div 12$ (I)	Periodic Interest Rate	0.833
4	1,135 (PMT)	Monthly Payment to be Received	1,135.00
5	Solve for (PV)	Present dollars to be Paid at 10%	−74,798.19

The price which could be paid today (present value) for the right to receive $1,135 per month for 8 years, with a 10 percent return on investment, is $74,798.19. Although the payments you will receive of $1,135.00 for the next 96 months total $108,960.00, you can only afford to pay $74,798.19 in today's dollars to receive a 10 percent return on your investment. A dollar to be received in the future is worth less than a dollar received today. Therefore, money received in the future must be discounted to reflect its present worth.

PERIODIC PAYMENT TO GROW TO $1 (SINKING FUND FACTOR)

The **periodic payment to grow $1** calculation provides an estimate of the periodic amount that must be set aside to accumulate to a certain amount in the future. This function is often used by appraisers when estimating what is commonly referred to as "reserves for replacement." **Reserves for replacement** is a fund whereby a property owner sets aside a certain amount of money periodically for the replacement of *short-lived* building components, or those components that will require replacement during the investment holding period, at a future point in time. Reserves for replacement and short-lived building components are subsequently discussed in Chapter 15.

For example, an appraiser estimates that the roof of the subject building will require replacement at the end of 5 years at an estimated cost of $25,000. What amount of money should be set aside each year to accumulate to $25,000 if the money is invested at 8.0%?

The periodic amount that would need to be set aside each year can be determined by using your financial calculator as follows:

Step	Entry	Comments	Display
1		Clear Financial Registers	0.00
2	5 (N)	Number of Periods	5.00
3	8 (I)	Periodic Interest Rate	8.00
4	25,000 (FV)	Future Value Required for Roof Replacement	25,000.00
5	Solve for (PMT)	Periodic Payment Required to Replace Roof at 8%	-4,261.41

The required amount to be set aside each year by the property owner, assuming an 8 percent investment rate, approximates $4,261.41. The owner would set aside $21,307.05 ($4,261.41 × 5 years) in actual dollars; however, investing the money at an 8 percent rate of interest would grow the money to $25,000 by the end of 5 years.

Another commonly used example to illustrate the periodic payment to grow $1 is, "How much money do I need to set aside each month to pay for college when my children are ready to enroll?" This problem can be solved using the same financial calculations as in the previous example.

PART TWO   Mortgage Calculations

■ CALCULATION OF A MORTGAGE PAYMENT

Using the basic financial calculator and the function keys previously discussed, you can calculate a **mortgage payment** if you know the mortgage terms and conditions (borrower's perspective).

Suppose the mortgage has monthly payments for 30 years, an interest rate of 10 percent, and a beginning loan balance of $250,000. The mortgage payment could be determined by using your financial calculator as follows:

Step	Entry	Comments	Display
1		Clear Financial Registers	0.00
2	30 × 12 = 360 (N)	Number of Periods	360.00
3	10 ÷ 12 = 0.833 (I)	Periodic Interest Rate	0.833
4	250,000 (PV)	Present Value of Mortgage	250,000.00
5	Solve for (PMT)	Calculates Payment	–2,193.93

The monthly payment is $2,193.93. It is in the register as a negative value because it is from the borrower's perspective.

To calculate **annual debt service**, multiply the payment amount by the number of payments to be made each year. In the previous example, the annual debt service would be $26,327.15, or $2,193.93 times 12 payments per year.

Now suppose the mortgage has quarterly payments for 20 years, an interest rate of 12 percent, and a beginning loan balance of $325,000:

Step	Entry	Comments	Display
1		Clear Financial Registers	0.00
2	20 × 4 = 80 (N)	Number of Periods	80.00
3	12 ÷ 4 = 3.00 (I)	Periodic Interest Rate	3.00
4	325,000 (PV)	Present Value of Mortgage	325,000.00
5	Solve for (PMT)	Calculates Payment	–10,761.32

The quarterly payment is $10,761.32. The annual debt service would be $43,045.27, or $10,761.32 times four (4) payments per year.

■ CALCULATION OF A MORTGAGE TERM

Using the basic financial calculator and the function keys, as previously discussed, you can calculate a **mortgage term** assuming the following mortgage terms and conditions (borrower's perspective).

Suppose the mortgage has a monthly payment of $1,254.66, an interest rate of 8 percent, and a beginning loan balance of $150,000. The mortgage term could be determined by using your financial calculator as follows:

Step	Entry	Comments	Display
1		Clear Financial Registers	0.00
2	8 ÷ 12 = .067 (I)	Periodic Interest Rate	0.67
3	150,000 (PV)	Present Value of Mortgage	150,000.00
4	–1,254.66 (PMT)	Periodic Mortgage Payment	–1,254.66
5	Solve for (N)	Calculates Number of Payments	240

The total number of payments required to amortize the debt applying monthly payments of $1,254.66 is 240, or 20 years.

Now suppose the mortgage has a semiannual payment of $32,682.56, an interest rate of 11 percent, and a beginning loan balance of $475,000:

Step	Entry	Comments	Display
1		Clear Financial Registers	0.00
2	11 ÷ 2 = 5.50 (I)	Periodic Interest Rate	5.50
3	475,000 (PV)	Present Value of Mortgage	475,000.00
4	−32,682.56 (PMT)	Periodic Mortgage Payment	−32,682.56
5	Solve for (N)	Calculates Number of Payments	30

The total number of payments required to amortize the debt applying semiannual payments of $32,682.56 is 30, or 15 years.

■ CALCULATION OF A MORTGAGE INTEREST RATE

Using the basic financial calculator and the function keys previously discussed, you can calculate a **mortgage interest rate** if you know the mortgage terms and conditions (borrower's perspective).

Suppose the mortgage has a monthly payment of $877.57, a mortgage term of 30 years, and a beginning loan balance of $100,000. The mortgage interest rate could be determined by using your financial calculator as follows:

Step	Entry	Comments	Display
1		Clear Financial Registers	0.00
2	30 × 12 = 360 (N)	Number of Periods	360.00
3	100,000 (PV)	Present Value of Mortgage	100,000.00
4	−877.57 (PMT)	Periodic Mortgage Payment	−877.57
5	Solve for (I)	Calculates Periodic Interest Rate	0.83
6	0.83 × 12 = 10	Calculates Annual Interest Rate	10.00

The annual interest rate is 10 percent.

Now suppose the mortgage has a quarterly payment of $21,063.35, a mortgage term of 15 years, and a beginning loan balance of $500,000.

Step	Entry	Comments	Display
1		Clear Financial Registers	0.00
2	15 × 4 = 60 (N)	Number of Periods	60.00
3	500,000 (PV)	Present Value of Mortgage	500,000.00
4	−21,063.35 (PMT)	Periodic Mortgage Payment	−21,063.35
5	Solve for (I)	Calculates Periodic Interest Rate	3.75
6	3.75 × 4 = 15	Calculates Annual Interest Rate	15.00

The annual interest rate is 15 percent.

■ CALCULATION OF A MORTGAGE CONSTANT

A **mortgage constant**, also known as the *rate to the mortgage*, is a function of the interest rate, the frequency of the payments (monthly, semiannual, etc.), and the term of the loan. The mortgage constant is simply what each dollar of debt service will cost at the mortgage terms and conditions given. There are two methods for calculating a mortgage constant. These two methods are discussed below.

Method 1: A mortgage constant is the annual debt service of a given mortgage divided by the original amount of the loan.

> For example, if you are given annual debt service of $12,000 (10% interest; 18 years, monthly payments) on an original loan of $100,000, the implied mortgage constant is 0.12. Stated another way, each dollar of debt is costing the borrower $0.12, or twelve cents per year.

Method 2: A mortgage constant can also be calculated by computing the annual payment of $1 given certain mortgage terms and conditions.

> For example, consider the mortgage terms and conditions from the previous illustration of 10% interest and a term of 18 years with monthly payments. What if you were not provided with the original loan amount? The mortgage constant could be calculated as follows:
>
> | Step | Entry | Comments | Display |
> |------|-------|----------|---------|
> | 1 | | Clear Financial Registers | 0.00 |
> | 2 | $18 \times 12 = 216$ (N) | Number of Periods | 216.00 |
> | 3 | $10 \div 12 = 0.83$ (I) | Periodic Interest Rate | 0.83 |
> | 4 | 1 (PV) | Present Value of Mortgage | 1.00 |
> | 5 | Solve for (PMT) | Calculates the Periodic Constant | −0.0100 |
> | 6 | -0.0100×12 | Calculates Mortgage Constant | −0.12 |

In order to test the calculated mortgage constant of 0.12, multiply the original loan amount of $100,000 given in the previous example by the mortgage constant of 0.12. The implied annual debt service is $12,000 per year which is accurate at the given mortgage terms and conditions.

Once you get a mortgage constant at certain mortgage terms and conditions, you can multiply that constant by any loan amount you are contemplating borrowing and instantly have the annual debt service that the loan amount will cost at those terms and conditions.

Problem: Find the mortgage constant for a $200,000 loan, paid monthly for 30 years at 10% interest.

You can use Method 1 to solve for the mortgage constant by calculating the annual debt service of $200,000 at the given terms and conditions, then simply dividing the annual debt service by $200,000 as follows:

Step	Entry	Comments	Display
1		Clear Financial Registers	0.00
2	30 × 12 = 360 (N)	Number of Periods	360.00
3	10 ÷ 12 = 0.833 (I)	Periodic Interest Rate	0.833
4	200,000 (PV)	Present Value of Mortgage	200,000.00
5	Solve for (PMT)	Calculates Monthly Payment	−1,755.14
6	−1,755.14 × 12	Calculates Annual Debt Service	−21,061.72

If annual debt service is $21,061.72, then the mortgage constant can be calculated by dividing $21,061.72 by the original loan amount of $200,000. The mortgage constant by Method 1 would approximate 0.1053.

Using Method 2, you can solve for the mortgage constant by calculating the annual debt service of $1 at the given terms and conditions as follows:

Step	Entry	Comments	Display
1		Clear Financial Registers	0.00
2	30 × 12 = 360 (N)	Number of Periods	360.00
3	10 ÷ 12 = 0.833 (I)	Periodic Interest Rate	0.833
4	1 (PV)	Present Value of Mortgage	1.00
5	Solve for (PMT)	Calculates the Periodic Constant	−0.0088
6	−0.0088 × 12	Calculates Mortgage Constant	−0.1053

Using either method, the mortgage constant of a loan at 10 percent for 30 years, monthly payments, is 0.1053. Therefore, each dollar of debt will cost the borrower $0.1053, or slightly over 10.5 cents per year.

1. If you purchased a tract of land for $250,000, what price (assume no sales cost) would you have to sell the property for in ten years to achieve an 8 percent annualized rate of return?
   a. $535,897
   b. $539,731
   c. $450,000
   d. $600,000

2. If you deposit $500 at the beginning of the year into an account that bears a nominal interest rate of 7.5 percent with annual compounding, how much will your investment be worth at the end of five years?
   a. $687.50
   b. $537.50
   c. $717.81
   d. $726.65

3. If you anticipate selling a rental property in five years for $750,000 and the appropriate discount rate is 12 percent, what is the present value?
   a. $1,321,756
   b. $425,570
   c. $450,000
   d. $417,628

4. If you have a rental property that is leased for $1,000 a month for the next 20 years, what could an investor pay for the property if their required rate of return was 11 percent (assume rent is collected at the end of each month)?
   a. $96,882
   b. $109,665
   c. $78,432
   d. $92,123

5. If a mortgage has eight years and four months remaining at $700 per month, what could a purchaser pay to achieve a 15 percent return on investment?
   a. $35,560
   b. $41,396
   c. $39,831
   d. $43,910

6. Calculate a mortgage payment assuming the mortgage has annual payments for 30 years, 8.5 percent interest, and an original loan amount of $325,000.
   a. $30,241.44
   b. $29,987.63
   c. $27,625.00
   d. $38,458.33

7. Calculate a mortgage payment assuming the mortgage has monthly payments for 15 years, 11 percent interest, and an original loan amount of $150,000.
   a. $1,738.32
   b. $1,375.00
   c. $1,704.90
   d. $2,208.33

8. Calculate a mortgage payment assuming the mortgage has semiannual payments for 10 years, 9 percent interest, and an original loan amount of $1,235,000.
   a. $96,218.91
   b. $92,612.98
   c. $91,247.71
   d. $94,942.04

9. Calculate the term of a mortgage assuming an interest rate of 7.75 percent, a monthly payment of $2,212.76, and an original loan amount of $280,000.
   a. 20 years
   b. 30 years
   c. 25 years
   d. 22 years

10. Calculate the term of a mortgage assuming an interest rate of 9.25 percent, an annual payment of $79,325.11, and an original loan amount of $435,000.
    a. 7 years
    b. 8 years
    c. 9 years
    d. 10 years

11. Calculate the nominal interest rate of a mortgage assuming a term of 30 years, a monthly payment of $2,738.79, and an original loan amount of $345,000.
    a.   8.00 percent
    b.   8.85 percent
    c.   7.25 percent
    d.   7.75 percent

12. Calculate the nominal interest rate of a mortgage assuming a term of 15 years, an annual payment of $115,385.96, and an original loan amount of $775,500.
    a.   12.25 percent
    b.   11.75 percent
    c.   12.50 percent
    d.   12.00 percent

13. Calculate the mortgage constant for a loan assuming a term of 25 years, an interest rate of 10.0 percent, and monthly payments.
    a.   0.11017
    b.   0.08333
    c.   0.10904
    d.   0.09181

14. Calculate the mortgage constant for a loan assuming a term of 30 years, an interest rate of 12.0 percent, a quarterly payment of $3,861.24, and an original loan amount of $125,000 (hint: There are two ways to solve this problem).
    a.   0.12414
    b.   0.12239
    c.   0.11885
    d.   0.12356

15. What is the annual debt service on a mortgage with an original loan amount of $642,000 and a mortgage constant of 0.10909?
    a. $72,193.12
    b. $70,035.78
    c. $69,203.86
    d.   Cannot determine from the information given

CHAPTER ELEVEN

Land and Site Valuation

■ LEARNING OBJECTIVES

Students will be able to

1. understand the underlying economic principles of land and site valuation including highest and best use, substitution, supply and demand, and anticipation.

2. understand and recognize the important influences on´ land and site valuation including physical characteristics, zoning, utilities, and site improvements.

3. recognize the six techniques for site valuation.

4. understand and apply three of the techniques for site valuation including allocation, extraction, and sales comparison.

■ KEY TERMS

allocation	element of comparison	principle of substitution
as if vacant	extraction	subdivision development
as improved	land residual	view

■ INTRODUCTION

Whether the property to be appraised is vacant or improved, an appraiser will undoubtedly perform the task of valuing land or a site. Generally speaking, there are two components that comprise the total value of an improved property: (1) the contribution of improvements and (2) the value of the site. In this book, we will first concentrate our efforts on the valuation of the site. A separate value for the site is required in arriving at a value indication by the Cost Approach. Other situations requiring a separate value of the land or site may include an estimation of casualty loss, an appeal of the tax assessment, estimating accrued depreciation or contribution of the improvements, eminent domain proceedings, a highest and best use analysis, a feasibility study, etc.

The economic principles were previously presented and discussed in Chapter 4. Several of these economic principles can be related to the valuation of land or a site: highest and best use, substitution, supply and demand, and anticipation. The relationship of these economic principles to land and site valuation is discussed below.

HIGHEST AND BEST USE

The *highest and best use* section of an appraisal report includes an analysis of the property's highest and best use **as if vacant** and highest and best use **as improved**. Highest and best use is a market force that drives the value and the ultimate development of land or a site. Therefore, land value must always be estimated in terms of its highest and best use as if vacant and available for development to its most economic and profitable use even when improved (i.e., improvements can be demolished). Comparable sales used in the valuation of land or a site should reflect a similar highest and best use in comparison to the property being appraised; otherwise, the estimate of value for the subject property may be unreliable or inaccurate.

Land is said to *have value* while improvements *contribute to value*. Land value may be equal to or greater than total property value even when substantial improvements are situated on the site.

As previously stated, there are two components that comprise the total value of an improved property: (1) the contribution of improvements and (2) the value of the site. The contribution of improvements is estimated by subtracting land or site value from total property value. When improvements no longer contribute to total property value (i.e., land value is equal to or greater than total property value as improved), demolition of the improvements and redevelopment of the site may occur.

SUBSTITUTION

The **principle of substitution** implies a prudent purchaser will not pay more for one site than for a comparable site offering similar utility and amenities (i.e., location, physical characteristics, zoning, etc.) In turn, the lower priced sites originate the greatest demand, all other things being equal.

SUPPLY AND DEMAND

The economic principle of *supply and demand*, as it relates to land and site valuation, implies that prices will rise when stable or increasing demand is coupled with a decrease in the availability (or supply) of land or a site. When an oversupply of land or available sites is coupled with stable or limited demand, prices will typically decline. When the demand for land or available sites increases within a particular market area, new supply may be created through new development, rezoning, demolition of existing improvements, etc.

Land values can also be substantially influenced by the supply and demand of a specific improved property type. For instance, an oversupply of single-family houses in an area may likely reduce the immediate demand for, and possibly the value of, vacant, residentially zoned land and sites. This example also relates to the principle of *balance* which suggests that the value of land or a site is created and sustained when supply and demand are in or near a state of equilibrium. Consistent with the principle of balance, the fluctuation in supply and demand significantly influences the economic use and market value of land or a site. Supply and demand must often be analyzed to arrive at a reliable indication of value.

ANTICIPATION

The principle of *anticipation*, as it relates to land and site valuation, implies that value is created by the expectation of future benefits associated with ownership of the land or a site. Occasionally, market participants are motivated to purchase land or a site in a specific location in "anticipation" of a future increase in demand, and hence value, even though current demand is quite limited.

PART TWO   Influences on Land and Site Valuation

Physical characteristics; zoning and/or deed restrictions; the availability, capacity, and proximity of utilities; and site improvements each influence a parcel of land or site's eventual use, development and market value. Each of these influences will be discussed below.

PHYSICAL CHARACTERISTICS

Physical characteristics that must be considered by the appraiser include the following:

1. Size

2. Shape or configuration

3. Frontage

4. Topography

5. Drainage

6. View

Size

The *size* of a parcel can limit its eventual use and development. For instance, a regional mall cannot physically be developed on a one-acre parcel.

Shape or Configuration

The *shape* or average width and depth of a parcel can limit its functional utility. For instance, a residential building lot may be so narrow that, after satisfying the required building setbacks (if applicable), the only style of house which can physically be constructed on the parcel is a two-story dwelling with the car storage attached to the rear of the residence.

Frontage and Access or Ingress/Egress

Frontage can either pertain to the street or it may pertain to an amenity such as a lake, golf course, etc. The amount of street frontage generally influences the visibility of and access to the building improvements. Access is how one gains entrance to a property, and it can greatly affect value. Ingress/egress relates to entry/exit of a property. A property may have excellent frontage, but it may have poor access (due to a roadway median) or inferior ingress/egress due to the absence of curb cuts along a roadway or due to topography problems.

Topography

The *topography* or slope of a parcel typically influences the visibility of the building improvements, as well as the costs associated with development of the site. For instance, if a parcel slopes significantly down from the street, the visibility and development costs of the building improvements will likely be adversely impacted. This would generally result in a lower price paid for the land parcel or site because the buyer will likely incur greater costs to develop the site.

Drainage

Problems associated with inadequate water *drainage* are both irritating and costly to correct. Sites with poor drainage generally command a lower price than sites with adequate drainage, all other things being equal.

View

The **view** from a site may add or detract from its market value. For instance, a cheerful view of a lake, mountains, golf course, etc. will generally increase the value of a site. Similarly, an offensive view (i.e., power line, landfill, etc.) will generally decrease the value of a site.

■ ZONING AND/OR DEED RESTRICTIONS

One of the four powers of government limiting fee simple ownership of real property is *police power*; this includes zoning and building codes. Also, private (deed) restrictions may be present. Most municipalities and counties have some form of public restrictions that identify what development can and cannot take place on a parcel of land. In addition to public restrictions, many jurisdictions have master, or land use, plans specifying long-term development goals as identified by the local government. Zoning and deed restrictions assist in defining a parcel's highest and best use (legally permissible) and are a primary consideration when selecting comparable sales for comparison to the property being appraised.

■ AVAILABILITY, CAPACITY, AND PROXIMITY OF UTILITIES

The availability, capacity and proximity of utilities (in relation to the subject site) such as electricity, natural gas, water, sewer, telephone, and cable television influence the use and development potential of a land parcel, and hence its market value. Utilities may be provided by off-site public facilities such as power lines, public water and natural gas mains, and sewer, or by on-site private facilities such as drilled or bored domestic wells, spring basins, liquid propane tanks, and septic tanks.

■ SITE IMPROVEMENTS

Site improvements can be classified into on-site and off-site improvements. *On-site improvements* include those improvements within the confines of the site such as grading, landscaping, paving, utility lines and hookups, etc. *Off-site improvements* include those improvements outside the confines of the site such as streets, curbs, gutters, sidewalks, storm sewer drains, connecting utility lines, etc.

PART THREE   Techniques for Site Valuation

There are six recognized methods for land and site valuation: allocation, extraction, sales comparison, subdivision development, land residual, and ground rent capitalization. Primary emphasis in this book will be accorded to allocation, market extraction, and sales comparison. The subdivision development method involves advanced procedures (i.e., forecasting, discounting, etc.) that are beyond the scope of this book. The land residual and ground rent capitalization methods are rarely used in day to day appraising.

■ ALLOCATION

Allocation is a technique used to estimate land value where an appraiser establishes a typical ratio of land value to total property value by analyzing recent sales of improved properties, and subsequently applies this ratio to the value of the property being appraised or sales price of the comparable sale being analyzed. When an inadequate number of comparable land or site sales are available to employ the sales comparison method, the allocation method may be used.

Allocation suggests that there is a typical ratio of land value to total property value for similar property types in a similar location. Allocation is generally more reliable when the subject improvements are relatively new. As improvements age, the ratio of land value to total property value typically increases.

> For example, assume you are appraising a house in the northern city limits and no sales of vacant sites have occurred recently. However, through your investigations, you determine that houses located in a similar city neighborhood on the south side have sold generally between $75,000 and $90,000, with vacant sites commanding a price of around $15,000. The land value would range from approximately 17% (0.17) to 20% (0.20) of total property value ($15,000 ÷ $90,000; $15,000 ÷ $75,000). If houses in the subject neighborhood are selling for between $60,000 and $75,000, the suggested land value by allocation would range from $12,000 ($60,000 × 0.20) to $12,750 ($75,000 × 0.17).

Procedure

The procedure for estimating site value by the allocation method is summarized as follows:

a. Locate a neighborhood comparable to the subject that features both improved sales and sales of vacant sites,

b. Obtain and verify several improved sales and sales of vacant sites from the comparable neighborhood,

c. Extract a typical land value to total property value ratio by dividing the sales price of the vacant sites by the sales price of the improved properties,

d. Multiply the reconciled land value ratio (in decimal format) by the sales price of improved comparable sales in the subject neighborhood to arrive at a range of value for the subject site by the allocation method.

Note: The allocation method does not establish a conclusive value for the subject site, but rather an indicated range of value.

> For example, assume in your attempt to estimate the value of the subject site that a search for vacant comparable land sales was unsuccessful. During the investigation, however, you uncovered a recent survey of local real estate brokers which supported a typical land value to total property ratio in the general neighborhood of 25% for homes between $50,000 and $75,000 and 20% for homes between $75,000 and $100,000. What is a reasonable value estimate for the subject site if your estimation of market value for the total property approximates $85,000?
>
> In this situation, the total property value falls within the $75,000 to $100,000 range; therefore, a 20% (0.20) allocation for the site would apply. An appropriate value for the subject site would thus approximate $17,000 ($85,000 × 0.20).

■ EXTRACTION

Extraction is a technique used to estimate land value where an appraiser estimates the contributory value (i.e., depreciated cost) of all improvements on an improved comparable sale and deducts this estimate from the total sale price of the comparable to arrive at an estimated contributory value for the land. This technique is generally most effective when the improvements contribute nominally to the value of the comparable property.

As with the Sales Comparison method of estimating accrued depreciation, subsequently presented in the course, the extraction method of estimating land value can best be understood by relating site value to the format of the Cost Approach. In its simplest form, the format of the Cost Approach (the topic of Chapters 12 and 13) is as follows:

$$
\begin{array}{ll}
& \text{Replacement or Reproduction Cost New (A)} \\
- & \text{Accrued Depreciation (B)} \\
\hline
& \text{Contributory Value of Improvements (C)} \\
+ & \text{Site Value (D)} \\
\hline
& \text{Total Property Value (E)}
\end{array}
$$

The market value (or eventual sales price) of a property (E) represents the summation of the property's contributory (or depreciated) value of improvements (C) and its site value (D). The site value (D) is merely the difference between the contributory value of the improvements (C) and total property value (E) as of the date of sale.

To arrive at an estimate of site value by the extraction method, the following three items of information are needed:

1. Actual sales price of the comparable

2. Accurate and reliable estimate of the comparable's reproduction cost new as of the date of sale

3. Accurate and reliable estimate of accrued depreciation as of the date of sale

Once these three items of information are obtained, site value can be estimated using the Cost Approach format previously presented.

For example, assume a comparable property sold for $85,000. You estimate the comparable's reproduction cost new at $92,000 and accrued depreciation at 25% of cost as of the date of sale. Site value would then approximate $16,000 as shown below:

$$
\begin{array}{lll}
& \text{Replacement or Reproduction Cost New (A)} & \$92,000 \\
- & \text{Accrued Depreciation at 25\% of Cost New (B)} & \underline{-\$23,000} \\
& \text{Contributory Value of Improvements (C)} & \$69,000 \\
+ & \text{Site Value (D)} & \underline{+\$16,000} \\
& \text{Total Property Value (E)} & \$85,000
\end{array}
$$

Algebraically, if $(A - B) + D = E$; then $D = E - (A - B)$. Therefore, site value (D) = $85,000 - ($92,000 - $23,000); $85,000 - $69,000 = $16,000. Site value (D) is thus $16,000.

Procedure

The procedure for estimating site value by the extraction method is summarized:

a. Find and verify the sales price of an improved comparable sale located in the subject (or similar) neighborhood, preferably with a site similar to the one being appraised,

b. Estimate the reproduction or replacement cost new of the comparable improvements as of the date of sale,

c. Estimate the accrued depreciation attributable to the comparable improvements as of the date of sale,

d. Deduct the estimated accrued depreciation (Step C) from the estimated reproduction or replacement cost new (Step B) to arrive at an indication of the contributory (or depreciated) value of the comparable improvements,

e. Deduct the contributory value of the comparable improvements (Step D) from the total sales price of the comparable (Step A) to arrive at an indication of the comparable's site value,

f. Adjust the indicated site value of the comparable (Step E), if necessary, for any dissimilarities between the comparable site and the one being appraised.

> For example, assume an improved sale that is located in the subject neighborhood on a site comparable to the property being appraised recently sold for $97,000. You estimate the reproduction cost new of the comparable improvements at $100,000 as of the date of sale. Further, you estimate accrued depreciation at 20% of cost new. What would be the indicated site value by this comparable sale?
>
> | | |
> |---|---:|
> | Estimated Reproduction Cost New (A) | $100,000 |
> | − Estimated Accrued Depreciation; 20% of Cost New (B) | − $20,000 |
> | Contributory Value of the Improvements (C) | $80,000 |
> | | |
> | Total Sales Price of the Improved Comparable Sale (E) | $97,000 |
> | − Contributory Value of the Improvements (C) | − $80,000 |
> | | |
> | Indicated Site Value by the Comparable Sale (D) | $17,000 |

■ SALES COMPARISON

Sales Comparison is the most common method of estimating the value of land or a site and should always be used when comparable sales are available.

Sales Comparison is a technique used to estimate land value where an appraiser directly compares the land parcel being appraised to similar properties that have recently sold in the marketplace. Derivation of a value estimate by the sales comparison technique requires the appraiser to identify dissimilarities between the subject property and comparable sales and to subsequently apply market-supported adjustments to the sales prices of the comparable properties for these dissimilarities.

To gain an understanding of Sales Comparison, it is first important to distinguish between *units of comparison* and *elements of comparison*. A discussion of each is subsequently presented.

Units of Comparison

A **unit of comparison** may be defined as a factor that expresses a relationship between value or price and a particular property feature or characteristic; a unit of comparison is often used for comparison purposes. Units of comparison typically used for the comparison and valuation of land or a site include total sales price, price per acre, price per square foot of land area, price per front foot, and price per subdivision lot. Any one or several of these units of comparison may be pertinent in the valuation of land or a site.

The units of comparison that are pertinent to the appraisal of a parcel or site differ depending upon the particular appraisal problem, location of the real estate market, and market characteristics and perceptions.

Similarly, the price per front foot may be an applicable unit of comparison for a lakefront lot in Boulder, Colorado; however, in Grand Rapids, Michigan, the appropriate unit of comparison for a lakefront lot may be total sales price or price per square foot of land area.

> For example, the price per developable subdivision lot may be an appropriate unit of comparison for a large acreage tract located in proximity to rapid residential growth/development; however, this unit of comparison may be meaningless when appraising a large acreage tract located in a remote rural area.

It is the responsibility of the appraiser to know which units of comparison are applicable when appraising certain properties or in certain geographic locations. Discussions during the verification process with real estate agents, brokers, buyers, sellers, appraisers, etc., will identify the appropriate unit of comparison for each market.

Elements of Comparison

An **element of comparison** is defined as features or characteristics of a property that create fluctuations in value or price. Elements of comparison that should be considered in appraising a parcel of land or site include (1) property rights conveyed; (2) financing; (3) conditions of sale (motivation); (4) market conditions (change in price over time); (5) location; (6) physical characteristics; (7) zoning and/or deed restrictions; and (8) availability, capacity, and proximity of utilities.

When percentage adjustments are applied, adjustments for elements (1) through (4) must be applied in the above sequence (see Chapter 9). Afterward, adjustments for elements (5) through (8) may be applied. Any percentage adjustments for elements (5) through (8) should be calculated using the adjusted base price through the adjustment for market conditions (4).

If lump-sum dollar adjustments are applied to the unit(s) of comparison, sequence of adjustments is not important. Rather, the adjustments may be *netted out*.

Procedure

The procedure for estimating site value by the Sales Comparison method is summarized:

a. Identify and verify recent sales, listings, and current or expired purchase contracts which are comparable to the property being appraised,

b. Select a relevant unit(s) of comparison (i.e., total sales price, price per acre, price per square foot, price per lot, price per front foot, etc.) and analyze each comparable sale accordingly,

c. Compare each comparable property directly to the subject property and identify all dissimilarities using the elements of comparison,

d. Adjust the comparable properties (using the selected unit(s) of comparison) for all dissimilarities in comparison to the subject property to arrive at an indication of value by each respective comparable,

    Note: If the comparable is inferior to the subject, an upward (+) adjustment is applied to the unit(s) of comparison; if the comparable is superior to the subject, a downward (−) adjustment is appropriate. If no dissimilarity exists, no adjustment is necessary.

e. Reconcile the various value indications into a final value estimate for the subject property.

For example, assume you are appraising a building site within an established single-family subdivision. From your investigations, you have uncovered three recent comparable sales and have organized them in a market data grid that follows.

Element	Subject	Sale No. 1	Sale No. 2	Sale No. 3
Sales Price	—	$17,000	$21,000	$12,500
Shape	Rectangular	Rectangular	Rectangular	Irregular
View	Good	Average	Good	Average
Topography	Average	Good	Good	Average

By *matched pair* analysis, you have extracted the following adjustments:

1. A rectangular site sells for $1,000 more than an irregular site,

2. A site with a good view sells for $5,000 more than a site with an average view,

3. A site with good topography sells for $3,000 more than a site with average topography.

Element	Subject	Sale No. 1	Sale No. 2	Sale No. 3
Sales Price	—	$17,000	$21,000	$12,500
Shape	Rectangular	Rectangular	Rectangular	Irregular
Adjustment	—	$0	$0	+$1,000
View	Good	Average	Good	Average
Adjustment	—	+5,000	$0	+$5,000
Topography	Average	Good	Good	Average
Adjustment	—	–$3,000	–$3,000	$0
Net Adjustment	—	+$2,000	–$3,000	+$6,000
Indicated Value for Subject	—	$19,000	$18,000	$18,500

■ SUBDIVISION DEVELOPMENT

Subdivision development is a technique used to estimate land value whereby the appraiser views the land parcel as if *subdivided* into smaller tracts or lots. The use of this technique requires the appraiser to first estimate the gross sales price of the finished lots as developed (i.e., *retail value*). From the estimate of *gross* sales price, the appraiser deducts an estimate of all costs (i.e., development, sales, marketing, holding, etc.) and developer's profit necessary to account for the disposition of and risk associated with the *sellout* of the individual lots to arrive at an estimate of the *net proceeds*. Finally, the *net* sales proceeds are discounted into a present value indication for the vacant land using a market-derived rate. The discounting procedure accounts for the period of time necessary to develop and sell off (*absorb*) the individual lots.

This method of estimating land is used when the highest and best use of the land is determined to be for the development of a subdivision. Because this method requires the appraiser to make numerous forecasts and projections associated with the development and subsequent sales of subdivision lots, the value estimate derived by this method should always be tested against recent undeveloped land sales that have occurred in the market, when available.

■ GROUND RENT CAPITALIZATION

Ground rent capitalization is a technique used to estimate land value whereby the *ground rent* generated by a land parcel is capitalized into an indication of value at a market-derived rate to the land.

This method of estimating land and site value may be used when vacant land and/or sites are actively leased in a particular location (ground rent) and land capitalization rates can be derived from the market. A surface parking lot in a downtown metropolitan area leased to an operator is representative of an appraisal assignment where this technique could be applicable.

■ LAND RESIDUAL

Land residual is a technique used to estimate land value whereby the appraiser isolates the portion of an improved property's total net operating income that is attributable to the land and capitalizes the income estimate into an indication of value.

This method is based on the principles of balance and contribution as they relate to equilibrium among the four agents of production; labor, capital, coordination, and land.

This method of valuing land or a site is rarely used. However, this method seeks to allocate the net operating income of an improved property between the income attributable to the building improvements and income attributable to the land, also known as residual income. Once identified, the income to the land is capitalized using a land capitalization rate derived from the market. This procedure and applications of the land residual technique are discussed at length in advanced appraisal courses.

1. The most reliable method of estimating land value is
   a. extraction.
   b. allocation.
   c. sales comparison.
   d. land residual technique.

Questions 2, 3, and 4 are based on the following information gathered in your investigation.

The subject site has a rectangular shape and a gently sloping topography. Sale 1 is rectangular in shape, has a severely sloping topography, and sold last week for $15,000. Sale 2 has a gentle topography and rectangular shape similar to the subject site and sold last week for $13,000. Sale 3 is irregularly shaped and reflects a severely sloping topography. This site sold one year ago for $10,000. Over the past one-year period, prices of similar sites have increased approximately 5 percent. The three comparable sales are similar to the subject in all other respects.

2. What is the adjustment for shape?
   a. + $4,500
   b. – $4,500
   c. + $3,000
   d. – $3,000

3. What is the adjustment for topography?
   a. +$1,500
   b. –$1,500
   c. +$2,000
   d. –$2,000

4. What is the adjusted sale price for Sale 3?
   a. $15,000
   b. $13,000
   c. $17,000
   d. $20,000

5. An improved 2,000 square foot residence recently sold for $150,000. You estimate its total cost new at $70 per square foot, excluding land. Properties in the area similar to the subject reflect accrued depreciation of approximately 20 percent. What is the estimated land value by extraction?
   a. $20,000
   b. $30,000
   c. $38,000
   d. $10,000

6. You are appraising a vacant single-family lot containing 32,000 square feet. In your investigations you uncover the following recent lot sales: Sale 1 contains 36,000 square feet and sold for $30,000; Sale 2 contains 28,000 square feet and sold for $27,200; and Sale 3 contains 30,000 square feet and sold for $28,500. The current market utilizes the price per square foot as the appropriate unit of comparison. What is the most appropriate indication of market value for the subject site?
   a. $26,000 – $27,000
   b. $31,000 – $32,500
   c. $28,000 – $29,500
   d. Cannot be determined

7. Your investigations revealed three recent improved sales. Comparable sale 1 sold for $135,000; comparable 2 sold for $100,000; and comparable 3 sold for $105,000. While no recent land sales were uncovered, a recent study showed typical land-value ratios for this neighborhood of 20 percent for homes between $90,000 and $110,000 and 15 percent for homes between $110,000 and $150,000. What is a reasonable value estimate for the subject site given these data?
   a. $27,000
   b. $20,500
   c. $16,000
   d. $22,500

Questions 8, 9, and 10 are based on the following information gathered in your investigation.

The subject site has a corner location and access to city water. Sale 1 features an interior location, has access to city water, and sold one year ago for $12,000. Sale 2 has access to city water and a corner location similar to the subject site and sold last week for $9,000. Sale 3 has an interior location and does not have access to city water. This site sold last week for $8,000. Over the past one year period, prices of similar sites have decreased approximately 10 percent. The three comparable sales are similar to the subject site in all other respects.

8. What is the adjustment for location?
   a. +$3,000
   b. −$3,000
   c. −$1,800
   d. +$1,800

9. What is the adjustment for access to city water?
   a. +$4,000
   b. −$4,000
   c. +$2,800
   d. −$2,800

10. What is the adjusted sale price for Sale 1?
   a. $ 9,000
   b. $15,000
   c. $10,800
   d. $12,000

12

Cost Approach: Overview and Estimation of Cost New

■ LEARNING OBJECTIVES

Students will be able to

1. understand the underlying economic principles of the Cost Approach.

2. understand the applicability and limitations of the Cost Approach.

3. recognize the various components of cost estimate including replacement cost, reproduction cost, direct cost, and indirect cost, as well as entrepreneurial profit.

4. understand the three methods of estimating cost with particular emphasis on the comparative-unit method.

■ KEY TERMS

comparative-unit method	indirect costs	sources of cost data
cost approach to value	quantity survey method	unit-in-place method
direct costs	replacement costs	
entrepreneurial profit	reproductive costs	

■ INTRODUCTION

Most experienced appraisers would probably agree that the vast majority of homeowners tend to link value, or the worth of a residence, to cost. Of the three approaches traditionally recognized to estimate property value, the Cost Approach is the sole procedure that identifies and attempts to reflect the relationship between the value of a property and its cost by permitting the appraiser to compare the property being appraised to a newly constructed building with optimum functional utility.

The Cost Approach is also the only approach of the three that provides and is dependent upon a separate value for the site. The value indication by the **Cost Approach** can therefore be easily allocated between site value and the contributory value of the building improvements. Of the three approaches to value, the Cost Approach is arguably the most difficult to comprehend.

PART ONE Underlying Economic Principles of the Cost Approach

The economic principles were previously presented and discussed in Chapter 4. Several of these economic principles can be related to the Cost Approach: substitution, balance, highest and best use, and externalities. Of these principles, perhaps the principle of substitution is most applicable and basic to the Cost Approach.

■ SUBSTITUTION

As it applies to the Cost Approach, the principle of *substitution* implies that a knowledgeable market participant would likely pay no more for a property than the cost to construct *comparable* improvements on a *similar* site in a *timely* manner. Comparison of the Cost Approach to the principle of substitution again emphasizes market participants' tendency to relate value or the worth of a property to its cost.

■ BALANCE

The principle of *balance* suggests that if value is to be maximized, the agents of production (land, labor, capital, and entrepreneurship) must be properly allocated. An improper allocation will likely result in overimprovement (excess) or underimprovement (deficiency) of the land, and thus, a loss in property value.

> For example, a real estate developer is considering construction of a motel on an appropriately zoned site. The principle of balance suggests that, relative to market demand and the value of land in the general area, there is an optimum number of rooms that should be constructed on the site. The construction of too few (underimprovement) or too many (overimprovement) motel rooms on the site would likely result in a loss in property value.

In the Cost Approach, this loss in value (later defined as depreciation) would be measured and subsequently deducted from the estimated cost new of the improvements to arrive at an indication of the contributory value of the building improvements.

■ HIGHEST AND BEST USE

As discussed in Chapter 8, land is valued *as if vacant* and available to be developed to its highest and best use. In the "Highest and Best Use" section of an appraisal, the appraiser forms an opinion as to the property's highest and best use both *as vacant* and *as improved*. It is feasible for the site of an improved property to reflect one highest and best use *as vacant*, while the same property (*as improved*) reflects a different highest and best use. Because land is said to *have* value, and improvements are said to *contribute* value, existing improvements that do not develop the land to its highest and best use are generally worth less than their cost new. This relates to the principle of change in that the building improvements can typically be renovated or demolished while the location and physical characteristics of a site remain relatively unchanged.

The *theory of consistent use* states that land may not be valued on the basis of one use while the improvements are valued on a different use. When the highest and best use of a property *as vacant* differs from its highest and best use *as improved*, an appraiser must use extreme caution in the Cost Approach so that the principle of *consistent use* is not violated. As discussed in Chapter 8, violation of the principle of consistent use would result in an erroneous indication of value. The improvement that is representative of market tastes and expectations (the *ideal improvement* for the site) as of the date of appraisal generally adds the greatest value or contribution to the site.

■ EXTERNALITIES

The principle of *externalities* implies that locational and/or economic conditions may positively or negatively influence property values. For instance, assume vacant lakefront sites in a particular community are scarce. At the same time, demand for lakefront properties in the community is strong. This would likely be an example of positive externalities, where the value of a newly constructed residence may be greater than its cost new. Conversely, consider a newly constructed residence that is adversely influenced by an unpleasant odor or perhaps is located in an area of high unemployment.

These would likely be examples of negative externalities, where the value of a newly constructed residence may be less than cost new. When supply and demand are in equilibrium, however, cost new, less accrued depreciation, plus land value tends to be generally representative of market value.

PART TWO   Applications of the Cost Approach

The applicability of the Cost Approach in a valuation assignment varies depending upon the age and physical condition of the property, the intended use or function of the property, the frequency in which the property type being appraised is exchanged in the market, and the type of value being sought by the user of the appraisal. The Cost Approach would typically be most applicable under the following three scenarios:

1. Proposed construction, new, and relatively new improvements where an estimation of site value can be well supported with market data, and the improvements are generally representative of the site's highest and best use as vacant (a recently constructed residence in a new single-family subdivision; a two-year old, functional office-warehouse facility located in an owner-occupied industrial park experiencing good market acceptance and demand, etc.).

2. Special-purpose properties designed and constructed for a specific use that are typically owner-occupied and are not frequently exchanged or leased in the marketplace (a museum, convention center, church, school, gymnasium, etc.).

3. When the client is specifically seeking an estimate of value-in-use or insurable value.

PART THREE   Limitations of the Cost Approach

The Cost Approach also has limitations that reduce its reliability in certain assignments. The dependence on the Cost Approach must be tempered somewhat under the following two scenarios:

1. When the improvements are older, the applicability of the Cost Approach is limited. As time passes, improvements are subject to greater physical deterioration and functional inutility (market tastes and demands change over time). Accrued depreciation becomes more and more difficult to estimate as the improvements age, thus reducing the accuracy of the value indication by the Cost Approach.

2. The Cost Approach has limited applicability in circumstances where the improvements no longer represent the highest and best use of the site *as vacant*, as previously discussed (the highest and best use of the site *as vacant* differs from the property's highest and best use *as improved*). Remember, it is a violation of consistent use to value the site on the basis of one use and the improvements on the basis of a different use. A violation of consistent use generally results in an artificially high value indication by the Cost Approach.

PART FOUR   Procedure and Format of Cost Approach

To derive an estimate of value via the Cost Approach, the following steps must be completed by the appraiser:

a. Estimate the value of the site by one of the six methods discussed in Chapter 11, Land and Site Valuation. As previously discussed, the valuation of the site should be consistent with the site's highest and best use *as vacant*. If the sales comparison technique is employed, the comparable sales used to estimate the site value should reflect a similar highest and best use in comparison to the subject site.

b. Estimate the cost new of the *building improvements* as of the effective appraisal date. The appraiser should be very clear as to whether the cost estimate represents reproduction or replacement costs, subsequently discussed in Part Five. Included in the estimate of cost should be direct (hard) costs, indirect (soft) costs, and an appropriate allowance for entrepreneurial profit, subsequently discussed in Part Five below.

c. Estimate accrued depreciation, or total loss in value, recognizing the three major classifications: physical deterioration, functional obsolescence, and external obsolescence.

d. Deduct accrued depreciation (Step c) from the cost new estimate of the building improvements (Step b) to provide an indication of the depreciated value or contributory value of the *building improvements*.

e. Estimate the "as is" or contributory value of the *site improvements*. Site improvements typically associated with a residence include utilities (well, septic tank system, etc.), landscaping, driveway, walkways, and other improvements made *to* the site.

f. Add the depreciated value of the *building improvements* (Step d) to the depreciated value of the *site improvements* (Step e) to arrive at an indication of the contributory value of *all* improvements.

g. Add the depreciated value or contribution of *all* improvements (Step f) to the previously estimated site value (Step a) to arrive at an indicated fee simple estimate of value by the Cost Approach.

The above procedure for the Cost Approach is consistent with the *Uniform Residential Appraisal Report (URAR)* form frequently used for appraisal of residential properties.

When reporting the appraisal in a narrative format, the following format for the Cost Approach is suggested:

Cost New of Building Improvements:

Direct Costs:	$105,000	
Indirect Costs:	$10,500	
Entrepreneurial Profit:	+ $17,325	
Total Cost New of Building Improvements:		$132,825

Less Accrued Depreciation:

Physical Deterioration	$12,500	
Functional Obsolescence:	$0	
External Obsolescence:	+ $0	
Total Accrued Depreciation:		− $12,500

Depreciated Cost of Building Improvements:	$120,325
Plus Depreciated Cost of Site Improvements:	+ $5,000
Depreciated Cost of All Improvements:	$125,325
Plus Site Value:	+ $25,000
Value Indication by Cost Approach:	$150,325
Rounded to:	$150,000

PART FIVE   Preparation of a Cost Estimate

■ DISTINCTION BETWEEN REPRODUCTION COST AND REPLACEMENT COST

When calculating cost new, the appraiser either estimates the *reproduction cost* or *replacement cost* new of the improvements.

Reproduction Cost

Reproduction cost is the cost to construct an exact duplicate or replica of the subject. In a reproduction cost estimate, deficiencies, superadequacies, and any existing inutility of the building are considered and included in the cost estimate.

Replacement Cost

Replacement cost is the cost to construct an improvement with similar or equal utility to the subject, but with materials, design, and layout indicative of standards currently reflected in the marketplace.

One major difference between reproduction and replacement cost is that an estimate of replacement cost tends to eliminate superadequate features associated with the improvements. For instance, consider an older house that originally used a gas-fired floor furnace for heating purposes. Recently, the owner installed a central forced air heating system due to its superior efficiency and lower utility cost. The floor furnace was inoperable and at the end of its physical life. If an appraiser is seeking an estimate of reproduction cost, he should include the cost new of both heating systems and consider the depreciation associated with the floor furnace. However, if an appraiser is estimating replacement cost, he should disregard the cost associated with the floor furnace and include only the cost new of the central forced air system. Therefore, it is essential that the appraiser know which cost is estimated, reproduction or replacement, so that a more accurate indication of accrued depreciation can be provided.

■ CATEGORIES OF COSTS

In preparing an estimate of reproduction or replacement cost, the appraiser must consider direct (hard) cost, indirect (soft) cost, and entrepreneurial profit (coordination).

Direct Costs

Direct costs, also commonly referred to as *hard costs*, include expenditures for labor and materials used for the construction of the improvements. It is important to distinguish between a subcontractor, a general contractor, and an entrepreneur. A *subcontractor* is an individual or firm typically responsible for one or more functions in the actual construction of a building (foundation, framing, plumbing, electrical, etc.). A *general contractor* is an individual responsible for the day to day coordination of the subcontractors and construction of the improvements. An *entrepreneur* is the individual or entity responsible for managing the development as a whole typically from acquisition of the land to the finished product. The subcontractor and general contractor charge the entrepreneur for their services inclusive of overhead and profit. This profit (contractor's profit) is considered a direct cost and should not be confused with entrepreneurial profit.

Indirect Costs

Indirect costs, or *soft costs*, include expenditures other than labor and materials and include items such as financing costs, construction loan interest, insurance and real estate taxes during construction, building permits, administrative costs, professional fees (appraisal, engineering, and architectural fees), and lease-up and marketing costs necessary to achieve a stabilized occupancy. Oftentimes, indirect costs are estimated as a percentage of direct costs.

Entrepreneurial Profit

Entrepreneurial profit is an increment of cost new that provides the incentive necessary for a developer to assume the risk associated with the development of real estate. Basically, entrepreneurial profit is the difference between the price paid for a new property less the total cost to deliver the property (direct and indirect costs, plus land value). Contrary to direct and indirect costs, the realization of entrepreneurial profit occurs only when the improved property sells.

Therefore, the inclusion of entrepreneurial profit in a cost estimate is actually an estimate of the anticipated profit to the entrepreneur upon sale of the property. Entrepreneurial profit should always be considered in a cost estimate because it is a necessary component of cost. It is important to note, however, that published cost manuals (Marshall and Swift, Means, etc.) do not include an allowance for entrepreneurial profit regardless of the cost estimation method used. Only when the cost is extracted from the market is an allowance for entrepreneurial profit included in the cost estimate.

The appraiser should be mindful of minimum profit ratios in a particular market. For instance, if a proposed development indicates only a 6 percent profit (market value less total cost) and the market standard is 10 percent to 12 percent, then it is not profitable or feasible.

Entrepreneurial profit is market sensitive and typically varies with changes in economic conditions.

> For example, when overbuilding occurs within a specific market ("buyer's market" or "lessee's market"), entrepreneurial profit may be diminished as a result of increased competition among local developers for fewer development opportunities (the principle of competition generally confines entrepreneurial profit to within a reasonable range). In these situations, a portion or all entrepreneurial profit may be deducted as obsolescence.

■ THREE RECOGNIZED METHODS OF ESTIMATING COST NEW

Following are the three recognized methods of estimating reproduction or replacement costs of a building:

1. Comparative-unit method

2. Unit-in-place method

3. Quantity survey method

Each of these three techniques is discussed below.

Comparative-Unit Method

The most straightforward and least complicated method of estimating cost is the **comparative-unit method**. The comparative-unit method is widely used by appraisers and is representative of the format presented in the Cost Approach section of the *Uniform Residential Appraisal Report (URAR)* form. The comparative-unit method estimates cost in terms of dollars per unit.

Common units of comparison include cost per square foot of gross living area, cost per square foot of gross building area, cost per leasable square foot, cost per cubic foot, and cost per rental unit.

> For example, the comparative-unit method would most likely estimate the cost new of a single-family residence as dollars per square foot of gross living area (2,000 square feet at $50 per square foot equals $100,000). For an apartment complex, the unit of comparison may be cost per rental unit (200 apartment units at $30,000 per unit equals $6,000,000) or per leasable square foot (200,000 leasable square feet at $40 per leasable square foot equals $8,000,000).

A cost estimate by the comparative-unit method may be (1) derived using various cost estimation services such as Marshall and Swift or Means; or (2) extracted from the market using recent sales of new houses. If the unit cost is derived using a cost estimation service, entrepreneurial profit is generally not included. However, if the unit cost is extracted from the market, the estimate includes direct costs, indirect costs, and entrepreneurial profit. Regardless, the comparative-unit method is based on known costs of comparable structures appropriately adjusted for differences in market conditions (time), physical characteristics, and sometimes location and/or availability of labor and materials.

Procedure

The procedure for estimating cost new by the comparative unit method using market extraction is summarized as follows:

1. Obtain and verify the sales price of a new, comparable property.

2. Estimate the site value of the comparable property.

3. Deduct the estimated site value of the comparable (Step 2) from its sales price (Step 1) to arrive at an indication of the cost new of the comparable improvement (cost new estimate includes direct costs, indirect cost, and entrepreneurial profit).

4. Adjust the estimated cost new of the comparable improvement (Step 3) for any dissimilarities in comparison to the subject improvements to arrive at an adjusted cost new.

5. Identify the appropriate unit of comparison associated with the property type being appraised (per square foot of gross living area, per unit, etc.).

6. Divide the adjusted cost new (Step 4) by the appropriate unit of comparison (Step 5) to arrive at an indication of cost new per unit for the respective comparable. (Note: When more than one comparable is used, the appraiser must reconcile these estimates into a point estimate or range of cost new for the subject improvements.)

7. Multiply the reconciled cost new per unit by the subject property's respective unit estimate to arrive at an estimated cost new for the subject improvements by the comparative-unit method.

For example, assume the sales price of a new single-family residence comparable to the subject property was verified at $100,000. You estimate the value of the comparable site at $20,000. The appropriate unit of comparison for a single-family residence is cost new per square foot of gross living area (GLA). You estimate the GLA of the comparable at approximately 2,000 square feet. What is the indicated cost new per square foot of GLA by this comparable?

Sales Price of Comparable Property	$100,000
Less Estimated Site Value of Comparable Property	− $20,000
Estimated Cost New of Comparable Improvements	$80,000
Divided by GLA of Comparable (2,000 square feet)	÷ $2,000
Estimated Cost New Per Square Foot of GLA	$40.00

Unit-In-Place Method

The **unit-in-place method**, commonly referred to the *segregated cost method*, estimates the various components of a structure as installed. This cost-estimating technique is widely used by building contractors. In a unit-in-place cost estimate, a cost *as installed* is assigned to each major component of the structure such as foundation, roof cover, exterior siding, carpeting, interior painting, etc., inclusive of labor and materials. Indirect costs and contractor's profit may be included separately. Published cost manuals (Marshall and Swift, Means, etc.) may be used to employ this technique.

An example of unit-in-place is presented in Figure 12.1. The residence is a two-story structure situated on a crawl space containing approximately 2,700 square feet of gross living area. The house features four bedrooms, two-and-one-half baths, and a two-car attached garage.

Quantity Survey Method

The **quantity survey method**, commonly referred to as the *engineering method*, is the most comprehensive and time-consuming method of estimating the reproduction or replacement cost of an improvement. Although the quantity survey method generally provides the most accurate estimate of cost new, it is seldom used by real estate appraisers. The quantity survey method produces a very detailed breakdown of direct costs (labor and materials) isolating the quantity and quality of the materials used and the labor hours required to construct the improvement. To this comprehensive estimate of direct costs, contractor's profit, indirect costs, and entrepreneurial profit are added to arrive at an estimate of reproduction or replacement cost by this method.

■ SOURCES OF COST DATA

To assist the appraiser with the preparation of a cost estimate, several **sources of cost data** are available. First and foremost, the appraiser should maintain an ongoing file of actual cost estimates. Other sources of cost data include building contractors, published cost manuals provided by cost-estimating services, on-line computer services, professional cost estimators, and recent sales of newly constructed buildings where the site value can easily be supported.

FIGURE 12.1 ■ Example of Unit-in-Place Method

RESIDENTIAL CONSTRUCTION COST ESTIMATE 2,700 SQUARE FEET, 2 STORY W/STUCCO EXTERIOR			ESTIMATED CONSTRUCTION
	UNIT	COST	COST
SITE PREPARATION & FOUNDATIONS			
EXCAVATION & BACKFILL	2,700 S F	$0.70	$1,900
CONCRETE FOOTINGS & CONCRETE BLOCK FOUNDATION	160 L F	$27.50	$4,400
STRUCTURE AND EXTERIOR WALLS, DOORS & WINDOWS			
FRAMING AND CARPENTRY (INCLUDING INTERIOR WALLS)	2,700 S F	$9.75	$26,300
INSULATION	2,700 S F	$0.50	$1,400
DOORS (INCLUDING HARDWARE)	4 EA	$450.00	$1,800
GARAGE DOOR	12 EA	$300.00	$3,600
STUCCO EXTERIOR WALLS	2,700 S F	$5.10	$13,800
EXTERIOR PAINTING	2,700 S F	$0.95	$2,600
ROOFING, EAVES, GUTTERS & DOWNSPOUTS			
ROOFING (SHINGLES & FELT)	50 SQ	$40.00	$2,000
VINYL OVERHANG, ALUM. GUTTERS DOWNSPOUTS	LUMP SUM	$2,500	$2,500
INTERIOR CONSTRUCTION & FINISHES			
DRYWALL	2,700 S F	$2.10	$5,700
INTERIOR DOORS	10 EA	$160	$1,600
FINISHED CARPENTRY & STAIRS	2,700 S F	$1.90	$5,100
INTERIOR PAINTING	2,700 S F	$1.33	$3,600
WALLPAPER	LUMP SUM	$1,500	$1,500
HARDWOOD FLOORING	705 S F	$5.25	$3,700
VINYL & CARPETING	225 S Y	$12.00	$2,700
KITCHEN CABINETS & VANITIES	LUMP SUM	$7,000	$7,000
KITCHEN APPLIANCES	LUMP SUM	$2,650	$2,650
BATHROOM ACCESSORIES	LUMP SUM	$940	$940
PREFABRICATED FIREPLACE	LUMP SUM	$2,100	$2,100
MISCELLANEOUS			
WOOD DECK (240 S.F.) AND FRONT STOOP	300 S F	$6.70	$2,000
PLUMBING, ELECTRICAL & MECHANICAL			
PLUMBING ROUGH-IN & FIXTURES	11 EA	$645.00	$7,100
ELECTRICAL SERVICE & WIRING	2,700 S F	$1.40	$3,800
LIGHTING FIXTURE	LUMP SUM	$4,200	$4,200
HEATING & AIR CONDITIONING	2,700 S F	$2.05	$5,500
WATER METER	1 EA	$1,000	$1,000
SITE IMPROVEMENTS			
DRIVEWAY & WALKS (CONCRETE)	1,650 S F	$2.00	$3,300
SEPTIC TANK & DRAINFIELD (1,500 GALLON)	LUMP SUM	$1,500	$1,500
LANDSCAPING	LUMP SUM	$7,800	$7,800

TOTAL DIRECT COSTS INCLUDING:
LABOR, MATERIALS, & CONTRACTOR'S OVERHEAD & PROFIT $134,090

INDIRECT COSTS INCLUDING:
INTEREST, TAXES, PLANS, SURVEYS, ETC. (5% OF DIRECT COST) $7,000

TOTAL DIRECT & INDIRECT COSTS $141,090
ENTREPRENEURIAL PROFIT
(10% OF DIRECT & INDIRECT COSTS) $14,100

TOTAL REPLACEMENT COST NEW **$155,190**

1. What underlying appraisal principle of the Cost Approach emphasizes that market participants tend to relate value or the worth of a property to cost?
   a. Balance
   b. Highest and best use
   c. Externalities
   d. Substitution

2. Which method of estimating cost new is widely used by building contractors?
   a. Comparative-unit
   b. Unit-in-place
   c. Quantity survey
   d. Engineering method

3. All labor and materials, including contractor's overhead and profit, is referred to as
   a. indirect cost.
   b. construction cost.
   c. direct cost.
   d. development cost.

4. Total direct cost to construct a single-family residence is $75,000. Indirect costs are estimated at 10 percent of direct costs. Land value in the subdivision is well-supported at $15,000. Entrepreneurial profit is supported throughout the market at 15 percent of the sum of direct costs, indirect costs, and land value. What is the estimated cost new of the subject improvement?
   a. $112,125
   b. $97,125
   c. $94,875
   d. $109,875

5. A survey of building contractors active in the subject subdivision indicated the following: Smith and Son constructed a 1,300 square foot, one-story house for $39 per square foot; BDR Construction built a 1,550 square foot, one-story house for $35 per square foot; and Unique Homebuilders built a 1,700 square foot, one-story house for $33.50 per square foot. Assume you are appraising a proposed 1,400 square foot, one-story dwelling. What would be a reasonable cost per square foot for the subject house (quality of construction and all other factors being equal)?
   a. $41 per square foot
   b. $39 per square foot
   c. $37 per square foot
   d. $34 per square foot

6. You are attempting to estimate the replacement cost of a recently completed, 1,200 square foot house in a new subdivision. During your investigations, you uncover two houses very similar to the subject that recently sold in an adjacent subdivision. The houses were all good quality, one-story dwellings with a two-car garage and large wood deck. Homestead Construction sold a 1,500 square foot home for $105,000 on a $25,000 lot; and Quality Homes sold a 1,100 square foot home for $93,000 on a $20,000 lot. What is the appropriate unit cost for the subject improvements?
   a. $63 per square foot
   b. $69 per square foot
   c. $54 per square foot
   d. $50 per square foot

7. You estimate the direct costs of the subject property at $90,000. Indirect costs in this market typically approximate 10 percent of direct costs and entrepreneurial profit is well supported at 10 percent of direct and indirect costs. The subject improvements reflect approximately $10,000 of accrued depreciation. The value of the site is well established at $15,000. What is the value estimate of the subject property by the Cost Approach?
   a. $113,900
   b. $115,400
   c. $123,000
   d. $113,000

8. Engineering fees, appraisal fees, construction interest, and legal services are all examples of what type of cost?
   a. Direct cost
   b. Development cost
   c. Construction cost
   d. Indirect cost

9. Which of the following statements is/are true regarding reproduction cost new?
   a. Cost of constructing a building using modern materials and current standards, design, and layout
   b. Includes costs associated with superadequate features such as high ceilings, etc.
   c. Tends to eliminate costs associated with superadequacies in the structure
   d. None of the above

10. Given the following data and the assumption that the minimum entrepreneurial rate is 15 percent, which alternative is justified?

	A	B	C
Estimated Market Value:	$100,000	$108,000	$115,000
Estimated Total Cost:	$96,000	$100,000	$102,000

   a. A
   b. B
   c. C
   d. None of the above

CHAPTER THIRTEEN

Cost Approach: Estimation of Accrued Depreciation

■ LEARNING OBJECTIVES

Students will be able to

1. understand the concept of accrued depreciation and accompanying key terms and definitions.

2. recognize and classify accrued depreciation into the three categories including physical deterioration, functional obsolescence, and external obsolescence.

3. recognize and properly employ the various methods of estimating accrued depreciation including economic age-life, modified age-life, market extraction or Sales Comparison method, and the breakdown method.

■ KEY TERMS

accrued depreciation	deterioration	long-lived item
actual age	economic life	market extraction
breakdown method	economic obsolescence	modified economic
cost-to-cure	effective age	age-life
curable depreciation	external obsolescence	obsolescence
curable functional obso-	functional obsolescence	physical deterioration
lescence	incurable functional	physical life
curable physical deterio-	obsolescence	remaining economic life
ration	incurable physical deteri-	short-lived item
deferred maintenance	oration	superadequacy
deficiency	locational obsolescence	total physical deterioration

■ INTRODUCTION

A critical step of the Cost Approach involves the estimation of accrued depreciation. To accurately estimate accrued depreciation, a clear understanding of the different classifications of depreciation is needed as well as an understanding of the various techniques available to assist the appraiser in estimating depreciation. In order to grasp the concept and methods of estimating accrued depreciation, it is essential to identify and understand several key terms.

PART ONE   Accrued Depreciation

■ KEY TERMS AND DEFINITIONS

Accrued Depreciation

Accrued depreciation is the difference between an improvement's cost new and its contributory (market) value as of the effective appraisal date. Accrued depreciation is a loss in value due to any cause including physical deterioration, functional obsolescence, or external obsolescence.

Deterioration

Deterioration is a loss in value due to the physical wear and tear on an improvement over time.

Obsolescence

Obsolescence is a loss in value due to a reduction in the improvement's desirability; it may be functional or external.

Curable Depreciation

Curable depreciation is an item of physical deterioration and/or functional obsolescence where the cost to cure the item is less than the resulting increase in value after repair, renovation, or replacement (as of the date of appraisal).

Actual Age

Actual age is the amount of time that has passed between the construction of an improvement and the date of appraisal. Also known as historical or chronological age, it is a fact or objective figure.

Effective Age

Effective age is a subjective estimate of age made by the appraiser that considers both the physical condition and functional utility of an improvement; may be less than, greater than, or equal to actual age depending upon design, quality, workmanship, materials used, maintenance, etc.

Economic Life

Economic life is the total number of years during which improvements on the land contribute to total property value; economic life is equal to effective age plus remaining economic life.

Remaining Economic Life

Remaining economic life is the estimated remaining number of years during which the improvements will continue to contribute to total property value; remaining economic life is equal to total economic life less effective age.

Physical Life

Physical life is the estimated number of years during which a building is expected to last if properly maintained.

Curable Physical Deterioration

Curable physical deterioration is an item of physical deterioration where the cost to cure the item is less than the resulting increase in value after repair or replacement (as of the date of appraisal); also known as deferred maintenance.

Cost-To-Cure

Cost-to-cure is the cost to repair or replace an item of deferred maintenance.

Incurable Physical Deterioration

Incurable physical deterioration is an item of physical deterioration where the cost to cure the item is greater than the resulting increase in value after repair or replacement (as of the date of appraisal); incurable physical deterioration is categorized into short-lived and long-lived items.

Short-Lived Item

A **short-lived item** is a building component with an expected physical life that is less than the remaining physical life of the structure as a whole; examples of short-lived items include roof cover, floor covering, painting, appliances, water heater, etc.

Long-Lived Item

A **long-lived item** is a building component with an expected economic life that is commensurate with the economic life of the structure as a whole; examples of long-lived items include the foundation, framing, etc.

Curable Functional Obsolescence

Curable functional obsolescence is an item of functional inutility where the cost to cure the item is less than the resulting increase in value after repair, replacement, or renovation.

Incurable Functional Obsolescence

Incurable functional obsolescence is an item of functional inutility where the cost to cure the item is greater than the resulting increase in value after repair, replacement, or renovation.

External Obsolescence

External obsolescence is a loss in value, generally incurable, that is the result of a negative or undesirable factor *external* to the site; external obsolescence may be classified as locational (attributable to the property's location) or economic (attributable to market forces such as supply and demand).

P A R T   T W O   Classifications of Accrued Depreciation

As defined above, *accrued depreciation* is simply the difference between an improvement's cost new and its market value (contribution) as of the effective date of appraisal. Accrued depreciation can be classified into three distinct categories: physical deterioration, functional obsolescence, and external obsolescence. Each category of accrued depreciation is subsequently discussed.

■ PHYSICAL DETERIORATION

Physical deterioration represents a loss in value attributable to normal wear and tear of an improvement over time. The physical deterioration of an improvement is inevitable and begins immediately following the completion or installation of a building component. Proper maintenance of an improvement will likely slow the process of physical deterioration; however, deterioration cannot be avoided. Items of physical deterioration may be curable (cost to cure is less than the resulting increase in value) or incurable (cost to cure is greater than resulting increase in value). The test of whether an item is curable or incurable occurs on the effective date of appraisal.

Curable Physical Deterioration

Curable physical deterioration, or **deferred maintenance**, represents items of deterioration that are in need of immediate repair or replacement on the date of appraisal. These items are considered to be 100 percent depreciated, thus adding no value contribution to the property. Items of deferred maintenance may reflect a needed repair (broken window pane) or may represent a short-lived building component that has expired (roof covering needs replacing). Curable physical deterioration is estimated as the **cost-to-cure**.

Incurable Physical Deterioration

Incurable physical deterioration may be further categorized into *short-lived* and *long-lived* building components. Items of deterioration classified into one of these two categories are not economically feasible to cure (incurable) as of the effective date of appraisal (these components still have remaining life and are physically contributing to value).

> For example, the roof covering (short-lived item) reflects an actual age of 10 years and a total physical life of 15 years as of the date of appraisal. The remaining physical life of the roof covering is 5 years (15 years less 10 years); thus, a prudent owner would not replace the roof at this time because the roof continues to contribute to the value of the property. The same logic would apply to a long-lived item such as the foundation or framing of an improvement. As of the effective date of appraisal, these items are only partially depreciated and are continuing to contribute to the value of the property. Further, the cost to replace these components would be greater than the resulting increase in value as replaced.

Incurable short-lived items are those components of a structure that have an expected physical life shorter than the physical life of the structure as a whole. Examples of short-lived items include roof cover, floor covering, appliances, water heater, etc.

Incurable long-lived items are those components of a structure that have an expected economic life equal to the total economic life of the structure as a whole. Examples of long-lived items include the structure's foundation, framing system, etc.

■ FUNCTIONAL OBSOLESCENCE

Functional obsolescence results when a component of a structure or the structure's design (floor plan, exterior appearance, quality, workmanship, etc.) does not conform and/or appeal to current market tastes or expectations. Functional obsolescence typically occurs within the confines of the subject's boundaries and may be curable or incurable as of the date of appraisal.

■ EXTERNAL OBSOLESCENCE

External obsolescence represents a loss in value resulting from factors or conditions outside the boundaries of the property; thus, the property owner has little or no control over these items. For this reason, external obsolescence is rarely curable.

PART THREE   Techniques for the Estimation of Accrued Depreciation

Accrued depreciation is typically estimated by the appraiser using any one of several acceptable techniques. The techniques subsequently discussed include the economic age-life method, modified economic age-life method, market extraction or sales comparison method, and the breakdown method.

ECONOMIC AGE-LIFE METHOD

The **economic age-life method** is a technique used for the purposes of estimating accrued depreciation whereby a percentage of accrued depreciation is calculated by dividing the building's effective age by its total economic life. The implied percentage is then multiplied by the current cost new of the improvements to obtain a lump sum estimate of accrued depreciation for the subject improvements. The economic age-life method is also known as the *straight line* technique for estimating accrued depreciation as it yields a lump-sum amount of accrued depreciation without allocating total depreciation between the three recognized categories; namely physical deterioration, functional obsolescence, and external obsolescence.

The formula for estimating accrued depreciation by the economic age-life method is presented below:

$$\frac{\text{Effective Age}}{\text{Total Economic Life}} \times \text{Cost New} = \text{Accrued Depreciation}$$

Effective age and total economic life were previously defined in Part One, Key Terms and Definitions. It is important to note that total economic life is merely the summation of effective age and remaining economic life.

For example, if the effective age of a structure is 20 years and the remaining economic life is 30 years, the total economic life is estimated at 50 years as illustrated below.

	Total Economic Life				
(Years) 0	10	20	30	40	50
	Effective Age		Remaining Economic Life		

Therefore, the formula for estimating accrued depreciation by the economic age-life method may also be expressed as:

$$\frac{\text{Effective Age}}{(\text{Effective Age} + \text{Remaining Economic Life})} \times \text{Cost New} = \text{Accrued Depreciation}$$

Procedure

The procedure for estimating accrued depreciation by the economic age-life method is summarized as follows:

a. Estimate the total reproduction or replacement cost new of the improvements.

b. Estimate the effective age of the property being appraised.

c. Estimate the total economic life of the property being appraised.

d. Estimate the rate of accrued depreciation by dividing the structure's effective age (Step b) by its total economic life (Step c).

e. Multiply the depreciation rate (Step d) by the estimated total cost new of the improvements (Step a) to arrive at an indication of accrued depreciation by the economic age-life method.

To arrive at an estimate of the contributory value of the improvements (also known as the depreciated value of the improvements) simply deduct the accrued depreciation estimate (Step e) from total cost new estimate (Step a).

For example, assume the property being appraised is a 15-year-old residence that has been well maintained over the years. Accordingly, you estimate the effective age of the subject at 10 years. In its current condition, you estimate the improvements will continue to contribute value to the overall property for an additional 40 years, indicating a total economic life of 50 years (effective age of 10 years plus remaining economic life of 40 years). The estimated total reproduction cost new of the residence approximates $100,000. What is the dollar amount of accrued depreciation estimated by the economic age-life method?

Total Reproduction Cost New of Residence	$100,000
Multiplied by Depreciation Rate (10 yrs. ÷ 50 yrs. = 0.20 or 20%)	× 0.20
Estimate of Accrued Depreciation by Economic Age-Life Method	$20,000

In the previous example, the contributory value of the improvements is $80,000 ($100,000 less $20,000). To arrive at an indication of value by the Cost Approach, simply add the estimated value of the site to the contributory value of the improvements.

Advantages and Disadvantages

The economic age-life method is the simplest method to employ, and it is the preferred method of most real estate appraisers. However, the economic age-life method assumes straight-line depreciation and does not recognize the various physical lives of the individual building components (short-lived and long-lived items). Thus, the depreciation estimate by the economic age-life method may be less accurate than depreciation estimates calculated by other techniques.

While the economic age-life method does provide an estimate of *accrued* depreciation, this technique does not allocate the estimate between the separate classifications of accrued depreciation (curable and incurable physical deterioration, functional obsolescence, and external obsolescence).

■ MODIFIED ECONOMIC AGE-LIFE METHOD

The **modified economic age-life method** is a technique used for the purposes of estimating accrued depreciation whereby the economic age-life ratio (a building's effective age divided by its total economic life) is applied to the current cost new of the improvements *after curable physical and functional items are deducted.*

The modified economic age-life method is very similar to the economic age-life method except that curable physical and functional items are identified and depreciated separately from the incurable building components.

The formula for estimating accrued depreciation by the modified economic age-life method is presented below:

$$(\text{Cost New} - \text{Curable Depreciation}) \times \frac{\text{Effective Age}}{\text{Total Economic Life}} = \text{Incurable Depreciation}$$

$$\text{Incurable Depreciation} + \text{Curable Depreciation} = \text{Accrued Depreciation}$$

Procedure

The procedure for estimating accrued depreciation by the modified economic age-life method is summarized as follows:

a.   Estimate the total reproduction or replacement cost new of the improvements.

b.   Estimate the cost to cure all items of curable physical and functional depreciation.

c.   Deduct the cost to cure the curable items (Step b) from the total estimated cost new of the improvements (Step a) to arrive at an indication of cost attributable to the incurable components only.

d.   Estimate the effective age and remaining economic life of the property being appraised assuming the curable depreciation has been corrected.

   Note: Often correction of the curable depreciation results in a decrease of the structure's effective age and possibly an increase in its remaining economic life expectancy.

e.   Estimate the rate of depreciation attributable to the incurable components by dividing the structure's effective age by its total economic life (equal to effective age plus remaining economic life).

f.   Multiply the depreciation rate (in decimal format) of the incurable components (Step e) by the estimated total cost new of the incurable components (Step c) to arrive at an indication of depreciation for the incurable components.

g. Add the estimated cost to cure of the curable items (Step b) to the depreciation estimate for the incurable components (Step f) to arrive at an indication of total accrued depreciation by the modified economic age-life method.

Again, to arrive at an estimate of the contributory value of the improvements (also known as the depreciated cost of the improvements) simply deduct the accrued depreciation estimate (Step g) from total cost new estimate (Step a).

For example, assume the property being appraised is a single-family residence that was constructed 21 years ago, and at that time, had a remaining life expectancy of 45 years. Based on a recent inspection of the residence, you identify curable physical deterioration (deferred maintenance) that you estimate will cost $5,000 to cure. By curing these items of deferred maintenance, you estimate the effective age of the improvements will be reduced to approximately 15 years and the remaining economic life will be extended to 60 years, indicating a total economic life of 75 years (effective age of 15 years plus remaining economic life of 60 years). The estimated total reproduction cost of the residence has reasonably been estimated at $125,000. What is the dollar amount of accrued depreciation estimated by the modified economic age-life method?

Cost New		Depreciation ($)		Contributory Value	
$125,000	(1)				
$5,000	(2)	$5,000	(3)	$0	(4)
$120,000	(5)				
$120,000	(6)	$24,000	(7)	$96,000	(8)
$0	(9)	$29,000	(10)	$96,000	(11)

Again, to estimate total accrued depreciation by the modified age-life method, consider the following table above that shows three columns: Cost New, Depreciation, and Contributory Value.

(1) Total reproduction cost new of the single-family residence (Step a).

(2) Cost new of the curable components, both physical and functional items (Step b).

(3) Depreciation estimate for curable components; same as the estimated "cost to cure."

(4) Contributory value of the curable components; items are 100% depreciated with no contributory value.

(5) Cost new of the incurable components only (Step c).

(6) Consider and depreciate the cost new of all incurable components.

(7) Depreciation estimate for the incurable components; cost new of incurable components multiplied by the depreciation rate in decimal format; $120,000 × 0.20 (15 years ÷ 75 years = 0.20) (Steps d, e, and f).

(8) Contributory value of the incurable components; components still contributing to value, hence the title "incurable."

(9) A $0 in the "Cost New" column means the *total* reproduction cost new of the residence has been considered and depreciated accordingly.

(10) Represents the *total accrued depreciation* of the single-family residence by the modified economic age-life method (Step g).

(11) Represents the remaining contributory value of the single-family residence (also known as the depreciated value of the improvements).

The total accrued depreciation by the modified economic age-life method is $29,000.

The total accrued depreciation (10) plus the remaining contributory value of the improvements (11) *must always* equal the total reproduction cost new of the improvement(s) (1). In this example, the final step of the Cost Approach would be to add the estimated site value to the estimated remaining contributory value of the improvements ($96,000).

Advantages and Disadvantages

In comparison to the economic age-life method, the modified economic age-life method more closely resembles the thought process of a knowledgeable buyer when contemplating a purchase. A prudent and knowledgeable buyer generally distinguishes between curable and incurable depreciation because curable items will often require immediate repair or replacement upon assuming ownership of a property.

Second, estimating depreciation of the curable items (cost to cure) is typically more objective and reliable than estimating depreciation of the incurable items. Therefore, deducting the cost to cure of the curable items from the total cost new of an improvement prior to estimating depreciation of the incurable items (estimated by the more subjective economic age-life ratio) generally results in a more accurate estimate of accrued depreciation (because the portion of the estimate that depends on the economic age-life ratio is smaller).

As with the economic age-life method, a disadvantage of the modified economic age-life method is that it does not distinguish between short-lived and long-lived building components nor does this method "break down" the depreciation estimate into the three categories of accrued depreciation, namely physical deterioration, functional obsolescence, and external obsolescence.

Further, a large portion of the structure's cost new is depreciated using the economic age-life ratio and that requires a great deal of judgment on the part of the appraiser.

■ MARKET EXTRACTION OR SALES COMPARISON METHOD

In its simplest form, the format of the Cost Approach is shown below:

$$
\begin{array}{rl}
 & \text{Replacement or Reproduction Cost New (A)} \\
- & \text{Accrued Depreciation (B)} \\
\hline
 & \text{Contributory Value of Improvements (C)} \\
+ & \text{Site Value (D)} \\
\hline
 & \text{Total Property Value (E)}
\end{array}
$$

The market value (or eventual sales price) of a property (E) represents the summation of the property's contributory (or depreciated) value of improvements (C) and its site value (D). Accrued depreciation (B) is the difference between an improvement's replacement or reproduction cost new (A) and its contributory value (C) as of the date of sale.

To arrive at an accurate estimate of accrued depreciation by the market extraction or Sales Comparison method, three items of information are needed: (1) the actual sales price of the comparable; (2) an accurate and reliable estimate of the comparable's site value as of the date of sale; and (3) an accurate and reliable estimate of the comparable's replacement or reproduction cost new as of the date of sale.

Once these three items of information are obtained, accrued depreciation can be estimated using the Cost Approach format.

For example, assume a comparable property sold for $110,000. You estimate the comparable's site value at $20,000 and its cost new at $100,000 as of the date of sale. Accrued depreciation would then approximate $10,000 as follows:

Replacement or Reproduction Cost New (A)	$100,000
− Accrued Depreciation (B)	− $10,000
Contributory Value of Improvements (C)	$90,000
+ Site Value (D)	+ $20,000
Total Property Value (E)	$110,000

If $A - B + D = E$; then $B = A + D - E$.

Therefore, accrued depreciation (B) = $100,000 + $20,000 − $110,000, or $10,000. Now, the comparable's accrued depreciation needs to be annualized.

Once the lump-sum dollar amount of accrued depreciation is estimated ($10,000 in the above example), the estimate must be converted into a meaningful unit of comparison that can be applied to the property being appraised. The most meaningful unit of comparison is the *average annual rate of accrued depreciation*. Conversion of the lump-sum dollar estimate of accrued depreciation into an average annual rate of accrued depreciation is a two-step process.

First, the lump-sum *dollar* estimate must be converted into a lump-sum *percentage* estimate of accrued depreciation. In the above example, the lump-sum dollar amount of accrued depreciation ($10,000) would be divided by the cost new ($100,000) to arrive at the lump-sum percentage estimate of accrued depreciation (0.10 or 10 percent). The lump-sum percentage estimate suggests that 10% of the improvement's cost new is charged as depreciation, while the remaining 90 percent, or $90,000, is the implied contributory value of the improvements.

The second step would be to divide the lump-sum percentage estimate of accrued depreciation by the comparable's effective age. If the comparable sale's effective age was estimated at 10 years in the above example, the average annual rate of accrued depreciation would approximate 1 percent per year (10 percent ÷ 10 years).

Unlike the lump-sum dollar and percentage estimates of accrued depreciation, the average annual rate of accrued depreciation is a refined unit of comparison which can be applied to the subject property's respective effective age for the purposes of estimating accrued depreciation.

Procedure

The procedure for estimating accrued depreciation by the market extraction or sales comparison method is summarized as follows:

a. Find and verify a minimum of two comparable, improved sales which reflect a similar amount of accrued depreciation in comparison to the property being appraised.

b. Deduct the estimated site value of the comparable from its respective sales price to arrive at an indication of the comparable's contributory value of improvements.

c. Estimate the comparable's replacement or reproduction cost new as of the date of sale.

d. Deduct the comparable's estimated contribution of improvements (Step b) from its estimated replacement or reproduction cost new (Step c) to arrive at an indication of the lump-sum dollar amount of accrued depreciation.

e. Convert the lump-sum dollar amount of accrued depreciation into a lump-sum percentage estimate of accrued depreciation by dividing the lump-sum dollar estimate (Step d) by the comparable's estimated replacement or reproduction cost new (Step c).

f. Estimate the effective age of the comparable property.

g. Convert the lump-sum percentage amount of accrued depreciation (Step e) into an average annual rate of accrued depreciation by dividing the lump-sum percentage estimate of accrued depreciation by the comparable's respective effective age (Step f).

h. Reconcile the individual indications of accrued depreciation from the comparable sales and multiply the estimated average annual rate of accrued depreciation by the effective age of the property being appraised to arrive at an indication (percentage) of total accrued depreciation for the subject property.

i. Multiply the percentage of total accrued depreciation (Step h) for the subject by the estimated reproduction or replacement cost new of the subject improvements to arrive at a dollar amount of accrued depreciation by the market extraction/sales comparison method.

For example, assume an improved sale, which you are using as a comparable in an appraisal report, recently sold for $80,000. Based on good comparable data, you estimate the site contributed approximately $15,000 to total property value. The effective age of the residence and the reproduction cost new were reasonably estimated at 15 years and $82,000, respectively. What would be the average annual rate of accrued depreciation indicated by this sale comparable?

Sales Price of Comparable (Step a)	$80,000
− Estimated Site Value (Step b)	− $15,000
Contributory Value of Improvements	$65,000
Estimated Reproduction Cost New (Step c)	$82,000
− Contributory Value of Improvements	− $65,000
Lump-Sum Accrued Depreciation ($) (Step d)	$17,000
Lump-Sum Accrued Depreciation ($) (Step d)	$17,000
÷ Estimated Reproduction Cost New	÷ $82,000
Lump-Sum Accrued Depreciation (%) (Step e)	0.207
Lump-Sum Accrued Depreciation (%) (Step f)	0.207
÷ Comparable's Effective Age (Years)	÷ 15
Average Annual Rate of Accrued Depreciation (Step g)	0.0138
	or 1.38% per year

The average annual rate of accrued depreciation in the preceding example would be 0.0138, or 1.38 percent. If the effective age of the subject property was, say, 20 years, the total amount of accrued depreciation would approximate 27.6 percent (1.38 percent × 20 years) of the estimated replacement or reproduction cost new of the subject property (Step h).

Advantages and Disadvantages

First, the market extraction or sales comparison method of estimating accrued depreciation provides an accurate and reliable estimate of accrued depreciation only in situations when good comparable improved sales are available. The comparable sales should reflect a similar amount of accrued depreciation (physical, functional, and external) in comparison to the property being appraised. Otherwise, this method of estimating accrued depreciation may be inaccurate and unreliable.

Second, the appraiser's estimate of site value and cost new for the improved comparable sale must be accurate and reliable for this method of estimating accrued depreciation to be dependable. When good market data are not available, the market extraction method is of little or no use.

The market extraction method does not allocate the estimate of accrued depreciation into the various classifications or categories (curable and incurable physical deterioration, functional obsolescence, and external obsolescence).

■ BREAKDOWN METHOD

In estimating accrued depreciation by the **breakdown method**, the appraiser analyzes each classification of depreciation (curable and incurable physical deterioration, functional obsolescence, and external obsolescence) separately and estimates the dollar or percentage amount of depreciation associated with each classification. The summation of the individual estimates equals the lump-sum estimate of accrued depreciation by the breakdown method. Because the breakdown method of estimating accrued depreciation is comprehensive and time-consuming, it is rarely used by appraisers.

Basically, the following five main classifications of accrued depreciation are recognized in the breakdown method:

1. Curable physical deterioration (also known as deferred maintenance)

2. Incurable physical deterioration (short-lived and long-lived items)

3. Curable functional obsolescence

4. Incurable functional obsolescence

5. External obsolescence

The procedure for estimating accrued depreciation by the breakdown method is discussed below.

Curable Physical Deterioration

Procedure The procedure for estimating curable physical deterioration is summarized as follows:

1. During the property inspection, identify each item of deferred maintenance.

2. Estimate the *cost to cure* or correct each item of deferred maintenance.

3. Add each respective estimate from Step 2 to arrive at an indication of total curable physical deterioration for the improvements.

For example, during the physical inspection of the subject property, you notice the 10-year old single-family residence needs repair of a broken window pane, painting of all exterior wood and trim, and replacement of several wood boards on the exterior of the home. From your cost files and conversations with several building contractors, you estimate the cost to repair the window pane at $75, the cost to paint the home's exterior at $1,700, and the cost to replace the deteriorated wood boards at $225.

The estimate of total curable physical deterioration, or *deferred maintenance*, would be $2,000 ($75 + $1,700 + $225).

Incurable Physical Deterioration, Short-Lived

Procedure The procedure for estimating incurable physical deterioration of a short-lived component is summarized:

1. Estimate the effective age of the short-lived component *Note: in most circumstances, the effective age of a short-lived component will be the same or very similar to its actual age.*

2. Estimate the total physical life of the short-lived component.

3. Divide the component's respective effective age (Step 1) by its estimated physical life (Step 2) to arrive at an estimate of straight-line physical deterioration for the short-lived component.

4. Estimate the reproduction or replacement cost new of the short-lived component as of the date of appraisal.

5. Multiply the straight-line physical deterioration estimate for the short-lived component (in decimal format) from Step 3 by the component's cost new estimate (Step 4) to arrive at the indicated amount of physical deterioration attributable to the respective short-lived component.

6. Repeat Steps 1 through 5 for each respective short-lived component of a structure depicting physical deterioration as of the date of appraisal.

7. Add the depreciation estimate (Step 5) for each short-lived component to arrive at an indication of the total physical deterioration of the incurable short-lived components.

In the depreciation of a short-lived component, the effective age of the component is divided by the component's respective total physical life to determine an approximate *straight-line* depreciation rate, as discussed above.

For example, the appliances in a single-family house are 10 years old and you estimate the total physical life expectancy of the appliances at 15 years. The appliances would suffer physical deterioration of approximately 67% of cost (10 years ÷ 15 years = 0.67, or 67%). The remaining 33% of cost (100% less 67%) is the contributory value of the appliances. The depreciation percentage estimate (67% in this case) is subsequently applied to the estimated cost new of the respective item to provide a dollar estimate of physical deterioration for this short-lived building component. This procedure is repeated for each individual short-lived item.

For example, in addition to the curable physical deterioration ($2,000) noted for the 10-year old, single-family residence discussed in the example on page 207, assume you estimate the total physical life of the roof covering at 20 years, the physical life of the appliances at 15 years, and the physical life of the floor covering and water heater at 12 years. Further, you estimate the reproduction cost new of these four short-lived items at $2,500, $2,000, $4,500, and $700, respectively. The incurable physical deterioration of the short-lived items would be estimated as follows:

Component	Effective Age (Yrs.)	Physical Life (Yrs.)	Depreciation Estimate (%)	Reproduction Cost New ($)	Depreciation Estimate ($)	Contributory Estimate ($)
Roof	10	20	10 ÷ 20 (50%)	$2,500	$1,250	$1,250
Appliances	10	15	10 ÷ 15 (67%)	$2,000	$1,340	$660
Flooring	10	12	10 ÷ 12 (83%)	$4,500	$3,735	$765
Water Heater	10	12	10 ÷ 12 (83%)	$700	$581	$119
Totals (Rounded)				$9,700	$6,900	$2,800
Percentages				100%	71%	29%

In the above example, the total physical deterioration of the incurable short-lived components is estimated at about $6,900. The reproduction cost new of the short-lived components is estimated at $9,700. The contributory value of these building components is thus $2,800 ($9,700 less $6,900).

Incurable Physical Deterioration, Long-Lived

Procedure The procedure for estimating incurable physical deterioration associated with long-lived components is summarized as follows:

1. Estimate the reproduction or replacement cost new of the *entire* building structure.

2. Derive the estimated reproduction or replacement cost new of the long-lived components as of the date of appraisal by subtracting the cost new of the curable physical components and the incurable short-lived components ($9,700 in the above example) from the total cost new of the entire building structure (Step 1).

3. Estimate the effective age of the entire building structure.

4 Estimate the total economic life of the entire building structure.

5. Divide the structure's effective age (Step 3) by its estimated total economic life (Step 4) to arrive at an estimated percentage of *straight-line* physical deterioration for the long-lived components.

6. Multiply the *straight-line* physical deterioration estimate for the long-lived components (in decimal format) from Step 5 by the long-lived component's cost new estimate (Step 2) to arrive at the indicated amount of total physical deterioration attributable to the long-lived components.

Because long-lived items are, by definition, items with a total economic life commensurate with the economic life of the entire structure, all long-lived items are depreciated using the same effective age and total economic life expectancy. As with the short-lived item, the effective age of the structure is divided by its estimated total life expectancy to determine an approximate *straight-line* depreciation rate. Once derived, this percentage estimate is applied to the reproduction or replacement cost of the long-lived items. To estimate the cost of the long-lived items, the cost new associated with the curable physical, or deferred maintenance items as well as the cost new associated with the incurable short-lived items must be deducted from the total cost new of the entire improvement (otherwise portions of cost new would be *double depreciated*, which would overstate the estimate of physical deterioration and understate the value indication by the Cost Approach).

In addition to the curable physical ($2,000) and incurable short-lived ($6,900) deterioration noted for the 10-year old, single-family residence discussed in the examples on page 207 and 208, assume you estimate the total reproduction cost new of the single-family residence at $100,000, and the residence's effective age and total economic life at 10 years and 50 years, respectively. The total incurable physical deterioration of the long-lived components would be estimated as follows:

Total Reproduction Cost New of Residence	$100,000
Less Cost New of Curable Physical Components	– $2,000
Less Cost New of Incurable Short-Lived Components	– $9,700
Total Reproduction Cost New of Long-Lived Components	$88,300
Times Depreciation Rate (10 Years ÷ 50 Years = 0.20)	× 0.20
Total Physical Deterioration of Long-Lived Components	$17,660

Total Physical Deterioration

Total physical deterioration is the summation of the depreciation estimates for curable physical (deferred maintenance) items, incurable short-lived components, and incurable long-lived components. To arrive at an indication of total physical deterioration from the above examples, as well as demonstrate physical deterioration as it relates to the Cost Approach, consider Table 13.1. The table depicts three columns: Cost New, Depreciation, and Contributory Value.

(1) Total reproduction cost new of the single-family residence.

(2) Cost new of the curable physical, or deferred maintenance, items.

(3) Depreciation estimate for curable physical items; same as the estimated *cost to cure*.

(4) Contributory value of the curable physical items; items are 100 percent depreciated with no contributory value.

(5) Cost new of the incurable physical components, both short-lived and long-lived components.

(6) Cost new of the incurable short-lived components.

(7) Depreciation estimate for the incurable physical short-lived components.

(8) Contributory value of the incurable physical short-lived components; components still contributing to value, hence the title *incurable*.

(9) Cost new of the incurable long-lived components; total cost new of residence less the cost of curable and incurable short-lived components.

(10) Cost new of the incurable long-lived components depreciated using the age-life method.

(11) Depreciation estimate for the incurable physical long-lived components.

(12) Contributory value of the incurable physical long-lived components; components still contributing to value, hence the title "incurable."

(13) A $0 in the Cost New column means the *total* reproduction cost new of the residence has been considered and depreciated accordingly.

TABLE 13.1 ■ Total Physical Deterioration of a 10-Year-Old Single-Family Residence

Cost New		Depreciation ($)		Contributory Value	
$100,000	(1)				
− $2,000	(2)	$2,000	(3)	$0	(4)
$98,000	(5)				
− $9,700	(6)	$6,900	(7)	$2,800	(8)
$88,300	(9)				
− $88,300	(10)	$17,660	(11)	$70,640	(12)
$0	(13)	$26,560	(14)	$73,440	(15)

(14) Represents the *total physical deterioration* of the single-family residence.

(15) Represents the remaining contributory value of the single-family residence (also known as the depreciated value of the improvements).

The total physical deterioration (14) plus the remaining contributory value of the improvements (15) *must always* equal the total reproduction cost new of the improvement(s) (1). In the above illustration, the final step of the Cost Approach would be to add the estimated site value to the remaining contributory value of the improvements (15), assuming no functional or external obsolescence were present.

Functional Obsolescence

Functional obsolescence may result from a *deficiency* (or underimprovement) and/or from a *superadequacy* (or overimprovement).

Deficiency   If functional obsolescence results from a **deficiency**, the solution may call for an addition or a replacement or renovation of the component or the structure itself.

1. *Addition:* This form of obsolescence results from the absence of an item currently required or expected by the market.

> For example, consider a three-story office building with no elevator service. The lack of an elevator has made it virtually impossible to lease the third floor space, as all competitive office buildings in excess of two stories feature elevator service. You determine there is ample space for the addition of an elevator, and that by adding an elevator, the third floor office space could be successfully leased. Given this scenario, an owner would consider the addition of an elevator.

The test of whether the deficiency in the example above is curable or incurable would require an analysis comparing the income potential associated with leasing the third floor office space to the cost associated with the addition and subsequent ownership of an elevator.

If curable, the loss in value attributable to this form of obsolescence is generally measured as the excess cost to cure, or the difference between the cost associated with adding the item as of the date of appraisal and the estimated cost assuming the item was included in the original construction of the improvement.

If incurable and the property generates income, the estimated loss in rent as a result of the deficiency would be capitalized using an appropriate gross rent multiplier or capitalization rate (discussed in Chapter 13). This form of incurable functional obsolescence may also be estimated by matched pair analysis if sufficient reliable market data are available.

2. *Replacement or Renovation:* This form of obsolescence typically results from an existing building component becoming outdated or obsolete by market standards. Correction of the obsolescence may require replacement (substitution) or renovation (modernization).

For example, consider an older house that still contains the original, outdated appliances. You determine that although the existing appliances are contributing nominally to value, the appliances are not reflective of market standards and need replacement. This form of functional obsolescence would be measured as the cost of replacing or updating the appliances less the remaining contributory value of the existing appliances (contributory value being the remaining value after physical deterioration has been charged). In essence, the entire cost of the obsolete item is deducted from cost new, a portion of the cost is allocated as physical deterioration, and the balance of cost as functional obsolescence.

Superadequacy This form of obsolescence, **superadequacy**, typically results when an existing building component, which was included in the original construction of the improvement, exceeds the expectations of the market or provides little or no benefit to the owner (also referred to as an *overimprovement*). The cost new of a superadequate item typically exceeds the item's contribution to value. In other words, the market is not willing to pay the full cost associated with the superadequate component. As previously discussed in Chapter 12, Part Five, Distinction Between Reproduction Cost and Replacement Cost, it is imperative to know what type of cost is being estimated in the Cost Approach, as replacement cost tends to eliminate the cost associated with most superadequate features of a property. Functional obsolescence due to a superadequacy may be either curable or incurable.

For example, consider a hotel that features both an indoor and outdoor swimming pool. From your investigation of the market, you conclude the hotel does not receive any monetary benefits from the indoor pool, not to mention the added expenses associated with ownership of the pool (maintenance, real estate taxes, liability insurance, etc.). In your opinion, the indoor pool area has several possible alternative uses (conference room, etc.) and is reflective of curable functional obsolescence-superadequacy. In this case, depreciation would likely be estimated as the current reproduction cost new of the pool, less physical deterioration previously charged (reflects the remaining contributory value of the pool), plus the cost associated with filling in the pool and refinishing the space into an alternative use.

As an example of incurable functional obsolescence-superadequacy, consider a modest priced single-family residence with an in-ground swimming pool. In your investigations, you determine that only a very small portion of the market demands a swimming pool and that, generally, the market will not pay the full cost associated with the construction of a swimming pool. By matched pair analysis, you estimate the market will pay about 50% of the physically depreciated value of a pool. Given this scenario, the estimate of obsolescence would approximate the current reproduction cost new of the pool, less physical deterioration previously charged (reflects the remaining contribution value of the pool), less approximately 50% of the physically depreciated, or contributory, value of the pool. In this example, the additional cost of ownership associated with the swimming pool would not be considered.

External Obsolescence

External obsolescence may be classified into two categories: locational and economic.

Locational **Locational obsolescence** results from the physical location (or proximity) of the subject property.

For example, consider single-family residences that are located adjacent to a heavily traveled thoroughfare or in proximity to the county landfill. All other elements of comparison being equal, these single-family residences are likely to sell for less than a similar residence unaffected by these adverse conditions (principle of substitution).

External obsolescence resulting from a property's location may be estimated by two techniques. First, if sufficient, reliable market sales data are available, the amount of obsolescence may be measured using *matched pair* analysis or direct comparison of market sales. As previously discussed, *matched pair* analysis would require one or more improved sales influenced by the negative factor or condition and a similar improved sale(s) unaffected by the *externality*. Often, sufficient market sales are not available to employ this technique.

The second technique estimates external obsolescence by capitalizing rent loss directly attributable to the negative locational factor or condition. The estimated rent loss may be either *gross rent* or *net income*. If *gross rent* loss is estimated by the appraiser, the rent loss must be multiplied by an appropriate *gross rent multiplier (GRM)*. A gross rent multiplier is simply the sales price of a comparable divided by the comparable's gross rental income and reflects a relationship between gross potential rent of a property and the eventual sales price paid for the property (see Chapter 15). If *net income* loss is estimated, the income loss must be divided by an appropriate capitalization rate.

A *capitalization rate* is simply the net income generated by a property divided by the property's eventual sales price.

Regardless of the technique used, the total estimated loss in value must be allocated between the improvement and site. Allocation is typically done using an estimated ratio of site value to building value. The rationale underlying the allocation between improvement and site is that a portion of the total obsolescence has previously been reflected in the valuation of the site (site value was less due to negative locational factor or condition).

Economic **Economic obsolescence** results from economic factors or conditions typically influencing supply and demand.

> For example, a recent downsizing by several significant employers within the community has resulted in a current oversupply of single-family residences directly competing with the property being appraised; in other words, it's a buyer's market. The principle of supply and demand implies that if supply is greater than demand, prices tend to decrease (all other things being equal). A buyer's market positively influences the negotiating ability of the purchaser and typically results in lower prices paid for real estate.

Economic obsolescence can best be measured by directly comparing a residence that sold prior to the negative economic climate with a residence (ideally the same property) that sold during the poor economic conditions. Generally speaking, the loss in value is attributable to a deterioration in market conditions over time. Again, the estimate of obsolescence should be allocated between the improvements and the site.

1. The difference between an improvement's cost new and its contribution to market value as of the date of the appraisal is referred to as
   a. physical deterioration.
   b. accrued depreciation.
   c. economic life.
   d. obsolescence.

2. The estimated period for which the improvements will continue to contribute to total property value, as of the effective date of the appraisal is known as
   a. total economic life.
   b. total physical life.
   c. remaining economic life.
   d. remaining physical life.

3. Functional obsolescence can result from which of the following?
   a. Fluctuation in local supply and demand
   b. Change in market tastes and standards
   c. Normal wear and tear from daily use
   d. All of the above

4. A defect caused by a flaw in the structure, material, or design of an improvement where the cost to cure the defect is less than the resulting increase in value (after the defect has been corrected) is known as
   a. curable physical deterioration.
   b. external obsolescence.
   c. curable functional obsolescence
   d. incurable functional obsolescence

5. The subject property is a 14-year-old residence that has been well maintained over the years. Accordingly, you estimate the effective age of the subject at 10 years. In its current condition, you estimate the improvements will continue to contribute value to the overall property for an additional 50 years. What is the percentage of accrued depreciation estimated by the economic age-life method?
   a. 28.0 percent
   b. 16.7 percent
   c. 20.0 percent
   d. 21.9 percent

6. You are appraising a single-family residence that was constructed 20 years ago, and at that time, had a remaining life expectancy of 40 years. Based on a recent inspection of the residence, you uncover curable depreciation that you estimate will cost $8,000 to cure. By curing these items, you estimate the effective age of the improvements will approximate 15 years and the remaining economic life will be extended to 45 years. The current reproduction cost of the residence has reasonably been estimated at $85,000. What is the lump-sum amount of accrued depreciation estimate using the modified economic age-life method?
   a. $21,250
   b. $33,640
   c. $27,250
   d. $19,250

7. An improved comparable sale recently sold for $92,000. Based on reliable comparable data, the site value was reasonably estimated at $18,000. The effective age of the residence and the reproduction cost new were reasonably estimated at 10 years and $98,000, respectively. What is the average annual rate of depreciation indicated by this sale comparable?
   a. 2.5 percent
   b. 1.3 percent
   c. 2.6 percent
   d. 2.0 percent

Questions 8, 9, and 10 are based on the following data. You are appraising a three-year-old residence and note the following observations:

A roof that has a total physical life of 15 years and a cost to replace of $3,500

Appliances that have a total physical life of 12 years and cost $2,500 to replace

Floor covering that has a total physical life of 10 years and cost $5,000 to replace

You estimate the cost new and the remaining physical life of the residence at $95,000 and 47 years, respectively. No curable physical deterioration, functional obsolescence, or external obsolescence were noted as of the effective date of the appraisal report.

8. What is the total amount of short-lived incurable physical deterioration for the property?
   a. $8,175.
   b. $4,250
   c. $11,000
   d. $2,825

9. What is the total amount of long-lived incurable physical deterioration for the property?
   a. $5,530
   b. $5,040
   c. $5,360
   d. $5,700

10. What is the total accrued depreciation by the breakdown method for the property?
    a. $7,865
    b. $8,185
    c. $13,215
    d. $8,525

11. During an inspection of the neighborhood, you note that the vast majority of homes feature a two-car, attached garage. The subject property features a one-car, attached garage. From you investigations, you conclude the market prefers a two-car, attached garage. What classification of depreciation is this?
    a. Curable physical deterioration
    b. Incurable physical deterioration
    c. Functional obsolescence
    d. External obsolescence

12. Total economic life is
    a. equivalent to the effective age plus remaining economic life.
    b. an estimate of how long improvements will contribute to total property value.
    c. the denominator (or bottom number) in the economic age-life ratio.
    d. all of the above.

13. In the highest and best use section, you formed a very specific and defensible conclusion with regard to the ideal improvement that , in your opinion, should be constructed on the subject site, if vacant. However, this ideal improvement reflects numerous differences in comparison to the subject property. What type of accrued depreciation may the improvement(s) suffer from?
    a. Physical deterioration
    b. Functional obsolescence
    c. External obsolescence
    d. The above comparison does not assist in determining depreciation for the improvements.

14. During the property inspection, you notice an offensive odor that you determine results from an industrial use located just outside the immediate subject area. Further investigation reveals market data that suggest an approximate 10 percent to 15 percent reduction in market value as a result of this odor. What classification of depreciation is this?
    a. Incurable physical deterioration
    b. Incurable functional obsolescence
    c. Curable obsolescence
    d. External obsolescence

15. An owner of a home asks your advice about whether she should add a central air-conditioning system to her home. Based on your analysis of sales in the neighborhood, the value of the home would increase approximately $3,000. The total cost to add the system is $6,000. This is an example of
    a. curable physical deterioration.
    b. external obsolescence.
    c. curable functional obsolescence.
    d. incurable functional obsolescence.

14

Applied Sales Comparison Approach

■ LEARNING OBJECTIVES

Students will be able to

1. understand the underlying appraisal principles of substitution and contribution as they relate to the Sales Comparison Approach.

2. understand the strengths and limitations of the Sales Comparison approach.

3. understand the difference between special purpose and limited market properties.

4. briefly review the land and site valuation concepts in Chapter 11.

5. identify and analyze units of comparison.

6. understand how to extract adjustments and apply the extracted adjustments in a market data grid both on a percentage and dollar adjustment basis.

■ KEY TERMS

comparison shopping   limited market property   special purpose property

■ INTRODUCTION

The Sales Comparison Approach is the most easily understood approach to value. It directly reflects considerations of buyers and sellers in a particular marketplace. In a sense, it is simply a means of interpreting **comparison shopping**. A potential, typical buyer may be unaware of the cost to reproduce a structure (Cost Approach) and be oblivious to the rental potential of a particular house (Income Approach). But, during the course of investigating numerous purchase alternatives, the potential buyer intuitively is going through a price comparison procedure, weighing the pluses and minuses for each housing alternative (Sales Comparison Approach).

This Chapter expands the application of the Sales Comparison Approach. There are no new concepts introduced in this Chapter; rather, the student is led to a familiarity with the adjustment process, using units of comparison, through numerous problems and case studies.

PART ONE   Underlying Economic Principles

■ SUBSTITUTION

The economic principle of *substitution* encompasses the premise that a prudent purchaser would pay no more for a component or commodity than the cost to acquire a component or commodity with equal utility. This principle is the basis for *comparison shopping*.

■ CONTRIBUTION

Contribution relates to the value of an item or component as it contributes to the entire entity. This principle becomes important when analyzing adjustments for items as they relate to the entire property.

PART TWO   Strengths and Limitations

■ STRENGTHS

The primary strength of the Sales Comparison Approach is that it is easily understood and is a direct reflection of actions of buyers and sellers in a particular marketplace. The average homebuyer may not understand cost or depreciation, and most home purchasers rarely have the ability to equate income-earning potential into a current value indication. Virtually all buyers and sellers, however, are aware of market competition for a particular product in a particular time period.

Even in more sophisticated real estate transactions, the Sales Comparison Approach is still appropriate. When investors consider acquiring shopping centers, hotels/motels, office buildings, and other income-producing type properties, competitive rates of return are considered as well as a broad range of physical comparisons such as price per unit, price per room, or price per square foot. Although a shopping center may not be similar in appearance to a high-rise office building, they are similar in that they are both investment alternatives competing for investment dollars. In addition to competing with each other, these real estate alternatives also compete for investment dollars in the stock market, bond market, savings accounts, etc.

■ LIMITATIONS

The primary limitation of the Sales Comparison Approach relates to the availability of comparable data. In many markets where sales activity is slow, there may not be a number of sales and listings that can be analyzed compared to the subject property in the valuation process. This is especially true in rural areas, where homes are scattered to begin with and residences may vary widely with regard to size, quality, condition, and style.

■ SPECIAL PURPOSE AND LIMITED MARKET PROPERTIES

Often the appraiser is confronted with an appraisal assignment that involves a property that appears to be unique.

Examples may be the following:

1. Bowling alleys

2. Automobile dealerships

3. Manufacturing facilities

4. Food processing facilities

5. Refineries

6. Churches

7. Golf courses

8. Municipal buildings

9. Ski resorts

When a property is in fact unique or one of a kind, no Sales Comparison Approach can therefore be applied. A property for which there is no identifiable market is said to be a **special purpose property**.

The appraiser can often confuse *special purpose properties* with *limited market properties*. A **limited market property** is one for which there is a market, although the market is not readily identifiable.

The previous nine examples above are more *limited market* in nature rather than *special purpose*.

When appraising limited market properties, the appraiser's market may be expanded significantly to a large geographic area. A golf course may appear to be a special purpose property; however, upon market investigations, the appraiser may find sales of golf courses that can be used for comparison purposes, although the golf courses that sold may be located throughout the state. The market for a food processing facility may be region-wide, encompassing several states in certain geographic regions of the United States. The appraiser may find an active market for churches in a community, although his initial impression is that churches are special purpose properties.

Determination as to whether or not a property is limited market or special purpose usually occurs after some investigation has been made into the market for that particular property.

PART THREE   Sales Comparison Procedure

The following four steps are used in the Sales Comparison Approach:

1. Identify and verify recent sales, listings, and expired purchase contracts on properties that are comparable to the property being appraised.

2. Select a relevant unit(s) of comparison (i.e., total sales price, price per acre, price per square foot, price per lot, price per front foot, etc.) and analyze each comparable sale accordingly.

3. Compare each comparable property directly to the subject property and identify all dissimilarities using the elements of comparison.

4. Adjust the comparable properties (using the selected unit(s) of comparison) for all dissimilarities in comparison to the subject property to arrive at an indication of value for the subject by each respective comparable.

PART FOUR   Units of Comparison

Appraisers continuously use *units of comparison* in analyzing market data to ascertain trends and tendencies. Data that may appear to be inconsistent and inconclusive may reveal obvious and apparent trends and tendencies once categorized into units of comparison.

Consider the following data on four sales of convenience stores:

Sale Number	1	2	3	4
Date	Current	6 Months	3 Months	4 Months
Price	$800,000	$750,000	$900,000	$550,000
Square Feet of Land	23,000	45,000	33,000	63,000
Square Feet of Building	3,000	2,300	2,500	3,200
Gross Sales per Year	$975,000	$880,000	$1,050,000	$690,000

The sales fluctuate fairly widely from $550,000 to $900,000. When converting to units of comparison, the following is discovered:

Sale Number	1	2	3	4
Price per Square Foot of Land	$34.78	$16.67	$27.27	$8.73
Price per Square Foot of Building	$266.67	$326.09	$360.00	$171.88
Price as a Percent of Gross Sales	82%	85%	86%	80%

The price per square foot of land varies significantly from $8.73 per square foot to $34.78 per square foot. The price per square foot of building also varies widely from $171.88 to $360.00 per square foot. No discernable tendencies can be isolated.

In the verification process, however, the appraiser may have discovered that the most significant determinant stressed by buyers and sellers is the gross business income. By analyzing the sales price related to gross sales, the appraiser discovers an obvious trend. The sales price as a percent of gross sales reflects a consistent pattern of 80 percent to 86 percent. The appraiser has now gone beyond the superficial step of viewing dirt and mortar to the more sophisticated level of understanding buyer and seller motivations.

Occasionally, the appraiser can overanalyze a property for units of comparison. Consider the following subdivision lot sales:

Sale Number	1	2	3	4	5
Price	$25,000	$25,000	$25,000	$25,000	$25,000
Corner/Interior	Corner	Interior	Interior	Interior	Corner
Square Feet	17,000	20,000	21,000	15,000	23,000
Front Feet	110	102	100	92	110
Price per Square Foot	$1.47	$1.25	$1.19	$1.67	$1.09
Price per Front Foot	$227.27	$245.10	$250.00	$271.74	$227.27

Although these sales reflect a somewhat inconsistent range in price per square foot and price per front foot, they all sold for exactly the same price, $25,000. Assuming the subject is a typical lot consistent with the other lots that have sold, little analysis is required.

PART FIVE   The Adjustment Process

As noted previously in Chapter 9, the appraiser is continually dealing with *adjustment extraction* and *adjustment application*. Adjustments can either be dollar or percentage. Adjustments are abstracted through paired sales analysis.

While the concept is simple, the application can often become very detailed and confusing because of the large volumes of data with which the appraiser works. To simplify the adjustment extraction process, the appraiser often prepares an analysis grid for comparison purposes.

Keep in mind that the following seven-step sequence of adjustments must always be followed:

1. Property rights conveyed

2. Financing

3. Conditions of sale

4. Market conditions (time)

5. Location

6. Physical characteristics

7. Income variances

When applying lump-sum adjustments, the sequence of adjustments is not critical in that the adjusted price will be the same regardless of the sequence.

Consider the following example:

Sequence 1		**Sequence 2**		**Sequence 3**	
Price	$100,000	Price	$100,000	Price	$100,000
Financing	+ $2,000	Market Conditions	+ $2,000	Location	– $4,000
Market Conditions	+ $2,000	Location	– $4,000	Physical Variances	– $3,000
Location	– $4,000	Physical Variances	– $3,000	Financing	+ $2,000
Physical Variances	– $3,000	Financing	+ $2,000	Market Conditions	+ $2,000
Net Adjustment	– $3,000	Net Adjustment	– $3,000	Net Adjustment	– $3,000
Adjusted Price	$97,000	Adjusted Price	$97,000	Adjusted Price	$97,000

When utilizing percentage adjustments, however, whether or not adjustments can be used in sequence or combined does become important. Consider the following:

Sales Price per Square Foot	$5.00
Market Conditions	+25% (Adjustment Factor 1.25)
Physical Variances	–20% (Adjustment Factor .80)

Alternative 1 (Combined)		**Alternative 2 (In Sequence)**	
Base	$5.00	Base	$5.00
Net Adjustment	× 1.05	Market Conditions Adjustment	× 1.25
Adjusted Price	$5.25	Adjusted Base	$6.25
		Physical Variances Adjustment	× 0.80
		Adjusted Price	$5.00

Under Alternative 1, the +25 percent and –20 percent adjustments are combined to yield a lump sum adjustment factor of 1.05, and an adjusted sales price of $5.25 per square foot. Under Alternative 2, however, a new base is created every time an adjustment is applied. After adjusting +25 percent for market conditions, an adjusted base of $6.25 per square foot is created. Applying the –20 percent adjustment for physical variances results in an adjusted price of $5 per square foot.

The question arises: Which is the proper technique? Technically, percentage adjustments are usually abstracted from the market data, one adjustment at the time. Accordingly, the appraiser should apply the adjustments one at the time, obtaining a new adjusted base after application of each adjustment.

In everyday practice, however, percentage adjustments are often combined because many paired sales from which the adjustments are abstracted reflect a range in adjustments that should be tempered with judgment, negating the impact of whether or not the adjustments are combined or a new base is created each time (cumulative).

P A R T   S I X   Adjustment Extraction

In abstracting adjustments, the appraiser is normally dealing with a large number of variables. Isolation of *matched pairs* usually requires formulating the variables into a grid that follows a logical pattern. Variables can then be put into this grid for a more refined comparison.

In the Table 14.1, all of the sales introduced represent fee simple transfers at cash or cash equivalent prices, with none of the sales occurring under duress conditions. No adjustments were therefore needed for rights conveyed, financing, or conditions of sale. What are the indicated adjustments for the items noted in Table 14.1?

TABLE 14.1 ■ Adjustment Extraction Variables Grid

Sale Number	1	2	3	4	5
Price	$93,000	$95,000	$100,000	$95,000	$96,000
Date of Sale (Market Conditions)	3 Months	2 Months	1 Month	4 Months	1 Month
Location	Typical Interior	Typical Interior	Typical Interior	Typical Interior	Typical Interior
Physical Variances					
Site Size	.43 Acre	.42 Acre	.41 Acre	.40 Acre	.43 Acre
Residence Size (Square Feet)	1,450	1,450	1,450	1,450	1,450
Bedrooms	3	3	3	3	4
Baths	2	2	2	2	2
Garage	No	No	Yes	Yes	No
Basement	Yes	Yes	Yes	No	Yes
Condition	Average	Good	Good	Good	Average

ANSWER

Comparison	Difference	Adjustment
1 versus 5	Bedrooms	$3,000
2 versus 3	Garage	$5,000
3 versus 4	Basement	$5,000
1 versus 2	Condition	$2,000

Frequently, it is necessary to convert lump sum adjustments abstracted from market data into units of comparison. In the following example, the four residence sales are all located in the same subdivision, and they all sold recently. The only major variance relates to the basement. The following analysis is offered:

	First Comparison		**Second Comparison**	
	Sale 1	Sale 2	Sale 1	Sale 3
Price	$105,000	$114,000	$105,000	$109,500
Square Feet of Basement	None	1,000	None	500

Difference Attributed to Basement
$114,000 − $105,000 = $9,000
Basement Contribution per Square Foot
$9,000 ÷ 1,000 = $9

Difference Attributed to Basement
$109,500 − $105,000 = $4,500
Basement Contribution per Square Foot
$4,500 ÷ 500 = $9

In this example, the data reflects an inconsistent absolute adjustment with regard to the presence of a basement, ranging from $4,500 to $9,000. When converted to a square foot basis, however, both show contributory value of $9 per square foot.

As noted previously, the adjustment extraction process is ongoing, with the appraiser rarely having to abstract adjustments each time with new paired sales for each appraisal assignment. In the course of archiving such data, the appraiser becomes aware of which adjustments tend to be consistent on a gross basis and which adjustments tend to be consistent on a per unit basis.

1. The principal of substitution encompasses which of the following premises?
   a. A prudent purchaser would pay no more for a property than the cost to acquire a substitute with equal utility.
   b. The value of an item may be substituted for another item.
   c. An income stream may be substituted for a component of a property.
   d. The principal of substitution relates to the substitution of adjustments in the Sales Comparison Approach.

2. What is the primary strength of the Sales Comparison Approach?
   a. It is the most mathematically correct approach to value.
   b. It is always the easiest approach to find data that has recently sold comparable to the subject.
   c. It considers the cost to reproduce the subject improvements plus land value.
   d. It is easily understood and a direct reflection of buyers and sellers in the marketplace.

3. What is the primary limitation of the Sales Comparison Approach?
   a. It is the least reliable approach to value.
   b. It always sets the upper limit of value.
   c. Confirmation of sales is very difficult.
   d. Comparable data is not always readily available.

4. What is the difference between a special purpose property and a limited market property?
   a. Sales of special purpose properties are restricted to local sales only.
   b. Sales of limited market properties are restricted to local sales only.
   c. Special purpose properties seldom if ever sell and limited market properties randomly sell.
   d. There is no difference between the two.

5. Which of the following is the correct order of sequence for adjustments in the Sales Comparison Approach?
   a. Time, property rights, conditions of sale, financing, other adjustments
   b. Property rights, financing, conditions of sale, time, other adjustments
   c. Financing, conditions of sale, time, property rights, other adjustments
   d. Conditions of sale, time, property rights, financing, other adjustments

CHAPTER FIFTEEN

Income Approach

■ LEARNING OBJECTIVES

Students will be able to

1. understand the underlying economic principles of the Income Approach including anticipation, supply and demand, substitution, and externalities.

2. understand the relationship between income, rent, and value (IRV).

3. recognize the three methods of income capitalization and properly employ the gross rent multiplier and direct capitalization techniques.

4. understand and analyze the components of an income and expense statement including gross income potential, and vacancy and collection loss allowance leading to the effective gross income estimate, as well as operating expenses leading to the estimate of the net income.

5. differentiate between net income ratios and expense ratios.

■ KEY TERMS

collection loss	Income Approach to value	property value
direct capitalization	net income ratio (NIR)	replacement allowance (reserves)
discounted cash flow	net operating income (NOI)	vacancy
effective gross income (EGI)	operating expenses (OER)	variable expenses
effective gross rent multiplier (EGRM)	overall capitalization rate	yield capitalization
fixed expenses	potential gross income (PGI)	
gross rent multiplier (GRM)		

■ INTRODUCTION

As in the Cost Approach where value is linked to cost, the **Income Approach** to value links value to the property's ability to produce income. In residential appraisals, the Income Approach is applicable only when potential buyers would consider the property's ability to produce income in their purchase decision. In neighborhoods that are predominantly owner-occupied, the Income Approach will likely have limited applicability. Typical units of comparison used for the analysis of rent for single-family residences include rent per month, rent per square foot of gross living area, and rent per room.

P A R T   O N E   Underlying Economic Principles

The economic principles were previously presented and discussed in Chapter 4. Several of these economic principles can be related to the Income Approach: anticipation, supply and demand, substitution, and externalities. The relationship of these four economic principles to the Income Approach is subsequently discussed.

■ ANTICIPATION

The principle of *anticipation* is the underlying principle of the Income Approach. In the Income Approach, value is a function of the owner's right to receive future benefits from the property in the form of rent and the eventual sale, or disposition of the property (sometimes referred to as the *reversion*). The Income Approach attempts to forecast these future ownership benefits and estimate their present worth or value as of the date of appraisal.

■ SUPPLY AND DEMAND

Since income-generating properties actively compete in the open market for tenants, the principle of *supply and demand* influences the rental rates that can be charged by a property owner/manager, as well as the occupancy level at which a property will likely perform. When the supply of rental properties outpaces demand, the rental rate and quite possibly the occupancy level of a property will decline because tenants have not only more properties from which to choose, but more leverage to negotiate. During these economic times, the value of income producing properties tends to decrease as the net income of the property is negatively impacted. The opposite of this is true when demand outpaces supply in a particular market area.

■ SUBSTITUTION

In the Income Approach, the principle of *substitution* implies that a knowledgeable tenant, or lessee, will not pay more in rent than the cost associated with leasing a property that provides equal utility. Similarly, income producing properties and financial markets in general compete with one another for investors; higher rates of return typically translate into greater demand, all other things being equal.

■ EXTERNALITIES

The principle of *externalities* implies that positive and negative external influences affect the ability of a particular property to produce income, and hence its market value. Examples of positive influences may include the property's location in proximity to shopping, public transportation, governmental (schools) or medical facilities, recreational amenities, etc; or stem from the fact that the general area is attractive with little pollution and/or crime. The opposite of these positive influences may be examples of negative influences affecting a property's value (i.e., inconvenience to support facilities, unattractive and/or polluted areas, neighborhood with high crime rate, etc.).

P A R T   T W O   Applications of the Income Approach

As previously noted, the Income Approach is most applicable and reliable when a property's ability to produce income would be considered in a potential buyer's purchase decision. The fact that a property is leased as of the date of appraisal may or may not be an indication as to the applicability of the Income Approach in an appraisal assignment. The primary questions are: "Who is likely going to purchase the subject property?" and "Will these individuals consider the income producing capabilities of the subject in their purchase decision?" For example, consider the following two scenarios.

■ SCENARIO 1

The subject property is located in the local country club development, but as a result of being transferred, the owner decides to lease the property. A survey of the neighborhood reveals that 98 percent of the single-family properties in the subdivision are owner-occupied. Is the Income Approach applicable in this situation?

It is highly unlikely because the vast majority of purchasers will owner-occupy the property and would not be concerned with the property's ability to produce income; thus, value is not related to or dependent on income. Further, there would likely be insufficient market data from which to derive a reliable value indication by the Income Approach.

■ SCENARIO 2

The owner of the subject property currently occupies the house and has for the past 30 years. Over the past several years, however, the neighborhood has undergone a transition and is presently predominantly tenant occupied. Is the Income Approach applicable in this situation?

Certainly, as the majority of homeowners in the neighborhood appear to be real estate investors who likely purchased the properties based on their income producing capabilities. In this situation, there is likely a direct relationship between income and value. Further, ample market data would likely be available from which to estimate a reliable value by the Income Approach.

With regard to commercial properties, the same two questions are again applicable: (1) Who is likely going to purchase the subject property? and (2) Will these individuals consider the income producing capabilities of the subject in their purchase decision?

> For example, the Income Approach would likely be applicable when appraising a multitenant office, retail, or industrial building, an apartment complex, a hotel or motel, golf course, etc. However, the Income Approach may not be applicable or as reliable when appraising a single-tenant property in an owner-occupied setting, or a special-purpose property such as a church or governmental building, etc.

PART THREE   Methods of Income Capitalization

Income estimates (gross income or net operating income) can generally be capitalized into a value indication by one of the following three generally recognized methods:

1. Gross rent multiplier (GRM)

2. Direct capitalization

3. Yield capitalization

Each of these methods is discussed below; however, direct capitalization and yield capitalization are advanced capitalization methods and are only briefly discussed here. The gross rent multiplier (GRM) will be the primary focus in this book as the GRM is generally the only capitalization method applicable to single-family residential properties.

■ GROSS RENT MULTIPLIER

A **gross rent multiplier (GRM)** is a market-derived factor that expresses the relationship between the potential gross rent of a property and its sales price. A GRM is extracted from improved sales of comparable properties similar to the property being appraised. Derivation of a GRM simply involves dividing the sales price of a comparable property by its potential gross market rent *as of the date the property sold* as shown below:

$$\frac{\text{Sales Price of Comparable}}{\text{Potential Gross Market Rent}} = \text{Gross Rent Multiplier (GRM)}$$

> For example, assume a comparable property that sold for $50,000 was rented for $500 per month as of the date of sale. The GRM would thus be 100 ($50,000 ÷ $500).

To arrive at a value indication using a GRM, simply multiply the estimated gross rent of the subject by an appropriate GRM. A GRM may be extracted using either monthly or annual potential gross rent, but it is generally extracted and applied using monthly rent for single-family residential properties. It is important to note, however, that after derivation of the gross income multiplier from the comparable sales, the GRM *must* be applied on the same basis as it was extracted from the market. In other words, if the sales price of a comparable is divided by potential gross *monthly* market (or actual) rent, then the GRM should be applied to the potential gross *monthly* market (or actual) rent of the subject.

In the example above, the GRM of 100 was extracted using the comparable's potential gross monthly rent; therefore, the GRM must be applied to the estimated gross monthly rent of the subject to arrive at a value indication by this method. Assuming the potential gross monthly rent of the subject was $550, the value indication by this capitalization method would approximate $55,000 ($550 x 100).

An **effective gross rent multiplier (EGRM)** is calculated the same way, but it includes an allowance for normal annual vacancy and collection losses. In the previous example, if vacancy and collection losses were estimated at $50 per month, or effective gross revenue was $500 per month, the EGRM would be 110 ($55,000 ÷ $500). Adjustments are not made to GRMs; they are a direct reflection of the market's participants. While adjustments are not made, the appraiser should be careful to have current and comparable sales as GRM indicators.

Suppose a house is leased at $400 per month, but the lease expires at the end of the current month. Market rent is $500 per month. Market rent would be used in this example, because of the minimal time remaining on the current contract.

■ DIRECT CAPITALIZATION

In order to comprehend **direct capitalization**, it is important to understand the relationship between net operating income (I), the overall capitalization rate (R), and property value (V).

(I) represents the net operating income of a property. The *net operating income (NOI)* of a property is simply the collected income generated by the property less typical operating expenses incurred by the property (i.e., real estate taxes, insurance, repairs, etc.). Debt service, book depreciation, and income taxes are not deducted to arrive at a NOI estimate.

(R) represents an **overall capitalization rate** which is simply the net operating income of a property at the time of sale divided by its sales price. Similar to the GRM, the overall capitalization rate expresses a relationship between income and price (value).

(V) represents the **property value** and is simply the net operating income generated by a property divided by an appropriate overall capitalization rate.

The triangles in Figure 15.1 illustrate the relationship among these three components. To define the relationship of each component, merely cover the respective component in the diagram.

In this capitalization method, the estimated NOI of the subject property is capitalized using an overall capitalization rate extracted from improved comparable sales.

> For example, assume a comparable property sold recently for $1,000,000, with a net operating income at the time of sale of $100,000. The implied overall capitalization rate (R) from the comparable sale would approximate 0.10 or 10% ($100,000 ÷ $1,000,000). If the estimated net operating income (*I*) of the subject is $90,000, then the value indication for the subject would approximate $900,000 ($90,000 ÷ 0.10).

■ YIELD CAPITALIZATION

Yield capitalization converts the forecasted future benefits of a property into a present worth, or value, by applying an appropriate yield, or discount, rate. Future benefits of a property typically include the NOI generated by the property during an estimated

FIGURE 15.1 ■ Direct Capitalization Relationships

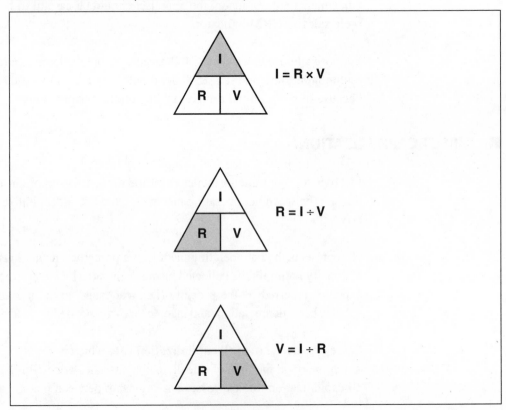

holding period and the eventual sale, or disposition, of the property or asset at the end of the holding period. Examples of yield capitalization include a **discounted cash flow (DCF)** analysis or estimating the value of land using the subdivision development approach (previously discussed in Chapter 11).

Yield capitalization and discounting are means of converting future benefits into a present worth or value; these are advanced concepts that are beyond the scope of this book.

P A R T   F O U R   Estimation of Income and Expenses

An accurate and reasonable projection of income and expenses for the subject property is crucial in producing a reliable value indication by the Income Approach. This section introduces several general terms and definitions and briefly discusses these terms in relation to the estimation of NOI for the property being appraised.

■ POTENTIAL GROSS INCOME (PGI)

Potential gross income (PGI) is the total potential income that a property can generate at full occupancy prior to a deduction for vacancy, collection loss, and operating expenses. PGI is the most frequent income estimate sought in the valuation of a residential property; it may be capitalized into a value indication using a GRM.

■ EFFECTIVE GROSS INCOME (EGI)

Effective gross income (EGI) is the potential gross income adjusted for anticipated vacancy and collection losses. This income estimate is commonly referred to as *collected income*, or the dollar amount of potential gross income that is actually realized by the property owner.

Vacancy

Vacancy is the portion of the property that is not occupied and/or leased. Vacancy is generally referred to as a percentage of PGI.

> For example, if 1,000 square feet of a 10,000 square foot, multitenant building is not occupied, the vacancy rate is commonly referred to as 10% (1,000 SF ÷ 10,000 SF).

Collection Loss

Collection loss is the portion of potential gross income that is forfeited by the landlord or owner due to the nonpayment of rent by a tenant(s). Collection loss is also generally referred to as a percentage of PGI.

> For example, if you estimate PGI and collection loss for the upcoming year at $100,000 and $2,000, respectively, collection loss may be referred to as 2% of potential gross income ($2,000 ÷ $100,000).

Collection loss typically varies from assignment to assignment and is generally dependent upon the property type being appraised (i.e., apartments, office, retail, etc.) and the quality of tenant (i.e., creditworthiness, etc.) associated with the specific property. For example, an apartment complex catering to business professionals and families may reflect a collection loss less than that of a similarly constructed apartment complex that caters to singles and/or young adults due to its *more stable* tenant profile.

■ OPERATING EXPENSES

Operating expenses are expenditures incurred by the owner or landlord necessary to maintain the production of effective gross income and adequately preserve the property. Operating expenses may be further divided into fixed expenses, variable expenses, and replacement allowance (also commonly referred to as *reserves*).

Fixed Expenses

Fixed expenses are those operating expenses that typically do not vary with occupancy and must be paid even when the property is vacant. The two primary fixed expenses influencing the vast majority of real property are real estate taxes and insurance (i.e., structural and liability). Although these expenses do typically vary from year to year, neither expense is dependent upon fluctuations in the occupancy level of the property.

Variable Expenses

Variable expenses are those operating expenses that typically vary with occupancy or the level of services offered. Examples of variable expenses include but are not limited to management fees, leasing fees, utilities, repairs and maintenance, cleaning and decorating, marketing, grounds maintenance, administrative, trash removal, etc.

Replacement Allowance (Reserves)

A **replacement allowance (reserve)** is a *reserve* fund set aside by the owner/landlord or manager of a property to fund the periodic replacement of short-lived building components. As discussed in Chapter 12, building components that reflect a life expectancy less than that of the entire building structure itself are called *short-lived* items. The replacement allowance, or reserves, is typically used for the replacement of short-lived building components such as roof covering, interior and exterior paint, appliances, floor covering, parking (paving) areas, etc.

An appraiser may decide to include or not include a deduction for reserves in the estimate of NOI for the property being appraised; either way is acceptable. The most important consideration, however, is not whether the appraiser chooses to deduct reserves prior to arriving at an NOI estimate for the property being appraised, but rather the method in which the overall capitalization rate is extracted from the market and subsequently applied to the net operating income estimate. An overall capitalization rate from a comparable property *must* be derived in a manner consistent with the NOI estimate for the property being appraised. In other words, if the appraiser deducts reserves prior to arriving at the NOI estimate for the subject property, reserves should also be deducted from the comparable sale's NOI estimate prior to derivation of an overall capitalization rate by the respective sale.

Net Operating Income

Net operating income (NOI) is the income remaining after the deduction of all operating expenses, both fixed and variable, from EGI; it is the income remaining prior to a deduction for debt service and depreciation. An estimate of NOI may or may not include a replacement allowance. A brief summary outline for estimating NOI is shown below:

Potential Gross Income (PGI)		$20,000
Less Vacancy and Collection Loss (5%)		− $1,000
Effective Gross Income (EGI)		$19,000
Less Operating Expenses		
Fixed Expenses	$2,000	
Variable Expenses	$1,500	
Replacement Allowance*	$1,000	
Total Operating Expenses/Replacements		− $4,500
Net Operating Income (NOI)		$14,500

*May or may not be deducted

Income and Expense Ratios

Income and expense ratios are two ratios that could prove helpful to an appraiser in an analysis of a property's income and expenses. Each of the two ratios expresses a relationship to the estimated EGI of the property being appraised. They are the *net income ratio (NIR)* and the *operating expense ratio (OER)*.

a. The *net income ratio (NIR)* is the NOI generated by a property divided by its EGI; the reciprocal of the OER. In other words, the net income ratio is one minus the OER (1 − OER).

b. The *operating expense ratio (OER)* is the total operating expenses incurred by a property divided by its EGI; the reciprocal of the NIR. In other words, the OER is one minus the NIR (1 − NIR).

c. The *applicability of the income and expense ratios* is twofold. First, these ratios tend to be fairly consistent when truly comparable properties are compared. A knowledgeable appraiser may likely be able to identify potential problems when the ratio(s) for the property being appraised falls outside the *typical* range reflected by a comparable property(ies). Secondly, the ratios are often beneficial to the appraiser in selecting an appropriate GRM used to capitalize the estimate of PGI for the subject property. The two ratios (NIR and OER) derived for the subject property (from the appraiser's income and expense estimate) may be directly compared to the respective ratios estimated from the comparable sales.

Generally, the GRM and the NIR reflect a *direct* relationship, and the GRM and the OER reflect an *inverse* relationship. In other words, the higher the NIR, the higher the GRM; the higher the OER, the lower the GRM. These relationships are sensible because:

- a higher NIR translates into the owner retaining a higher percentage of collected income (i.e., lower operating expenses = higher NIR); therefore, the owner is willing to pay a higher multiple of PGI for the property because the property is less susceptible to expenses (and expense increases).

- a higher OER translates into the owner retaining a lower percentage of collected income (i.e., higher OEs = lower NIR); therefore, the owner is willing to pay a lower multiple of PGI for the property.

For example, assume the comparable sales reflect the following indications (data is arranged from highest to lowest NIR and lowest to highest OER):

No.	GRM	NIR	OER
1	6.5	58%	42%
4	6.2	55%	45%
3	5.9	54%	46%
2	5.4	51%	49%
5	4.8	48%	52%

Further, assume the NIR and OER for the subject were 52% and 48%, respectively. Based on the above data, a GRM between 5.4 and 5.9 would be reasonable.

PART FIVE Valuation by the Income Approach—Gross Rent Multiplier (GRM)

In the valuation of single-family residential properties, GRMs are more often used to estimate property value than the capitalization of NOI. Due to the similarities in the leasing structure of most residential properties, the proportion of net income collected by the landlord (as it relates to gross income) tends to be about the same (comparables versus subject) if truly comparable properties are being compared to the subject. Thus, the GRM can be a reliable method of valuation when adequate comparable sales are available.

■ PROCEDURE FOR ESTIMATING VALUE USING A GROSS RENT MULTIPLIER

The formula for deriving a value indication using a GRM is shown below:

$$\text{PGI of Subject Property} \times \text{GRM} = \text{Value Indication}$$

The procedure for using a GRM to arrive at a value indication is discussed below.

Estimation of Potential Gross Rent

One-half of the valuation equation when using a GRM stems from a reliable estimate of the potential gross rent for the property being appraised. The procedure for estimating potential gross rent for the subject property is summarized below:

Procedure

1. If applicable, analyze the present rental agreement for the subject property.

2. Obtain and verify comparable rentals, preferably from the same or similar neighborhood as the subject property.

3. Identify dissimilarities between the comparable rental properties and the subject property.

4. Adjust the monthly rent of the comparable rentals for dissimilarities in comparison to the subject property to arrive at a separate indication of market rent for the subject from each comparable rental.

   Elements of comparison considered in the market rent analysis include legal rights conveyed, conditions of rental (motivation of parties involved), market conditions, location, physical characteristics, and lease terms (who pays what expenses).

5. Reconcile the rent indications from the comparable rentals into a final conclusion of market rent (monthly) for the subject property.

For example, the property you are appraising is presently leased for $500 per month. A survey of the neighborhood yields two comparable rentals that are very similar to the subject property. Details of the two comparables are summarized below.

Comparable 1 presently rents for $435 per month with lease terms similar to the subject property. The physical characteristics of the comparable are similar in all respects to the subject except that the comparable has one less bedroom than the subject property. You estimate the additional bedroom of the subject is worth approximately $50 per month in the marketplace. Therefore, the adjusted monthly rent indication for the subject by Comparable 1 is $485 ($435 + $50).

Comparable 2 rents for $540 per month with lease terms similar to the subject property. The physical characteristics of the comparable are similar in all respects to the subject except that the comparable has one extra bathroom in comparison to the subject property. You estimate the additional bathroom of the comparable is worth approximately $30 per month in the marketplace. Therefore, the adjusted monthly rent indication for the subject by Comparable 2 is $510 ($540 − $30).

The present rent of the subject is $500 which appears well-supported in the marketplace (Comparables 1 and 2 indicate $485 and $510 per month, respectively, for the subject property); therefore, your market rent estimate for the subject is $500 per month.

Derivation of a Gross Rent Multiplier

The second one-half of the valuation equation when capitalizing with a GRM is the derivation of an appropriate GRM from comparable sales for application to the estimated potential gross rent of the subject property. The procedure for the derivation of a GRM is summarized below.

Procedure

1. Obtain and verify comparable sales, preferably from the same or similar neighborhood as the subject property, *which were rented at the time of sale*.

2. Divide the sales price of each comparable sale by its respective gross monthly rent to derive a GRM by each sale.

3. *Reconcile* the GRM indications from the comparable sales into an appropriate gross rent multiplier to be applied to the estimated potential gross rent of the subject property.

4. Notice the word *reconcile* in 3. An appraiser should not *adjust* GRMs. All other things being equal, GRMs will tend to be higher in more stable neighborhoods with higher occupancy rates. In other words, real estate investors are willing to pay a higher price

for gross rental income in stable neighborhoods than for a similar gross rental income stream in a less desirable neighborhood. There are other circumstances that influence gross rent multipliers discussed in more advanced books.

> In the previous example, the estimated potential gross rent of the subject property was reconciled at $500 per month. During your investigations, you obtain and verify three comparable sales. The sales price and potential gross rent (monthly) of each comparable is summarized:
>
> *Comparable 1* recently sold for $50,000 and was rented for $510 per month at the time of sale. The GRM thus approximates 98 ($50,000 ÷ $510).
>
> *Comparable 2* recently sold for $55,000 and was rented for $535 per month at the time of sale. The GRM thus approximates 103 ($55,000 ÷ $535).
>
> *Comparable 3* recently sold for $48,500 and was rented for $475 per month at the time of sale. The GRM thus approximates 102 ($48,500 ÷ $475).
>
> The GRMs indicated by the three comparable sales range from approximately 98 to 103. Based on these data, it appears an appropriate GRM would approximate 100.

Value Indication—Gross Rent Multiplier Method

As previously illustrated, the formula for estimating value by the gross rent multiplier method is simply the estimated PGI of the subject multiplied by an appropriate GRM. The procedure for arriving at a value indication using the Gross Rent Multiplier Method is summarized below.

Procedure

1. Multiply the estimated PGI for the subject property by the reconciled GRM.
2. If necessary, round the final value indication appropriately.

> In the two previous examples, the estimated PGI for the subject property and an appropriate GRM were reconciled at $500 per month and 100, respectively. Thus, the final value indication for the subject property by the Gross Rent Multiplier Method is $50,000 ($500 × 100).

■ APPLICABILITY AND LIMITATIONS OF GROSS RENT MULTIPLIERS

The gross rent multiplier method is a very simple technique to derive a value indication for the property being appraised when current, reliable, and accurate market data is available. This method of capitalization is the most straightforward technique of the three methods previously identified for the capitalization of income into a value estimate.

The gross rent multiplier method can be very reliable when the comparable sale's ratio of NOI to gross income is similar to the property being appraised. When the subject or comparable properties experience a dissimilar ratio level, the reliability of the Gross Rent Multiplier Method is diminished. A dissimilar ratio level may result when the comparable sales and subject property reflect different vacancy rates, different operating expenses, and/or dissimilar leasing structure.

1. Units of comparison used for the analysis of rental income for residential properties include
   a. rent per square foot of gross living area.
   b. rent per room.
   c. rent per month.
   d. all of the above.

2. In which of the following appraisal assignments would the Income Approach likely be considered a reliable indication of market value?
   a. Single-family home in a predominantly owner-occupied neighborhood
   b. Church facility
   c. Multitenant office building
   d. None of the above

3. Of the three methods available for the capitalization of income, which method is most applicable in a single-family residential appraisal?
   a. Gross rent multiplier (GRM)
   b. Direct capitalization
   c. Yield capitalization
   d. None of the above

4. Which of the following represents a method for estimating value by the Income Approach?
   a. Net operating income (NOI) divided by an overall capitalization rate
   b. Potential gross rent multiplied by an appropriate gross rent multiplier (GRM)
   c. Net operating income (NOI) multiplied by an overall capitalization rate
   d. A and B only

5. An operating expense ratio
   a. equals the total operating expenses divided by PGI.
   b. equals 1 minus the NIR.
   c. has a direct relationship with a GRM.
   d. includes all of the above.

6. The subject property is currently leased on a month-to-month basis to a college student from his grandmother for $425 per month. Homes similar to the subject typically rent for $550 per month in the neighborhood. The gross rent multiplier is 110. What is the market value indication for the subject property by the Income Approach?
   a. $46,750
   b. $64,000
   c. $45,000
   d. $60,500

7. The single-family house that you are appraising has been occupied by the owner for the past 25 years. The predominant occupancy of the subject neighborhood is by tenants. Which would likely be considered a reliable technique(s) for estimating market value of the property under these circumstances?
   a. Cost Approach
   b. Sales Comparison Approach
   c. Income Approach—Gross Rent Multiplier Method
   d. B and C only

8. The owner of the three-year old house that you are appraising was recently transferred to another state. In the interim, the owner elects to lease the property to a young professional. The house is located in an upscale, owner-occupied neighborhood adjacent to the municipal golf course. Which would likely be considered a reliable technique(s) for estimating market value of the property under these circumstances?
   a. Cost Approach
   b. Sales Comparison Approach
   c. Income Approach—Gross Rent Multiplier Method
   d. A and B only

9. You are appraising a vacant house. Market rent is estimated at $800 per month. A GRM of 100 is representative of the market. What is the value indication of the house?
   a. $96,000
   b. $80,000
   c. $6,700
   d. Cannot be determined because the house is vacant

10. Based on data in the previous question, if the effective gross revenue is $775 per month, what is the EGRM?
    a. 103.2
    b. 8.60
    c. 120.0
    d. Cannot be determined because the house is vacant

16

Reconciliation and Final Value Estimate

■ LEARNING OBJECTIVES

Students will be able to

1. recognize and understand the criteria of reconciliation.

2. recognize for each approach its appropriateness.

3. recognize for each approach its accuracy.

4. recognize for each approach its quantity of evidence.

5. select a final value estimate based on the appropriateness, accuracy, and quantity of evidence.

■ KEY TERMS

accuracy	final value estimate	reconciliation
appropriateness	quantity of evidence	

■ INTRODUCTION

Reconciliation is the section of an appraisal report in which the appraiser summarizes the value indications by the various approaches presented in the appraisal, reviews the methods and data used in arriving at the value indications, and *reconciles* the indications into a final estimate of value for the property being appraised. However, reconciliation occurs throughout a good appraisal report and requires sound judgment and logic by the appraiser. For instance, the appraiser will likely be required to reconcile when estimating reproduction or replacement cost new for the subject improvements, when estimating site value for the subject from comparable sales, when estimating potential rental income for the subject from comparable sales, etc. Of course, the ultimate objective of any appraisal assignment is to estimate a defined value in defined real property as of an effective date. To achieve this goal, the appraiser must reconcile the value indications from the applicable approaches to value (Cost, Sales Comparison, and Income Approaches) to arrive at a final value estimate for the property as of the effective date of appraisal.

P A R T   O N E   Criteria of Reconciliation

The criteria relied upon by the appraiser in the reconciliation process include appropriateness, accuracy, and the quantity of evidence. These criteria are used to analyze the value indication(s) from each applicable approach to value and to reconcile these indications into a final, defensible value estimate for the property being appraised. The appraiser should carefully consider the significance, applicability, and accuracy of each value indication within the appraisal report, and place primary emphasis on the approach or approaches which most accurately depict the reasoning and logic of potential purchasers in the marketplace. The criteria of reconciliation are discussed below.

■ APPROPRIATENESS

The criterion of **appropriateness** is used by the appraiser to (1) judge the relevance of each comparable property in comparison to the property being appraised, and (2) judge the applicability of each approach in light of the purpose and use of the appraisal.

For instance, assume the subject property is a residence located in a transitional neighborhood that is gradually changing from residential to commercial uses. Further, assume that after a thorough search for market data, two of the three comparable sales presented in the Sales Comparison Approach are houses located in the same transitional neighborhood as the subject, but the third comparable sale is a residence located in an established residential neighborhood with no commercial influence.

Based on the criterion of appropriateness, the appraiser would likely place primary emphasis on the two sales located in the same neighborhood as the subject that are influenced by surrounding commercial land uses. The potential buyers of the one comparable sale located in the established residential neighborhood may very well be different from those purchasers interested in the subject property and the two comparable sales.

The appropriateness of a particular approach to value is generally heavily related to the property type and/or the type of purchaser who would most likely buy the property being appraised. Depending upon these two factors, the appropriateness of the three approaches to value will differ from assignment to assignment.

For example, an older apartment complex or a multitenant office or retail facility would most likely be purchased by a real estate investor as opposed to an owner/user. Therefore, the value indication by the Income Approach would likely yield the most appropriate and reliable estimate of value while the value indication from the Sales Comparison Approach would likely provide added support. The Cost Approach, however, may reflect limited applicability in this appraisal assignment.

In the appraisal of a residential property, the Income Approach typically has very limited applicability when appraising a single-family residence located in a predominantly owner-occupied neighborhood (Scenario 1); however, the Income Approach is most appropriate when appraising a single-family residence located in a predominantly tenant-occupied neighborhood (Scenario 2). The primary difference in these two scenarios is that in Scenario 1, the most likely purchaser of the property would be an owner-occupant who would give very little or no consideration to the income-producing capabilities of the property. However, in Scenario 2, the most likely purchaser of the property may be a real estate investor who is primarily concerned with the income-producing capabilities of the subject property. The Income Approach would thus be given more weight in determining the final value estimate in Scenario 2 than in Scenario 1.

■ ACCURACY

The criterion of **accuracy** measures the appraiser's confidence in the precision, or *accuracy*, of the market data analyzed, the calculations performed in each of the approaches to value, and any necessary adjustments applied to the comparable properties for comparison with the property being appraised. At the time of reconciliation, appraisers should ask themselves questions regarding the accuracy of the data used in the appraisal assignment.

For example, during final reconciliation, an appraiser may question the accuracy of

- the site value conclusion as it relates to the value indication by the Cost Approach;
- the reproduction or replacement cost new estimate for the subject property;
- the accrued depreciation estimate for the subject property;
- the improved comparable sales and the necessary adjustments for dissimilarities;
- the estimate of potential rental income for the subject property;
- the estimate of vacancy and typical operating expenses for the subject property; and
- the capitalization estimates (i.e. gross rent multipliers, overall capitalization rates, etc.).

The accuracy and the appraiser's confidence in the market data analyzed to arrive at the value indications by the applicable approaches to value should influence the reconciliation process, and thus, the final selection of the defined value estimate.

■ QUANTITY OF EVIDENCE

The criteria of appropriateness and accuracy judge the quality and applicability of the value indications from the applicable approaches to value; however, these criteria should be analyzed in relation to the **quantity of evidence** provided by a specific comparable or approach. The lack of sufficient evidence may weaken the market data analyzed, and therefore, the value indication(s) derived by the approach(es) to value that relied upon the particular market data.

For example, assume you are analyzing three comparable sales of single-family residences in the Sales Comparison Approach, and you personally appraised and inspected two of the three properties. Suppose information on the third comparable was provided by a real estate broker and a distant inspection of the property from the street. Although the three properties are "appropriate" comparables and the information you have obtained is "accurate," in your opinion, you may place primary emphasis on the two comparable properties which you appraised and inspected because more complete data was available. The *quantity of evidence* regarding the third comparable sale is inferior in comparison to the other two comparables; therefore, you may likely have less confidence in the value indication by this comparable.

| P A R T   T W O   Selection of a Final Value Estimate |

A **final value estimate** is usually reported as a single dollar figure. Occasionally, it may be reported as a range. The selection of the final value estimate should reflect the appraiser's comfort level based upon the reconciliation criteria (appropriateness, accuracy, and quantity of evidence). If the appraiser is comfortable with the final value estimate, the estimate may likely imply greater precision than those times when the final value estimate is judged more subjective. Nevertheless, most clients typically require the appraiser to select a single dollar figure as the final estimate of value.

For example, assume you derived the following value indications by the three approaches to value:

Cost Approach	$125,000
Sales Comparison Approach	$115,000
Income Approach	$100,000

In your opinion, the Sales Comparison and Income Approaches reflect the most applicable indications of value for the subject property in this specific case. Depending upon your comfort level, you may report a final value estimate range of between $100,000 and $115,000, or select a single dollar figure of $110,000. The reconciliation criteria can assist the appraiser in determining his or her level of comfort.

Typically, the final value conclusion(s) is (are) rounded to reflect the lack of precision associated with each particular value estimate. Again, the appraiser's degree of comfort should be considered when rounding the final value estimate(s). For instance, a value conclusion of $146,125 may be rounded to $145,000 if the appraiser has a high level of confidence in the accuracy of the estimate. On the other hand, if the appraiser has only a moderate level of confidence in the accuracy of the estimate, he or she might round the final conclusion upward to $150,000.

As another example, suppose that all we know is that the value indications from five sales are $100,000 (Sale 1), $110,000 (Sale 2), $104,000 (Sale 3), $98,000 (Sale 4), and $108,000 (Sale 5). What is the value indication? It cannot be determined by the data. Yes, the average of the sale prices is $104,000, but suppose Sale 4 is next door and sold last week, while the other sales are from 1.0 miles to 2.0 miles away and sold from 2 months to 6 months ago. In this case, the value may very well be closer to $98,000, emphasizing Sale 4.

1. Reconciliation
   a. occurs throughout the entire appraisal.
   b. is the final step in the valuation process.
   c. is both A and B.
   d. is none of the above.

2. The criterion of appropriateness is often influenced by
   a. the property type being appraised.
   b. the potential purchasers who would likely consider buying the property.
   c. the amount of reliable information available regarding a particular comparable sale.
   d. both A and B.

3. Assume you are appraising an older single-family residence in a predominantly owner-occupied neighborhood. Which of the three approaches to value would likely be most applicable in this assignment?
   a. Cost Approach
   b. Sales Comparison Approach
   c. Income Approach
   d. Highest and Best Use Approach

4. Assume you are appraising a three-year-old special-purpose property that is typically constructed for owner occupancy. In your investigations, you determine these properties are rarely leased or sold in the marketplace. Which of the three approaches to value would likely be most applicable in this assignment?
   a. Cost Approach
   b. Sales Comparison Approach
   c. Income Approach
   d. Highest and Best Use Approach

5. Assume you are appraising a new single-family residence in a rapidly developing, owner-occupied subdivision. Which of the three approaches to value would likely be most applicable in this assignment?
   a. Cost Approach
   b. Sales Comparison Approach
   c. Income Approach
   d. Both A and B

CHAPTER SEVENTEEN

Partial Interests

■ LEARNING OBJECTIVES

Students will be able to

1. understand and redefine the concept of a fee simple estate.

2. understand that a fee simple estate can be subdivided into various partial interests.

3. recognize the difference between a leased fee estate and leasehold estate.

4. understand other fractional or partial interests such as vertical interests and easements.

■ KEY TERMS

air right	leased fee estate	shop tenants
anchor tenants	leasehold estate	subsurface right
contract rent	market rent	vertical interests
easement	positive leasehold estate	

■ INTRODUCTION

The first step of the valuation process requires the appraiser to *define the appraisal problem*. Although most homeowners hold fee simple title to their property, appraisal of commercial properties (i.e., apartments, offices, retail centers, etc.) may require the real estate appraiser to understand partial interests in order to define the appraisal problem. Standard 1 of *The Uniform Standards of Professional Appraisal Practice (USPAP)* requires an appraiser to clearly identify within the appraisal report the property rights to be valued. Because many forms of real estate ownership and lease agreements involve less than the complete bundle of rights, valuations of partial interests are often required. Real property rights may be retained, sold, leased, or mortgaged. This Chapter focuses on the most common and basic types of partial or fractional interests typically encountered by a real estate appraiser.

P A R T   O N E   Fee Simple Estate

The most complete form of real property ownership is a *fee simple estate*; however, fee simple ownership is limited by the four powers of government, namely taxation, eminent domain, police power, and escheat, previously discussed in Chapter 2.

The fee simple estate is the property interest most frequently appraised in the valuation of single-family residential properties.

P A R T   T W O   Partial Interests Created by a Lease

When a lessor (owner) and lessee (tenant) enter into a lease agreement, the bundle of rights is divided or separated. A **lease** is a written contract whereby the rights to use and occupy a described property are transferred by the owner (lessor) to another party (lessee) subject to a predetermined rent and various terms and conditions for a specified period of time. The divided interests which result from a lease are the *leased fee estate* and the *leasehold estate*. These two estates continue for the term, or duration, of the lease agreement. The appraiser must analyze the financial arrangements stipulated within the lease agreement so as to value each interest created by the lease correctly and appropriately.

■ LEASED FEE ESTATE

The **leased fee estate** represents the lessor's, or owner's, estate. Whereas there can be multiple leasehold estates (created by subleasing the property), there can only be one leased fee estate. A leased fee estate is the interest retained by the owner/landlord in which the right to use and occupy the property has been transferred in a lease to another party. When a lease agreement is entered into, the lessor must surrender possession of the property to the tenant and abide by the terms and conditions set forth or stipulated within the lease.

The rights of the lessor, or owner, as they relate to market value (valuation of the leased fee estate) generally include: (1) the right to receive rent payments as stipulated by the lease agreement (contract rent) and (2) the right of repossession upon termination of the lease.

■ LEASEHOLD ESTATE

The **leasehold estate** represents the lessee's, or tenant's, estate. Through the process of subleasing the property (Tenant 1 leases to Tenant 2, etc.), more than one leasehold estate may be created. A leasehold estate encompasses the rights and interest of the tenant (lessee) that were conveyed within a lease from the owner/landlord (lessor). When a lease agreement is entered into, the lessee must pay rent consistent with the terms and conditions set forth by the lease, and upon termination of the lease, the lessee must surrender possession of the property to the lessor, or owner.

The rights of the lessee, or tenant, generally include: (1) the right to possess the property for the lease period, (2) the right to sublease the property unless otherwise stated within the lease agreement, and (3) the right to improve the property as agreed upon in the lease.

Valuation of the leasehold estate focuses upon the relationship between *contract rent* and *market rent*. **Contract rent** is the actual stated rental set forth in a lease. **Market rent** is the estimated amount of rent that a particular property would most likely achieve in an open market. The leasehold estate has a positive value when the contract rent is less than the market rent.

> For example, consider an anchored shopping center in an established urban neighborhood. The *anchor tenant* in this particular shopping center occupies approximately 60% of the center with the *shop tenants* occupying the balance, or 40% of the center. (Note: **Anchor tenants** typically *draw* patrons to a particular center that benefits the **shop tenants**. Therefore, anchor tenants generally pay less rent per square foot of leased space than *shop tenants*). Suppose there are five years remaining on the anchor tenant's lease, and that during the past several years, the local market has intensified and the success of the *shop tenants* are no longer dependent upon the anchor tenant. Thus, the landlord believes, if available, the anchor space could be divided and leased at a substantially higher rental rate than currently being paid by the anchor tenant, thereby increasing the net income and market value of the shopping center.

In the example above, the anchor tenant is paying a lower rent (contract rent) than is currently achievable in the open market (market rent). Hence, contract rent is less than market rent. The anchor tenant would thus have a positive leasehold interest in the property. If contract rent is greater than market rent, the leasehold estate will have a negative value.

The example above represents an actual situation where the landlord offered the anchor tenant over $500,000 in exchange for the anchor tenant's leasehold rights and immediate termination of the lease. The landlord's intention was to lease the anchor tenant space as additional *shop space* at a higher rental rate. The anchor tenant rejected the landlord's offer because its contract rent was substantially below current market rent. This is an example of positive leasehold interest.

In a **positive leasehold estate**, the value of the lessee's (or tenant's) interest is the present value of the excess rent (i.e., difference between contract rent and market rent) for the remainder of the lease term, plus options if applicable.

Generally, most residential leases are for a 12-month period or less. Therefore, the leases are so short that the leased fee interest is essentially the same as the fee simple estate, and the leasehold estate has no value.

P A R T   T H R E E   Other Fractional Interests

Other partial, or fractional, interests typically encountered by a real estate appraiser include *vertical interests* and *easements*.

■ VERTICAL INTERESTS

The fee simple estate of a property includes vertical interests based on the legal concept of land as a volume of space with boundless height and depth. Vertical interests may be further divided into the following two rights:

1   **Subsurface Rights**—A **subsurface right** relates to the right to use and profit from portions of the real estate under the surface of the land. The right to extract iron ore from below the surface is an example of the subsurface right. Another example would be the acquisition of a defined volume below the surface for installing a subterranean rail line in a central city.

2. **Air Rights**—The defined volume of space above the surface of the earth is an **air right**. These rights, however, are normally restricted to the extent of the air space controlled by the Federal Aviation Administration or other governmental agencies. Usually air rights also include some surface or subsurface rights known as *touch down rights*. A building constructed over an existing five-level parking lot in a central city is an example of air rights. These air rights will normally include the right to construct foundations adjacent to the parking deck (touch down rights).

■ EASEMENTS

An **easement** conveys the right to use part of the land for a specific purpose. Easements thus divide the bundle of rights. When a condemning authority needs work space to widen a road, a *temporary construction easement* is usually required; this conveys the right to work on the defined area for a specific period of time for the purpose of road reconstruction. The *use* may be conveyed in perpetuity or for a limited period of time. An easement can be created by a legal contract between two parties or through the exercise of eminent domain. The recipient of an easement is the beneficiary, while the grantor forfeits a property right. The value of an easement is typically determined by comparing the value of the grantor's property *before* forfeiting the easement with the value *after* the easement has been conveyed.

An example of a common easement is the right associated with the ingress and egress across one property for purposes of gaining access to another property. This type of easement is illustrated by the survey in Figure 17.1.

In Figure 17.1, the owner of Tract B has given an easement to the owner of Tract D. The owner of Tract D is therefore the beneficiary of the easement, and the owner of Tract B has forfeited a property right.

FIGURE 17.1 ■ Easement Example

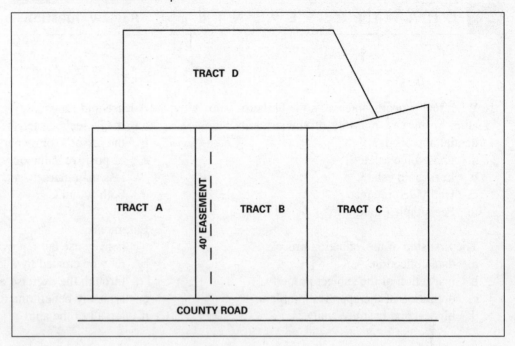

Another example of an easement may be a public utility company that acquires the right to locate underground or overhead utility lines across a property. This type of easement is common and often has little or no influence on property value.

1. What real property interest is the basis for valuation in the vast majority of single-family residential appraisals?
   a. Leased fee estate
   b. Leasehold estate
   c. Undivided interest
   d. Fee simple estate

2. The first step of the valuation process is
   a. data collection.
   b. inspection of the subject property.
   c. definition of the appraisal problem.
   d. highest and best use analysis.

3. A leased fee estate is
   a. the lessee's, or tenant's, interest.
   b. the lessor's, or owner's, interest.
   c. a right to use and occupy real estate for conditions conveyed by a lease.
   d. both B and C.

4. A leasehold estate is
   a. the lessee's, or tenant's, interest.
   b. the lessor's, or owner's, interest.
   c. of positive value only when contract rent is less than market rent.
   d. both A and C.

5. Easements
   a. convey use but not ownership.
   b. may be created by a legal contract or through the exercise of eminent domain.
   c. typically benefit the recipient.
   d. are all of the above.

American Institute of Architects (AIA)
www.aia.org

American Society of Appraisers
www.appraisers.org

American Society of Farm Managers
and Rural Appraisers, Inc.
www.asfmra.org

American Society of Home Inspectors (ASHI)
www.ashi.com

Appraisal Foundation
www.appraisalfoundation.org

Appraisal Institute
www.appraisalinstitute.org

Appraisal Institute of Canada
www.aicanada.org

Appraisal Qualifications Board
www.appraisalfoundation.org/aqb.htm

Building Owners and Managers
Association International (BOMA)
www.boma.org

Bureau of Labor Statistics
http://stats.bls.gov

Bureau of Land Management
www.glorecords.blm.gov

Bureau of Transportation Statistics
www.bts.gov

Commercial Investment Real Estate Institute
www.ccim.com

Department of Housing and
Urban Development (HUD)
www.hud.gov

Department of Veterans Affairs (DVA)
www.va.gov

Environmental Protection Agency
www.epa.gov

Fannie Mae
www.fanniemae.com

Federal Deposit Insurance Corporation (FDIC)
www.fdic.gov

Federal Emergency Management Agency (FEMA)
www.fema.gov

Federal Reserve System (the FED)
www.federalreserve.gov

Freddie Mac
www.freddiemac.com

Ginnie Mae
www.ginniemae.gov

Internal Revenue Service (IRS)
www.irs.ustreas.gov

International Association of Assessing Officers
www.iaao.org

International Real Estate Digest
www.ired.com

Manufactured Housing Institute
www.mfghome.org

National Association of Home Builders
www.nahb.com

National Association of Independent Fee Appraisers
www.naifa.com

National Association of REALTORS® (NAR)
www.realtor.com

National Association of the
Remodeling Industry (NARI)
www.nari.org

National Association of Review Appraisers and
Mortgage Underwriters
www.iami.org/nara.cfm

National Safety Council
www.nsc.org

Office of the Comptroller of Currency (OCC)
www.occ.treas.gov

Real Estate Educators Association (REEA)
www.reea.org

U.S. Census Bureau
www.census.gov

U.S. Farm Service Agency
www.fsa.usda.gov

■   **LAND AND SITE VALUATION**

Classroom Problems

1.   You have been asked to appraise the last remaining vacant site in an older established residential neighborhood. A search for recent sales of comparable vacant sites was unsuccessful; however, you were able to find and verify five recent sales of improved properties that were situated on a similar site in comparison to the subject property. The sale prices of the five improved comparables were $72,000, $75,000, $76,500, $70,000, and $74,500. From conversations with local building contractors and real estate brokers, you determine that a ratio of 20% of the eventual sales price should be allocated to the land.

What is a reasonable site value range given this market data using the allocation method?

2.   You have been asked to appraise a vacant building site located in an older residential neighborhood. While there were no recent comparable sales of vacant building sites in the area, you did locate and verify three recent comparable sales of improved properties on similar lots in comparison to the subject property.

Comparable 1 sold recently for $125,000. You estimate the reproduction cost of the improvements at $130,000, and the accrued depreciation at 25% as of the date of sale.

Comparable 2 sold recently for $151,000. You estimate the reproduction cost of the improvements at $125,000. Because the improvements were new and functional, you estimate there was no depreciation evident at the time of sale.

Comparable 3 sold recently for $132,000. You estimate the contributory value (or depreciated value) of the improvements at $104,000.

What is a reasonable site value for the subject given this market data using the extraction method?

3.   The subject site is located at the corner of Park Street and Garden Boulevard. The site features a rectangular shape and a gently sloping topography. From your investigations, you find and verify the four following comparable sales. All sales are similar with regard to property rights conveyed, financing, conditions of sale and market conditions. The only dissimilar elements of comparison between the comparables and subject property are location (corner versus interior), shape

(rectangular versus irregular), and topography (gently sloping versus steep). The specific data on the comparable sales are summarized:

Comparable 1 features a corner location, an irregular shape, and a steeply sloping topography. This site sold for $15,000.

Comparable 2 features a corner location, a rectangular shape, and a steeply sloping topography. This site sold for $18,000.

Comparable 3 features an interior location, a rectangular shape, and a steeply sloping topography. This site sold for $20,000.

Comparable 4 features a corner location, an irregular shape, and a gently sloping topography. This site sold for $17,000.

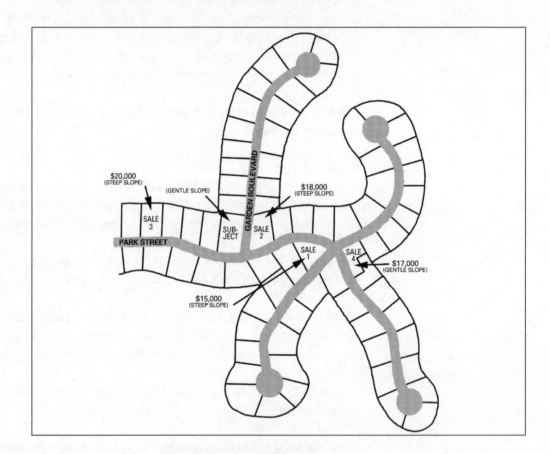

What is a reasonable value indication for the subject site by the Sales Comparison method? (Hint: Adjustments are derived by "matched pair" analysis)

Homework Problems

1. You have been asked to appraise the last remaining vacant site in an older established residential neighborhood. A search for recent sales of comparable vacant sites was unsuccessful; however, you were able to find and verify five recent sales of improved properties that were situated on a similar site in comparison to the subject property. The sale prices of the five improved comparables were $120,000, $123,000, $118,000, $154,000, and $156,000. From conversations with local building contractors and real estate brokers, you determine that a ratio of 20% of the eventual sales price should be allocated to the land for properties ranging in value from $110,000 to $130,000, and that a ratio of 15% is appropriate for properties ranging in value from $130,001 to $160,000.

    What is a reasonable site value range given this market data using the allocation method?

2. You have been asked to appraise a vacant building site located in an older residential neighborhood. While there were no recent comparable sales of vacant building sites in the area, you did locate and verify three recent comparable sales of improved properties on similar lots in comparison to the subject property.

    Comparable 1 sold recently for $160,000. You estimate the reproduction cost of the improvements at $156,000 and the accrued depreciation at 20% as of the date of sale.

    Comparable 2 sold recently for $152,000. You estimate the contributory value (or depreciated value) of the improvements at $116,000.

    Comparable 3 sold recently for $184,000. You estimate the reproduction cost of the improvements at $148,000. Because the improvements were new and functional, you estimate there was no depreciation evident at the time of sale.

    What is a reasonable site value for the subject given this market data using the extraction method?

3. The subject site is a wooded building lot that fronts on a municipal golf course and has adequate drainage. From your investigations, you find and verify the four following comparable sales. All sales are similar with regard to property rights conveyed, financing, and conditions of sale. Sale 1, however, sold approximately one year ago; values have increased approximately 10% since that time. All other comparables are recent transactions.

    The only dissimilar elements of comparison between the comparables and the subject property are location (golf front versus non-golf), drainage (adequate versus problems), and coverage (wooded versus open).

    Comparable 1 is an open golf front lot with adequate drainage. This site sold one year ago for $40,000.

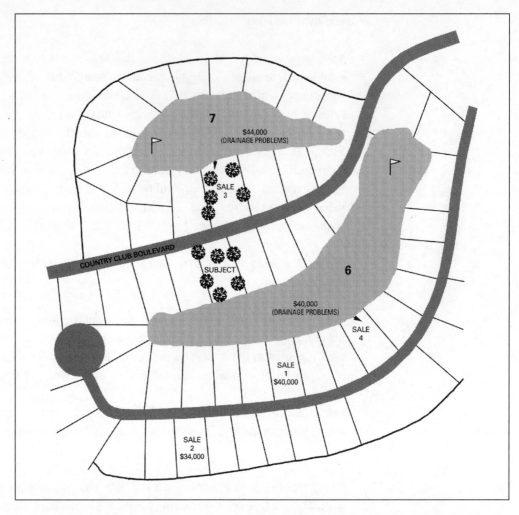

Comparable 2 is an open non-golf lot with adequate drainage. This site sold recently for $34,000.

Comparable 3 is a wooded golf front lot with noted drainage problems. This site sold recently for $44,000.

Comparable 4 is an open golf front lot with noted drainage problems. This site sold recently for $40,000.

What is a reasonable value indication for the subject site by the Sales Comparison method? (Hint: Adjustments are derived by *matched pair* analysis)

■   **COST ESTIMATION**

Classroom Problems

1. You are asked to appraise a two-story residence containing 1,950 square feet of gross living area. The subject property contains four bedrooms and two-and-one-half baths with a two-car attached garage. The improvements are situated on an approximate two-acre site in a new rapidly developing subdivision.

In your search for market data, you find three closed sales of new comparable two-story residences located in the subject subdivision. All of the comparable sales contained four bedrooms, two-and-one-half baths, and a two-car attached garage similar to the subject. Verification of the three recent comparable sales revealed the following:

Comparable 1 represents the sale of a 2,050 square foot house situated on an approximate three-acre site. The residence sold for $164,500.

Comparable 2 represents the sale of an 1,850 square foot house situated on an approximate one-and-one-half-acre site. The residence sold for $138,500.

Comparable 3 represents the sale of a 1,975 square foot house situated on an approximate two-acre site. The residence sold for $150,000.

Market data in your files suggest that small acreage tracts (one to five acres) generally sell for approximately $10,000 per acre.

a. What is the indicated cost new for the subject improvements by the comparative-unit method?

b. Assuming the subject property reflects no accrued depreciation, what is the indicated market value by the Cost Approach?

2.   You are asked to appraise a three-year-old, one-story home located in a steadily developing residential neighborhood. The subject house contains approximately 1,500 square feet of GLA, three bedrooms, and two bathrooms. Other distinguishing features include a one-car garage and fireplace. The improvements are situated on a typical subdivision lot that you estimate contributes $15,000 to property value.

In your search for market data, you find three closed sales of recently constructed, one-story residences located in the subject neighborhood. All of the comparable sales were similar quality, three-bedroom and two-bath homes situated on a typical $15,000 subdivision lot. Verification of the three comparable sales revealed the following:

Comparable 1 represents the sale of a 1,550 square foot house containing a two-car attached garage and a fireplace. The residence sold for $92,200.

Comparable 2 represents the sale of a 1,410 square foot house featuring a one-car attached garage but no fireplace. The residence sold for $81,750.

Comparable 3 represents the sale of a 1,495 square foot house containing a two-car attached garage but no fireplace. The residence sold for $88,400.

Based on several cost data sources, you estimate that a two-car garage costs about $3,500 more to construct than a one-car garage, and a fireplace costs approximately $2,000.

a. What is the indicated cost new for the subject improvements by the comparative-unit method?

b. Assuming you estimate accrued depreciation for the subject at approximately $5,000, what is the market value indicated by the Cost Approach?

Homework Problems

1. You are asked to appraise an average quality, one-story residence containing 2,275 square feet of gross living area. The subject property contains four bedrooms and three baths with a two-car attached garage. The improvements are situated on an approximate one-acre site in a steadily developing single-family subdivision.

    In your search for comparables, you find three closed sales of new, comparable one-story residences located in the subject subdivision. All of the comparable sales contained four bedrooms, three baths, and a two-car attached garage. Verification of the three recent comparable sales revealed the following:

    Comparable 1 represents the sale of a 2,150 square foot house situated on an approximate one-acre site. The residence sold for $136,750.

    Comparable 2 represents the sale of a 2,310 square foot house situated on an approximate one-acre site. The residence sold for $137,000.

    Comparable 3 represents the sale of a 2,350 square foot house situated on an approximate two-acre site. The residence sold for $147,750.

    Market data in your files suggest that one-acre sites generally sell for approximately $25,000, and two-acre sites for about $35,000.

    a. What is the indicated cost new for the subject improvements by the comparative-unit method?

    b. Assuming the subject property reflects no accrued depreciation, what is the market value indicated by the Cost Approach?

2. You are asked to appraise a two-year-old, one-story home located in a steadily developing residential neighborhood. The subject house contains approximately 1,125 square feet of GLA, two bedrooms, and one bathroom. Other distinguishing features of the house include a fireplace and brick veneer exterior walls. The improvements are situated on a typical subdivision lot that you estimate contributes $12,000 to property value.

    In your search for market data, you find three closed sales of recently constructed one-story residences located in the subject neighborhood. All of the comparable sales featured two bedrooms and one bath and were situated on a typical subdivision lot ($12,000). Verification of the three comparable sales revealed the following:

Comparable 1 represents the sale of a 1,025 square foot house featuring a fireplace and wood siding exterior walls. The residence sold for $47,450.

Comparable 2 represents the sale of a 1,250 square foot house featuring brick veneer exterior walls but no fireplace. The residence sold for $52,300.

Comparable 3 represents the sale of a 1,100 square foot house featuring wood siding exterior walls and no fireplace. The residence sold for $46,900.

Based on several cost data sources, you estimate that a fireplace costs about $1,500 to install and brick veneer exterior walls cost approximately $2 per square foot more than wood siding.

a. What is the indicated cost new for the subject improvements by the comparative-unit method?

b. Assuming you estimate accrued depreciation for the subject at approximately $2,500, what is the market value indicated by the Cost Approach?

■   ACCRUED DEPRECIATION

Classroom Problems

1. The subject property is a 25-year-old residence that has been well maintained over the years. Accordingly, you estimate the effective age of the improvements at 20 years. As of the effective appraisal date, you estimate the reproduction cost new and the remaining economic life of the improvements at $150,000 and approximately 30 years, respectively.

    a. What is the implied total economic life of the improvements?

    b. What is the percentage amount of accrued depreciation for the subject improvements by the economic age-life method?

    c. What is the lump-sum dollar amount of accrued depreciation for the subject improvements?

    d. What is the contributory value (also known as depreciated value) of the improvements?

    e. Assuming a land value of $20,000, what is the value indication by the Cost Approach?

2. You are appraising a single-family residence that was constructed 10 years ago, and at the time, had a remaining life expectancy of 50 years. Based on your recent inspection of the residence, you determine the improvements suffer from approximately $5,000 in curable depreciation. By curing these items, you estimate the effective age of the improvements will approximate 5 years and the remaining economic life will be extended to 55 years. The current reproduction cost of the residence has reasonably been estimated at $80,000.

   a. What is the estimated cost new of the incurable components?

   b. What is the estimated percentage amount of accrued depreciation applicable to the incurable components?

   c. What is the lump-sum dollar amount of accrued depreciation estimated by the modified economic age-life method?

3. The two improved comparable sales that you are using as comparables in an appraisal report recently sold. Sale 1 sold for $112,000, and Sale 2 sold for $126,000. Based on recent land sales in the neighborhood, the site values for the two comparable properties were estimated at $30,000 each.

   Sale 1 reflects an estimated effective age of 11 years and an estimated reproduction cost new of $100,000.

   Sale 2 reflects an estimated effective age of 16 years and an estimated reproduction cost new of $128,000.

   You estimate the effective age of the subject property at 14 years and its reproduction cost new at $120,000. The subject site value is estimated at $32,000.

   a. What is the average annual rate of depreciation indicated by the two comparable properties?

   b. What is an appropriate percentage depreciation rate for the subject improvements considering the two comparable sales?

   c. What is the approximate lump-sum dollar amount of accrued depreciation applicable to the subject improvements by the market extraction or Sales Comparison method of estimating accrued depreciation?

   d. What is the value indication by the Cost Approach for the subject property?

4. You are appraising a 5-year-old residence and observe the following:

   • The roof has a total physical life of 20 years and a cost to replace of $5,000.

   • The appliances have a total physical life of 15 years and cost $3,000 to replace.

- The floor covering has a total physical life of 10 years and cost $7,000 to replace.

- The water heater has a total physical life of 10 years and cost $800 to replace.

You estimate the cost new and the remaining physical life of the residence at $150,000 and 45 years, respectively. Curable physical deterioration was estimated at $4,000. No functional or external obsolescence was noted as of the effective date of the appraisal report.

a. What is the total amount of short-lived incurable physical deterioration for the property?

b. What is the total amount of long-lived incurable physical deterioration for the property?

c. What is the total accrued depreciation by the breakdown method for the property?

Homework Problems

1. The subject property is a 10-year-old residence that has been poorly maintained over the years. Accordingly, you estimate the effective age of the improvements at 15 years. As of the effective appraisal date, you estimate the reproduction cost new and the remaining economic life of the improvements at $65,000 and approximately 35 years, respectively.

   a. What is the implied total economic life of the improvements?

   b. What is the percentage amount of accrued depreciation for the subject improvements by the economic age-life method?

   c. What is the lump-sum dollar amount of accrued depreciation for the subject improvements?

   d. What is the contributory value (also known as depreciated value) of the improvements?

   e. Assuming a land value of $20,000, what is the value indication by the Cost Approach?

2. You are appraising a single-family residence that was constructed 20 years ago and, at the time, had a life expectancy of 50 years. Based on your recent inspection of the residence, you determine the improvements suffer from approximately $10,000 in curable depreciation. By curing these items, you estimate the effective age of the improvements will be approximately 10 years and the total economic life will be 60 years. The current reproduction cost of the residence has reasonably been estimated at $120,000.

a. What is the estimated cost new of the incurable components?

b. What is the estimated percentage amount of accrued depreciation applicable to the incurable components?

c. What is the lump-sum dollar amount of accrued depreciation estimated by the modified economic age-life method?

3. Two improved comparable sales that you are using as comparables in an appraisal report recently sold. Comparable 1 sold for $95,000, and Comparable 2 sold for $93,500. Based on recent land sales in the neighborhood, the site values for the two comparable properties are estimated at $20,000.

   Comparable 1 reflects an estimated effective age of 6 years and an estimated reproduction cost new of $82,500.

   Comparable 2 reflects an estimated effective age of 17 years and an estimated reproduction cost new of $98,000.

   You estimate the effective age of the subject property at 8 years and its reproduction cost new at $90,000. The subject site value is estimated at $18,000.

   a. What is the average annual rate of depreciation indicated by the two comparable properties?

   b. What is an appropriate percentage depreciation rate for the subject improvements considering the two comparable sales?

   c. What is the approximate lump-sum dollar amount of accrued depreciation applicable to the subject improvements by the market extraction or sales comparison method of estimating accrued depreciation?

   d. What is the value indication by the Cost Approach for the subject property?

4. You are appraising a 2-year-old residence and observe the following:

   • The roof has a total physical life of 20 years and a cost to replace of $3,000;

   • The appliances have a total physical life of 12 years and cost $2,000 to replace;

   • The floor covering has a total physical life of 10 years and cost $4,000 to replace;

   • The water heater has a total physical life of 10 years and cost $600 to replace.

   You estimate the cost new and the total physical life of the residence at $60,000 and 50 years, respectively. Curable physical deterioration was estimated at $2,000. No functional or external obsolescence was noted as of the effective date of the appraisal report.

a. What is the total amount of short-lived incurable physical deterioration for the property?

b. What is the total amount of long-lived incurable physical deterioration for the property?

c. What is the total accrued depreciation by the breakdown method for the property?

■ APPLIED COMPARISON APPROACH

Classroom Problems

1. Complete the grid in the following three examples including an indication for the subject:

APARTMENT PROPERTY

Rental Number	Subject	1	2	3	4
Unit Type	2BR/2BA	2BR/2BA	2BR/2BA	2BR/2BA	2BR/2BA
Square Feet	950	917	850	770	1,003
Monthly Rent		$525	$535	$530	$520
Monthly Rent/SF					

APARTMENT PROPERTY

Rental Number	Subject	1	2	3	4
Unit Type	2BR/2BA	2BR/2BA	2BR/2BA	2BR/2BA	2BR/2BA
Square Feet	1,150	1,200	950	1,150	1,100
Monthly Rent		$600	$495	$585	$580
Monthly Rent/SF					

COMMERCIAL LAND

Sale Number	Subject	1	2	3	4
Date		3 Months	6 Months	4 Months	1 Month
Price		$120,000	$123,500	$115,500	$115,000
Square Feet	25,000	24,000	26,000	22,000	23,000
Front Feet	100	75	135	170	100
Price per Square Foot					
Price per Front Foot					

2. You are given the following report:

MARKET DATA GRID

Sale Number	1	2	3	4	5
Price	$200,000	$215,000	$185,000	$225,000	$210,000
Date of Sale (Market Conditions)	Current	Current	Current	Current	Current
Location/View	Interior	Lake View	Interior	Lake View	Interior
Physical Variances					
Site Size	.5 Acre	.5 Acre	.5 Acre	.5 Acre	1.0 Acre
Residence Size (Square Feet)	3,000	3,000	3,000	3,000	3,000
Bedrooms	4	4	4	4	4
Baths	2.5	2.5	2.5	2.5	2.5
Garage	Yes	Yes	No	Yes	Yes
Basement	Yes	No	No	Yes	Yes
Condition	Good	Good	Good	Good	Good

a. Solve the following:

Comparison	Dollar Adjustment
Location	
Site Size	
Residence Size	
Bedrooms	
Baths	
Garage	
Basement	
Condition	

b. Apply the extracted adjustments from Part A to arrive at a value indication for the subject property:

MARKET DATA GRID

Sale Number	Subject	1	2	3	4	5
Price	?	$200,000	$215,000	$185,000	$225,000	$210,000
Date of Sale (Market Conditions)	Current	Current	Current	Current	Current	Current
Adjustment:						
Location/View	Interior	Interior	Lake View	Interior	Lake View	Interior
Adjustment:						
Physical Variances						
Site Size	1.0 Acre	.5 Acre	.5 Acre	.5 Acre	.5 Acre	1.0 Acre
Adjustment:						
Residence Size (Square Feet)	3,000	3,000	3,000	3,000	3,000	3,000
Adjustment:						
Bedrooms	4	4	4	4	4	4
Adjustment:						
Baths	2.5	2.5	2.5	2.5	2.5	2.5
Adjustment:						
Garage	No	Yes	Yes	No	Yes	Yes
Adjustment:						
Basement	Yes	Yes	No	No	Yes	Yes
Adjustment:						
Condition	Good	Good	Good	Good	Good	Good
Adjustment:	___	___	___	___	___	___
Net Adjustment:	___	___	___	___	___	___
Indicated Value:		$	$	$	$	$

Homework Problems

1. You are given the following report:

MARKET DATA GRID

Sale Number	1	2	3	4	5
Price	$225,000	$200,000	$210,000	$215,000	$235,000
Date of Sale (Market Conditions)	Current	Current	Current	Current	Current
Location/View	Golf View	Interior	Golf View	Interior	Golf View
Physical Variances					
Site Size	1.0 Acre	1.0 Acre	1.0 Acre	1.0 Acre	1.0 Acre
Residence Size (Square Feet)	2,000	2,000	2,500	2,000	2,000
Bedrooms	3	3	3	3	3
Baths	2	2.5	2	2	2.5
Garage	Yes	Yes	No	Yes	Yes
Basement	No	No	No	No	No
Condition	Avg.	Avg.	Avg.	Avg.	Avg.

a. Solve the following:

Comparison	Dollar Adjustment
Location	
Site Size	
Residence Size	
Bedrooms	
Baths	
Garage	
Basement	
Condition	

b. Apply the extracted adjustments from Part A to arrive at a value indication for the subject property:

MARKET DATA GRID

Sale Number	Subject	1	2	3	4	5
Price	?	$225,000	$200,000	$210,000	$215,000	$235,000
Date of Sale						
(Market Conditions)	Current	Current	Current	Current	Current	Current
Adjustment:						
Location/View	Golf View	Golf View	Interior	Golf View	Interior	Golf View
Adjustment:						
Physical Variances						
Site Size	1.0 Acre	1.0 Acre	1.0 Acre	1.0 Acre	1.0 Acre	1.0 Acre
Adjustment:						
Residence Size						
(Square Feet)	2,500	2,000	2,000	2,000	2,500	2,000
Adjustment:						
Bedrooms	3	3	3	3	3	3
Adjustment:						
Baths	2.5	2	2.5	2	2	2.5
Adjustment:						
Garage	No	Yes	Yes	No	Yes	Yes
Adjustment:						
Basement	No	No	No	No	No	No
Adjustment:						
Condition	Avg	Avg.	Avg.	Avg.	Avg.	Avg.
Adjustment:						
Net Adjustment:						
Indicated Value:		$	$	$	$	$

◼ INCOME APPROACH

Classroom Problems

1. You are appraising a small apartment complex containing 20 two-bedroom units. From your investigation of the market, you estimate a two-bedroom apartment similar to the subject units commands a rent of $700 per month. Vacancy and collection loss rates are estimated at 10% and 2% of PGI, respectively, based on similar apartment projects in the area. Operating expenses for similar projects typically approximate 40% of EGI which is in line with historical expenses at the property being appraised.

    a. What is the annual PGI for the subject property?

    b. What is the estimated EGI for the subject property?

    c. What is the approximate amount of operating expenses to be incurred at the subject property?

d. What is the approximate OER for the subject property?

e. What is the approximate NOI for the subject property?

f. What is the approximate NIR for the subject property?

2. You are appraising a single-family residence located north of the central business district. The subject house contains three bedrooms and features a fenced backyard.

Collection of market data has focused on two residential subdivisions where the economic, social, governmental, and environmental forces are fairly similar. Your investigations have revealed the following market data that you personally have verified with various parties. The market data has been organized in a market data grid shown below:

Element	Subject	Rental No. 1	Rental No. 2	Rental No. 3	Rental No. 4
Monthly Rent	—	$375	$425	$300	$325
Location	North	North	South	North	South
Bedrooms	3	3	3	2	2
Fence	Yes	No	Yes	No	No

To derive a GRM, your search for market data revealed the following comparable sales that were rented at the time of sale. The below sales are not the same properties used for the estimation of PGR above. The market data has been organized in a market data grid shown below:

Element	Subject	Rental No. 1	Rental No. 2	Rental No. 3	Rental No. 4
Sales Price	—	$52,000	$37,500	$35,000	$39,500
Monthly Rent $ (from A)		$620	$500	$485	$520
Location	North	South	North	North	North
Indicated GRM	_____	_____	_____	_____	_____

a. What is the estimated monthly rent for the subject property by these comparables using *matched pair* analysis?

b. What is an appropriate GRM applicable to the estimated potential gross rent of the subject property?

c. What is the value indication for the subject property by the gross rent multiplier method?

Homework Problems

1. You are appraising an apartment complex containing 200 total units; 80 one-bedroom units and 120 two-bedroom units. From your investigation of the market, you estimate one-bedroom and two-bedroom apartments similar to the subject units command a rent of $400 and $600 per month, respectively. Vacancy and collection loss rates are estimated at 5% and 1% of PGI, respectively, based on similar apartment projects in the area. Operating expenses for similar projects typically

approximate $3,000 per apartment unit which is in line with historical expenses at the property being appraised.

a. **What is the annual PGI for the subject property?**

b. **What is the estimated EGI for the subject property?**

c. **What is the approximate amount of operating expenses to be incurred at the subject property?**

d. **What is the approximate OER for the subject property?**

e. **What is the approximate NOI for the subject property?**

f. **What is the approximate NIR for the subject property?**

2. You are appraising a single-family residence located west of the city limits. The subject house contains three bedrooms and two bathrooms and features a two-car garage.

Collection of market data has focused on several residential subdivisions where the four forces influencing property values are fairly similar. Your investigations have revealed the following market data that you personally have verified with various parties. The market data has been organized in a market data grid shown below. All comparables have three bedrooms.

Element	Subject	Rental No. 1	Rental No. 2	Rental No. 3	Rental No. 4
Monthly Rent	—	$500	$425	$625	$500
Location	West	East	West	East	West
Bathrooms	2	1	1	2	2
Car Storage	2-Car	1-Car	1-Car	2-Car	1-Car

To derive a GRM, your search for market data revealed the following comparable sales which were rented at the time of sale. The sales below are not the same properties used for the estimation of PGR above. The market data has been organized in a market data grid shown below.

Element	Subject	Sale No. 1	Sale No. 2	Sale No. 3	Sale No. 4
Sales Price	—	$62,500	$60,000	$59,500	$75,000
Monthly Rent	$ (from A)	$635	$575	$600	$625
Location	West	West	West	West	East
Indicated GRM	____	____	____	____	____

a. **What is the estimated monthly rent for the subject property by these comparables?**

b. **What is an appropriate GRM applicable to the estimated potential gross rent of the subject property?**

c. **What is the value indication for the subject property by the gross rent multiplier method?**

C A S E   S T U D Y   1

128 Kentucky Avenue, NE

■ LEARNING OBJECTIVES

Students will be able to

1. apply the valuation process as it relates to a specific appraisal assignment.

2. perform a subject property inspection, gathering all appropriate information.

3. analyze the subject property related to its physical condition, functional utility, and external concerns.

4. analyze the applicable market area.

5. extract market adjustments.

6. apply the cost approach including cost, depreciation, and land value.

7. perform the proper reconciliation of the approaches to value.

8. prepare a Fannie Mae appraisal form.

■ BACKGROUND

You are part owner in a small independent fee appraisal shop with four active appraisers and one support staff person. You have been in business for approximately 30 years in Gardendale, Brickton County, have been active in the professional organizations, and currently hold the certified general designation of your particular state. You have appraised all types of real estate in the past but prefer to focus on single-family residential properties within your particular home county.

■ CITY/COUNTY

You live in a midsize southeastern city in the United States named Gardendale. The city contains about 50,000 people, while the county contains an additional 150,000 people. The city lies about 100 miles from any major metropolitan area. Its economic base is fairly diversified, although it primarily relies on industry for its employment base. Employment has shifted from textile manufacturing to a more diversified base with a particular emphasis on high-tech industrial manufacturing over the last 10 years to 20 years. The population has been increasing steadily at about 2 percent to 3 percent per year. One interstate highway traverses the eastern limits of this city, and several U.S. and state routes intersect within the corporate limits.

Unemployment has been around 4 percent to 5 percent over the last 10 to 20 years, slightly less than the state average overall. A continuation of the stability in employment and steady growth in the population base is anticipated over the next several years.

■ ASSIGNMENT

You have been called by a local lending institution to appraise a single-family residential property in an older, in-town neighborhood for mortgage loan purposes. The owner does not intend to sell the home but has lived in the home for approximately ten years and is refinancing in order to procure funds for college education expenses. You are asked to complete the appraisal on the Fannie Mae Form 1004 6-93.

■ SUBJECT

The subject property is located at 128 Kentucky Avenue, NE, about 5.0 miles northeast of the central business district. The property lies just off Lanier Boulevard, a major collector road that serves the northeast section of the city, leading to the downtown area.

You call the owner and arrange an inspection, which is scheduled for the next day.

■ SUBJECT PROPERTY

The client furnishes a recently completed "Plat/Site Plan," included as Exhibit I in this case study. The street address is 128 Kentucky Avenue, NE. You identify the subject property related to its geographic location on the Area Map, included as Exhibit II.

During your inspection of the property, you measure and do an interior layout sketch of the residence. The sketch, which will be included as part of the submitted appraisal report, is included as Exhibit III. After sketching the improvements, you complete a detailed checklist related to the physical characteristics of the residence and site, which is included as Exhibit IV.

The site is generally level at street grade with no apparent drainage problems or detrimental soil or subsoil conditions. There is perimeter landscaping around the residence as well as several trees to the rear of the residence. There are no low-lying areas or indications of any potential contamination. The subject has a typical view for the area, along an aesthetically pleasing, well-kept residential subdivision street. The driveway is concrete. A review of the Federal Emergency Management Agency (FEMA) map indicates that the subject is not located within a special flood hazard area.

The FEMA map checked was GZ000384, completed in November of the previous year. The site plan shows no easements, other than typical utility easements.

All utilities serve the subject, including electricity, gas, water, sanitary sewer, and telephone service. The street is well served by a storm sewer system. All utilities are public.

The street is asphalt paved with concrete curbs and gutters. There is no sidewalk, but the street is well lit with street lights.

The two-story residence was constructed about 30 years ago. Resting on a continuous wall concrete block foundation built over crawl space, the residence has brick over wood frame exterior walls and a gable roof with composition asphalt shingles and gutters and downspouts. The windows are double-hung, single pane with screens but no storm windows. There is no basement. It is centrally heated (gas fired, two units) and air-conditioned with two slab-mounted air-conditioning units. There is a small patio at the rear of the house.

Your inspection of the property indicates that there is no dampness in the crawl space or apparent settlement problems. There is also no evidence of insect infestation.

You consult the owner and find out that the roof cover was replaced about five years ago, the air-conditioning units were replaced about seven years ago, and one of the furnaces was replaced about two years ago. The entire exterior trim was repainted about three years ago.

The interior is well kept with no obvious needed items of deferred maintenance such as painting, carpet replacement, etc. The interior walls are sheetrock. Insulation was noted in the ceiling and walls. Trim and finish are judged average.

Your overall assessment is that the residence is somewhat superior to typical residences in the neighborhood with regard to condition. The effective age is estimated at 20 years, and the total economic life is estimated at 50 years.

The interior floors are hardwood with some areas having received carpet cover. The bath floors are ceramic tile, with ceramic tile wainscot walls and tub/shower enclosures. The interior doors are hollow-core.

The kitchen has never been modernized, but is in very good condition. The refrigerator is freestanding, but there is a built-in range and double built-in oven, disposal, dishwasher, and vent hood with fan. A microwave oven is not permanently installed. There is a small attic storage area, accessible by a drop stair.

■ NEIGHBORHOOD

After leaving the subject, you spend about one hour driving and analyzing the area. You conclude that the neighborhood boundaries coincide with the original subdivision development. The neighborhood boundaries are delineated on Exhibit V.

The neighborhood is suburban in character and was about 90 percent built out during the initial development phase about 30 years ago. You find that the typical lots range in size from 0.4 to 0.75 acre and are arranged on the curvilinear subdivision streets, several of which end in cul-de-sacs. The homes are mostly two-story in design and are built in conformity with the rolling, wooded contours of the area.

The predominant zoning is R-100, a single-family classification that requires minimum lot width of 100 feet at the building line and minimum lot area of 15,000 square feet. The minimum residence size is 1,200 square feet, with front, side, and rear yard setbacks of 40 feet, 10 feet, and 30 feet, respectively.

Within the neighborhood, there are two small land tracts that have recently been sub-divided and rezoned for cluster-type development. These in-fill properties were bypassed by the original development trend because of their topographical problems, but they have become more desirable in recent years because of the scarcity of available land in this relatively close-in subdivision. These two land tracts were rezoned about two years ago and now support two small cluster-type subdivisions, one known as Princeton Oaks, the other known as Wood Creek.

You have done work in the subject neighborhood for a number of years. Based on your experience, conversations with brokers in the area, and your continuing analysis of sales data documented in the local multiple-listing service, you know that the neighborhood has always been desirable, with most homes generally selling in the three-month to six-month time period, assuming proper marketing. Supply and demand typically tend to be in balance. Prices in the older residences have generally ranged from $170,000 to $200,000. The two new "in-fill" subdivisions, however, reflect homes that are priced from $200,000 to $250,000, although the lots are much smaller than typical neighborhood lots. Virtually all residences are owner-occupied, and the only vacancies occur when homes are listed for sale. Typically, no more than 2 percent to 3 percent of the homes are listed in the neighborhood at any particular time.

Located along North Highland Avenue in proximity to the subject are neighborhood commercial uses, including strip shopping centers and a variety of freestanding commercial uses, such as branch banks, restaurants, and convenience stores. This commercial corridor has been relatively stable over the last 10 years to 20 years, consistent with the relative stability of the supporting residential base. There is virtually no multifamily development or duplexes in the vicinity of the subject.

No change in the land use pattern is anticipated over the next several years.

Property values have generally been increasing at a consistent pace, at to slightly below the rate of inflation over the last several years.

Your final conclusion is that the subject property reflects typical quality of construction compared to other residences in the area of the same age and vintage as the subject. It has received superior upkeep during the years and is in superior condition when compared to most residences in the area. As a consequence, the effective age is estimated at 20 years, compared to the chronological age of 30 years.

■ VALUATION METHODOLOGY

After analyzing the subject property related to the overall neighborhood, you decide that the Cost Approach is appropriate because of the effective age of the subject. You find that the area has been fairly active with regard to sales of residences; accordingly, the Sales Comparison Approach is deemed appropriate as a valid indicator of the market value of the property as improved. Because of the scarcity of rental data in the neighborhood, you decide that the Income Approach is inappropriate and exclude this approach from the appraisal.

■ MARKET DATA

Land

Because you decide the Cost Approach is appropriate, you begin your market investigations by trying to locate sales of vacant lots in the neighborhood. Because the area was approximately 90 percent built out during the initial development phase about 30 years ago, you find only one vacant lot sale that is located about one mile northeast of the subject. Occupying a typical fronting site, this lot became available because the residence was completely demolished by fire about two years ago. After a lengthy insurance settlement dispute, the original owner sold the lot about six months ago for $40,000. You interview the buyer and find that the sale was arm's length after the lot had been marketed for about four months. Because the foundation of the home was not demolished by fire and the utility lines were still in place, the buyer felt like a slight premium may have been paid for the lot because of the existing improvements. A plat of the lot that sold is included as Exhibit VI.

Further investigation into the neighborhood reveals that the two cluster-type subdivisions have been selling lots and homes over the past two years. You locate three current lot sales in Princeton Oaks and four lot sales in Wood Creek. The lot sales in Princeton Oaks range from 4,000 square feet to 5,000 square feet, and all sold for $40,000. Recent home prices in Princeton Oaks have ranged from $200,000 to $210,000. Wood Creek is a slightly higher priced subdivision. These lots are 6,000 square feet to 8,000 square feet in size. Current lot prices have averaged $50,000. Homes are currently selling in the $240,000 to $260,000 price range.

Cost Data

You keep an ongoing file of cost data related to construction costs for homes in your market area. You conclude that single-family residential dwellings such as the subject would likely cost $80 per square foot for the basic structure, including all direct and indirect expenditures. The garage reflects a cost of $30 per square foot, also including all direct and indirect expenditures. The estimated contribution of the site improvements is $5,000, including the driveway, landscaping, sidewalks, etc.

A reasonable allowance for entrepreneurial profit in your market area is 15 percent of all direct and indirect costs.

Residence Sales

After reviewing all data sources in your office, you find there have been 10 recent sales in the subject neighborhood that all occurred within the last 12 months. You locate these on a map and do a field inspection. From this field inspection, you then verify the five that you deem most appropriate and finally conclude that there are three most appropriate sales that you decide to analyze as direct indicators of the market value of the subject. These are identified as to location on Exhibit VII and summarized on Exhibit VIII. All data was confirmed with the broker involved in each transaction. All were cash to seller transactions with the buyer utilizing typical mortgage financing.

You have a file which you continually update related to adjustment extraction. From the paired sales analyses, you conclude that the following adjustments are appropriate in this price range in this market area:

Square Footage Adjustment	$20 to $25 Per Square Foot
Basement	$10 to $15 Per Square Foot
Good versus Very Good Condition	$5 to $7 Per Square Foot of Total Residence Area
Garage	$6,000
Pool	$3,000

■ VALUATION

Complete the Fannie Mae Form 1004 6-93.

EXHIBIT I ■ Plat Site Plan

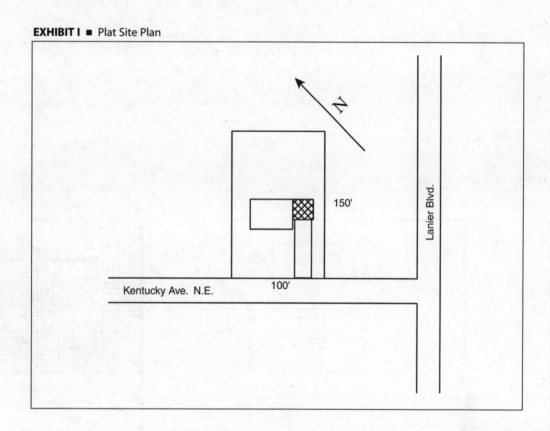

EXHIBIT II ■ Area Map

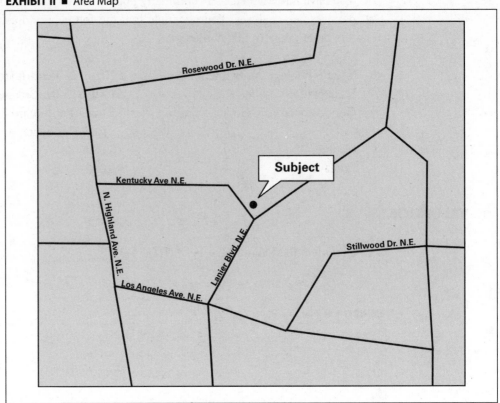

EXHIBIT III-A ■ Floor Plan: First Floor

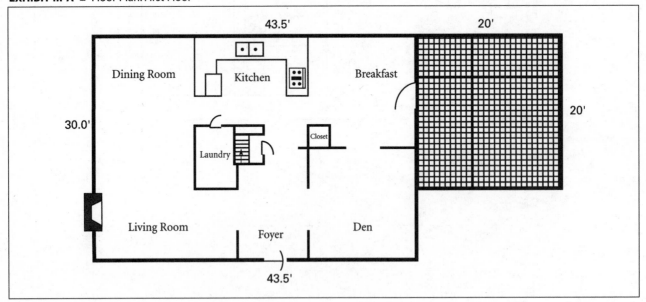

EXHIBIT III-B ■ Floor Plan: Second Floor

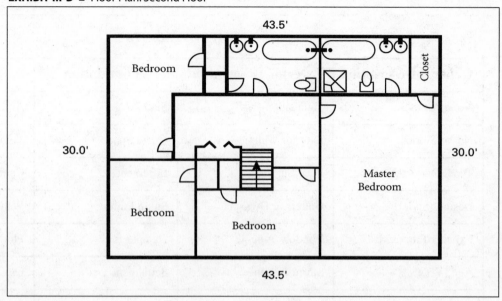

EXHIBIT IV-A ■ Inspection Check List: Site

SITE

Location:	
Dimensions:	
Area:	
Topography:	
Shape:	
Drainage:	
View:	
Landscaping:	
Driveway Surface:	
Apparent Easements:	
Low-Lying Areas:	
Utilities—	
Electricity:	
Gas:	
Water:	
Sanitary Sewer:	
Street	
Curb/Gutter:	
Sidewalk:	
Street Lights:	
Alley:	

EXHIBIT IV-B ■ Inspection Check List: Improvements

IMPROVEMENTS

General Description	Exterior Description	Foundation	Basement
No. of Units	Foundation	Slab	Area Sq. Ft.
No. of Stories	Exterior Walls	Crawl Space	% Finished
Type (Det./Att.)	Roof Surface	Basement	Ceiling
Design (Style)	Gutters & Dwnspts.	Sump Pump	Walls
Existing/Proposed	Window Type	Dampness	Floor
Age (Yrs.)	Storm/Screens	Settlement	Outside Entry
Effective Age (Yrs.)	Manufactured House	Infestation	

Insulation	Interior (Materials/Condition)	Heating	Cooling
Roof	Floors	Type	Central
Ceiling	Walls	Fuel	Other
Walls	Trim/Finish	Condition	Condition
Floor	Bath Floor		
None	Bath Wainscot		
Unknown	Doors		

Kitchen Equipment	Attic	Amenities	Car Storage
Refrigerator	None	Fireplace(s) #	None
Range/Oven	Stairs	Patio	Garage # of cars
Disposal	Drop Stair	Deck	Attached
Dishwasher	Scuttle	Porch	Detached
Fan/Hood	Floor	Fence	Built In
Microwave	Heated	Pool	Carport
Washer/Dryer	Finished		Driveway

EXHIBIT V ■ Neighborhood Map

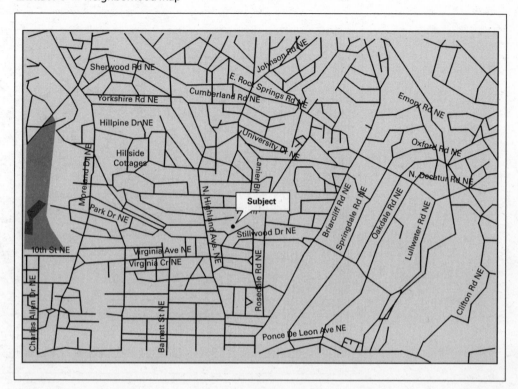

EXHIBIT VI ■ Lot Sale 1

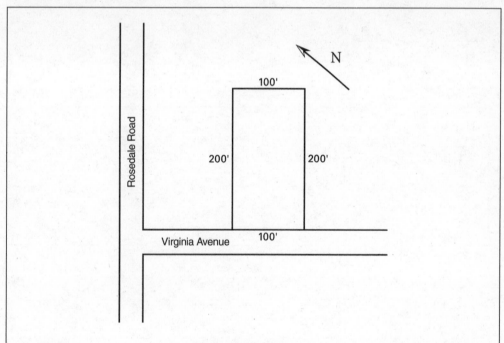

Location:	North side of Virginia Avenue just east of Rosedale Road.
Seller (Grantor):	Richard Simpson
Buyer (Grantee):	Greg Builder
Date:	April 6, 1998
Price:	$40,000
Financing:	Cash to Seller
Size:	0.45 Acres
Remarks:	Buyer indicated that the prior residence was gutted by a fire and razed prior to sale date.

EXHIBIT VII ■ Sale Location Map

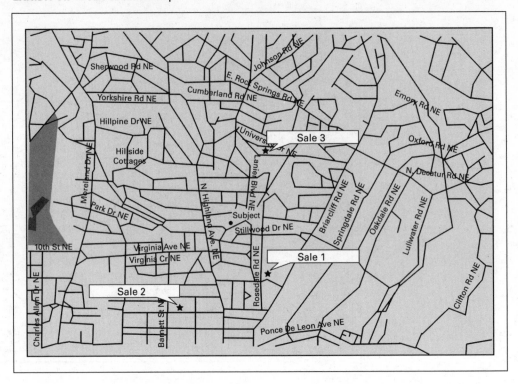

EXHIBIT VIII ■ Improved Sales Locations

IMPROVED SALES LOCATIONS

Item	Subject			Comparable No. 1			Comparable No. 2			Comparable No. 3		
Address	128 Kentucky Avenue, NE			148 Johnson Street			152 Mitchell Street			119 Cantrell Street		
Proximity to Subject												
Sales Price				$180,000			$189,000			$198,000		
Data and/or Verification Sources				Broker			Broker			Broker		
Value Adjustments	**Description**			**Description**			**Description**			**Description**		
Sales or Financing Concessions				Cash			Cash			Cash		
Date of Sale/Time				Current			Current			Current		
Site Size	15,000 Square Feet			15,000 Square Feet			15,000 Square Feet			15,000 Square Feet		
View	Good			Good			Good			Good		
Design and Appeal	Good/Typical			Good/Typical			Good/Typical			Good/Typical		
Quality of Construction	Good			Good			Good			Good		
Age	30 Years			30 Years			29 Years			31 Years		
Condition	Very Good			Good			Very Good			Very Good		
Above Grade	Total	Bedrooms	Baths	Total	Bedrooms	Baths	Total	Bedrooms	Baths	Total	Bedrooms	Baths
Room Count	8	4	2.5	7	4	2.5	7	4	2.5	7	4	2.5
Gross Living Area	2,610 Square Feet			2,550 Square Feet			2,610 Square Feet			2,750 Square Feet		
Basement and Finished Rooms Below Grade	None			None			None			None		
Functional Utility	Good			Good			Good			Good		
Heating/Cooling	Central			Central			Central			Central		
Energy Efficient Items	Typical			Typical			Typical			Typical		
Garage/Carport	2-Car Garage			2-Car Garage			None			2-Car Garage		
Porch, Patio, Deck, Fireplace(s), etc.	Patio			Patio			Patio			Patio		
Fence, Pool, etc.	None			None			None			Pool		

CASE STUDY 2

722 Black Fox Drive, NE

■ LEARNING OBJECTIVES

Students will be able to

1. apply the valuation process as it relates to a specific appraisal assignment.

2. perform a subject property inspection, gathering all appropriate information.

3. analyze the subject property related to its physical condition, functional utility, and external concerns.

4. analyze the applicable market area.

5. recognize and measure through market activity the financial feasibility of a construction option (enclosed carport).

6. extract market adjustments.

7. apply the cost approach including cost, depreciation, and land value.

8. perform the proper reconciliation of the approaches to value.

9. prepare a Fannie Mae appraisal form.

■ BACKGROUND

You are a staff appraiser in a small appraisal department owned by a local lending institution. Your specialty is single-family residential, and you primarily work the five major counties comprising a major metropolitan area. The entire metro area includes about two million people in the southeastern part of the United States.

The economy is fairly well diversified. The city is primarily a distribution center and financial center, although there is a substantial amount of high-tech manufacturing. Associated retail services and government employment are well in balance.

Although there is a central city, major employment in recent years has shifted to northern sections of a perimeter loop road that encircles this city, and this has led to substantial suburbanization over the last 20 years to 40 years.

■ ASSIGNMENT

You have been asked to appraise a single-family residential home in an older, suburban section of the metropolitan area. One of the first counties to experience suburbanization, Smith County, the county in which your subject property lies, has been fairly stable over the last 20 years to 30 years since the initial surge about 30 years to 40 years ago.

■ SUBJECT PROPERTY

The subject property is a 20-year old, single-family, one-story residence situated on an approximate 11,250 square foot lot along a curvilinear subdivision street. The street address is 722 Black Fox Drive, NE.

You call the owner and arrange an inspection, which is scheduled for the next day.

In the loan package sent to you, you have a recently completed Plat/Site Plan, included as Exhibit I in this case study. You identify the subject property related to its geographic location on the Area Map, included as Exhibit II.

You begin your inspection by measuring the house and notice that the old carport has been enclosed and is now part of the finished area. After sketching the improvements, detailed on Exhibit III, you complete a detailed checklist related to the physical characteristics of the residence and site, included as Exhibit IV.

The site is gently rolling and slightly above street grade. Your observation indicates that there is a small drainage problem toward the rear, but this could easily be accommodated with minor grading and regrassing. Otherwise, you observe no apparent detrimental soil or subsoil conditions or evidence of any site contamination. The residence is circumscribed by typical low-level foliage.

The subject has a typical view along the aesthetically pleasing subdivision street which is well kept. The driveway is concrete. You review the Federal Emergency Management Agency (FEMA) map, and find that the subject is not located within a special flood hazard area. The FEMA map is Number GZ00921, completed in December of the previous year. The site plan shows typical utility easements but no unusual easements otherwise.

The subject site is served by all publicly owned utilities, including electricity, natural gas, water, sanitary sewer, and telephone service. The street drains well by a storm sewer system. All utilities are underground.

The two-lane asphalt-surfaced street is served by sidewalks and is well lit.

The one-story ranch residence was constructed about 20 years ago. During the development period, three basic floor plans were constructed within the subdivision, and there is good uniformity among the residences.

The residence rests on a concrete block foundation built over a crawl space. The exterior is wood siding over wood frame. The gable roof is covered with composition asphalt shingles with gutters and downspouts. The windows are double-hung, single-pane, with screens. There is no basement. There is a small patio off the rear of the house.

The house is centrally heated with a gas-fired system that was replaced about five years ago, and the air conditioning is central with a slab-mounted single unit. The air conditioning compressor was replaced about seven years ago. All systems were reported to be in good working condition. You noted insulation in the ceiling and walls.

You inspect the crawl space and observe no dampness or settlement problems. You also note no evidence of insect infestation.

Consulting with the owner, you discover that the roof cover is about three years old, and the entire exterior was painted about five years ago.

The interior is fairly well kept, but several items of deferred maintenance are observed. The interior needs painting, and the carpet is about ten years old and severely worn. The kitchen has never been modernized, but it is in fairly good condition. The refrigerator is freestanding and is not considered part of the real estate. There is a built-in range, disposal, dishwasher, and vent hood with fan. There is no microwave oven. The small attic storage area is accessible by a drop-stair system.

The interior floors are mostly plywood over wood joists, except in the bathrooms and kitchen. The baths and kitchen both have sheet vinyl. The tub/shower combinations are fiberglass. The interior doors are hollow core, and the interior walls are sheetrock. The inside trim and finish are rated average.

Your overall assessment is that the residence is somewhat below the typical neighborhood residence with regard to overall condition because of its deferred maintenance. You estimate that all items of deferred maintenance could be corrected for about $3,000. In its "as is" condition, the effective age is estimated at 25 years, and the total economic life is estimated at 50 years. After restoration of the items of deferred maintenance, however, the effective age would be reduced to 20 years, more in line with the typical residences in the neighborhood.

◼ NEIGHBORHOOD

After driving away from the subject, you spend about 45 minutes driving the subject area and conclude that the neighborhood boundaries are basically as identified on Exhibit V. The neighborhood is typical of other suburban neighborhoods that were developed during the initial suburbanization phase in this metropolitan area about 20 years ago. During that time, about 90 percent to 95 percent of the available single-family land was built out with single-family subdivisions ranging from 50 lots to 150 lots. The typical lots range in size from about 0.23 to 0.5 acre and are arranged on the curvilinear subdivision streets with cul-de-sacs.

The homes are generally one of three floor plans as the builder in this neighborhood was more of a tract-type developer. Most homes are one-story ranch, containing about 1,260 square feet, three bedrooms, and two baths. Many of the ranch dwellings have experienced enclosure of their carport areas into the finished living area. There are also a number of split-levels and two-story residences, although the predominant residence is ranch in design.

The predominant zoning is R-75. This single-family residential classification requires a minimum lot width of 75 feet at the building line and minimum lot area of 10,000 square feet. The minimum residence size is 1,000 square feet. The front, side, and rear yard setbacks are 40 feet, 10 feet, and 30 feet, respectively.

Although the neighborhood was about 20 years old, there has been a shift in desirability back toward closer-in living, and a few lots that were never built on during the initial development phase have been selling. Also, several property owners who had purchased additional lots for expanded yard areas several years ago have sold the excess lots, and they have been developed with single-family residences.

Neighborhood shopping is conveniently located, and the area is well served by a blend of private and public schools, parks, recreational amenities, and places of worship. There is virtually no multifamily development in the vicinity of the subject.

No change in the land use pattern is anticipated over the next several years. Property values have been increasing at a consistent pace, generally consistent with the rate of inflation over the last several years.

Your final conclusion is that the subject property reflects typical quality of construction compared to other residences in the area of the same age and vintage as the subject. It has received inferior upkeep during the years, however, with about $3,000 noted in items of deferred maintenance.

■ VALUATION METHODOLOGY

After analyzing the subject property related to the overall neighborhood, you decide that the Cost Approach is appropriate because of the effective age of the subject. You find that the area has been fairly active with regard to sales of residences, and the Sales Comparison Approach is deemed appropriate.

Only one or two rental properties were located in the neighborhood during your investigation, so you decided that the income approach is inappropriate and have excluded this approach from the appraisal.

■ MARKET DATA

Land

You are able to locate several lot sales that are identified as to location on Exhibit VI.

Sale 1 is located along a typical subdivision street in the neighborhood. It was originally part of a double lot that the original purchaser had bought as additional yard area. Six months ago, the owner sold the lot to an individual builder who constructed a new residence on the lot. The 75 foot by 100 foot lot is typical for the area as to topography, view, etc. It sold for $30,000, but no commission was paid in that the seller personally knew the builder who purchased the lot. Although they were acquainted and no real estate commission was paid, the purchaser stated that he felt the transfer was at market value.

Sale 2 is also a typical subdivision lot in the neighborhood. It contains about 30,000 square feet but is located on a cul-de-sac and backs up to a low-lying area adjacent to a creek, and part of the land area is located within a flood plain. The lot had inferior topography compared to most lots in the area, and it sold for $32,000 about three months ago.

Your conversations with the buyer disclosed that the purchaser had few available lots from which to choose in this neighborhood, and he wanted to be in the neighborhood because of the good school system, proximity to his employment, and other factors.

Sale 3 is a typical lot along an interior subdivision street in the neighborhood. The 75 foot by 100 foot lot sold about two months ago for $32,500. It is typical for the area. It was purchased by a local builder who intends to construct a residence on the lot for his own occupancy.

Cost Data

You keep an ongoing file of cost data related to construction costs for homes in your market area. You conclude that single-family dwellings such as the subject would likely cost $70 per square foot for the basic structure, including all direct and indirect expenditures. The carport reflects a cost of $20 per square foot, also including all direct and indirect expenditures. Site improvements contribute an estimated $5,000 to value, including the driveway, landscaping, etc.

A reasonable allowance for entrepreneurial profit in your market area is 10 percent of all direct and indirect costs.

Residence Sales

You review all of the data sources in your office and find that there have been a number of sales in the neighborhood, but few have occurred recently. You locate these on a map and do a field inspection. In performing the field inspection, you are able to locate 16 sales, of which six are ranch-style residences like the subject and are deemed most appropriate. These are identified as to location on Exhibit VI and summarized on Exhibit VII.

All data was confirmed with the broker involved. All were cash to seller transactions with the buyer utilizing typical mortgage financing.

You have a file that you continually update related to adjustment extraction. From the paired sales analysis, you conclude that the following adjustments are appropriate in this price range in this market area:

Square Footage Adjustment	$40 to $45 Per Square Foot
Basement	$10 to $15 Per Square Foot
Average versus Good Condition	$2 to $3 Per Square Foot of Total Residence Area
Single Carport	$1,000
Pool	$1,000

■ VALUATION

Complete the Fannie Mae Form 1004 6-93.

EXHIBIT I ■ Plat Site Plan

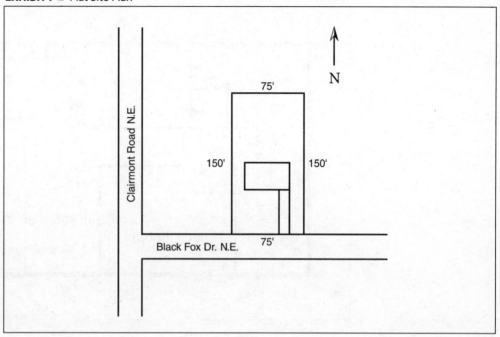

EXHIBIT II ■ Area Map

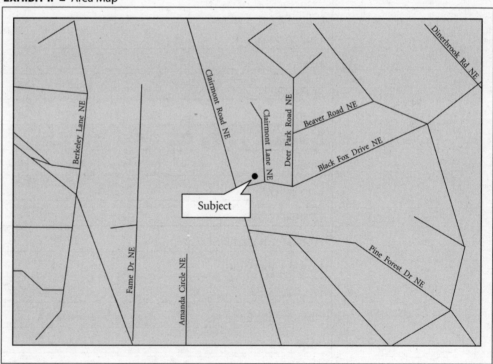

EXHIBIT III ■ Floor Plan

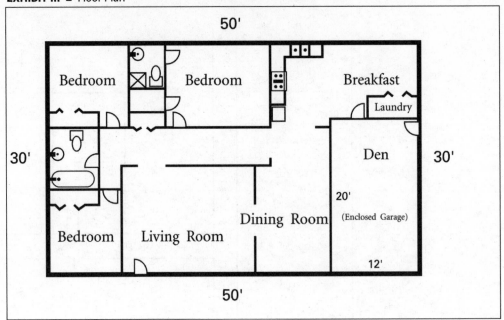

EXHIBIT IV-A ■ Inspection Check List: Site

SITE

Location:	
Dimensions:	
Area:	
Topography:	
Shape:	
Drainage:	
View:	
Landscaping:	
Driveway Surface:	
Apparent Easements:	
Low-Lying Areas:	
Utilities—	
Electricity:	
Gas:	
Water:	
Sanitary Sewer:	
Street	
Curb/Gutter:	
Sidewalk:	
Street Lights:	
Alley:	

EXHIBIT IV-B ■ Inspection Check List: Improvements

IMPROVEMENTS

General Description	Exterior Description	Foundation	Basement
No. of Units	Foundation	Slab	Area Sq. Ft.
No. of Stories	Exterior Walls	Crawl Space	% Finished
Type (Det./Att.)	Roof Surface	Basement	Ceiling
Design (Style)	Gutters & Dwnspts.	Sump Pump	Walls
Existing/Proposed	Window Type	Dampness	Floor
Age (Yrs.)	Storm/Screens	Settlement	Outside Entry
Effective Age (Yrs.)	Manufactured House	Infestation	

Insulation	Interior (Materials/Condition)	Heating	Cooling
Roof	Floors	Type	Central
Ceiling	Walls	Fuel	Other
Walls	Trim/Finish	Condition	Condition
Floor	Bath Floor		
None	Bath Wainscot		
Unknown	Doors		

Kitchen Equipment	Attic	Amenities	Car Storage	
Refrigerator	None	Fireplace(s) #	None	
Range/Oven	Stairs	Patio	Garage	# of cars
Disposal	Drop Stair	Deck	Attached	
Dishwasher	Scuttle	Porch	Detached	
Fan/Hood	Floor	Fence	Built In	
Microwave	Heated	Pool	Carport	
Washer/Dryer	Finished		Driveway	

EXHIBIT V ■ Neighborhood Map

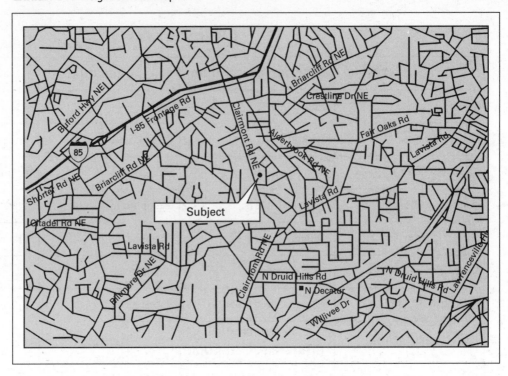

EXHIBIT VI ■ Sale Location Map

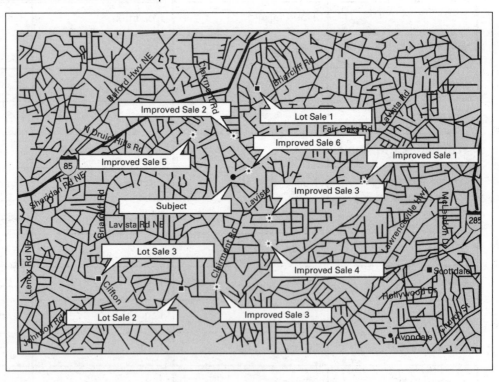

EXHIBIT VII ▪ Improved Sales Locations

IMPROVED SALES LOCATIONS

Item	Subject	Comparable No. 1	Comparable No. 2	Comparable No. 3
Address	722 Black Fox Drive, NE	819 Clinton Drive	816 Hillary Place	216 Washington Road
Proximity to Subject				
Sales Price		$86,000	$96,000	$85,000
Data and/or Verification Sources		Broker	Broker	Broker
Value Adjustments	**Description**	**Description**	**Description**	**Description**
Sales or Financing Concessions		Cash	Cash	Cash
Date of Sale/Time		3 Years	3 Years	3 Years
Site Size	11,250 Square Feet	11,250 Square Feet	11,250 Square Feet	11,250 Square Feet
View	Good	Good	Good	Good
Design and Appeal	Good/Typical	Good/Typical	Good/Typical	Good/Typical
Quality of Construction	Good	Good	Good	Good
Age	20 Years	20 Years	20 Years	20 Years
Condition	Average	Average	Average	Average

Above Grade	Total	Bedrooms	Baths	Total	Bedrooms	Baths	Total	Bedrooms	Baths	Total	Bedrooms	Baths
Room Count	7	3	2	6	3	2	7	3	2	6	3	2

Value Adjustments	Subject	Comparable No. 1	Comparable No. 2	Comparable No. 3
Gross Living Area	1,500 Square Feet	1,260 Square Feet	1,500 Square Feet	1,260 Square Feet
Basement and Finished Rooms Below Grade	None	None	None	None
Functional Utility	Good	Good	Good	Good
Heating/Cooling	Central	Central	Central	Central
Energy Efficient Items	Typical	Typical	Typical	Typical
Garage/Carport	Enclosed	Single Carport	Enclosed	Single Carport
Porch, Patio, Deck, Fireplace(s), etc.	Patio	Patio	Patio	Patio
Fence, Pool, etc.	None	None	None	Pool

EXHIBIT VII (CONT'D) ■ Improved Sales Locations

IMPROVED SALES LOCATIONS

Item	Subject	Comparable No. 4	Comparable No. 5	Comparable No. 6
Address	722 Black Fox Drive, NE	919 Victory Street	313 Lovely Lane	502 Gore Place
Proximity to Subject				
Sales Price		$103,000	$99,000	$93,000
Data and/or Verification Sources		Broker	Broker	Broker
Value Adjustments	**Description**	**Description**	**Description**	**Description**
Sales or Financing Concessions		Cash	Cash	Cash
Date of Sale/Time		Current	2 Years	Current
Site Size	11,250 Square Feet	11,250 Square Feet	11,250 Square Feet	11,250 Square Feet
View	Good	Good	Good	Good
Design and Appeal	Good/Typical	Good/Typical	Good/Typical	Good/Typical
Quality of Construction	Good	Good	Good	Good
Age	20 Years	20 Years	20 Years	20 Years
Condition	Average	Average	Average	Average
Above Grade	Total / Bedrooms / Baths	Total / Bedrooms / Baths	Total / Bedrooms / Baths	Total / Bedrooms / Baths
Room Count	7 / 3 / 2	7 / 3 / 2	7 / 3 / 2	6 / 3 / 2
Gross Living Area	1,500 Square Feet	1,500 Square Feet	1,500 Square Feet	1,260 Square Feet
Basement and Finished Rooms Below Grade	None	None	None	None
Functional Utility	Good	Good	Good	Good
Heating/Cooling	Central	Central	Central	Central
Energy Efficient Items	Typical	Typical	Typical	Typical
Garage/Carport	Enclosed	Enclosed	Enclosed	Single Carport
Porch, Patio, Deck, Fireplace(s), etc.	Patio	Patio	Patio	Patio
Fence, Pool, etc.	None	None	None	None

CASE STUDY 3

717 Dick Boyd Way

■ LEARNING OBJECTIVES

Students will be able to

1. apply the valuation process as it relates to a specific appraisal assignment.

2. perform a subject property inspection, gathering all appropriate information.

3. analyze the subject property related to its physical condition, functional utility, and external concerns.

4. analyze the applicable market area.

5. extract market adjustments.

6. apply the cost approach including cost, depreciation, and land value.

7. determine when historical market data may not be sufficient to reflect a significant change in external conditions and apply reason and judgment.

8. perform the proper reconciliation of the approaches to value.

9. prepare a Fannie Mae appraisal form.

■ BACKGROUND

You are an associate appraiser with a small independent fee appraisal shop. There are two owners, four associate appraisers including yourself, and one support staff person. You have been in the appraisal business for approximately three years. You began your appraisal career after graduating from the state university with a major in real estate. You have appraised all types of real estate in the past, and your work portfolio is evenly divided between single-family residential and small commercial properties. You work mostly in your home county, but do occasionally work in adjacent counties.

■ CITY/COUNTY

You live in a small to midsize southeastern city in the United States named Smithville, Carter County. This is a somewhat isolated midsize city of about 50,000 residents, with an additional 50,000 in the county. The closest metropolitan area of about 2,000,000 people lies about 150 miles to the north, and the next closest major metropolitan area lies about 300 miles to the south in an adjacent state.

From the turn of the century until about 1940, Smithville was a small rural community, being the governmental seat and economic focal point for Carter County. Carter County had long been an agrarian community with farmers specializing in row crops and cattle production to a lesser degree. In 1950, the United States military announced plans for a major Air Force installation at the outer fringe of Smithville. The military installation is oriented toward the training of Air Force fighter pilots, and it also serves as a major reconnaissance center. The base has experienced steady growth through the years. Currently, there are about 15,000 military personnel, with an additional 15,000 in the civilian labor force.

Over the past 50 years, Smithville and Carter County have experienced steady economic growth without major fluctuations, either up or down. Population has grown steadily at about 2 percent per year. Although heavily dependent upon the military base for employment, the community does have some high-tech manufacturing, but these industries are also related to the aerospace installation at the base. Over the past 10 years to 20 years, the base has been known as a critical installation by the United States government, and the local congressmen have successfully lobbied for various military expenditures that tend to benefit the military base and community in general.

As the base has evolved, agricultural endeavors in the county have diminished over the past 20 years to 40 years. Most of the old farms are now utilized for timber production, a much less labor-intensive industry.

Two years ago, Smithville was shocked at the announcement by the president that the air base would be scaled back dramatically, as most of the operations will be consolidated into another base located in another section of the United States. It is anticipated that military personnel will decrease by 80 percent and the civilian labor force will be decreased by 70 percent.

The plan has been enacted and is underway. Last year, about 2,000 military personnel were transferred, and plans call for about 2,000 per year to be transferred to other bases over the next five years. About 2,000 in the civilian force were laid off, and plans call for the elimination of about 1,500 jobs per year over the next several years.

ASSIGNMENT

You have been called by an out-of-state lending institution to appraise a duplex located along a fairly heavily used collector road that leads into the base. The appraisal is to be used to assess the asset since the borrower is about two months behind on mortgage payments.

SUBJECT PROPERTY

The subject property is located at 717 Dick Boyd Way. The property lies midway between the old downtown area and the air base.

You call the owner and arrange an inspection, which is scheduled for the next day.

The client furnishes a recently completed Plat/Site Plan, included as Exhibit I in the Case Study. You identify the subject property related to its geographic location on the Area Map, included as Exhibit II.

You begin your inspection of the property by measuring the duplex. The sketch is included as Exhibit III. After sketching the improvements, you complete a detailed checklist related to the physical characteristics of the residence and site, included as Exhibit IV.

The site is generally level at street grade with no apparent drainage problems or detrimental soil or subsoil conditions. The landscaping around the residence is minimal, and the lot is barren of tree cover. You do observe that there are no low-lying areas, with good drainage. The driveway is concrete. A review of the Federal Emergency Management Agency (FEMA) Map indicates that the subject is not located within a specific flood hazard area. The Panel Number is LQ000982, completed in December of the previous year. The site plan shows no easements, other than normal utility easements.

The owner of the duplex lives in one of the units and works at the adjacent air base in the maintenance department that services utility vehicles. You notice several old drums at the rear of the site that apparently contain some unknown chemicals. Part of the lawn area around the drums is barren of grass groundcover, and there appears to be a greenish-gray tint to the soil.

The site is served by all utilities including electricity, natural gas, water, sanitary sewer, and telephone service. The street is served by a storm sewer system. All utilities are public.

The fronting street is asphalt paved with concrete curbs and gutters. There is no sidewalk, but the street is well lit with street lights.

The duplex was constructed about 40 years ago. Resting on a concrete slab, the structure has painted concrete block exterior walls and a hip roof with composition asphalt shingles and gutters and downspouts. The windows are single-hung, wood frame with single-pane windows, but there are no storm windows or screens.

The duplex is centrally heated and air-conditioned. The heating system is natural gas.

You observe no evidence of insect infestation or evidence of settlement problems.

Neither kitchen has ever been modernized, but they are both in fairly good condition. The refrigerator in the rental unit has always remained with this unit and is included in the rent. There is a built-in range and dishwasher, as well as a vent hood with fan. There is no disposal. Neither unit has attic storage.

The interior reflects carpet over concrete floors and paneled walls. The baths and kitchens, however, are sheet vinyl. The bathroom wainscoting is fiberglass. The interior doors are hollow-core. Insulation was noted in the ceiling only.

Overall, the exterior has been fairly well maintained. The roof cover was replaced about eight years ago, and the exterior was completely repainted about three years ago. All heating and air-conditioning units are reported to be in working condition. The interiors also have been fairly well maintained, with overall condition rated average. The effective age is estimated at 40 years, commensurate with the chronological age. The total economic life is estimated at 60 years.

■ NEIGHBORHOOD

The subject is somewhat unusual in that it lies along a collector road that leads directly from the downtown area into the air base. The street is occupied primarily by several duplexes and older single-family residences that are rented. These older residences were constructed during the 1950s and have been continuously operated as rental units since that time. The old downtown area is fairly static, but it still serves as the economic focal point for the county and city. Other supporting commercial facilities are well located. The community is well served by public schools and various parks and recreational facilities.

The predominant zoning along the subject street, including the subject property, is R-2A. This is a residential classification that permits attached duplex units on lots containing at least 10,000 square feet. The minimum duplex size is 800 square feet per rental unit, with front, side, and rear yard setbacks of 40 feet, 10 feet, and 20 feet, respectively.

Over the last several years, the residential development that has taken place in the community has largely been on more outlying tracts, at least 4.0 to 5.0 miles away from the downtown area. Almost no residential development activity has occurred in the city limits of Smithville, except for some sporadic renovation, expansions, and very limited new construction.

■ VALUATION METHODOLOGY

After analyzing the subject property related to the overall neighborhood, you decide that the Cost Approach is not appropriate because of the age of the improvements and speculation involved in accurately measuring accrued depreciation. There have been several sales of duplex units; accordingly, you do decide to employ the Sales Comparison Approach. Because this is an income-producing property, you do decide to do the Income Approach and conclude that the GRM is the most appropriate technique of the Income Approach.

■ MARKET DATA

Land

Because you are not including the cost approach, no land valuation is necessary.

Duplex Sales

You interview the owner and discover that one unit has been continuously owner-occupied for over 20 years. The other unit is leased, usually to military personnel. The typical occupancy period is about one year to two years. The most recent rental rate was $450 per month, with the tenant paying utilities and the owner paying taxes, insurance, general maintenance, and grounds upkeep. The rental unit is currently vacant, but the owner anticipates a new tenant will be moving in soon, although there is no written lease in place.

You discover two duplex sales that have both occurred within the subject's market area. These are summarized as Comparable 1 and Comparable 2 on the Data Sheet, included as Exhibit V.

You are also aware of the recent bank foreclosure on the property directly adjacent to the subject. This duplex is the same floor plan as the subject, and it is generally similar to the subject with regard to quality and condition. It was recently foreclosed upon by a local lending institution which "bid in" $60,000, which was the same as the existing balance on the three year-old mortgage. There were no other bidders, and the sale was confirmed by the court.

There is also a listing of a duplex unit located across the street from the subject, included as Comparable 3. The listing price was originally $105,000 about two years ago, but it was reduced to $95,000 a year later, and is now listed for $90,000. Favorable seller financing is also offered as a part of this listing.

■ VALUATION

The lender simply wants to know the value of the property because the owner is two months behind on his mortgage payments. The lender says a fancy report isn't necessary; a bottom line number will be sufficient. You suggest that a limited appraisal be performed using a restricted use format. The client agrees.

EXHIBIT I ■ Plat Site Plan

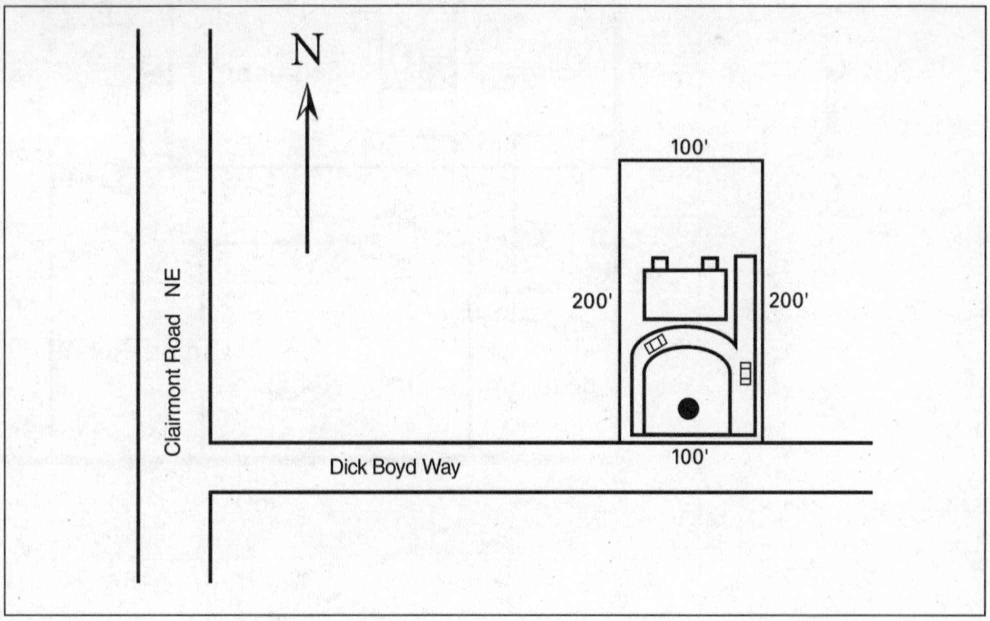

EXHIBIT II ■ Area Map

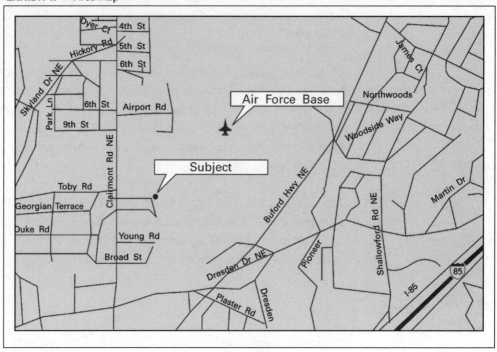

EXHIBIT III ■ Floor Plan: First Floor

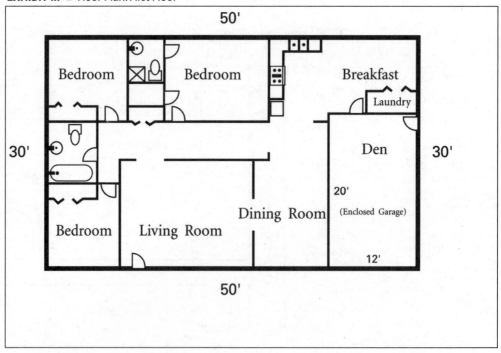

EXHIBIT IV-A ■ Inspection Check List: Site

SITE

Location:	
Dimensions:	
Area:	
Topography:	
Shape:	
Drainage:	
View:	
Landscaping:	
Driveway Surface:	
Apparent Easements:	
Low-Lying Areas:	
Utilities—	
Electricity:	
Gas:	
Water:	
Sanitary Sewer:	
Street	
Curb/Gutter:	
Sidewalk:	
Street Lights:	
Alley:	

EXHIBIT IV-B ■ Inspection Check List: Improvements

IMPROVEMENTS

General Description	Exterior Description	Foundation	Basement	
No. of Units	Foundation	Slab	Area Sq. Ft.	
No. of Stories	Exterior Walls	Crawl Space	% Finished	
Type (Det./Att.)	Roof Surface	Basement	Ceiling	
Design (Style)	Gutters & Dwnspts.	Sump Pump	Walls	
Existing/Proposed	Window Type	Dampness	Floor	
Age (Yrs.)	Storm/Screens	Settlement	Outside Entry	
Effective Age (Yrs.)	Manufactured House	Infestation		
Insulation	**Interior (Materials/Condition)**	**Heating**	**Cooling**	
Roof	Floors	Type	Central	
Ceiling	Walls	Fuel	Other	
Walls	Trim/Finish	Condition	Condition	
Floor	Bath Floor			
None	Bath Wainscot			
Unknown	Doors			
Kitchen Equipment	**Attic**	**Amenities**	**Car Storage**	
Refrigerator	None	Fireplace(s) #	None	
Range/Oven	Stairs	Patio	Garage	# of cars
Disposal	Drop Stair	Deck	Attached	
Dishwasher	Scuttle	Porch	Detached	
Fan/Hood	Floor	Fence	Built In	
Microwave	Heated	Pool	Carport	
Washer/Dryer	Finished		Driveway	

EXHIBIT V ■ Improved Sales Locations

IMPROVED SALES LOCATIONS

Item	Subject	Comparable No. 1	Comparable No. 2	Comparable No. 3
Address	717 Dick Boyd Way	148 Oak Street	152 Oak Street	119 Oak Street
Proximity to Subject				
Sales Price		$90,000	$91,000	$90,000
Data and/or Verification Sources		Broker	Broker	Broker
Value Adjustments	**Description**	**Description**	**Description**	**Description**
Sales or Financing Concessions		Cash	Cash	Favorable Owner Financing
Date of Sale/Time		3 Years	4 Years	Current Listing
Site Size	20,000 Square Feet	20,000 Square Feet	20,000 Square Feet	20,000 Square Feet
View	Good	Good	Good	Good
Design and Appeal	Good/Typical	Good/Typical	Good/Typical	Good/Typical
Quality of Construction	Average	Average	Average	Average
Age	40 Years	40 Years	40 Years	30 Years
Condition	Average	Average	Average	Average
Above Grade	Total	Bedrooms	Baths	Total	Bedrooms	Baths	Total	Bedrooms	Baths	Total	Bedrooms	Baths

Above Grade	Total	Bedrooms	Baths	Total	Bedrooms	Baths	Total	Bedrooms	Baths	Total	Bedrooms	Baths
Room Count	8	4	2	8	4	2	8	4	2	8	4	2
Gross Living Area	1,800 Square Feet			1,750 Square Feet			1,720 Square Feet			1,800 Square Feet		
Basement and Finished Rooms Below Grade	None			None			None			None		
Functional Utility	Good			Good			Good			Good		
Heating/Cooling	Central			Central			Central			Central		
Energy Efficient Items	Typical			Typical			Typical			Typical		
Garage/Carport	None			None			None			None		
Porch, Patio, Deck, Fireplace(s), etc.	Patio			Patio			Patio			Patio		
Fence, Pool, etc.	None			None			None			Pool		
Rent/Unit/Month	$450			$450			$460			$450		

1. Subsurface and air rights are examples of what type interest?
   a. Fractional interests
   b. Rights that may be divided and sold separately
   c. Vertical interests
   d. All of the above are correct

2. Frontage relates to
   a. roadways.
   b. streams.
   c. golf courses.
   d. all of the above

3. Given the following, what is the area?

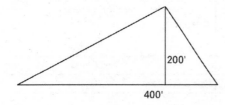

   a. 60,000 square feet
   b. 80,000 square feet
   c. 40,000 square feet
   d. 35,000 square feet

4. Generally, the most direct and easily understood approach is the
   a. Income Approach.
   b. Cost Approach.
   c. Technical Approach.
   d. Sales Comparison Approach.

5. Which type of study is site-specific?
   a. Market study
   b. Supply and demand study
   c. Marketability study
   d. Trade area analysis

6. The principle of contribution encompasses which of the following premises?
   a. The income stream as a component of the Sales Comparison Approach
   b. The value of an item or component as it contributes to the entire entity
   c. The income approach expresses the contribution of the income stream to the value estimate
   d. The depreciated replacement cost expresses the principle of contribution in the Cost Approach

7. Anticipation is the primary basis of which approach to value?
   a. Cost Approach
   b. Income Capitalization Approach
   c. Sales Comparison Approach
   d. Traditional Approach

8. If you deposited $150 a month in an account for replacement reserves at 6.25 percent interest for five years, how much money would accumulate?
   a. $9,000
   b. $11,128
   c. $9,562
   d. $10,533

9. The criteria of reconciliation include
   a. appropriateness.
   b. quantity of evidence.
   c. accuracy.
   d. all of the above

10. The difference between an improvement's reproduction or replacement cost new and its contributory value as of the date of the appraisal is referred to as
    a. physical deterioration.
    b. accrued depreciation.
    c. economic life.
    d. obsolescence.

11. Does market value equal cost?
    a. Yes, always
    b. No, never
    c. No, definitively; market value cannot equal cost
    d. Maybe

12. Given the following, what is the area expressed in acres?

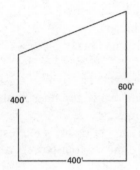

    a. 5.50 acres
    b. 5.00 acres
    c. 3.67 acres
    d. 4.59 acres

13. A comparable property recently sold for $80,000. At the time of sale, the property was leased for $640 per month. Based on similar properties in the neighborhood, the gross monthly income earned by the subject property is reflective of the "market" rate. What is the gross monthly rent multiplier indicated by this comparable?
    a. 90
    b. 125
    c. 10.4
    d. 140

14. What principle involves a buyer paying for the right to receive future benefits?
    a. Expectation
    b. Substitution
    c. Consistency
    d. Anticipation

15. Under which scenario would the cost approach likely be the LEAST reliable?
    a. The appraisal of a special-purpose property
    b. The appraisal of a proposed industrial building
    c. The appraisal of a 12-year old single-family residence
    d. The appraisal of a museum

16. In measuring the building exterior, the appraiser usually uses a
    a. yardstick.
    b. flexible measuring tape.
    c. measurements verbally delivered by the owner.
    d. none of the above

17. If a sale is influenced by special or creative financing, can it be used as a sale that meets the market value definition?
    a. Yes, with an adjustment if necessary.
    b. No, it absolutely cannot be used.
    c. Yes, with no comments or adjustments.
    d. Yes, with a standard adjustment of 5 percent.

18. If the comparable has an inferiority, the adjustment is
    a. upward.
    b. downward.
    c. not made.
    d. omitted.

19. When supply and demand are at equilibrium, what is achieved?
    a. Conformity
    b. Balance
    c. Change
    d. Contribution

20. The method of appraising land that deals with the percent contribution of land to total property is called
    a. allocation.
    b. sales comparison.
    c. subdivision analysis.
    d. extraction.

21. Gross building area is
    a. total measured area of heated space.
    b. total first floor area only.
    c. total site area.
    d. total measured area, excluding unenclosed areas.

22. What are the four tests of highest and best use?
    a. Physical, legal, financial, maximum productivity
    b. Physical, legal, probably, and utility
    c. Scarcity, utility, purchasing power, and capital
    d. Land, labor, capital, and entrepreneurship

23. Published data sources such as multiple-listing services
    a. should be used as a beginning point only.
    b. should be used as a final document worthy of no further analysis.
    c. should only be given partial weight in the analysis.
    d. should be discarded.

24. The correct formula for calculating the area of a triangle is
    a. length x width = area.
    b. ½ length x width = area.
    c. ½ base x height = area.
    d. 3 x base x height = area.

25. The best way for an appraiser to detect environmental hazards is to
    a. use an extremely sensitive camera.
    b. read the environmental assessment prepared by a qualified environmental company.
    c. check for obnoxious odor.
    d. check for dying vegetation.

26. A trend of rising interest rates is what type of force on real estate?
    a. Social
    b. Economic
    c. Governmental
    d. Physical/Environmental

27. What is the first step in the valuation process?
    a. Highest and best use analysis
    b. Inspection of the subject property
    c. Data collection
    d. Definition of the appraisal problem

28. If the value to be addressed is not conveyed to the appraiser as part of the assignment, the appraiser should
    a. assume market value is to be addressed.
    b. consult with the client to affirm the value to be addressed.
    c. pick any value.
    d. leave it up to the borrower.

29. Topography is most important as it relates to
    a. a site's ultimate development potential.
    b. the ability to grow trees.
    c. subsoil conditions.
    d. none of the above

30. Extracting adjustments from the market yields _____ for that item.
    a. market value
    b. value in use
    c. investment value
    d. contributory value

31. Income after deductions for taxes and other government payments is called
    a. net income.
    b. disposable income.
    c. gross income.
    d. effective income.

32. Fee simple estate is
    a. absolute ownership unencumbered by any other interest.
    b. the lessor's or owner's interest.
    c. subject only to four powers of government.
    d. both A and C

33. A neighborhood has a beautiful view of the mountains. This is an example of which kind of force?
    a. Environmental
    b. Economic
    c. Governmental
    d. Social

34. The identification of the real property as it relates to the valuation is
    a. absolutely critical.
    b. nice to have.
    c. occasionally useful.
    d. inappropriate data.

35. An installed under-the-counter dishwasher is
    a. a fixture.
    b. personal property.
    c. a part of the real estate.
    d. both A and C

36. When inspecting a building, the appraiser usually
    a. measures the exterior then proceeds to the interior.
    b. measures the interior then proceeds to the exterior.
    c. examines the substructure.
    d. takes a photograph.

37. The underlying appraisal principle of the Income Approach is
    a. supply and demand.
    b. substitution.
    c. anticipation.
    d. externalities.

38. Given the following, what is the area of the residence?

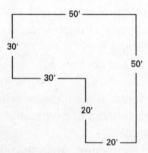

    a. 2,200 square feet
    b. 1,500 square feet
    c. 1,900 square feet
    d. 1,750 square feet

39. Which is *NOT* one of the four agents of production?
    a. Land
    b. Labor
    c. Contribution
    d. Entrepreneurship

40. Real property rights may be
    a. sold.
    b. retained by owner.
    c. leased.
    d. all of the above

41. What is the first step in a market analysis?
    a. Establishing market boundaries
    b. Supply analysis
    c. Demand analysis
    d. Calculation of months or years of supply

42. Forces outside the boundaries of the subject site are called
    a. the neighborhood.
    b. the market.
    c. governmental forces.
    d. external economies or external forces.

43. What is the last step in the valuation process?
    a. Preparing and submitting the report
    b. Gathering data
    c. Sending the invoice
    d. Property inspection

44. A commercial parcel selling for $225,000 and containing 20,500 square feet sold for what per square foot?
    a. $10.98
    b. $10.00
    c. $9.56
    d. $12.20

45. A group of homogenous land uses is called a(n)
    a. area.
    b. neighborhood.
    c. district.
    d. region.

46. Which of the following is a step in the Sales Comparison Approach?
    a. Estimate land value by sales comparison
    b. Estimate market rent for the subject and each of the sales
    c. Estimate the depreciated replacement cost of the sales
    d. Select a relevant unit of comparison and analyze each sale accordingly

47. Which approach uses market data?
    a. Cost Approach
    b. Income Approach
    c. Sales Comparison Approach
    d. All of the above

48. The process by which appraisers measure market reaction to items of dissimilarity is called
    a. adjustment process.
    b. computer analysis.
    c. market surveys.
    d. first-hand interviews.

49. Horizontal framing members are called
    a. studs.
    b. joists.
    c. a sleeping workman.
    d. none of the above

50. The allowable apartment density in an area is 12 units per acre. A 10-acre parcel sold for $400,000 per acre. What is the indicated price per unit?
    a. $2,500
    b. $1,800
    c. $3,500
    d. $3,333

51. Additional land not directly utilized by an improvement that could be sold off to support an additional improvement is known as
    a. plottage.
    b. excess land.
    c. developable land.
    d. assemblage.

52. An inspection of the subject property reveals that the subject improvement needs a new water heater immediately. What type of depreciation is this?
    a. Incurable, short-lived physical deterioration
    b. Incurable, long-lived physical deterioration
    c. Curable physical deterioration
    d. Curable functional obsolescence

53. Mobile homes can be considered part of the real estate when
    a. attached to the ground with a permanent foundation.
    b. underskirting is in place.
    c. at the appraiser's discretion.
    d. at the direction of the client.

54. Which type of legal description uses a system based on a recorded subdivision plat?
    a. Metes-and-bounds description
    b. Monument system
    c. Governmental (rectangular) survey system
    d. Lot-and-block system

55. Which is *NOT* a fundamental condition of market value?
    a. Buyer and seller are typically motivated.
    b. Buyer and seller are paying all cash in the transaction.
    c. A reasonable time is allowed for exposure on the open market.
    d. Both parties are well informed.

56. Calculate the term of a mortgage assuming an interest rate of 6.5 percent, a quarterly payment of $36,124.31, and an original loan amount of $1,750,000.
    a. 20 years
    b. 22 years
    c. 24 years
    d. 27 years

57. The highest and best use analysis applies to
    a. the land as if vacant.
    b. the property as improved.
    c. both A and B
    d. none of the above

58. The four forces that influence value are
    a. social, economic, environmental, and statistical.
    b. social, economic, environmental, and governmental.
    c. economic, environmental, contractual, and social.
    d. governmental, environmental, social, and highest and best use.

59. An improved 2,500 square-foot residence recently sold for $220,000. You estimate its total cost new at $80 per square foot. Properties in the area similar to the subject reflect accrued depreciation of approximately 10 percent What is the estimated land value by extraction?
    a. $40,000
    b. $22,000
    c. $20,000
    d. $26,000

60. High vacancy rates and stagnant rent levels as a result of an oversupplied market generally cause an income-producing property to suffer from what form of depreciation?
    a. Physical deterioration
    b. Functional obsolescence
    c. External obsolescence
    d. None of the above

61. Which is a money market instrument?
    a. Corporate bond
    b. Commercial paper
    c. Mortgage
    d. Treasury bond

62. The formula for calculating the area of a rectangle is
    a. length x width = area.
    b. length x width x height = area.
    c. width x ½ the volume x height = area.
    d. ½ base x height = area.

63. Condemnation is the process of the government taking property. Which power of government is this a process of?
    a. Police power
    b. Eminent domain
    c. Escheat
    d. Taxation

64. A mortgage that is secured by numerous properties is called a
    a. blanket mortgage.
    b. chattel mortgage.
    c. purchase money mortgage.
    d. package mortgage.

65. Which type of value is synonymous with market value?
    a. Going-concern value
    b. Insurable value
    c. Investment value
    d. Value-in-exchange

66. Specific data relates to the
    a. subject and comparables.
    b. subject only.
    c. comparables only.
    d. general market trends.

67. If you needed $5,000 in three years to replace the roof on your house, how much would you have to set aside each month if you were investing the money at 6.5 percent?
    a. $138.89
    b. $126.16
    c. $147.92
    d. $119.84

68. Assume you are appraising an older single-family residence located in a predominantly tenant-occupied location. Which of the three approaches to value would likely be most applicable in this assignment?
    a. Cost Approach
    b. Sales Comparison Approach
    c. Income Approach
    d. Highest and Best Use Approach

69. Land in its unimproved state is defined as a
    a. tract.
    b. site.
    c. real property.
    d. subdivision.

70. Given the following, what is the area expressed in acres?

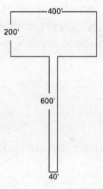

    a. 2.39 acres
    b. 1.84 acres
    c. 0.88 acres
    d. 3.79 acres

71. The term real estate relates to
    a. land.
    b. improvements.
    c. leased fee.
    d. both A and B

72. Rounding should
    a. rarely be employed within an appraisal report.
    b. reflect the appraiser's level of comfort regarding a value conclusion.
    c. only be used for reporting the final estimate of defined value.
    d. include none of the above.

73. The right to extract coal, minerals, oil, gas, and other hydrocarbon substances is an example of
    a.   an easement.
    b.   subsurface rights.
    c.   air rights.
    d.   none of the above

74. An improved 1,500 square foot residence recently sold for $80,000. You estimate its total cost new at $60 per square foot, excluding land. Properties in the area similar to the subject reflect accrued depreciation of approximately 30 percent. What is the estimated land value by extraction?
    a. $10,000
    b. $17,000
    c. $24,000
    d. $34,000

75. If the percentage adjustment is down 15 percent, the appraiser can simply multiply the unadjusted number by which of the following?
    a.   115
    b.   110
    c.   1.15
    d.   0.85

76. How many square feet are included in one acre?
    a.   5,280
    b.   6,000
    c.   750
    d.   43,560

77. When extracting adjustments, the contributory value may be
    a.   equal to cost.
    b.   greater than cost.
    c.   less than cost.
    d.   any of the above.

78. A zoning code prohibits fences taller than five feet around houses. What type of force is this?
    a.   Economic
    b.   Physical/Environmental
    c.   Social
    d.   Governmental

79. When can the bundle of rights be separated?
    a.   Never
    b.   Through a lease
    c.   By zoning
    d.   None of the above

80. The preferred method of estimating cost new in a single-family residence, and the method reflected in the Cost Approach on a standard residential appraisal form, is
    a.   unit-in-place method.
    b.   comparative unit method.
    c.   quantity survey method.
    d.   segregated cost method.

81. Most appraisal assignments involved the use of which business machine?
    a.   Hand electronic calculator
    b.   Desktop computer
    c.   Mainframe computer
    d.   Abacus

82. The highest and best use analysis tends to identify markets for
    a.   land sales.
    b.   improved sales.
    c.   rent comparables.
    d.   all of the above

83. Monetary policy is controlled by
    a.   the Office of Management and Budget.
    b.   the President of the United States.
    c.   the U.S. Congress.
    d.   the Federal Reserve Board.

84. Converting 0.375 to a percentage yields
    a.   0.375 percent.
    b.   3.75 percent.
    c.   37.5 percent.
    d.   375.0 percent.

85. When appraising properties as of a previous date, the appraiser should
    a.   increase their fee the further in time they are asked to go back.
    b.   assume the role of a broker active in the area on that date.
    c.   consider events that happened after the date of value.
    d.   assume the role of a typical buyer/seller with typical market knowledge on that date.

86. The N ½ of the SW ¼ of a section contains how many acres?
    a.   20
    b.   40
    c.   60
    d.   80

87. Effective gross income (EGI) is
   a. the total amount of income that may possibly be generated by a property in an open market.
   b. the potential gross income less vacancy and collection loss.
   c. the total amount of income actually collected by a property.
   d. B and C only

88. A mortgage that is secured by personal property is called a
   a. conventional mortgage.
   b. chattel mortgage.
   c. package mortgage.
   d. blanket mortgage.

89. A simple way to classify building improvements is
   a. interior and superstructure.
   b. exterior and interior.
   c. superstructure and basement.
   d. building plans.

90. If the comparable has a superiority, the adjustment is
   a. downward.
   b. omitted.
   c. upward.
   d. no adjustment.

91. The term *function* relates to the
   a. date of the appraisal.
   b. use of the appraisal.
   c. addressee of the appraisal.
   d. consequences of the appraisal.

92. Which of the following statements is/are true regarding *replacement cost* new?
   a. Tends to eliminate costs associated with superadequacies in the structure
   b. Cost of constructing a building using modern materials and current standards, design, and layout.
   c. Estimates cost to construct an equally desirable substitute improvement
   d. All of the above

93. A net income ratio
   a. equals net operating income (NOI) divided by effective gross income (EGI).
   b. has a direct relationship with a gross rent multiplier (GRM).
   c. equals 1 minus the operating expense ratio (OER).
   d. all of the above

94. Zoning is an example of which type of governmental power that limits real estate ownership?
   a. Escheat
   b. Eminent domain
   c. Police power
   d. Condemnation

95. The approach emphasized most by the appraiser depends upon
   a. the appraisal problem at hand and the applicability of each approach.
   b. the appraiser's discretion.
   c. the client's discretion.
   d. none of the above

96. Land's uniqueness, immobility, durability, finite supply, and utility are
   a. influences on real estate.
   b. forces on real estate.
   c. attributes of land.
   d. concepts of land.

97. Which type of title transfer ensures the buyer that the seller will guarantee all title claims against a property?
   a. Title insurance
   b. Special warranty deed
   c. General warranty deed
   d. Quitclaim deed

98. All improvements are
   a. building improvements or site improvements.
   b. building improvements or entrepreneurial profit.
   c. site improvements or site valuation.
   d. none of the above

99. If the percentage adjustment is plus 25 percent, the appraiser can simply multiply the unadjusted number by which of the following?
    a. 1.50
    b. 0.75
    c. 1.25
    d. 0.50

100. For federally related transactions, appraisal formats are governed by
    a. the President of the United States.
    b. the U.S. Congress.
    c. the Standards Board of the Appraisal Foundation.
    d. the Appraisal Institute.

CHAPTER REVIEW QUESTIONS ANSWER KEY

Chapter 1

1. D
2. C
3. B
4. A
5. A
6. D
7. C
8. C
9. A
10. D
11. B
12. C
13. C
14. A
15. A

Chapter 2

1. A
2. A
3. B
4. C
5. D
6. B
7. A
8. C
9. C
10. A
11. D
12. C
13. A
14. D
15. B
16. C
17. B
18. A
19. D
20. B

Chapter 3

1. A
2. D

3. B
4. C
5. C
6. D
7. C
8. C
9. B
10. D

Chapter 4

1. C
2. D
3. D
4. B
5. C
6. D
7. B
8. A
9. C
10. A
11. D
12. B
13. C
14. A
15. B

Chapter 5

1. B
2. C
3. B
4. D
5. C
6. D
7. D
8. A
9. A
10. A
11. D
12. A
13. B
14. C
15. D

Chapter 6

1. B
2. D
3. A
4. D
5. A
6. C
7. A
8. C
9. B
10. A
11. D
12. B
13. A
14. B
15. C
16. A
17. B
18. C
19. C
20. D
21. B
22. A
23. C
24. C
25. A
26. C
27. D
28. A
29. B
30. C

Chapter 7

1. C
2. B
3. B
4. D
5. A
6. A
7. C
8. C
9. C
10. A

11. B
12. A
13. A
14. C
15. B
16. A
17. C
18. A
19. C
20. D

Chapter 8

1. D
2. B
3. C
4. B
5. C
6. B
7. B
8. A
9. A
10. A

Chapter 9

1. C
2. C
3. D
4. A
5. D
6. A
7. C
8. D
9. C
10. D
11. B
12. A
13. C
14. B
15. A
16. C
17. A
18. A

19. A
20. C

Chapter 10

1. B
2. C
3. B
4. A
5. C
6. A
7. C
8. D
9. D
10. B
11. B
12. A
13. C
14. D
15. B

Chapter 11

1. C
2. A
3. D
4. B
5. C
6. C
7. B
8. C
9. C
10. A

Chapter 12

1. D
2. B
3. C
4. A
5. C
6. A
7. A
8. D

9. B
10. D

Chapter 13

1. B
2. C
3. B
4. C
5. B
6. C
7. A
8. D
9. B
10. A
11. C
12. D
13. B
14. D
15. D

Chapter 14

1. A
2. D
3. D
4. C
5. B

Chapter 15

1. D
2. C
3. A
4. D
5. B
6. D
7. D
8. D
9. B
10. A

Chapter 16   **Chapter 17**

1. A   1. D
2. D   2. C
3. B   3. B
4. A   4. D
5. D   5. D

■ PRACTICE EXAM ANSWER KEY

1. D	18. A	35. D	52. C	69. A	86. D
2. D	19. B	36. A	53. A	70. A	87. D
3. C	20. A	37. C	54. D	71. D	88. B
4. D	21. A	38. C	55. B	72. B	89. B
5. C	22. A	39. C	56. C	73. B	90. A
6. B	23. A	40. D	57. C	74. B	91. B
7. B	24. C	41. A	58. B	75. D	92. D
8. D	25. B	42. D	59. A	76. D	93. D
9. D	26. B	43. A	60. C	77. D	94. C
10. B	27. D	44. A	61. B	78. D	95. A
11. D	28. B	45. B	62. A	79. B	96. C
12. D	29. A	46. D	63. B	80. B	97. C
13. B	30. D	47. D	64. A	81. A	98. A
14. D	31. B	48. A	65. D	82. D	99. C
15. C	32. D	49. B	66. A	83. D	100. C
16. B	33. A	50. D	67. B	84. C	
17. A	34. A	51. B	68. C	85. D	

■ APPENDIX B SUGGESTED SOLUTIONS

Land and Site Valuation Classroom Problems

1. The five recent comparable sales indicate a value for the subject site ranging from $14,000 to $15,300. Excluding the two extreme indications, the range narrows to between $14,400 and $15,000. A value estimate for the subject of $14,500 to $15,000 appears reasonable and well supported based on the market data analyzed.

    $$\$72,000 \times 0.20 \ (20\%) = \$14,400$$
    $$\$75,000 \times 0.20 \ (20\%) = \$15,000$$
    $$\$76,500 \times 0.20 \ (20\%) = \$15,300$$
    $$\$70,000 \times 0.20 \ (20\%) = \$14,000$$
    $$\$74,500 \times 0.20 \ (20\%) = \$14,900$$

2. Recall the format of the Cost Approach, fill in the known, and solve for the unknown (site value):

    Replacement or Reproduction Cost New (A)
    − Accrued Depreciation (B)
    _____
    Contributory Value of Improvements (C)
    + Site Value (D)
    _____
    Total Property Value (E)

Sale No.	1	2	3
Reproduction Cost New	$130,000	$125,000	Unknown
Less Accrued Depreciation	− $32,500 (25%)	$0	Unknown
Contributory Value of Improvements	$97,500	$125,000	$104,000
Plus Site Value (?)	**+ $27,500**	**+ $26,000**	**+ $28,000**
Total Property Value	$125,000	$151,000	$132,000

    The indicated site value is merely the sales price of the comparable (total property value) less the contributory value of the improvements as shown above. A value indication between $26,000 and $28,000 is indicated for the subject site.

3. What is a reasonable value indication for the subject site by the Sales Comparison method? *(Hint: Adjustments are derived by "matched pair" analysis).*

    Step 1: Arrange the data in a market data grid to isolate dissimilarities between the subject and comparable sales.

Element	Subject	Sale No. 1	Sale No. 2	Sale No. 3	Sale No. 4
Sales Price	—	$15,000	$18,000	$20,000	$17,000
Location	Corner	Corner	Corner	Interior	Corner
Shape	Rectangular	Irregular	Rectangular	Rectangular	Irregular
Topography	Gentle	Steep	Steep	Steep	Gentle

Step 2: Comparable Sales 1 and 2 are identical except for "shape." Compare Sales 1 and 2 for "shape" difference and apply the adjustment to Sales dissimilar to subject (Sales 1 and 4).

- The difference in price is $3,000 ($18,000 versus $15,000).

- A site with a rectangular shape ($18,000) sells for $3,000 more than a site with an irregular shape ($15,000).

- Because the subject features a rectangular shape, no adjustment is required for the Sales with a rectangular shape (Sales 2 and 3).

- All Sales featuring an irregular shape (Sales 1 and 4) are *inferior* to the subject and require an upward (+) $3,000 adjustment.

Element	Subject	Sale No. 1	Sale No. 2	Sale No. 3	Sale No. 4
Sales Price	—	$15,000	$18,000	$20,000	$17,000
Shape Adjustment		+ $3,000	$0	$0	+ $3,000
Adjusted Price		$18,000	$18,000	$20,000	$20,000
Location	Corner	Corner	Corner	Interior	Corner
~~Shape~~	~~Rectangular~~	~~Irregular~~	~~Rectangular~~	~~Rectangular~~	~~Irregular~~
		(inferior)	(same)	(same)	(inferior)
Topography	Gentle	Steep	Steep	Steep	Gentle

Step 3: After the shape adjustment, compare Sales 1 and 3 for "location" difference and apply the adjustment to Sales that are dissimilar to subject (Sale 3).

- The difference in price is $2,000 ($20,000 versus $18,000); analysis is based on the adjusted price, after shape adjustment.

- An interior site ($20,000) sells for $2,000 more than a site on the corner ($18,000).

- Because the subject features a corner location, no adjustment is required for Sales with a corner location (Sales 1, 2, and 4).

- All Sales featuring an interior location (Sale 3) are *superior* to the subject and require a downward (−) $2,000 adjustment.

Element	Subject	Sale No. 1	Sale No. 2	Sale No. 3	Sale No. 4
Sales Price	—	$15,000	$18,000	$20,000	$17,000
Shape Adjustment		+ $3,000	$0	$0	+ $3,000
Adjusted Price		$18,000	$18,000	$20,000	$20,000
Location Adjustment		$0	$0	− $2,000	$0
Adjusted Price		$18,000	$18,000	$18,000	$20,000
~~Location~~	~~Corner~~	~~Corner~~	~~Corner~~	~~Interior~~	~~Corner~~
		(same)	(same)	(superior)	(same)
Topography	Gentle	Steep	Steep	Steep	Gentle

Step 4: After the shape and location adjustments, compare Sale 4 with any of the three remaining Sales for the "topography" difference and apply adjustment to Sales dissimilar to subject (Sales 1, 2, and 3).

- The difference in price is $2,000 ($20,000 versus $18,000); analysis is based on the adjusted price, after shape and location adjustments.

- A site featuring a gentle topography ($20,000) sells for $2,000 more than a site with steep topography ($18,000).

- Because the subject features a gentle topography, no adjustment is required for the Sales with a gentle topography (Sale 4)

- All Sales with steep topography (Sales 1, 2, and 3) are *inferior* to the subject and require an upward (+) $2,000 adjustment.

Element	Subject	Sale No. 1	Sale No. 2	Sale No. 3	Sale No. 4
Sales Price	—	$15,000	$18,000	$20,000	$17,000
Shape Adjustment		+ $3,000	$0	$0	+ $3000
Adjusted Price		$18,000	$18,000	$20,000	$20,000
Location Adjustment		$0	$0	− $2,000	$0
Adjusted Price		$18,000	$18,000	$18,000	$20,000
Topography Adjustment		+ $2,000	+ $2,000	+ $2,000	$0
Estimated Value for Subject		**$20,000**	**$20,000**	**$20,000**	**$20,000**
~~Topography~~	~~Gentle~~	~~Steep~~	~~Steep~~	~~Steep~~	~~Gentle~~
		(inferior)	(inferior)	(inferior)	(same)

Cost Estimation Classroom Problems

1.a. What is the indicated cost new for the subject improvements by the comparative-unit method?

Sale No.	1	2	3
Sales Price of Comparable	$164,500	$138,500	$150,000
Less Site Value ($10,000 per Acre)	− $30,000	− $15,000	− $20,000
Indicated Cost New of Improvements	$134,500	$123,500	$130,000
Gross Living Area (GLA) of Comparable	÷ 2,050	÷ 1,850	÷ 1,975
Cost New Per Square Foot of GLA	$65.61	$66.76	$65.82

(Note: The cost new estimates per square foot include direct and indirect costs and entrepreneurial profit.)

No.	Size of House	Unit Cost
2	1,850	$66.76
Subject	1,950	?
3	1,975	$65.82
1	2,050	$65.61

As noted above, the larger the homes, the lower the unit cost (cost per square foot in this example). The subject house lies between Sale 2 and Sale 3, but at 1,950 square feet, it is closer to Sale 3. The correct selection would approximate $66 per square foot of gross living area, or $128,700 (1,950 square feet at $66 per square foot).

1.b.   Assuming the subject property reflects no accrued depreciation, what is the market value indicated by the Cost Approach?

Cost New of Subject Improvements (1,950 SF @ $66 per SF)	$128,700
Less Accrued Depreciation	– $0
Contributory Value of the Improvements	$128,700
Plus Site Value (2.0 Acres @ $10,000 per Acre)	+ $20,000
Indicated Value by Cost Approach	$148,700

2.a.   What is the indicated cost new for the subject improvements by the comparative-unit method?

Sale No.	1	2	3
Sales Price of Comparable	$92,200	$81,750	$88,400
Less Site Value	- $15,000	- $15,000	- $15,000
Indicated Cost New of Improvements	$77,200	$66,750	$73,400
Garage Adjustment	- $3,500	$0	- $3,500
Fireplace Adjustment	$0	+ $2,000	+ $2,000
Adjusted Cost New of Improvements	$73,700	$68,750	$71,900
GLA of Comparable	÷ 1,550	÷ 1,410	÷ 1,495
Cost New Per Square Foot of GLA	$47.55	$48.76	$48.09

(Note: The cost new estimates per square foot include direct and indirect costs and entrepreneurial profit.)

No.	Size of House	Unit Cost
2	1,410	$48.76
3	1,495	$48.09
Subject	1,500	?
1	1,550	$47.55

Again, notice the larger the home, the lower the unit cost. The subject house lies between Sale 1 and Sale 3, but at 1,500 square feet, it is closer to Sale 3. The correct selection would approximate $48 per square foot of gross living area.

2.b.   Assuming you estimate accrued depreciation for the subject at approximately $5,000, what is the market value indicated by the Cost Approach?

Cost New of Subject Improvements (1,500 SF @ $48 per SF)	$72,000
Less Accrued Depreciation	– $5,000
Contributory Value of the Improvements	$67,000
Plus Site Value (2.0 Acres @ $10,000 per Acre)	+ $15,000
Indicated Value by Cost Approach	$82,000

Accrued Depreciation Classroom Problems

1.a.   What is the implied total economic life of the improvements?

Because total economic life is the sum of effective age and remaining economic life, the implied economic life of the improvements equals 50 years (20 years plus 30 years) as shown below.

	Total Economic Life				
(Years) 0	10	20	30	40	50
	Effective Age		Remaining Economic Life		

1.b.   What is the percentage amount of accrued depreciation for the subject improvements by the economic age-life method?

The rate of depreciation estimated by the economic age-life method divides the effective age by the total economic life of the improvement. Therefore the percentage amount of accrued depreciation equals 0.40, or 40% (20 years ÷ 50 years).

1.c.   What is the lump-sum dollar amount of accrued depreciation for the subject improvements?

The estimated percentage rate of depreciation is always applied to the reproduction or replacement cost new. Therefore, the lump-sum dollar amount of accrued depreciation approximates $60,000 ($150,000 × 0.40).

1.d.   What is the contributory value (also known as depreciated value) of the improvements?

The contributory value (or depreciated value) of the improvements is simply the reproduction or replacement cost new less accrued depreciation. Therefore, the contributory value equals $90,000 ($150,000 – $60,000).

1.e.   Assuming a land value of $20,000, what is the value indication by the Cost Approach?

The value indication by the Cost Approach is simply the contributory value of the improvements plus the estimated value of the site. Therefore, the value indication by the Cost Approach approximates $110,000 ($90,000 + $20,000).

2.a.   What is the estimated cost new of the incurable components?

The estimated cost new of the incurable components equals the *total* cost new less the cost new of the curable components. In the modified economic age-life method, curable depreciation is estimated at the *cost to cure*; therefore, the curable depreciation estimate is equal to the cost new of the curable components, or $5,000 (the curable components are 100% depreciated). The cost new of the incurable components is thus $75,000 ($80,000 – $5,000).

2.b. What is the estimated percentage amount of accrued depreciation applicable to the incurable components?

In the modified economic age-life method, incurable components are estimated assuming correction of the curable depreciation. Therefore, the effective age and total economic life *after curable depreciation is corrected* are used to estimate the rate of accrued depreciation applicable to the incurable components. The rate of depreciation estimate divides the effective age by the total economic life of the improvement. Therefore the percentage amount of accrued depreciation applicable to the incurable components equals 0.0833, or 8.33% (5 years ÷ 60 years).

2.c. What is the lump-sum dollar amount of accrued depreciation estimated by the modified economic age-life method?

Cost New		Depreciation ($)		Contributory Value	
$80,000	(1)				
– $5,000	(2)	$5,000	(3)	$0	(4)
$75,000	(5)				
–$75,000	(6)	+ $6,250	(7)	+ $68,750	(8)
$0	(9)	$11,250	(10)	$68,750	(11)

(1) Total reproduction cost new of the single-family residence.

(2) Cost new of the curable components.

(3) Depreciation estimate for curable components; same as the estimated *cost to cure*.

(4) Contributory value of the curable components; items are 100% depreciated with no contributory value.

(5) Cost new of the incurable components only.

(6) Consider and depreciate the cost new of all incurable components.

(7) Depreciation estimate for the incurable components; cost new of incurable components multiplied by the depreciation rate in decimal format; $75,000 × 0.0833 (5 years ÷ 60 years = 0.0833).

(8) Contributory value of the incurable components; components still contributing to value, hence the title *incurable*.

(9) A $0 in the *Cost New* column means the *total* reproduction cost new of the residence has been considered.

(10) Represents the *total accrued depreciation* of the single-family residence by the modified economic age-life method.

(11) Represents the remaining contributory value of the single-family residence (also known as the depreciated value of the improvements).

The total accrued depreciation by the modified economic age-life method is $11,250.

3.a.   What is the average annual rate of depreciation indicated by the two comparable properties?

Sale No.	1	2
Sales Price of Comparable	$112,000	$126,000
− Estimated Site Value	− $30,000	− $30,000
Contributory Value of Improvements	$82,000	$96,000
Estimated Reproduction Cost New	$100,000	$128,000
− Contributory Value of Improvements	− $82,000	− $96,000
Lump-Sum Accrued Depreciation ($)	$18,000	$32,000
Lump-Sum Accrued Depreciation ($)	$18,000	$32,000
÷ Estimated Reproduction Cost New	÷ $100,000	÷ $128,000
Lump-Sum Accrued Depreciation (%)	0.180	0.250
Lump-Sum Accrued Depreciation (%)	0.180	0.250
÷ Comparable's Effective Age (Years)	÷ 11	÷ 16
Average Annual Rate of Accrued Depreciation	0.0164	0.0156
Converted to Percentage Format	1.64%	1.56%

3.b.   What is an appropriate percentage depreciation rate for the subject improvements considering the two comparable sales?

The two comparable sales indicate an average annual rate of depreciation of 1.64% and 1.56%, respectively. It appears a reasonable estimate of depreciation for the subject would approximate 1.6% per year.

The subject property has an estimated effective age of 14 years old. Therefore, the appropriate percentage depreciation rate for the subject would approximate 0.224 or 22.4% (0.016 per year × 14 years).

3.c.   What is the approximate lump-sum dollar amount of accrued depreciation applicable to the subject improvements by the market extraction or sales comparison method of estimating accrued depreciation?

The estimated percentage rate of depreciation is always applied to the reproduction or replacement cost new. Therefore, the lump-sum dollar amount of accrued depreciation approximates $26,880 ($120,000 × 0.224).

3.d.   What is the value indication by the Cost Approach for the subject property?

Estimated Reproduction Cost New (a)	$120,000
Less Accrued Depreciation (b)	− $26,880
Contributory Value of Improvements (c)	$93,120
Plus Estimated Site Value (d)	+ $32,000
Value Indication by Cost Approach (e)	$125,120

4.a.   What is the total amount of short-lived incurable physical deterioration for the property?

Component	Effective Age (Yrs.)	Physical Life (Yrs.)	Depreciation Estimate (%)	Reproduction Cost New ($)	Depreciation Estimate ($)	Contributory Estimate ($)
Roof	5	20	5 ÷ 20 (25%)	$5,000	$1,250	$3,750
Appliances	5	15	5 ÷ 15 (33%)	$3,000	$1,000	$2,000
Flooring	5	10	5 ÷ 10 (50%)	$7,000	$3,500	$3,500
Water Heater	5	10	5 ÷ 10 (50%)	$800	$400	$400
Totals (Rounded)				$15,800	$6,150	$9,650
Percentages				100%	38.9%	61.1%

The total amount of short-lived incurable physical deterioration is $6,150.

4.b.   What is the total amount of long-lived incurable physical deterioration for the property?

Total Reproduction Cost New of Residence	$150,000
Less Cost New of Curable Physical Components	– $4,000
Less Cost New of Incurable Short-Lived Components	– $15,800
Total Reproduction Cost New of Long-Lived Components	$130,200
Times Depreciation Rate (5 years ÷ 50 years = 0.10)	× 0.10
Total Physical Deterioration of Long-Lived Components	$13,020

4.c.   What is the total accrued depreciation by the breakdown method for the property?

Cost New		Depreciation ($)		Contributory Value	
$150,000	(1)				
– $4,000	(2)	$4,000	(3)	$0	(4)
$146,000	(5)				
– $15,800	(6)	+ $6,150	(7)	+ $9,650	(8)
$130,200	(9)				
$130,200	(10)	$13,020	(11)	$117,180	(12)
$0	(13)	$23,170	(14)	$126,830	(15)

(1) Total reproduction cost new of the single-family residence.

(2) Cost new of the curable physical, or deferred maintenance, items.

(3) Depreciation estimate for curable physical items; same as the estimated "cost to cure."

(4) Contributory value of the curable physical items; items are 100% depreciated with no contribution value.

(5) Cost new of the incurable physical components, both short-lived and long-lived components.

(6) Cost new of the incurable short-lived components.

(7) Depreciation estimate for the incurable physical short-lived components.

(8) Contributory value of the incurable physical short-lived components; components still contributing to value, hence the title "incurable."

(9) Cost new of the incurable long-lived components; total cost new of residence less the cost of curable and incurable short-lived components.

(10) Cost new of the incurable long-lived components.

(11) Depreciation estimate for the incurable physical long-lived components (5 years ÷ 50 years = 0.10 x $130,200).

(12) Contributory value of the incurable physical long-lived components; components still contributing to value, hence the title "incurable."

(13) A $0 in the "Cost New" column means the *total* reproduction cost new of the residence has been considered and depreciated accordingly.

(14) Represents the *total physical deterioration* of the single-family residence.

(15) Represents the remaining contributory value of the single-family residence (also known as the depreciated value of the improvements).

The total accrued depreciation by the breakdown method approximates $23,170. Remember, the total physical deterioration (14) plus the contributory value of the improvements (15) *must* equal the total cost new (1) in this exercise.

Applied Comparison Approach Classroom Problems

1. Complete the grid in the following three examples including an indication for the subject.

APARTMENT PROPERTY

Rental Number	Subject	1	2	3	4
Unit Type	2BR/2BA	2BR/2BA	2BR/2BA	2BR/2BA	2BR/2BA
Square Feet	950	917	850	770	1,003
Monthly Rent		$525	$535	$530	$520
Monthly Rent per Square Foot		$0.57	$0.63	$0.69	$0.52

Subject would likely fall between the indication from Sale 1 ($0.57 per SF for 917 square feet) and Sale 4 ($0.52 per SF for 1,003 square feet).

APARTMENT PROPERTY

Rental Number	Subject	1	2	3	4
Unit Type	2BR/2BA	2BR/2BA	2BR/2BA	2BR/2BA	2BR/2BA
Square Feet	1,150	1,200	950	1,150	1,100
Monthly Rent		$600	$495	$585	$580
Monthly Rent per Square Foot		$.050	$.052	$0.51	$0.53

Subject would command monthly rent per square foot of around $0.51.

COMMERCIAL LAND

Sale Number	Subject	1	2	3	4
Date		3 Months	6 Months	4 Months	1 Month
Price		$120,000	$123,500	$115,500	$115,000
Square Feet	25,000	24,000	26,000	22,000	23,000
Front Feet	100	75	135	170	100
Price per Square Foot		$5.00	$4.75	$5.25	$5.00
Price per Front Foot		$1,600	$915	$679	$1,150

Subject would likely fall between the indication from Sale 1 ($5.00 per SF for 24,000 square feet) and Sale 2 ($4.75 per SF for 26,000 square feet). On a price per front foot basis, the subject would likely command a price of around $1,150.

2. Adjustment Extraction

MARKET DATA GRID

	Sale No. 1	Sale No. 2	Sale No. 3	Sale No. 4	Sale No. 5
Price	$200,000	$215,000	$185,000	$225,000	$210,000
Date of Sale (Market Conditions)	Current	Current	Current	Current	Current
Location/View	Interior	Lake View	Interior	Lake View	Interior
Physical Variances					
Site Size	.5 Acre	.5 Acre	.5 Acre	.5 Acre	1.0 Acre
Residence Size (Square Feet)	3,000	3,000	3,000	3,000	3,000
Bedrooms	4	4	4	4	4
Baths	2.5	2.5	2.5	2.5	2.5
Garage	Yes	Yes	No	Yes	Yes
Basement	Yes	No	No	Yes	Yes
Condition	Good	Good	Good	Good	Good

2.a.   Solve the following:

Comparison	Dollar Adjustment	Comments
Location	$25,000	Sale 1 vs. Sale 4
Site Size	$10,000	Sale 1 vs. Sale 5
Residence Size	$0	No Adjustment
Bedrooms	$0	No Adjustment
Baths	$0	No Adjustment
Garage	$5,000	Sale 1 vs. Sale 3
		(after + $10,000 basement adjustment)
Basement	$10,000	Sale 2 vs. Sale 4
Condition	$0	No Adjustment

2.b.   Apply the extracted adjustments from Part a to arrive at a value indication for the subject property:

MARKET DATA GRID

Sale Number	Subject	1	2	3	4	5
Price	?	$200,000	$215,000	$185,000	$225,000	$210,000
Date of Sale						
(Market Conditions)	Current	Current	Current	Current	Current	Current
Adjustment:		$0	$0	$0	$0	$0
Location/View	Interior	Interior	Lake View	Interior	Lake View	Interior
Adjustment:		$0	– $25,000	$0	– $25,000	$0
Physical Variances						
Site Size	1.0 Acre	.5 Acre	.5 Acre	.5 Acre	.5 Acre	1.0 Acre
Adjustment:		+ $10,000	+ $10,000	+ $10,000	+ $10,000	+ $0
Residence Size						
(Square Feet)	3,000	3,000	3,000	3,000	3,000	3,000
Adjustment:		$0	$0	$0	$0	$0
Bedrooms	4	4	4	4	4	4
Adjustment:		$0	$0	$0	$0	$0
Baths	2.5	2.5	2.5	2.5	2.5	2.5
Adjustment:		$0	$0	$0	$0	$0
Garage	No	Yes	Yes	No	Yes	Yes
Adjustment:		– $5,000	– $5,000	$0	– $5,000	– $5,000
Basement	Yes	Yes	No	No	Yes	Yes
Adjustment:		$0	+$10,000	+$10,000	$0	$0
Condition	Good	Good	Good	Good	Good	Good
Adjustment:		$0	$0	$0	$0	$0
Net Adjustment:		+ $5,000	– $10,000	+ $20,000	– $20,000	– $5,000
Indicated Value:		$205,000	$205,000	$205,000	$205,000	$205,000

Income Approach Classroom Problems

1.a.   What is the annual PGI for the subject property?

20 units × $700 per month per unit × 12 months = $168,000 annually

1.b.   What is the estimated EGI for the subject property?

Potential Gross Income (PGI)	$168,000
Less Vacancy (10% of PGI)	– $16,800
Less Collection Loss (2% of PGI)	– $3,360
Effective Gross Income (EGI)	$147,840

1.c.   What is the approximate amount of operating expenses to be incurred at the subject property?

Operating expenses approximate 40% of effective gross income. Therefore, $147,840 × 0.40 = $59,136

1.d.   What is the approximate OER for the subject property?

The OER is simply total operating expenses divided by effective gross income, or $59,136 ÷ $147,840 = 0.40 or 40%

1.e.   What is the approximate NOI for the subject property?

Potential Gross Income (PGI)	$168,000
Less Vacancy (10% of PGI)	– $16,800
Less Collection Loss (2% of PGI)	– $3,360
Effective Gross Income (EGI)	$147,840
Less Operating Expenses	– $59,136
Net Operating Income (NOI)	$88,704

1.f.   What is the approximate NIR for the subject property?

The NIR is simply net operating income divided by effective gross income, or 1 – OER. Therefore, the NIR approximates 60% as follows:

$$\$88,704 \div \$147,840 \text{ or } 1 - 0.40 = 0.60 \text{ or } 60\%$$

2.a.   What is the estimated monthly rent for the subject property by these comparables using matched pair analysis?

Step 1: Comparable rentals 1 and 3 are identical except for bedrooms. Compare rentals 1 and 3 for bedrooms difference and apply the adjustment to rentals dissimilar to subject (Rentals 3 and 4).

- The difference in rent is $75 ($375 versus $300).

- A three-bedroom house ($375) rents for $75 more than a two-bedroom house ($300).

- Because the subject has three bedrooms, no adjustment is required for the rentals with three bedrooms (Rentals 1 and 2).

- All two-bedroom rentals (Rentals 3 and 4) are *inferior* to the subject and require an upward (+) $75 adjustment.

Element	Subject	Rental No. 1	Rental No. 2	Rental No. 3	Rental No. 4
Monthly Rent	—	$375	$425	$300	$325
Bedroom Adjustment		$0	$0	+ $75	+ $75
Adjusted Rent		$375	$425	$375	$400
Location	North	North	South	North	South
~~Bedrooms~~	3	3	3	2	2
		(same)	(same)	(inferior)	(inferior)
Fence	Yes	No	Yes	No	No

Step 2: After bedrooms adjustment, compare rentals 1 and 4 for location difference and apply the adjustment to rentals dissimilar to subject (Rentals 2 and 4).

- The difference in rent is $25 ($400 versus $375).

- A house located south of town ($400) rents for $25 more than a house on the north side of town ($375).

- Because the subject is located on the north side of town, no adjustment is required for the rentals located on the north side of town (Rentals 1 and 3).

- All rentals located on the south side of town (Rentals 2 and 4) are **superior** to the subject and require a downward (–) $25 adjustment.

Element	Subject	Rental No. 1	Rental No. 2	Rental No. 3	Rental No. 4
Monthly Rent	—	$375	$425	$300	$325
Bedroom Adjustment		$0	$0	+ $75	+ $75
Adjusted Rent		$375	$425	$375	$400
Location Adjustment		$0	– $25	$0	– $25
Adjusted Rent		$375	$400	$375	$375
~~Location~~	~~North~~	~~North~~	~~South~~	~~North~~	~~South~~
		(same)	(superior)	(same)	(superior)
Fence	Yes	No	Yes	No	No

Step 3: After the bedrooms and location adjustment, compare rental 2 with any of the three remaining rentals for the fence difference and apply adjustment to rentals dissimilar to subject (Rentals 1, 3, and 4).

- The difference in rent is $25 ($400 versus $375).

- A house with a fence ($400) rents for $25 more than a house without a fence ($375).

- Because the subject has a fence, no adjustment is required for the rentals with a fence (Rental 2).

- All rentals without a fence (Rentals 1, 3, and 4) are *inferior* to the subject and require an upward (+) $25 adjustment.

Element	Subject	Rental No. 1	Rental No. 2	Rental No. 3	Rental No. 4
Monthly Rent	—	$375	$425	$300	$325
Bedroom Adjustment		$0	$0	+ $75	+ $75
Adjusted Rent		$375	$425	$375	$400
Location Adjustment		$0	– $25	$0	– $25
Adjusted Rent		$375	$400	$375	$375
Fence Adjustment		+ $25	$0	+ $25	+ $25
Estimated Rent for Subject		**$400**	**$400**	**$ 400**	**$400**
~~Fence~~	~~Yes~~	~~No~~	~~Yes~~	~~No~~	~~No~~
		~~(inferior)~~	~~(same)~~	~~(inferior)~~	~~(inferior)~~

2.b.   What is an appropriate GRM applicable to the estimated potential gross rent of the subject property?

Element	Subject	Sale No. 1	Sale No. 2	Sale No. 3	Sale No. 4
Sales Price	—	$52,000	$37,500	$35,000	$39,500
Monthly Rent	$400	$620	$500	$485	$520
Location	North	South	North	North	North
Sales Price	—	$52,000	$37,500	$35,000	$39,500
Monthly Rent		÷ $620	÷ $500	÷ $485	÷ $520
Indicated GRM (Rounded)	—	84	75	72	76

The GRMs range from 72 to 84. The comparable sales located on the north side of town range from 72 to 76. Because the subject property is located on the north side of town, a GRM around 75 is considered reasonable.

2.c.   What is the value indication for the subject property by the GRM method?

The estimated market rent for the subject is $400 per month. The appropriate GRM is 75. The indicated market value by the GRM method is $30,000 ($400 × 75).

absolute mean Absolute average, as opposed to the weighted average; calculated by adding the value of all the variables then dividing by the number of variables; e.g., $2.50 + 2.22 + 20.62 = 25.34 \div 3 = 8.45$, the absolute mean.

access A path of entry to a property or the physical and legal means of entrance. Most property owners have a right to access to their property from a public street that includes the right to unimpeded flow of light and air. Landlords also have rights to access a rented property under reasonable conditions.

accrued depreciation In real estate appraisal, the total deduction from cost new due to physical deterioration, functional obsolescence and/or external obsolescence. Accrued depreciation represents the total difference between an improvement's reproduction cost or replacement cost and its contributing value in the cost approach. Typical methods of estimating accrued depreciation include the economic age-life method, the modified economic age-life method, and the breakdown method. *See also* breakdown method, curable physical deterioration, incurable physical deterioration, curable functional obsolescence, incurable functional obsolescence, external obsolescence.

accuracy Criterion that measures the appraiser's confidence in the precision or accuracy of the market data analyzed, the calculations performed in each of the approaches to value, and any necessary adjustments applied to the comparable properties for comparison with the property being appraised.

actual age The amount of time that has passed since construction of a structure was completed. It is also called chronological, physical or historical age. *See also* effective age, economic life, physical life, remaining economic life.

adjustment process Means by which appraisers measure market reaction to items of dissimilarity. *See also* application, extraction.

adverse possession The acquiring of title to real property owned by another by means of open, actual, continuous, and hostile possession for a statutory period of time that is stipulated by state law.

air rights The legal rights to use, occupy, control, and regulate the airspace above a parcel of real estate. Air rights can be sold, leased, and created through easements.

allocation The division of the value of a property between land and improvements; an appraisal method in which the land value is found by deducting the value of improvements from the overall sales price of the property. The value of the improvements may be established by developing a typical ratio of site value to total property value and applying this ratio to the property to be appraised. Allocation is most frequently used in appraisals of vacant lots in which comparable sales of vacant lots cannot be found and improved sites must be used as comparables, e.g., in urban areas where few vacant lots exist or in rural areas where few sales exist. Allocation is also called abstraction or extraction method. *See also* land.

allowance for replacements A non-cash expense item included in many forecasted income and expense statements to compensate for the future replacement of building components that may wear out in the future, such as a new roof or replacement of heating, ventilating and air-conditioning (HVAC) equipment. The annual allowance for reserves should reflect the amount that must be set aside each year to have the funds required to replace the item at the time it must be replaced. Also called an allowance for reserves or a reserve for replacement.

amortization (1) The process of retiring a debt through repayment of principal. It occurs when the payment on the debt exceeds the required interest payment for a particular time period. For example, suppose a loan has a balance at the beginning of a year of $100,000, annual payments of $12,000, and a 10% interest rate. Interest for the year would be 10% of $100,000, or

Glossary based on selected terms from the 2002 printing of *Language of Real Estate Appraisal* by Jeffrey D. Fisher, Rober S. Martin, and Paige Mosbaugh ©1991 by Dearborn Financial Publishing, Inc.®

$10,000. Amortization would be equal to $12,000 less $10,000, or $2,000 per year. (2) Annual deductions allowed in the calculation of federal income taxes. For example, points paid on a loan on income property are amortized over the loan term. If points amount to $25,000 and the loan has a 25-year term, then $1,000 can be deducted each year for tax purposes.

anchor tenant The major store that attracts or generates traffic within a shopping center. Anchors are strategically placed to maximize sales for all tenants. The type of anchor depends on the type of shopping center, e.g., a supermarket is a typical anchor for a neighborhood shopping center, whereas a major chain or department store is a typical anchor for a regional shopping mall.

annual debt service The total mortgage payments, including interest and principal, required in one year by a particular loan or for a particular property. *See also* amortization.

anticipation The appraisal principle that states that value is created by the expectation of benefits to be received in the future.

application Step in the comparison process where the appraiser applies the isolated contributory value of an isolated property.

appropriateness Criterion used by appraiser to judge the relevance of each comparable property in comparison to the property being appraised and the applicability of each approach in light of the purpose and use of the appraisal.

area The surface space defined by two-dimensional boundaries of a building, lot, market, city or other such space, measured in square units. For example, a rectangular building that measures 30 feet by 100 feet has an area of 3,000 square feet.

as if vacant Highest and best use analysis without improvements.

as improved Highest and best use analysis with improvements.

assessed value The value or worth of a property according to tax rolls on which *ad valorem* taxes are based.

balance The appraisal principle that states that property value is created and maintained when contrasting, opposing, or interacting elements are in a state of equilibrium.

breakdown method A method of estimating accrued depreciation by which each cause of depreciation is analyzed and measured separately. (The five causes measured include curable physical deterioration, incurable physical deterioration, curable functional obsolescence, incurable functional obsolescence, and external obsolescence.) The different types of depreciation are then summed to find the total depreciation. *See also* accrued depreciation, curable physical deterioration, incurable physical deterioration, curable functional obsolescence, incurable functional obsolescence, external obsolescence.

building improvements Valuable additions made to property that relate to the structure itself, classified as exterior, interior, and equipment and mechanical.

building inspection Process in which the appraiser measures both exterior and interior improvements and takes detailed notes on construction features as well as on condition of improvements with emphasis on those that may need future correction or replacement.

bundle of rights An ownership concept that describes real property by the legal rights associated with owning the property. It specifies rights such as the rights to sell, lease, use, occupy, mortgage, and trade the property, among others. These rights are typically purchased by the buyer in a sales transaction unless specifically noted or limited in the sale.

capital The accumulated wealth including money and/or property owned or used by a person or business.

cash equivalency An adjustment made to a comparable property sale that was financed in a manner not typical of the marketplace. The adjusted sales price should reflect the price that would have been paid, assuming typical financing were used. Thus, a sale with the seller carrying back a no-interest loan would be adjusted downward based on cash equivalency principles.

change An appraisal principle that recognizes the fact that a property and its environment are always in transition and are impacted by economic and social forces that are constantly at work.

collection Gathering of information for appraisal purposes.

collection loss Income that is lost when payment is not collected from tenants.

comparative-unit method A method used to estimate the cost of a building based on the value of comparable properties that were recently constructed and adjusted for time and physical differences. The total value is based on the sum of the value per square foot or cubic foot. Values may also be determined through a recognized cost service.

comparison shopping Choosing a property by comparing one to another; potential buyer intuitively compares prices of various properties, weighing the pluses and minuses for each housing alternative.

competition An appraisal concept that states that value is affected by the interaction of supply and demand in a market.

compounding Paying interest on both the accrued interest and the principal. *See also* future value of $1.

conclusion Final step in a market analysis; reconciles or correlates the results of the supply and demand analysis in the identified market.

condemnation The exercise of the power of eminent domain by the government, i.e., the right of the government to take private property for public use.

condominium A multiunit structure or property in which persons hold fee simple title to individual units and an individual interest in common areas.

conformity An appraisal principle that states that the more a property is in harmony with its surroundings, the greater the contributory value.

consistent use theory An appraisal concept that states that land and improvements to that land must be valued on the same basis. Improvements to the land must contribute to the land value to have any value themselves.

contract rent The actual rental payment specified in a lease. Contract rent may be greater than, less than or equal to economic rent and/or market rent.

contribution An appraisal concept that states that the value of a particular component is equal to the amount it contributes to the property as a whole. The value of the component is not measured as its cost but by the amount that its absence would detract from the entire property value.

cooperative apartment A unit in a building in which the resident purchases stock in the corporation or trust that owns the building in an amount representative of the value of a single apartment. The resident receives a lease for that apartment.

cost approach One of the three traditional appraisal approaches to estimating value. In this approach, value is based on adding the contributing value of any improvements (after deduction for accrued depreciation) to the value of the land as if it were vacant, based on its highest and best use. If the interest appraisal is other than fee simple, additional adjustments may be necessary for non-realty interest and/or the impact of existing leases or contracts. *See also* replacement cost, reproduction cost.

cost to cure The dollar amount needed to restore an item of deferred maintenance to a new or reasonably new condition. *See also* curable physical deterioration.

curable depreciation Items of physical deterioration and functional obsolescence in which the cost to cure the item is less than or the same as the anticipated increase in value after the item is cured. Curable depreciation is reasonable and economically feasible to cure. *See also* curable functional obsolescence, curable physical deterioration.

curable functional obsolescence A loss in value due to a defect in design, in which the cost to cure the item is less than or the same as the anticipated increase in value after the item is cured, for example, flaws in materials or design or materials and design that have become obsolete over time; an element of accrued depreciation. Includes superadequacies and deficiencies requiring additions, substitutions, or modernization.

Deficiencies requiring additions are measured by how much the cost of the addition exceeds the cost if it were installed new during construction. For example, an office building is hard to rent because it has no windows on the top floor. The cost to install new windows in the existing structure is $10,000. If the windows were installed in a new building, the cost would be $7,000. The loss in value, therefore, is $3,000.

Deficiencies requiring substitutions or modernization are measured as the cost of installing the modern component minus the remaining value of the existing component. For example, an office building has outdated tile on the floor in the lobby. New tile, including the cost of installation, will be $4,000. The remaining value of the outdated tile is $300. Therefore, the loss in value is $3,700.

Superadequacies are measured as the current *reproduction* cost of the item minus any physical deterioration already charged plus the cost to install a normally adequate or standard item. For example, a small office building lobby has 12-foot ceilings that cause the electrical bill to be too high. The cost of lowering the ceiling will be $1,000. The salvage value of the old ceiling is zero. The estimated savings from decreased electrical bills is $240 per year, which would equal a capitalized value of $1,846 at a 13% building capitalization rate. Since the capitalized gain in net operating income ($1,846) is greater than the cost to cure ($1,000), the superadequacy is deemed curable. The depreciation due to the superadequacy is estimated as follows: The current reproduction cost of the ceiling is $700 and the physical deterioration already charged is $200. Therefore, the loss in value is $1,500 ($700 – $200 + $1,000).

However, if a replacement cost is used as the basis of the current cost, the expenditure to reproduce the superadequacy and the charge for physical deterioration are not deducted. Therefore, the total amount of depreciation charged would be $1,000 (the cost to cure only).

curable physical deterioration Items of deferred maintenance or in need of repair in which the cost to repair is reasonable and economically feasible, measured as the cost to restore the item to new or reasonably new condition. An element of accrued depreciation. For example, a building has wood siding and needs to be painted. The cost to restore the building to a reasonably new state is $1,500, which is the cost of curable physical deterioration.

current date Actual date of inspection by appraiser who conveys a type of value conclusion as of that date.

data analysis Step in appraisal process where the appraiser begins to identify and understand trends and to focus in on those specific items of data that are most appropriate in leading to the final value conclusion.

decimals Parts of the whole expressed by using the decimal point; e.g., 0.10 or 0.100, which is the result of 1/10, or 1 (numerator) ÷ 10 (denominator).

decline Stage in the economic life cycle; in real estate, indicates neighborhood can no longer compete with other neighborhoods; improvements functionally inadequate, loss of market appeal, maintenance levels decline.

deed restriction A clause in the deed of a property that limits its type of use or intensity of use; usually passes with the land regardless of the owner.

deferred maintenance Items that are in need of repair because upkeep and repairs have been delayed, the result of which is physical depreciation or loss in value of a building; a type of physical deterioration that is usually curable. *See also* curable physical deterioration.

deficiency An inadequate feature in a structure or one of its components. *See also* functional obsolescence.

demand unit In economics, an individual component capable of expressing demand for a product.

desirability An economic characteristic of value; real estate is worth seeking or possessing as advantageous, beneficial, or useful.

deterioration *See* curable physical deterioration, incurable physical deterioration.

direct capitalization The capitalization method whereby forecasted first-year net operating income is divided by an estimated overall capitalization rate in order to arrive at a value estimate for the total property. *See also* income capitalization approach, yield capitalization.

For example, a property produces a first-year NOI of $20,000. The market indicates an overall capitalization rate of 0.09. The indicated value would be $222,222 ($20,000/0.09).

direct costs Expenditures necessary for the labor and materials used in the construction of a new improvement, including contractor's overhead and profit. Also called hard costs. *See also* indirect costs.

direct sales comparison approach One of the three traditional appraisal approaches to estimating value. Value is estimated by comparing to the subject property similar properties that have sold recently. Formerly referred to as the "market approach." *See also* land.

discounted cash flow analysis (DCF) In appraisal, any method whereby an appraiser prepares a cash flow forecast (including income from operations and resale) for the interests appraised, selects a discount rate that reflects the return expected for the interest and uses the rate to calculate the present value of each of the cash flows. The total present value of the cash becomes the value estimate for that interest.

Sometimes the cash flow forecast is based on an assumed pattern of change, e.g., compound growth. Also referred to as discounted cash flow. *See also* income capitalization approach, yield capitalization.

discounting The process of converting future income to a present value by mathematically reducing future cash flow by the implied interest that would have been earned assuming an initial investment, an interest rate, and a specified period (possibly divided into shorter equal periodic increments). *See also* income capitalization approach.

district A type of neighborhood that represents homogeneous land use, e.g., residential, industrial, agricultural. *See also* tax district.

drainage A system of gradually drawing off water and moisture from land, naturally or artificially, by means of pipes and conduits.

durable Long lasting; an attribute of land.

easement A legal interest in real property that conveys use or enjoyment but not ownership of the property.

easement appurtenant An easement attached to the dominant estate. An easement appurtenant is passed with the conveyance of the dominant estate and continues to burden the servient estate. *See also* easement.

easement in gross A limited right of one person to use another's property when the right is not created for the benefit of land owned by the owner of the easement. An easement in gross is not attached to any particular estate or land, nor is it transferred through the conveyance of title. Examples include pipelines and telephone lines. *See also* easement.

economic forces In appraisal theory, one type of force that affects property value. Includes effects on value such as supply and demand, employment, wage levels, industrial expansion, and availability of mortgage credit.

economic life The estimated time period during which an improvement yields a return over the economic rent attributable to the land itself; the estimated time period over which an improved property has value in excess of its salvage value. The economic life of an improvement is usually shorter than its actual physical life. *See also* remaining economic life, actual age, effective age.

economic obsolescence A type of external obsolescence in which value loss is caused by an occurrence or situation that adversely affects the employment, quality of life, or economics of an area, e.g., loss of a major employer, a high tax base, or changes in zoning. *See also* external obsolescence.

effective age The age of an improvement determined by its current condition and utility based on its design, location, and current competitive market conditions. The effective age may be greater than or less than the actual age. *See also* actual age, economic life, remaining economic life.

economics of scale Theory based on the idea that the greater the volume of an item, the less each incremental volume would cost; theory suggests that a 2,800 square foot home is less expensive per square foot than a 2,000 square foot home, all else being equal.

effective gross income (EGI) The anticipated income from the operation of a project after adjustment for vacancy and credit loss. The effective income can be further classified as actual, market, and/or economic effective gross income depending on which rent levels were considered when making the calculation. *See also* effective gross income multiplier (EGIM), potential gross income (PGI).

For example, a property has 100,000 square feet of leasable space. Current rental rates are $12 per square foot. Vacancy is expected at 15%, and a collection loss of $20,000 is expected. The effective gross income is calculated as follows:

$$10,000 \text{ sq. ft} \times 12 \text{ sq. ft} = \$1,200,000$$
$$\$1,200,000 \times (1-.15) = \$1,020,000$$
$$\$1,020,000 - \$20,000 = \$1,000,000 = EGI$$

effective gross income multiplier (EGIM) The ratio of the sales price, after adjustment for non-realty interests and favorable financing divided by the projected first-year effective gross income. For income-producing properties, the EGIM can be derived from comparable sales as one method of estimating a property value in the direct sales comparison approach. *See also* effective gross income (EGI), potential gross income multiplier (PGIM), direct sales comparison approach.

For example, the value of an apartment building that produces an annual effective gross income of $400,000 is being estimated. The EGIMs of comparable apartment buildings range from 3.24 to 4.1.

The indicated value range for the subject property would then be $1,296,000 to $1,640,000. ($400,000 × 3.24 = $1,296,000, $400,000 × 4.1 = $1,640,000).

effective purchasing power The ability to participate, economically speaking, in an activity, such as buying a home; what people can afford to buy.

efficient market A market where goods and services are easily produced and readily transferable, with a large readily identified group of active buyers and sellers.

elements of comparison A categorization of property characteristics that causes real estate prices to vary, e.g., property rights, financing terms, conditions of sale, date of sale (or market conditions), location, and physical characteristics. *See also* direct sales comparison approach.

eminent domain The governmental right to take private property for public use upon the payment of just compensation.

encroachment A part of real estate that physically intrudes upon, overlaps, or trespasses the property of another.

entrepreneur A manager, owner, or developer who assumes the risk and management of a business or enterprise; a promoter, in the sense of one who undertakes to develop.

entrepreneurial profit The sum of money an entrepreneur expects to receive in addition to costs for the time and effort, coordination, and risk bearing necessary to create a project. The portion associated with creation of the real estate by a developer is referred to as developer's profit. Properties that also include an operating business may include additional entrepreneurial profit that is reflected in the going-concern value of the property. *See also* going-concern value.

environmental forces In appraisal theory, one of four categories of forces that affect property value; environmental forces include effects on value such as climate, location, topography, natural barriers and transportation systems.

environmental hazards Toxic materials and conditions, such as chemical spills, mine tailings, nuclear waste, and a host of industrial substances harmful to life and health.

equity The owner's capital investment in a property; the property value less the balance of any debt as of a particular point in time. Equity is equal to the property value if there is no debt on the property. For example, a property is purchased for $100,000. A loan equal to $70,000 is used to purchase the property. The remaining balance, $30,000, is provided by the buyer. The equity in the property then equals $30,000.

escheat The government right to transfer property ownership to the state when the owner dies without a will or any ascertainable heirs.

excess land On an unimproved site, land that is not needed to accommodate a site's highest and best use. On an improved site, excess land is the surplus land that is not needed to serve or support the existing improvement.

external obsolescence A loss in property value resulting from negative influence outside the property itself. An element of accrued depreciation. External obsolescence is generally incurable and can be further defined as either economic obsolescence or locational obsolescence. Economic obsolescence is caused by a negative economic force that affects an entire area whereas locational obsolescence is caused by environmental or social forces that negatively affect a specific property due to its location. In the cost approach, the total loss in value from external obsolescence is distributed between the land and the improvements. External obsolescence can be measured by either capitalizing the income loss due to the negative influence or by comparing sales of similar properties that are subject to the negative influence and similar properties that are not subject to the negative influence. *See also* accrued depreciation, economic obsolescence, locational obsolescence. For example, several retail stores in an urban center have moved to the suburbs, leaving a large percentage of vacant spaces in the center. A retail space in this center currently produces a net operating income (NOI) of $14,000 after physical and functional accrued depreciation are cured. Comparable stores in other leased-up centers in the same market area indicate that the NOI on the subject property would equal $18,000 after physical and functional accrued depreciation are cured if the center was more fully leased. An overall capitalization rate of 12.5% is estimated, and the overall loss attributable is 50% to the building and 50% to the land. The external obsolescence attributable to the building is calculated as follows:

Estimated NOI with no external obsolescence	$ 18,000
NOI with external obsolescence	− 14,000
Estimated annual NOI loss ($18,000−$14,000)	$ 4,000
Capitalized NOI loss ($4,000/.125)	$ 32,000
Loss attributable to building ($32,000/2)	$ 16,000

externalities An appraisal concept that states that economies or diseconomies outside a property's boundaries may have a positive or negative effect on its value.

extraction Step in comparison process where the appraiser compares two properties that are highly similar to each other in all pertinent characteristics except for one factor. *See also* paired sales, paired rentals.

feasibility analysis According to the *Uniform Standards of Professional Appraisal Practice*, a study of the cost-benefit relationship of an economic endeavor.

feasibility study *See* feasibility analysis.

federal discount rate Interest rate at which member banks can borrow funds from the Federal Reserve Bank; raising and lowering the federal discount rate helps balance economic growth and inflation.

Federal Open Market Committee (FOMC) Arm of the Federal Reserve Bank that buys and sells government securities, in effect spurring or discouraging market economic activity.

fee simple estate Absolute ownership of real estate that is unencumbered by any other interest or estate and is subject to the limitations of eminent domain, escheat, police power, and taxation. A fee simple estate can be valuated by the present value of market rents. *See also* leased fee estate, leasehold estate. For example, suppose a building produces a net operating income of $500,000 at market rents. This income will increase at 3% per year over a 5-year holding period. With leases at the market rate as indicated above, the property value (fee simple) will also increase 3% per year. Assuming a 13% discount rate, the value of the fee simple estate (V) can be calculated as follows:

Year	NOI (increase of 3%/yr.)	Resale
1	500,000	
2	515,000	
3	530,450	
4	546,364	
5	562,754	$(1.03)^5 \times V$

$$V = \frac{500,000}{1.13} + \frac{515,000}{(1.13)^2} + \frac{530,450}{(1.13)^3}$$
$$+ \frac{546,364}{(1.13)^4} + \frac{562,754}{(1.13)^5} + \frac{(1.03)^5 \times V}{(1.13)^5}$$

$V = 442,478 + 403,321 + 367,628 + 335,095$
    $+ 305,441 + (0.629207 \times V)$
$V = 1,853,962 + (0.629207 \times V)$
$V - (0.629207 \times V) = 1,853,962$
$0.370792 \times V = 1,853,962$
$V = 5,000,000$

Now that we know the value (V), we can calculate the resale price after 5 years as follows:

Resale price $= \$5,000,000 \times (1.03)^5 = \$5,796,370$

The value of this fee simple estate could also be calculated by another method: Because income and value are increasing at the same compound rate, the going-in cap rate is equal to the discount rate (Y_0) minus the compound growth rate (g). The value can be calculated as follows:

$$V = \frac{NOI_1}{Y_0 - g}$$

$$V = \frac{500,000}{.13 - .03}$$

$$V = \$5,000,000$$

final value estimate A range of values or a single dollar amount given at the end of an appraisal report that has been derived from the reconciliation of the different methods of valuation used in the report.

financially feasible A requirement of highest and best use; refers to a project that satisfies the economic objectives of the investor.

finite in supply Something that is not continually created; an attribute of land.

fiscal policy Government management of revenues (taxes) and expenses (appropriations).

fixed expense An operating expense that does not vary with the occupancy level of a property, e.g., property taxes, insurance, repairs and maintenance, advertising and promotions. *See also* variable expense.

fixture Personal property that becomes real property after it is attached to the land or building in a permanent manner. To determine if an item can be considered a fixture, it must meet three criteria: (1) it must be able to be removed without serious injury to itself or the real estate; (2) the character of the item must be such that it is specifically constructed for or carries out the purpose for which the building was built; (3) it must be the intention of the party that attached the item to leave it attached on a permanent basis. Examples of fixtures include built-in dishwashers, furnaces, and garage door openers. Trade fixtures are not considered real property.

floodplain A geographic area close to a river or stream that is subject to flooding. In some areas, floodplains are mapped by the Federal Emergency Management Agency so that they may be covered by the National Flood Insurance Plan.

fractions Parts of the whole expressed by using a numerator and denominator; e.g., ½.

frontage The length of a property that abuts the street line or other landmark such as a body of water. Frontage differs from width, which may vary from the front of the lot to the back.

function (1) In relation to a building, the intended use, activity, or purpose for which a building was designated or altered. (2) In appraisal, the intended use or uses of an appraisal report by the client or a third party.

functional obsolescence A loss in the value of real estate improvements due to functional inadequacies or subadequacies due to poor design and/or change in market standards or requirements for building components. *See also* curable functional obsolescence, incurable functional obsolescence.

functional utility The extent to which a property is able to be used for the purpose that it was intended. Functional utility includes factors such as current trends in tastes and styles, architectural style, design and layout, and traffic patterns.

future benefits In appraisal, anticipated positive cash flows or appreciation in property value. A premise of the income approach.

future date Prospective date or projected date upon which appraiser is asked to estimate a type of value; future date valuations must carry appropriate qualifiers.

future value annuity of $1 per period (S$_n$) A compound interest factor that represents the sum to which a constant periodic investment of $1 per period will grow assuming compound growth at a specific rate of return for a specific number of compounding periods. In an appraisal, these payments are generally assumed to be made at the end of each period. The factor can be calculated through the following formula:

$$\frac{(1 + i)^n - 1}{i}$$

where i equals the periodic interest rate and n equals the number of periods.

Also called amount of $1 per period and future value interest factor-annuity.

future value of $1 (S^n) The amount to which an investment of $1 grows with compound interest after a specified number of years at a specified interest rate. The factor is arrived at by adding $1 to the interest per period (i) and taking this to the exponent of the number of years (n), i.e., $(1 + i)^n$. Also called the amount of $1, future value interest factor, and future worth of $1.

general data Information that is not specific to a certain property, e.g. interest rates, employment rates, and census information.

general warranty deed Conveys a covenant of warranty in which the seller guarantees to the buyer that the title is unclouded or clean of any prior claims or heirs.

going concern value The value of a property which includes the value due to a successful operating business enterprise which is expected to continue. Going-concern value results from the process of assembling the land, building, labor, equipment, and marketing operation and includes consideration of the efficiency of plant, the know-how of management, and the sufficiency of capital. The portion of going concern value that exceeds that of the real property and tangible personal property is an intangible value that is referred to as business value.

governmental forces In appraisal theory, one of four forces thought to affect real estate value, e.g., government controls and regulations, public services, fiscal policies, and zoning and building codes.

gross building area (GBA) The total floor area of a building measured in square feet from the external walls, excluding unenclosed areas. Unlike gross living area measurements, GBA does include basement areas. *See also* gross living area.

gross living area (GLA) Residential space measured by finished and habitable above-grade areas, excluding finished basements or attic areas. Gross living area is measured by the outside perimeter of the building. *See also* gross building area (GBA).

gross rent multiplier (GRM) The ratio of sales price or value divided by the potential or effective gross rent; a measure similar to the gross income multiplier but used exclusively for residential properties that receive rent only and no other types of income.

The gross rent multiplier can be used in appraising to give a rough estimate of value. For example, a small rental house is being appraised. Two other similar rental properties have recently sold in the same neighborhood. The sales can be summarized as follows:

	Comp #1	Comp #2
Adjusted sales price	$100,000	$115,000
Gross rent	$11,500	$13,500
GRM	8.70	8.52

If the subject property rents for $12,000 per year, the value of the property indicated by the comparable sales would be $102,240 to $104,400.

$$\$12,000 \times 8.70 = \$104,400$$
$$\$12,000 \times 8.52 = \$102,240$$

growth Initial stage of expansion and development in a neighborhood or district life cycle.

heated areas Those parts of a building that include enclosed, heated areas measured in from the outside walls.

highest and best use (HBU) The reasonable and probable use that results in the highest present value of the land after considering all legally permissible, physically possible, and economically feasible uses. Capitalization rates or discount rates for each feasible use should reflect typical returns expected in the market. Highest and best use is usually determined under two different premises: as if the site was vacant and could be improved in the optimal manner or as the site is currently improved.

In the latter premise, the highest and best use of the site will either be to keep the existing building or to demolish the building and develop a building that is the highest and best use. In general, it is not feasible to demolish an existing building as long as it contributes to the value of the site.

holding Speculative retention of a parcel until underlying land economics mature to justify more clear determination of the use that is physically possible, legally permissible, financially feasible, and maximally productive.

income approach *See* income capitalization approach.

income capitalization approach One of the three traditional appraisal approaches to estimating value. In this approach, value is based on the present value of future benefits of property ownership. In direct capitalization, a single year's income is converted to a value indication using a capitalization rate. In yield capitalization, future cash flows are estimated and discounted to a present value using a discount rate. *See also* direct capitalization, yield capitalization.

increasing and decreasing returns, principle of An economic principle that states that the addition of more factors of production will increase the output at an increasing rate until a maximum is reached (the asset's maximum value). Then as more input factors are added, income will increase at a decreasing rate, producing an output value that is less than the cost of the added factor.

incurable functional obsolescence A defect caused by a deficiency or superadequacy in the structure, materials, or design of a structure. The defect is deemed incurable if the cost to cure the defect is greater than the anticipated increase in value after the defect is cured. A component of accrued depreciation. Incurable functional obsolescence due to a deficiency is measured as the net income loss attributable to the deficiency in comparison with otherwise competitive properties. The net income loss can be divided by the overall cap rate to find the amount of the obsolescence. For example, the estimated net income loss due to an incurable deficiency is estimated to be $1,000 per year. The overall cap rate is 10%. The estimated incurable functional obsolescence due to the deficiency would equal $1,000 \div 10\% = \$10,000$.

Incurable functional obsolescence due to a superadequacy based on the *reproduction* cost is measured as the current reproduction cost of the superadequacy minus any physical deterioration already charged plus the present value of the added cost of ownership due to the superadequacy. For example, the current reproduction cost of a superadequacy is $2,000. Physical deterioration already charged equals $200. The cost of ownership of the superadequacy (additional taxes, insurance, maintenance, and utility charges) equals $50 per year (with a present value of $500). The estimated amount of the incurable functional obsolescence equals:

Current *reproduction* cost of superadequacy	$2,000
Less physical deterioration	200
Plus present value cost of ownership	500
Total incurable functional obsolescence	$2,300

Incurable functional obsolescence due to a superadequacy based on the *replacement* cost does not consider physical deterioration, because the replacement cost does not include the cost to construct a superadequacy. For example, the replacement cost of a superadequacy equals $1,500. The present value of the additional cost of ownership due to the superadequacy equals $400. The estimated amount of the incurable functional obsolescence equals:

Current *replacement* cost of superadequacy $1,500
Plus present value cost of ownership   400
Total incurable functional obsolescence $1,900

Sometimes a superadequacy will cause the rent for the property to be higher than that of an equivalent property but not enough to justify the capital requirements of the item's cost. In this instance, the obsolescence is measured as the capitalized rent plus the superadequate item's current cost minus the physical deterioration plus the present value of the added cost of ownership. *See also* accrued depreciation, breakdown method, deficiency, superadequacy.

incurable physical deterioration A defect caused by physical wear and tear on the building that is unreasonable or uneconomical to correct. An element of accrued depreciation. Incurable physical deterioration can be further classified as long-lived or short-lived. Long-lived items are expected to have a remaining economic life that equals the remaining economic life of the structure. Short-lived items are expected to have a remaining economic life that is less than the remaining economic life of the structure. Both types of incurable physical deterioration are measured by the physical age-life method, which calculates depreciation by multiplying the ratio of effective age divided by the total physical life of the item by the reproduction or replacement cost of the item minus any curable physical deterioration already charged. Incurable physical deterioration for shortlived items is calculated first and subtracted from the reproduction or replacement cost before the depreciation for long-lived items is calculated. *See also* accrued depreciation, breakdown method. For example, the roof and plumbing on a building each have an effective age of 10 years. The roof has a total physical life of 20 years, and the plumbing has a total physical life of 25 years. Outdoor paint was applied 5 years ago and has a total physical life of 10 years. The reproduction cost after curable physical depreciation was subtracted for the roof, plumbing and paint are $20,000, $12,000, and $6,000 respectively. The short-lived incurable physical deterioration can be estimated as follows:

	Repro-duction Cost Remaining	Effec-tive Age	Total Physical Life	Ratio	Short-lived Incurable Physical Depreciation
Roof	$20,000	10	20	0.50	$10,000
Plumbing	$12,000	10	25	0.40	$4,800
Paint	$ 6,000	1	10	0.10	$600
Total short-lived incurable physical depreciation					$15,400

Assume that the above building's reproduction cost of longlived items equals $350,000. Depreciation due to curable physical deterioration and short-lived incurable deterioration equals $20,000. The building has an effective age of 10 years and has a total physical life of 50 years. The amount of incurable physical deterioration for long-lived items can be estimated as follows: Reproduction cost = $350,000 - $20,000 = $330,000.

Reproduction Cost Remaining	Effective Age	Total Physical Life	Ratio	Long-lived Incurable Physical Depreciation
$330,000	10	50	0.20	$66,000

indirect costs Construction expenses for items other than labor and materials, e.g., financing costs, taxes, administrative costs, contractor's overhead and profit, legal fees, interest payments, insurance costs during construction, and lease-up costs. Also called soft costs. *See also* direct costs.

insurable value The value of the destructible parts of a property. This value is used to determine the amount of insurance carried on the property.

interest Money paid for the use of money over time; a return on capital. Interest payments are deductible for income tax purposes, although payments of principal are not.

inefficient market A market where goods and services are not easily produced or readily transferable, with no readily identified group of active buyers and sellers.

interim use A temporary use for a property when the highest and best use of the property is different from the highest and best use of the land as if vacant.

investment value The value of a property to a particular investor.

joint tenancy Joint ownership by two or more persons with right of survivorship in which each person has an identical interest and right of possession. *See also* tenancy.

labor Direct and indirect costs and wages associated with workers; includes materials used by labor in the production of a commodity.

land The earth's surface including the solid surface of the earth, water, and anything attached to it; natural resources in their original state, e.g., mineral deposits, timber, soil. In law, land is considered to be the solid surface of the earth and does not include water. Common methods used to provide legal descriptions of land include the metes and bounds system, rectangular survey (government survey) system, geodetic survey system and lot and block system. Land valuation techniques include the direct sales comparison approach, allocation, extraction, subdivision development, land residual, and ground rent capitalization.

land residual technique A technique used to find the value of a property by subtracting income attributable to the building from the net operating income and valuing the residual land income, for example, by dividing the land income by a land capitalization rate to arrive at a land value indication. The land value is then added to the building value to arrive at an estimate of value for the total property. The land residual technique is one way of evaluating the highest and best use of a site. Under its highest and best use, the building value should equal its development cost and the highest land value will result for this use. *See also* land.

For example, a property's building is valued at $100,000. Net operating income (NOI) for the property equals $30,000. The land cap rate equals 10% and building cap rate equals 13%. The land value and property value can be calculated as follows:

Building value	$100,000
NOI	$30,000
Building value $\times R_B$ (100,000 $\times$ 0.13)	$- 13,000$
Residual income to land	17,000
Land value (17,000/0.10)	170,000
Total property value	$270,000

lease A written contract between a building owner and a tenant that transfers the right to occupy a specific property to the tenant for a specific period of time in return for a specified rent. The lease may also establish other rules, conditions and terms regarding the use and occupancy of the property under which the lease will be valid.

leased fee estate An ownership interest in the real estate held by a landlord who has transferred the right of occupancy to a property through the execution of a lease. The landlord retains the right to receive rental payment throughout the term of the lease and the right to possess the property at the termination of the lease. The leased fee estate can be valued as the present value of the lease income plus the right to the reversion at the end of the lease. The discount rate used to value the leased fee estate may be higher or lower than the discount rate used to value the fee simple estate, depending on the risk associated with the lease. Characteristics such as the creditworthiness of the tenants and terms of the lease should be considered. Care must also be taken when using the cost approach to value a leased fee

estate. The cost approach always gives a fee simple value. *See also* fee simple estate, leasehold estate.

For example, assume that a building is leased so that NOI is $400,000 per year for a holding period of 5 years, at which time the lease expires with no renewal option. The resale value at the end of the 5 years is estimated to be $5,796,370. Assume a discount rate of 12.5%. The value of the leased fee estate (V) can now be calculated as follows:

$$V = \frac{400,000}{1.125} + \frac{400,000}{(1.125)^2} + \frac{400,000}{(1.125)^3}$$
$$+ \frac{400,000}{(1.125)^4} + \frac{400,000}{(1.125)^5} + \frac{5,796,370}{(1.125)^5}$$

$$V = \$4,640,801$$

leasehold estate An ownership interest in real estate held by a tenant during the term of a lease. The tenant is given the right to use and occupy a property for a time and based on the restrictions contained in the lease. The leasehold estate can be valued as the present value of the difference between the market rent and the rent specified by the lease. The value of the leasehold estate is not necessarily equal to the difference between the value of the fee simple estate and the leased fee estate. The leasehold estate may be more or less risky than the fee simple estate or the leased fee estate. Any change in market rent will have the most effect on the value of the leasehold estate. Therefore, the leasehold estate may be discounted at a higher or lower rate than the fee simple estate or leased fee estate. *See also* fee simple estate, leased fee estate.

For example, assume that a building is leased at a rate of $400,000 per year for a holding period of 5 years, at which time the lease expires with no renewal option. Market rates for this property equal $500,000 in the first year, increasing at a rate of 3% per year. Assume a discount rate of 18%, The value of the leasehold estate (V) can now be calculated as follows:

Year	1	2	3	4	5
Market rent	500,000	515,000	530,450	546,364	562,754
Actual rent	400,000	400,000	400,000	400,000	400,000
Difference	100,000	115,000	130,450	146,364	162,754

$$V = \frac{100,000}{1.18} + \frac{115,000}{(1.18)^2} + \frac{130,450}{(1.18)^3}$$
$$+ \frac{146,364}{(1.18)^4} + \frac{162,754}{(1.18)^5}$$

$$V = \$393,367$$

legally permissible Required in highest and best use; that which is allowable by law. To be the highest and best use of a site, the use must be legally permissible.

lien A charge created by agreement or law against a property in which the property serves as the security for a debt.

life cycle *See* neighborhood life cycle.

life estate An estate that is limited to the lifetime of a designated party and conveys the rights to use, occupy and control the property.

limited market property Property for which there is a market, although the market is not readily identifiable. *See also* special purpose property.

limited warranty deed *See* special warranty deed.

liquidation value The price received when a property is sold as a quick sale.

loan to value ratio (M) The ratio of the outstanding loan balance divided by the total property value. For example, a property is purchased for $15,000,000 with an $11,250,000 loan. The loan to value ratio could be calculated as follows: M = 11,250,000/15,000,000 = 0.75.

locational obsolescence A type of external obsolescence in which value loss is caused by a negative influence outside the property due to its location, e.g., a corner location in a residential area, a health hazard close to the property, or a change of property use close to the property. *See also* external obsolescence.

long-lived item A component with an expected remaining economic life that is the same as the remaining economic life of the entire structure.

lot and block survey system A legal description of subdivided land that refers to the lot by lot and block numbers that appear on survey maps and plats of recorded subdivided land. *See also* land.

market analysis According to the *Uniform Standards of Professional Appraisal Practice*, a study of real estate market conditions for a specific type of property.

market extraction *See* direct sales comparison method.

market rent The rental income that a property would command if exposed for lease in a competitive market.

market segmentation The identification and analysis of submarkets within a larger market. *See also* market disaggregation.

market study *See* market analysis.

market value According to the *Uniform Standards of Professional Appraisal Practice*, market value is the major focus of most real property appraisal assignments. Both economic and legal definitions of market value have been developed and refined. A current economic definition agreed upon by federal financial institutions in the United States is:

The most probable price which a property should bring in a competitive and open market under all conditions requisite to a fair sale, the buyer and seller each acting prudently and knowledgeably, and assuming the price is not affected by undue stimulus. Implicit in this definition is the consummation of a sale as of a specified date and the passing of title from seller to buyer under conditions whereby:

1. buyer and seller are typically motivated;

2. both parties are well-informed or well-advised, and acting in what they consider their best interests;

3. a reasonable time is allowed for exposure in the open market;

4. payment is made in terms of cash in United States dollars or in terms of financial arrangements comparable thereto; and

5. the price represents the normal consideration for the property sold unaffected by special or creative financing or sales concessions granted by anyone associated with the sale.

Substitution of another currency for United States dollars in the fourth condition is appropriate in other countries or in reports addressed to clients from other countries.

Persons performing appraisal services that may be subject to litigation are cautioned to seek the exact legal definition of market value in the jurisdiction in which the services are being performed.

maximally productive One of four criteria in highest and best use analysis which states that a use is the highest and best use if it produces the highest value or price. *See also* highest and best use (HBU).

mean An average of a set of numbers; the sum of a group of values divided by the number of values in the group; a measure of the central tendency of data. The mean is affected by extreme values. For example, the mean of the set of numbers 1, 4, and 500 is 168.33

[(1+4+500)/3]. The mean of the set of numbers 1, 4, and 5 is 3.33 [(1+4+5)/3]. *See also* median, mode, weighted average.

median The middle figure in a numerically ordered set of data having an equal number of values lying above and below the middle figure; a measure of the central tendency of data. If an even number of data points are present in the data set, then the median is the average of the middle two figures. The median is not affected by extreme values as is the mean. For example, the median of the set of numbers 1, 4, and 500 is 4. The median of the set of numbers 1, 4, and 5 is also 4. *See also* mean, mode.

metes and bounds method A legal description of land in which land boundaries are referred to by a point of origin, metes, and bounds. The point of origin is extended by a line in a specified direction (metes). The points at which these lines change direction are called bounds. This process continues until the line has returned to the point of origin. The metes and bounds method is the oldest known land survey method and the primary method of describing property in many states. *See also* land.

mode The most frequent value in a set of numbers or most frequent response in a set of responses. The mode is not affected by extreme numbers. If the sample size is very small and no duplicate numbers exist, a mode does not exist. For example, in the set of numbers 1, 3, 4, 4, 2, 2, 6, and 4, the mode is 4. In the set of numbers 1, 3, 4, and 5, there is no mode. *See also* mean, median.

modified economic age-life method A method of estimating accrued depreciation in which the ratio of effective age to total economic life is multiplied by the reproduction or replacement cost minus curable physical and functional obsolescence to calculate the incurable accrued depreciation. *See also* accrued depreciation.

For example, the reproduction cost of a building equals $80,000. Curable physical and functional obsolescence is estimated to be $800. The total economic life equals 40 years and the effective age equals 20 years. The indicated incurable accrued depreciation can be calculated as follows:

$(20/40) \times (80,000 - 800) = 39,600$
The indicated property value equals $80,000 - 800 - 39,600 = $39,600$.

money market The interaction of buyers and sellers of short-term money instruments.

monument system Land description system that utilizes natural and human-made landmarks to describe land; generally no longer used.

mortgage A legal document in which real estate is named under certain conditions as the security or collateral for the repayment of a loan.

mortgage capitalization rate (R_M) The mortgage capitalization rate that is the ratio of the first-year debt payment divided by the beginning loan balance. In some instances, the ratio may be calculated using one month's payment but typically it is the total of the loan payment for an entire year. Also referred to as a mortgage loan constant.

For example, a $100,000 loan has terms of 10% interest, monthly payments, and a 20-year term. Monthly payments equal $965.02. The mortgage capitalization rate can be calculated as follows:

$$R_M = \frac{\$965.02 \times 12}{\$100,000} = 0.116, \text{ or } 11.6\%$$

mortgage constant *See* mortgage capitalization rate (R_M).

mortgage interest rate The sum paid or accrued in return for the use of money, as in a mortgage loan.

mortgage payment (PMT) Money paid to a lender to decrease the principal and/or interest on a mortgage. The amount of the mortgage payment varies depending on the type of loan. On a level-payment mortgage, the payment can be calculated as the annuity to pay the principal at the specified interest rate and mortgage term. *See also* amortization schedule.

For example, the payment on a $100,000 mortgage at 10% over a 15-year term with level monthly payments can be calculated as follows:

$\text{PMT} = 100,000 \times 1/a_{\overline{n}|(10\%, \text{ 15 years})}$
$1/a_{\overline{n}|(10\%, \text{ 15 years})} = 0.010746$ using a monthly compound interest table or financial calculator
$\text{PMT} = 100,000 \times 0.010746$
$\text{PMT} = \$1,074.61$

mortgage term The length of time, specified in a mortgage contract, over which a mortgage loan must be paid off.

neighborhood A geographical area delineated by geographical or political boundaries that is characterized by having complementary land uses.

neighborhood life cycle The changes that occur in a neighborhood over time. The cycle is defined by four stages: growth, stability, decline, and revitalization. Gentrification is not part of the natural neighborhood life cycle.

net income multiplier (NIM) The ratio of the price or value of a property divided by its net operating income; the reciprocal of the overall rate. For example, a property is purchased for $12,000,000. The first-year net operating income equals $1,000,000. The net income multiplier equals $12,000,000/$1,000,000 = 12. The overall rate (R_O) would equal 1/12 = 0.083.

net income ratio (NIR) The ratio of net operating income divided by effective gross income. For example, a property produces an effective gross income of $75,000. The net operating income equals $50,000. The net income ratio would equal: $50,000/$75,000 = 0.67. The complement of this ratio is the operating expense ratio, i.e., the operating expense ratio plus the net income ratio equals 1. In this example, the operating expense ratio would equal 0.33.

net operating income (NOI) The actual or anticipated income remaining during a year after deducting operating expenses from effective gross income but before any deductions for debt service payment or income taxes.

For example, an office building consists of 10,000 square feet that is rented at the rate of $12 per square foot. The vacancy rate equals 15%, and there is no collection loss. Operating expenses equal $6 per square foot. The net operating income can be calculated as follows:

Potential gross income: (10,000 sf × $12/sf)	$120,000
Vacancy loss ($120,000 × 0.15)	− 18,000
Effective gross income	102,000
Operating expenses (10,000 sf × $6/sf)	− 60,000
Net operating income	$ 42,000

objective value Economic theory holding that value is inherent in the object itself: "Because something is, it has value."

obsolescence A loss in value resulting from defects in design or forces outside the boundaries of a property. May be either functional or external. *See also* accrued depreciation, curable functional obsolescence, external obsolescence, incurable functional obsolescence.

on-site improvements Physical improvements that are constructed within the boundaries of a parcel of land,

for example, buildings, structures, and other support facilities installed within the boundaries of the property.

operating expenses Expenditures necessary to maintain the real property and continue the production of income. Includes both fixed expenses and variable expenses but does not include debt service, depreciation, or capital expenditures. *See also* fixed expense, variable expense.

opportunity cost The cost of options forgone or opportunities that are not chosen.

original loan amount Face amount of the original loan.

overall capitalization rate (R_O) A single year's cash flow ratio that is calculated by dividing the net operating income (NOI) by the total value of the property. When calculated using NOI for the first year of operations, the overall capitalization rate is sometimes referred to as a "current yield." However, it is *not* a yield rate that considers NOI over the entire holding period, nor does it consider resale proceeds. Thus it should not be confused with an overall yield rate. Frequently used to find the value of a property by dividing the first year's net operating income by the overall capitalization rate. The inverse of the overall capitalization rate is the net income multiplier. Also called overall cap rate. *See also* yield capitalization, direct capitalization, income capitalization approach, net income multiplier (NIM).

For example, a property is valued at $100,000. The net operating income equals $9,000. The overall capitalization rate would equal $9,000/$100,000 = 0.09. The net income multiplier would equal 1/0.09, or 11.11.

payment *See* mortgage payment (PMT).

paired rentals Appraiser's comparison of two properties highly similar to each other except for the one factor, rent rate.

paired sales Appraiser's comparison of two properties highly similar to each other except for the one factor, sales price.

percentage adjustments The adjustment of the price of a comparable property when the amount of adjustment is based on a percentage of either the price of the subject property or a percentage of the price of the comparable property. For example, suppose the comparable property sold for $100,000. If the subject was

10% inferior to the comparable property, then the adjusted price would be $100,000 − .10 × 100,000 or .90 × $100,000 = $90,000. It should be noted that this is not the same as if the comparable property was stated as being 10% better than the subject. In this case, the adjustment would be $100,000/(1.10) = $90,909. The adjustment is slightly different because in this case the percentage adjustment (10%) is applied to the subject's price. That is, $90,909 + $90,909 × .10 = $90,000 × (1.10) = $100,000.

percentages Parts of the whole expressed as percents of the whole; when the decimal is moved two places to the right it becomes a percentage, e.g., 0.3500 = 35.00%.

periodic payment to grow to $1 Provides an estimate of the periodic amount that must be set aside to accumulate to a certain amount in the future.

personal property According to the *Uniform Standards of Professional Appraisal Practice*, identifiable, portable, and tangible objects, which are considered by the general public as being personal, e.g., furnishings, artwork, antiques, gems and jewelry, collectibles, machinery, and equipment. All property that is not classified as real estate.

physical deterioration *See* curable physical deterioration, incurable physical deterioration.

physical life The actual time period over which a structure is considered habitable, in contrast to economic life. *See also* actual age, economic life, effective age, remaining economic life.

physically possible One of four criteria in highest and best use analysis. For a use to be the highest and best use, the size, shape, and terrain of the property must be able to accommodate the use. *See also* highest and best use (HBU).

plottage An increment of value that results when extra utility is created by combining two or more sites under a single ownership.

point A fee charged by a lender to issue a loan; one point equals 1 percent of the loan. For example, a borrower who wishes to borrow $100,000 but will be charged 2 points must actually borrow $102,041 [$100,000/(1-.02)]. In this case, payments would be based on the full amount of the loan ($102,041), but the borrower will only receive $100,000 and the lender will receive a fee of $2,041. The effect of points is the raise the effective rate of the loan. Also called discount point.

police power The governmental right to regulate property for the purpose of protecting public safety, health and general welfare, e.g., condemnation, rent control, zoning.

positive leasehold estate Value of the lessee's (or tenant's) interest is the present value of the excess rent (i.e., difference between contract rent and market rent) for the remainder of the lease term, plus options if applicable.

potential gross income (PGI) The amount of theoretical income a property could potentially generate assuming 100% occupancy at market rental rates. For example, an office building contains 20,000 square feet of leasable area. Market rates for this type of building are currently $11 per square foot. The potential gross income equals $220,000 (20,000 sf × $11/sf). *See also* effective gross income (EGI), net operating income (NOI).

present value annuity of $1 per period (a) $_{\overline{n}|}$) A compound interest factor typically calculated for an annual interest rate that is used to discount a series of equal future cash flows in order to arrive at a current present value of the total stream of income. The factor is calculated through the following formula:

$$\frac{1[1/(1 + i)^n]}{i}$$

where i equals the periodic interest rate and n equals the number of periods. Also called present value interest factor annuity, present value of an annuity, present worth of $1 per period.

previous date Date in past upon which appraiser is asked to estimate a type of value; also referred to as a *back-dated appraisal*.

price The amount of money paid or asked for in a specific transaction; the price may include non-realty items such as personal property or a financing premium. The price does not necessarily equal the market value.

property value (V) The monetary worth of interests held in real estate arising from property ownership. A property may have several different values depending on the interest or use involved. Common methods of estimating property value include the cost approach, direct sales comparison approach, and income approach.

principle of substitution States that the maximum value of a property tends to be set by the cost of acquiring, through purchase or construction, an equally desirable and valuable substitute property, assuming no costly delay is encountered in making the substitution.

purchase money mortgage A mortgage taken back by a seller in lieu of cash from a buyer.

purpose A section of the appraisal report that identifies the real property and type of value addressed in the report.

quality/condition survey Appraiser's survey of the property improvements, noting quality standards met, or ones that are lacking or that are above standard for the market, particularly short-lived items such as paint, gutters, appliances, carpeting, and items with lives less than the property itself.

quantity of evidence Appropriateness and accuracy of appraisal analyzed in relation to criterion of quantity of evidence; lack of sufficient evidence may weaken the market data analyzed and, therefore, the value indication(s) derived by the approach(es) to value that relied upon the particular market data.

quantity survey method The most comprehensive method of estimating building construction or reproduction costs in which the quantity and quality of all materials and labor are estimated on a current unit cost basis to arrive at a total cost estimate. The method duplicates the contractor's method of developing a bid. Also called builder's breakdown method, price take-off method.

quitclaim deed A legal instrument by which an estate or ownership interest in real property is conveyed by a grantor to a grantee without warranty of title.

range An interval in numbers ordered sequentially from the lowest to the highest number.

real estate According to the *Uniform Standards of Professional Appraisal Practice*, an identified parcel or tract of land, including improvements if any. *See also* real property.

real property According to the *Uniform Standards of Professional Appraisal Practice*, the interests, benefits, and rights inherent in the ownership of real estate.
    Comment: In some jurisdictions, the terms real estate and real property have the same legal meaning. The separate definitions recognize the traditional dis-

tinction between the two concepts in appraisal theory. *See also* personal property.

reconciliation In the appraisal process, the analysis of value indications from different appraisal approaches to arrive at a final value estimate.

rectangular survey method A method initially used by the federal government of legally describing land by east-west lines (base lines) and north-south lines (principal meridians). Further lines are drawn located 6 miles apart. These east-west lines are called township lines and north-south lines are called range lines. The location within the township and range lines are called townships (measuring 36 square miles). Townships are further divided into 36 sections that measure 1 square mile. To account for the curvature of the earth, guide meridians are drawn every 24 miles east and west of the principal meridian and standard parallels are drawn every 24 miles north and south of the base line. Also called the government survey method. *See also* land.

remaining economic life The time period over which an improvement is expected to add value above the value of the land as if vacant and valued at its highest and best use. *See also* actual age, effective age, economic life, physical life.

replacement allowance *See* allowance for replacements.

replacement cost The cost of constructing a building today with a structure having the same functional utility as a structure being appraised. The cost includes construction using modern materials and modern techniques. *See also* reproduction cost.

reproduction cost The cost of constructing a building today with an exact duplicate or replica of a structure being appraised including all deficiencies, superadequacies, and obsolescence that are in the current building. *See also* replacement cost.

reserve for replacement *See* allowance for replacements.

reserve requirement Percentage of deposits that must be retained by banks to ensure balanced economic expansion and inflation control.

revitalization Stage in neighborhood or district life cycle showing regain of momentum, rebirth, or reentry into new growth cycle; in older areas, sometimes called *gentrification*.

scarcity An environment in which demand is greater than supply for a particular product and an increase in value for the good typically results.

scope In an appraisal report, the data program or extent of the process of collecting, confirming, and reporting appraisal data.

shape Geometric configuration of land site; of importance is market preference and utility attributed to the shape as it relates to the site's highest and best use.

shop tenants Tenants in a shopping center who benefit from the presence of anchor tenants who draw patrons or shoppers to the center. *See also* anchor tenant.

short-lived item A structural component with an expected remaining economic or useful life that is shorter than the remaining economic life of the structure as a whole. *See also* curable physical deterioration, incurable physical deterioration.

site A plot of land improved for a specific purpose.

site improvements *See* on-site improvements.

size Dimensions of land site, usually expressed in square feet or acres; of importance is the size of the parcel related to zoning requirements.

social forces In appraisal theory, one of four forces thought to influence property value. Refers to population characteristics such as population age and distribution.

sources of cost data Compendium of cost data gathered from appraiser's own ongoing files of actual cost estimates, building contractors, published cost manuals by cost-estimating services, online computer services, professional cost estimators, and recent sales of newly constructed buildings where site value can easily be supported.

special purpose property A property that is appropriate for only one use or a very limited number of uses. Its highest and best use will probably be continued at the current use or the building will be demolished so the property can be used for another use.

special warranty deed Warrants to the grantee by the grantor that the seller will defend the buyer against all claims by the actions or omissions of the grantor but not any claims that precede the grantor's ownership. Also known as a limited warranty deed.

standard deviation In statistics, the square root of the arithmetic mean of the squares of the deviations from the arithmetic mean of the frequency distribution. The standard deviation measures the extent of variability in a frequency distribution and it is often used as a measure of risk. *See also* mean.

For example, the standard deviation of the set of numbers 3, 4, 6, 8, 10, and 5 can be calculated as follows:

the mean of the distribution = $(3+4+6+8+10+5)/6 = 6$
the variance = $[(3-6)^2 + (4-6)^2 + (6-6)^2 + (8-6)^2 + (10-6)^2 + (5-6)^2]/6 = 5.67$
the square root of $5.67 = 2.38$ (standard deviation)

specific data Refers in appraisal data collection to the subject property itself as well as to the comparable sales, improved sales, and rent utilized in the three approaches to value.

stability Stage in neighborhood or district life cycle manifesting slower growth rate; supply of vacant land may be depleted or prohibitively expensive.

statistical analysis Process by which appraisers analyze large samples of data through the use of various mathematical relationships. *See also* mean, median, mode, range, standard deviation, and weighted average.

subdivision development Technique used to estimate land value where the appraiser views the land parcel as subdivided into smaller tracts or lots.

subjective value Economic theory holding that value is in the eye of the beholder, not in the object itself: "The worth of a thing is what it will bring."

submission of report Final step in the appraisal process; while the report format will be specified by the client, the allowed report formats are outlined in the *Uniform Standards of Professional Appraisal Practice (USPAP)*.

substitution The appraisal principle that states that a buyer will pay no more for a property than the cost of obtaining an equally desirable substitute. If several similar goods are supplied, the good with the lowest price will produce the greatest demand and quantity sold. Substitution is one of the key principles for both the direct sales comparison approach and the cost approach to appraisal.

subsurface rights The right to the use and profit from the land that lies below the surface of a property, for example, the right to extract minerals or construct and maintain underground sewers and lines.

superadequacy A type of functional obsolescence that is caused by a structural component that is too large or of a higher quality than what is needed for the highest and best use of the property; an item in which its cost exceeds its value; an overimprovement (e.g., high ceilings in an office, built-in bookshelves in a building to be used as a restaurant). *See also* curable functional obsolescence, incurable functional obsolescence.

supply and demand An appraisal principle that states that the value of a property depends on the quantity and price of the property type available in the market, and on the number of market participants and the price that they are willing to pay.

surplus land Unlike excess land, surplus land cannot be sold off as a separate use; it is additional land over and above what is typical for a specific property in an area.

surplus productivity The net income remaining after the costs of labor, capital, and coordination have been deducted from total income.

survey (1) The process by which the boundaries and area of a parcel of land is measured. Information such as the location of improvements, physical features of the land, easements, encroachments, and lines of ownership are typically specified. (2) A map or plan that illustrates the results of the survey.

taxation Right granted to government to levy taxes on properties.

tenancy (1) The ownership of property by a title. (2) As conveyed in a lease, the right to use and occupy a space. *See also* joint tenancy, tenancy by the entireties, tenancy in common.

tenancy by the entireties An equal, indivisible estate held by a husband and wife in which neither has a disposable interest in the property during the lifetime of the other, except by joint action. The property passes to the survivor upon death of one spouse. *See also* tenancy.

tenancy in common An indivisible estate held by two or more persons that may be equal or unequal interests. The property passes to the heirs, not the survivor(s), on the death of one. *See also* tenancy.

total physical deterioration Summation of the depreciation estimates for curable physical (deferred maintenance) items, incurable short-lived components, and incurable long-lived components.

time-sharing A sale of limited, undivided ownership interests in a property in which each purchaser receives a deed conveying title to the unit for a specific period of time.

topography The features and contour of the land.

tract A lot; often refers to a lot that will be subdivided into smaller parcels.

unique in composition An attribute of land where no two parcels are identical in their geological composition.

unique in location An attribute of land; no two parcels are identical in terms of location.

unit-in-place method A method of estimating building costs in which total building cost is estimated by summing prices for various building components as installed, based on specific units of use such as square footage or cubic footage. Also called the segregated cost method, unit costs method.

useful Land's attribute of usefulness or utility to people.

user value The value of a property or space to a specific user. Sometimes more particularly the value of a property designed or adapted to fit the specific requirements of the user. In the latter case, such value often applies to the classification of special purpose property. Also called value in use.

utilities The operating services required by a developed area and provided by a public utility company, e.g., electricity, telephone, water, and gas.

utility In economics, the enjoyment gained from a good in relationship to its risk and return.

vacancies Unoccupied space available for rent.

value in use *See* user value.

variable expense An operating expense that varies with the occupancy level or intensity of use of a property, e.g., utilities, management, and maintenance. *See also* fixed expense.

verification Step in appraisal process where specific data collected by the appraiser is confirmed and verified; general data collected by the appraiser, on the other hand, can be accepted at face value, assuming data sources are reliable and reputable.

vested interest A right or estate that grants possession and use of a property at some later date but does not grant current use of the property. The vested interest, however, may be currently conveyed to another party.

view Scene or prospect; may add or detract value: a pretty view increases value; an offensive view decreases value.

volume Building measurement in terms of cubic feet; often used in warehouse rentals and in reproduction or replacement cost estimates used in the cost approach.

weighted average The mean of a set of numbers that is calculated by applying a weight factor to each component, representing its size compared to the whole. For example, as used in a band of investment technique to find an overall capitalization rate, the weighted average of the land and building capitalization rates is calculated by multiplying each by its percentage value as compared to the whole value. *See also* mean.

For example, the weighted average of an 8% land cap rate and an 11% building cap rate, when the building value equals $100,000 and the total property value equals $340,000 is:

weighted average = $(100,000/340,000) \times 0.11 + (1 - (100,000/340,000)) \times 0.08 = 0.089 = R_O$

wetlands Hydraulic (water) influence on the land; however, soil type and vegetation can lead to wetland designations. Wetlands are generally protected from development in the interests of aquifer and wildlife preservation and aesthetics.

yield capitalization A method of estimating property value by discounting all expected future cash flows to a present value by a rate typical for investors in the marketplace for the interest being valued. The approach may or may not explicitly include financing. Algebraic formulas have been developed to discount future cash flows; however, these are no longer needed with the availability of computer spreadsheets.

For example, a property produces cash flows of $235,000 per year. The property is held for 8 years. The reversion value at this time is $2,000,000. The appropriate discount rate is 11%. The property value can be estimated as follows:

$PV = 235,000 \times a_{\overline{n}|(11\%,\ 8\ \text{yrs.})} + \$2,000,000 \times 1/S^n_{(11\%,\ 8\ \text{yrs.})}$
$a_{\overline{n}|(11\%,\ 8\ \text{yrs.})} = 5.146123,\ 1/S^n_{(11\%,\ 8\ \text{yrs.})} = 0.433926$

using annual compound interest tables
$PV = 235,000 \times 5.146123 + \$2,000,000 \times 0.433926$
$PV = \$2,077,191$

Therefore, the property value is approximately $2,077,191.

INDEX